# BRAZIL ON SCREEN

Cinema Novo, New Cinema, Utopia

Lúcia Nagib

I.B. TAURIS

LONDON · NEW YORK

Published in 2007 by I.B.Tauris & Co. Ltd
6 Salem Road, London W2 4BU
175 Fifth Avenue, New York, NY 10010
www.ibtauris.com

In the United States of America and Canada distributed by Palgrave Macmillan, a division
of St Martin's Press, 175 Fifth Avenue, New York, NY 10010

ISBN: 978 1 84511 328 5 (PB)
ISBN: 978 1 84511 448 0 (HB)

A full CIP record for this book is available from the British Library
A full CIP record for this book is available from the Library of Congress

Library of Congress catalog card: available

Typeset in Goudy Old Style by A. & D. Worthington, Newmarket, Suffolk
Printed and bound in Great Britain by TJ International Ltd, Padstow, Cornwall

# CONTENTS

# ILLUSTRATIONS

Images captured from the films by the author.

*To Stephen*

# ACKNOWLEDGEMENTS

This book originated from research on the New Brazilian Cinema that I conducted with a brilliant team of graduate students at the State University of Campinas and the Catholic University of São Paulo in the second half of the 1990s. I would like to thank them in the first place and also the National Council for Scientific and Technological Development (CNPq) and the State of São Paulo Research Foundation (FAPESP), in Brazil, which financed a substantial part of the research.

Between 2003 and 2004, at Laura Mulvey's invitation, I spent a year at Birkbeck College, University of London, as Leverhulme Trust Visiting Professor. During this period I had the opportunity of structuring and writing most of the chapters of this book. My heartfelt gratitude goes to Laura for her support and critical suggestions, as well as to the Birkbeck graduate students and the Leverhulme Trust.

For the collection of documents and illustrations, I am grateful for the invaluable help and good will of filmmakers, casts, crews, assistants and producers, in particular Fernando Meirelles, Beto Brant, Carlos Diegues, Toni Venturi, Débora Duboc, Rosemberg Cariry, Luiz Alberto Pereira, Bia Lessa, Dany Roland, Paulo Caldas, Lírio Ferreira, Paloma Rocha, Walter Salles, Fernanda Torres and Walter Carvalho. My special thanks go to actor Rodrigues Santoro, photographer Christian Cravo and VideoFilmes, who generously granted me permission to use the cover image.

Previous versions of some of the chapters were published in the journals *Framework*, *Novos Estudos*, *Aletria*, *Revista USP*, *Third Text*, *New Cinemas* and *Studies in European Cinema* to which I am grateful. The School of Modern Languages and Cultures, University of Leeds, contributed funds for the illustrations and research travel. Lisa Shaw and Roderick Steel made a decisive contribution to the translation of the Portuguese original. Thanks are also due to Philippa Brewster for her perceptive editing.

My deepest gratitude goes to my friends and relatives who read and commented on the whole or parts of the manuscript, especially Cecília Antakly de Mello, Ismail Xavier, Davi Arrigucci Jr, Maria Helena Arrigucci, Gustavo Nagib, Luiza Nagib Eluf, Roberto Schwarz, Song Hwee Lim and Stephanie Dennison.

Stephen Shennan is my constant source of inspiration and indispensable reader. I dedicate this book to him.

# FOREWORD

Since its rebirth in the mid-1990s, Brazilian cinema has consistently demonstrated, in a coherent and dynamic fashion, that fiction continues to be an important means for gaining a better understanding of Brazil's contemporary historical experience, set against a backdrop of various failed political projects.

Indeed, films have provided Brazilians with not only an outlet for their dreams, even when there is little to dream about, but equally a means for getting to grips with their self-image, their inner turmoil, even when they find it difficult to recognize themselves in the mirror, given the extent to which they have been disfigured over the years. Cinema has almost always, even when it has got it wrong, acted as a kind of moral opinion poll, sounding out the collective soul of the Brazilian people, as well as playing a significant role in documenting the nation's historical process.

The distinction between what is an effective artistic accomplishment, with the power to shed light on the historical process, and that which is nothing more than a record of facts or raw document, is not always easy to achieve. The same is true of the role of the mere document within artistic production with a realist intent. But this study takes a risk in its very undertaking, which reflects a sense of daring without which meaningful criticism could not exist. One only has to consider the lamentable spectacle of reviews published in newspapers or top-selling magazines, which no longer take any risks and habitually demonstrate a total lack of care in their preparation or the most blatant commercial self-interest, reproducing the prejudices of the editorial staff with no evidence of intellectual rigour or investigative impulses and, much less, any attempt to try to say something that, from an artistic point of view, could be deemed of critical importance.

The first merit of this book is that it takes on the challenge of presenting in an organized and elucidating manner, in clear prose that shifts effortlessly between multiple approaches to very different films, central aspects of the rich and complex material that contemporary Brazilian cinema attempts to shape.

The organization of such a varied subject, which has no obvious common thread, so as to convey to the reader with thorough coherence a problematic theme, is no mean feat. Lúcia Nagib, whose observational skills and stylistic flair have already been evidenced in numerous essays and articles on Brazilian and world cinemas, reveals once again her great ability for getting to the crux of a question, namely, that of utopia and its variations, a topic which today is almost exclusively referred to in disheartening terms, but which the author uses as a means for organizing her wealth of material.

In the thesis put forward in this book, the question of utopia finds its historical roots within the decisive current of Brazilian cinematic tradition, that of Cinema Novo, and spreads its branches through all contemporary film production. The latter is the main focus of Nagib's critical approach, which unearths from recent political events and their deep-rooted historical origins the basis for the current cinematic landscape.

Nagib's analysis focuses first on the matrix found in the work of Glauber Rocha, at a time when utopia was identified with revolution. In his films the utopian vision drew on imagery of the sea – 'The *sertão* will become the sea, and the sea will become the *sertão*' – a motif whose genesis Nagib researches at length in order to shed light on all its subsequent symbolic reworkings.

This becomes clear when the author studies the films of Walter Salles, in which the inaugural sense of the Glauberian sea is still central to the image of the nation, as well as in the vision of the *sertão*-sea of filmmaker Rosemberg Cariry. But the motif continues to echo throughout her analysis when it focuses on the new Brazilian utopia in more recent films, made in the wake of the virtual paralysis of film production during the Collor government. The study recognizes images linked to the formation of Brazil and national identity, highlighting the nostalgic reworking of myths from the past, which to a certain extent represents a characteristic feature of postmodern cinema's vision of history.

However, it is also in Glauber Rocha's work that the author searches for the roots of anti-utopia. After the revolutionary perspective of *Black God, White Devil*, the schism, that is, the dissociation between utopia and the Edenic myth, is already perceptible in *Land in Anguish*. In this film, Eldorado is turned into the stage for bourgeois decadence, and the utopian sea, linked to the genesis of Brazil, into the origin of authoritarianism and class oppression.

Glauber Rocha's dual and contradictory view of the future of Brazil shows how a film can act as a seismograph, sensitive to a film artist's reactions to the directions that society is taking and the intricate feelings of those affected by the expectations the country inspires. The filmmaker's visionary antennae capture these subtleties in the art form, through which the complexity of historical experience is expressed in its totality, symbolically condensed in the film.

Capturing the various dimensions of a totality is, as ever, no easy task. This book's second major achievement is that it makes us aware of this, even when it insists on detailing the good intentions of films such as Carlos Diegues's *Orfeu*, a film which, in my opinion, does not live up, in terms of its artistic merit, to the author's meticulously crafted critical reconstruction of his project. However, even in this case, it must be admitted that the richness of the material collected, in itself illuminating, makes it worthy of discussion.

The book's forte lies in showing how a given artistic intention is translated into film language. The author's aptitude for critical analysis comes to the fore when confronted with this most delicate and subtle challenge. The high points of the book include, first, the incisive study of the nuances and differences between the various films that focus on cannibalism and issues of national identity; second, the shrewd analysis that formulates, in general terms, through meaningful details, the distinctions between the prose of Paulo Lins's novel *City of God* and the language of Fernando Meirelles and Kátia Lund's film version. Nagib's achievement is that she does not reduce the former to the latter, but rather looks for structural correspondences, affinities between their sometimes very disparate stylistic devices and narrative modes, judiciously evaluating the film's artistic merits, which in my opinion are superior to those of the novel, which I consider powerful mainly as a document.

The strength of this study lies, above all, in its treatment of urban dystopia in relation to Beto Brant's film *The Trespasser*. The author provides an illuminating and penetrating analysis of the limits of the document in the construction of a work of fiction. The analytical dismantling of *The Trespasser* inverts, from the outset, certain audience expectations created by some of the film's images themselves and to a large extent by its critical reception. It captures the contradictions between the naturalism, with its allegorical intent, of the metaphors for corruption, and the truly creative and innovative aspects of the film, in the grotesque and expressionist style in which it characterizes the central protagonist and deals with the São Paulo cityscape.

I believe that this book's principal critical revelation lies in this line of analysis, which demonstrates that fiction does not directly translate immediate reality. Rather, a film invents its own imaginary truth by means of language techniques and structural devices, distancing itself from the mere document. In the last analysis, this invented human truth is much more vivid and revealing of historical experience and of a terrifying reality than any attempt to simply reproduce facts relating to an apparent reality. The author's reasoning allows the reader to infer that expressionist deformation and other techniques of film language that hold symbolic power do not constitute an obstacle to the creation of an impression of true reality, something that *The Trespasser* ends up transmitting via ugly, base, frightening elements, which produce powerful metaphors of highly evocative effect. The result is a film that, turning its back on immediate realistic facts, ultimately results in a work of extreme realism.[1]

In this way, the study recognizes, with a finely tuned critical ear, the intense poetry that permeates the most penetrative and complex images of *The Trespasser* in the midst of the ugliness and poverty of the outskirts of São Paulo. Similarly, the author captures the pervasive power of the rapper Sabotage, who himself becomes, beyond the work of art which he 'invades' as a trespasser, a symbolic figure, since, as we know, he subsequently became yet another victim of Brazil's urban war shortly after the film was completed. This unexpected blurring of reality and fiction points to the precariousness and the unavoidably ironic, tragic quality of our own art, when it focuses on class conflicts in a society whose overlapping historical stages and clashing lifestyles move the population further and further away from the civilized co-existence and utopian dreams that films have sometimes evoked. This encounter with the poetic where one would least expect it, in the most debased aspects of the city, perhaps holds the key to another dream, one that is unrelated to traditional utopias.

Ultimately, when the book is viewed in its entirety it becomes apparent that, while providing an organizing principle around which to structure the varied subject-matter of the films analysed so as to create a coherent thread of discussion and debate, the theme of utopia ends up also restricting further development of the analysis. The latter is its most incisive precisely when it turns to issues that stray beyond the overarching thematic structure, taking an unexpected detour.

From the very way in which the language and structure of the films, together with their relationship to reality, are dealt with, it becomes apparent that the theme of utopia and its corollaries facilitates, on the one hand, the general organization of the subject-matter. On the other hand, however, when applied to all the films as an obligatory theoretical framework, the theme ends up moulding them to an externally imposed perspective, which is not necessarily the one that we are most likely to draw from the internal structure of a given film or even from the auteurist intentions it contains.

The choice of an overarching point of view can lead to a predictable format in the evolution of the argument. In this case, however, it does not hinder the free movement of the author's critical gaze, which is always attentive, alert and astute in its treatment of concrete details, which are fundamental for the understanding of individual films in isolation, and subsequently in linking each to the wider theme of the book.

Thus, notwithstanding the contradictions that the very choice of a fixed thematic approach could lead to, the book is a lively and knowledgeable guide to contemporary Brazilian cinema in all its many guises. The richness and impact of the analyses and the precise choice of the films as a whole will allow readers to gain a firm foothold in both the inner workings of the films themselves and, at the same time, the world to which in some way they relate, enabling them to evaluate for themselves the subtle and expressive relationships between the two. You cannot ask more of a critical work.

Davi Arrigucci Jr

# INTRODUCTION

The fall of the Berlin Wall on 9 November 1989 marks the end of the socialist utopia and the victory of postmodern anti-utopian neo-liberalism. A few months later, in 1990, Francis Fukuyama was already publishing his polemical article 'The End of History and the Last Man', which was expanded into a bestselling book that elaborated on the end of history as conceived by Hegel and Marx, expounding the virtues of liberal democracy over communism.[1]

Fredric Jameson defined this era as 'late capitalism', characterized by the end of hermeneutics, dialectics and the 'utopian gesture',[2] and the installation of intellectual, counter-revolutionary *ressentiment*. It was the realm of superficiality and simulacra, derived from the postmodern condition, which levelled inner and outer worlds, appearance and essence, signifier and signified.[3] In relation to cinema, Jameson identified in this era the 'nostalgia film', which trained the spectator 'to consume the past in the form of glossy images'.[4] Indeed, tied as it was to a present without a future and devoid of any avant-garde ambitions, cinema tended, from the mid-1980s onwards, to recycle the past through citation, parody of conventional genres and aestheticized violence, a trend epitomized by the likes of David Lynch and, a little later, Quentin Tarantino, whose films combined historical scepticism with black humour and political cynicism.

In 1990, Jean-Luc Godard made a symbolic film about the fall of the Wall called *Allemagne 90 neuf zéro*. Revolving around the end of history in reunified Germany, the film evokes the Berlin razed to the ground of Rossellini's *Germany, Year Zero*, shot just after the end of the Second World War, as well as the ruins of narrative and the death of cinema itself. In Brazil, 1990 was cinema's real year zero. It saw the sudden closure of Embrafilme, the state film company, by the newly elected President Fernando Collor de Mello, which brought film production to a halt for the following two years. Before that, Brazilian cinema had also undergone a brief phase of postmodern self-reflexivity and disbelief in history and narrative. With headquarters in the São Paulo district of Vila Madalena, a group of filmmakers including Guilherme de Almeida Prado, Chico Botelho, Walter Rogério and Wilson Barros, and musicians such as Arrigo Barnabé, had been producing urban films, conceived as parodies and citations of the American film noir and vaguely akin to the porn output of the Boca do Lixo (literally, the 'garbage mouth', or the red-light district). Basking in scintillating neon effects, which illuminated nostalgic cinephilias in artificial settings, these films cultivated the ludic superficiality of the cartoon and the electronic game,[5] and remained immune to the nation's cultural peculiarities.

This was the Brazilian response to a process that, throughout the 1980s, had kept cinema under the threat of imminent death through narrative dissolution, nostalgic metalanguage and the rise of video, whose adepts rejoiced in forecasting cinema's complete disappearance. But it somehow managed to survive and even experienced an international boom after the fall of the Berlin Wall, which Godard had suggested was cinema's own end. The emergence of cultural studies, which made room for the expression of ethnic and sexual minorities, accompanied the return of the film *engagé*. At the same time, new, enlightened audiences, no longer motivated by old left-wing imperatives, but duly imbued with political correctness, were formed around the proliferating film festivals and alternative venues. Gradually, the interest in local and national peculiarities reappeared in response to the cultural homogenization entailed by globalization, as well as to the postmodern deconstructive superficiality.

From the end of the 1980s onwards, new cinemas started to appear in various parts of the world, particularly in Asia (Iran, China, Taiwan and Japan), all of them strongly narrative and committed to the recuperation of history. Filmmakers such as Zhang Yimou, Edward Yang, Hou Hsiao-Hsien, Abbas Kiarostami and Mohsen Makhmalbaf demonstrated that the mastery of a wide range of aesthetic tools, including the deconstructive ones, made them all the more capable of apprehending and analysing the historical processes of their own countries.

In the mid-1990s, it was the turn of Latin America, where, after repeated declines and silences, cinema returned with renewed energy, especially in Brazil, Argentina and Mexico. In these countries, the film revival derived in the first place from the establishment of democratic governments, which instituted favourable cultural policies and film incentives. But it also resulted from a global situation which welcomed multicultural expressions, especially when they combined auteurist impulses with local colour and certain doses of conventional genres. In Brazil, the utopian gesture, lost in the past of Cinema Novo, returned with a new impetus, particularly notable in the first years of President Fernando Henrique Cardoso's neo-liberal reforms, propelled by a euphoria which reflected the return of the belief in Brazil as a viable country. However, this new utopia never attained full development, subjected as it was to another realistic tendency which pointed to the continuation of the country's historical problems.

This book studies the resurgence of the utopian gesture in Brazilian cinema from the mid-1990s onwards, as well as its variations and negations. The analysis identifies trajectories of rise and fall, which reflect oscillations in the political scenario, and includes a retrospective look at utopian traditions of the Brazilian cinematic past, in turn derived from the nation's foundational myths. At the same time, it considers the ways in which recent Brazilian film production transcends Cinema Novo's national project to interact with modern, postmodern and commercial cinemas of the world, thus benefiting from and contributing to a new transnational cinematic aesthetics.

Chapter 1 introduces the dialectic matrix of utopia and anti-utopia which was established by Glauber Rocha in the films he shot immediately before and after the 1964 military coup. Focusing on images of the sea, it begins by looking at Brazilian cinema's most famous utopian prophecy, presented in Glauber's Black God, White Devil (1964): 'The backlands will turn to sea, and the sea into backlands.' The formula combines the discoverers' dreamed paradise with popular millennarian beliefs as a means of proposing revolution in the present. The chapter goes on to describe the prophecy's anti-utopian inversion which is presented in Glauber's Land in Anguish (1967). Here, the opening maritime images, rather than fulfilling utopian prophecies, lead to a rotten Eldorado in the New World, which accounts for the failure of the revolutionary project in the present.

The work of retracing the genesis of Glauber's maritime imaginary finally leads to Thomas More's island of Utopia itself. My argument here is based on Afonso Arinos de Melo Franco's creative cartography, which locates Utopia on the island of Fernando de Noronha, in the northeast of Brazil. Described by its first European visitor, Amerigo Vespucci, in one of his letters as paradise regained, the island caught More's fancy and led him to install his perfect society, by mere chance, in Brazil. Rather than this geographic coincidence, what draws my interest is the obsession with the mythic 'island' that moves the characters in Black God, White Devil.

Remaining invisible to the spectator, the main character's dreamed island stands for a project which is both practical and unfeasible, or the 'best place' and the 'no place' encapsulated by the ambivalent term 'utopia'.

Endowed, like the myths at their origin, with foundational power, Glauber's images offered an effective aesthetic resource to recent film directors who were interested in reconnecting with the nation. Walter Salles, an intellectual filmmaker who is entirely aware of the imaginary he manipulates, was the first to return to Glauber's maritime tropes. In his programmatic film *Foreign Land* (co-directed by Daniela Thomas, 1995), he uses images of the sea to mark the end of utopia and Cinema Novo's national project during the Collor period. Centred on the mythology of discovery and including in its title the word 'land' borrowed from Glauber's films,[6] *Foreign Land* is the starting point of the recent utopian curve, which follows an ascending trajectory in the two following years, reflecting the country's momentary economic improvement.

Many films produced in this brief period revisit Cinema Novo's dry backlands with an updated yet nostalgic look. Works such as *Corisco and Dadá* (Rosemberg Cariry, 1996), *Perfumed Ball* (Lírio Ferreira and Paulo Caldas, 1997) and *Believe Me* (Bia Lessa and Dany Roland, 1997) present colourful backland settings in combination with sea and water imagery, which indicate the possibility, or even realization, of the promised paradise. In the following years, however, the utopian project is challenged, especially in the films about the *favelas* (slums) set in urban territories of exclusion. The utopian curve comes full circle with *Behind the Sun* (Walter Salles, 2001), in which the final sea is cinephilic abstraction, reminiscent both of Glauber and of Truffaut's *The 400 Blows* (1959), which inspired the ending of *Black God, White Devil*.

Chapter 2 extends the boundaries of the maritime imaginary to include the motifs of the zero and the centre, which turn around the search for the nation and its definition. In focus are again two films by Walter Salles, *Central Station* (1998) and *Midnight* (co-directed by Daniela Thomas, 1999), as well as Toni Venturi's *Latitude Zero* (2000). The analysis draws parallels between them and new-wave films which also elaborate on the motif of the zero, with examples picked from Italian neo-realism, the Brazilian Cinema Novo and the New German Cinema. In *Central Station*, the homeland is re-encountered in the archaic backlands, where political issues are resolved in the private sphere and the social drama turns into family melodrama. *Midnight* recycles Glauber's backlands–sea prophecy in the new millennium's hour zero, when the earthly paradise represented by the sea is re-encountered by the middle-class character, but not by the poor northeastern migrant who dies on the beach. Finally, *Latitude Zero* focuses on an emptied, 'zeroed' Eldorado in an abandoned goldmine in the heart of Brazil, to mark the end of the masculine predatory utopia and the installation of the feminine principle.

Chapter 3 returns once again to the mythology of the discovery to discuss the famous 'anthropophagic utopia', a centrepiece of the 1920s modernist project inspired by the Renaissance ideal of paradise regained in the land of Brazil and the classical theory of the noble savage. Under Oswald de Andrade's leadership, the modernists defined the anthropophagic Indian as the holder of the national identity, an idea which was re-elaborated by late Cinema Novo, especially in *Macunaíma* (Joaquim Pedro de Andrade, 1969) and *How Tasty Was My Little Frenchman* (Nelson Pereira dos Santos, 1970–72), and more recently in *Hans Staden* (Luiz Alberto Pereira, 1999). Seen in sequence, these three films describe yet another curve of rise and fall, this time with reference to the cannibal Indian, and present an interesting migration of the national identity through Brazilian society's different ethnic components. Originally proposed by the modernists as a libertarian attitude, anthropophagy is turned, in the film *Macunaíma*, into the general rule of a self-devouring humanity. In *How Tasty Was My Little Frenchman*, it is celebrated as sexual revolution that unites the oppressed among both the natives and the European colonizers. Finally, *Hans Staden*, at the end of the 1990s, focuses on cannibalism through the European's exclusive point of view and dismisses it as a relic of the past, devoid of any utopian potential.

Another mythology that has found fertile ground in Brazilian cinema is the Greek, with the invention of the black Orpheus. This is the theme of Chapter 4, which looks at Vinicius de Moraes's play *Orfeu da Conceição* and its adaptation into the world-cinema classic *Black Orpheus* (Marcel Camus, 1959). The analysis includes other related artistic landmarks, such as *Rio, Northern Zone* (Nelson Pereira dos Santos, 1957), a precursor of Cinema Novo which influenced Camus and its idyllic vision of Rio's *favelas*; Cocteau's various films on Orpheus; and, more importantly, Sartre's negritude project as expressed in 'Black Orpheus', his preface to an anthology of black poetry in French. The objective is to evaluate the way in which the racial question is presented in a more recent film, *Orfeu*, by Carlos Diegues (1999), which proposes to update the image of the black and the *favela*. The idealized black paradise, staged in previous re-workings of the Orphic myth, receives, in this film, a realistic counterpoint which includes problems such as overcrowding, criminality and drug trafficking that pervade Brazilian present-day *favelas*.

The last two chapters dispense with the method of historic affiliation and comparison, as the films in question, unlike those analysed in the previous chapters, do not present a structure of citation, nostalgia and revision. Chapter 5 is devoted to *City of God* (Fernando Meirelles and Kátia Lund, 2002), Brazilian cinema's greatest international success of all time. The film's inventive narrative structure, I argue, owes much to the extraordinary novel it was based on, Paulo Lins's *City of God*. The book's language, which incorporates the *favela* slang and the speed of the gunshots that put an end to lives barely begun, is turned, in the film, into realistic acting and quick-fire editing to describe the inferno of crime that interrupted the *favela*'s 'golden age' of samba and solidarity. However, the valorization of the protagonists' personal stories is directed towards ensuring that the interruption of utopia will not put an end to history, thus decidedly taking the side of narrative cinema against postmodern fragmentation.

Finally, Chapter 6 focuses on *The Trespasser* (Beto Brant, 2003) as a dystopian portrait of urban Brazil. The film, which describes the social ascent of a professional killer from a São Paulo *favela*, was regarded by many critics as revelatory of Brazil's moral decadence. In my analysis, I suggest that its revelatory quality is of an aesthetic kind: the representation of the supposedly protected universe of the ruling class is in fact permeated by the misery that surrounds it. Such an aesthetic contamination, I argue, passes for an ethical diagnosis of Brazil as a whole thanks to the film's skilful combination of genre and documentary elements.

The interest of recent Brazilian film production – the variety of which is by no means exhausted in this book – goes necessarily beyond the way they update the national project. Films such as *Central Station* and *City of God*, which turned their directors into international names, are products of globalized culture as much as of Brazil, a theme I have been exploring elsewhere.[7] Walter Salles feels equally at ease making films in Portuguese, English and Spanish, as proven by his recent Latin American work *Motorcycle Diaries* (2004). Salles's and Fernando Meirelles's latest directorial outputs, respectively *Dark Water* (2005) and *The Constant Gardener* (2005), are international productions to which present-day critics are drawn, just as Truffaut was towards the American cinema in his time, to decipher their secret auteurist features. If the Brazilian utopia is still far from reality, that of Brazilian cinema, at least on the aesthetic level, seems to have come about.

## CHAPTER ONE

# IMAGES OF THE SEA

**Films**

*Black God, White Devil* (*Deus e o diabo na terra do sol*, Glauber Rocha, 1964)

*Land in Anguish* (*Terra em transe*, Glauber Rocha, 1967)

*The 400 Blows* (*Les quatre cents coups*, François Truffaut, 1959)

*Foreign Land* (*Terra estrangeira*, Walter Salles and Daniela Thomas, 1995)

*Corisco and Dadá* (*Corisco e Dadá*, Rosemberg Cariry, 1996)

*Perfumed Ball* (*Baile perfumado*, Paulo Caldas and Lírio Ferreira, 1997)

*Believe Me* (*Crede-mi*, Bia Lessa and Dany Roland, 1997)

*Behind the Sun* (*Abril despedaçado*, Walter Salles, 2001)

# IMAGES OF THE SEA

Danger and the abyss God gave the sea,
But gave it a mirror for the sky to see.
(*Deus ao mar o perigo e o abismo deu,*
*Mas nele é que espelhou o céu*)
Fernando Pessoa, 'Portuguese Sea' ('Mar português')

In 1964, *Black God, White Devil* formulated Brazilian cinema's most famous utopia: 'The backlands will turn to sea, and the sea will turn into backlands' ('O *sertão vai virar mar, e o mar vai virar sertão*').[1] The phrase is the chorus of a song in *cordel* style,[2] which punctuates the film, and is sung by Sérgio Ricardo, who wrote the music to lyrics by Glauber Rocha. This prediction is also the *leitmotiv* of the dialogues. It is uttered both by the religious leader Sebastião and the *cangaceiro* Corisco,[3] then repeated by the cowherd Manuel, who successively follows these two leaders in an attempt to free himself from the *sertão*'s poverty and drought. The film ends with the apparent fulfilment of the utopian prophecy: the famous image of the sea, which replaces that of the backlands.

New meanings are added to the Glauberian sea in *Land in Anguish* (1967), whose opening sea imagery harks back to his 1964 film. An aerial camera glides across a silver, round, cosmogonic sea that fills the entire frame, arriving at green coastal mountains, over which appears the title 'Eldorado'. The arid backlands, with their wretched characters yearning for a revolutionary miracle, are here substituted for a land of opulence, confirming the existence of paradise which, it seems, remains beyond the reach of the poor.

Thanks to its richness and complexity, Glauber's maritime imagery became the main source of utopian motifs available to recent Brazilian cinema. The Film Revival of the mid-1990s brought back inaugural myths and impulses attached to Brazil's formation and national identity, favouring the return of utopian thought. But in a globalized, post-utopian world,

3

virtually devoid of political ideas, where national projects have long since given way to transnational aesthetics and relationships, a new Brazilian utopia could only emerge as a reference to the past and a re-evaluation of old proposals centred on the nation. Thus, as it sought to recover a utopian nation lost in time and space, recent Brazilian cinema followed the route of the 'nostalgia cinema', which Jameson once classified as 'the current dominant Western or postmodern form of telling history'.[4] Nostalgia, homage, cross-reference and a desire for historic continuity gave shape to the utopian sea which has re-emerged with all its symbolic power in the new cinema.

Ismail Xavier has written extensively about the totalizing capacity of Glauber's backlands and sea as national allegories.[5] Xavier has also detailed the dialectics of this process, which is capable of incorporating both the unifying myth and the fragmented discourse and narrative. As a result, he says, the utopian prophecy of the backlands–sea contains in itself an anti-utopia.[6] In line with this thought, I propose to examine, first, the Glauberian sea's genesis and aesthetic characteristics and how it is propelled by impulses of affirmation and negation of the utopia; and, second, the way it has been re-appropriated by recent Brazilian cinema.

From its beginnings Brazilian cinema has abounded in sea images, although no other filmmaker before Glauber had provided them with such symbolic power. The pioneering filmmaker Humberto Mauro, who was fond of water and river images to the point of defining cinema as 'waterfall', made a founding film about the Portuguese navigators, *The Discovery of Brazil* (*Descobrimento do Brasil*, 1937), in which the sea's scattered appearances are merely decorative. The famous *Limit* (*Limite*, 1929-31) by Mário Peixoto, who has a legion of worshippers among contemporary filmmakers, including Walter Salles, evolves around maritime images which are romantic expressions of subjective deserts rather than suggestions of social utopia. The films *Black God, White Devil* and *Land in Anguish* will therefore be considered here as aesthetic matrices, as they describe a trajectory of rise and fall of the maritime utopia, from the revolutionary early 1960s to the decline following the military coup in 1964, which is mirrored in the curve of the rise and fall of the neo-liberal, globalized utopia of the 1990s.

*Foreign Land* (Walter Salles and Daniela Thomas, 1995) offers a starting point for the recent utopian trajectory. It portrays the dark period of President Collor's government, when the transition to democracy seemed doomed to failure, Brazil had become a nation of emigrants, and the sea, once crossed by the Portuguese discoverers, led the characters towards defeat and death instead of the expected paradise. From that moment on, the curve rises, with the advent of films that return to Cinema Novo's dry backlands with an updated yet nostalgic look. Films like *Corisco and Dadá* (Rosemberg Cariry, 1996), *Perfumed Ball* (Paulo Caldas and Lírio Ferreira, 1997) and *Believe Me* (Bia Lessa and Dany Roland, 1997) present colourful backlands alongside sea and water imagery, pointing to the possibility, or even realization, of the promised paradise. The trajectory comes full circle with *Behind the Sun* (Walter Salles, 2001), in which the final utopian sea is cinephilic abstraction, reminiscent both of Glauber and of Truffaut's *The 400 Blows* (*Les quatre cents coups*, 1959), which inspired the ending of *Black God, White Devil*. Another kind of solution, completing the utopian curve's downturn, is offered by *Midnight* (*O primeiro dia*, Walter Salles and Daniela Thomas, 1999), to be discussed in detail in Chapter 2. In this film, the earthly paradise represented by the sea is re-encountered by the middle-class character, though not by the poor northeastern migrant who dies on the beach.

As well as these works, several other recent Brazilian films present images of sea and large expanses of water, either in their opening scenes or at key moments in which they acquire totalizing, allegorical meaning. Examples are *Landscapes of Memory* (*Sertão das memórias*, José Araújo, 1996), *Bocage, the Triumph of Love* (*Bocage – o triunfo do amor*, Djalma Limongi Batista, 1998), *Friendly Fire* (*Ação entre amigos*, Beto Brant, 1998), *Sea Land* (*Terra do mar*, Eduardo Caron and Mirella Martinelli, 1998) and *Hans Staden* (Luiz Alberto Pereira, 1999). The list itself, by no means exhaustive, attests to the importance of the maritime trope in recent Brazilian cinema and to Glauber's inaugural role in the formation of Brazil's cinematic imaginary.

### The inaugural sea

The genealogy of Glauber's sea overlaps Brazilian history, popular myths and the history of cinema. According to Glauber, the images of sea in his films convey, above all else, 'the *sertanejo's*[7] primal obsession, which is to see the sea'. He says:

> The northeastern migrants always move towards the shore. As for 'The backlands will turn to sea, and the sea will turn into backlands', this was Antônio Conselheiro's widespread prophecy, and while it does not really contain such an idea, it gives you the liberty to interpret it in a revolutionary way. I appropriated the symbol and used it in my film.[8]

Glauber ascribes the prophecy's authorship to Antônio Conselheiro on the basis of two main sources: the book *Rebellion in the Backlands* (*Os sertões*) by Euclides da Cunha, and the northeastern oral tradition. In Euclides's book, which recounts the rebellion led by the messianic leader Antônio Conselheiro in the hinterlands of Bahia in 1896-97, the prophecy actually announces that 'the backlands will turn into seacoast and the seacoast into backlands'.[9] Its authorship remains unclear, as it was transcribed by Euclides from small apocryphal notebooks found in Canudos, where the rebellion took place. The term 'seacoast', in its turn, conveys a more practical sense than 'sea', as it suggests the rich coastline beyond the reach of the poor *sertanejo*. But the grandiose idea of the sea seems to have suggested utopian possibilities also to Euclides, who drew on controversial ideas of the period to create the 'geological fantasy', in Roberto Ventura's words,[10] according to which the recent formation of the *sertão*, in the state of Bahia, indicated the previous existence of a sea:

> however inexpert the observer may be, upon leaving behind him the majestic perspectives which unfold to the south and exchanging them here for the moving sight of Nature in torment, he cannot but have the persisting impression of treading the newly upraised bed of a sea long extinct, which still preserves, stereotyped in its rigid folds, the agitation of the waves and the stormy deeps.[11]

Glauber was also familiar with the northeastern oral tradition, which is equally riddled with aquatic prophecies. The filmmaker and researcher Rosemberg Cariry, who reworked the Glauberian backlands–sea binomial in *Corisco and Dadá*, suggests that the origin of the prophecy is linked to the belief in an 'enchanted lake', passed down from Cariri Indians to their living descendants as the mystic seat of creation. According to him, the Cariris believed that,

> the giant water snake slept underground, with its tail curled up inside the Batateira Rock. ... The Cariri shamans (*pajés*) prophesied that the rock would tumble, water would flood the Cariri valley and in its fury would devour all the bad men who had stolen land and enslaved the Indians. Once the waters had settled, the land would once again be fertile and free, and the Cariris would return to inhabit Paradise.[12]

Cariry believes that, in the days when Antônio Conselheiro wandered through the backlands of the state of Ceará trading sugar cane spirit (*cachaça*), he heard this legend from local Indians (*caboclos*). He then used it to formulate his own prophecy that 'the backlands will turn to sea, and the sea into backlands', which he later spread throughout the hinterlands of Bahia. Still according to Cariry:

This messianic discourse found favour with the *caboclos* living in the backlands of Bahia. Cariri Indians from Mirandela and Saco do Morcego, who had been converted by Capucin monks, provided 300 archers to help defend Conselheiro's Sacred Empire of Canudos.[13]

Hélène Clastres, in her classic book *The Land Without Evil: Tupi-Guarani Prophetism*, which is certainly among Cariry's sources, had already observed the importance of deluge mythology among Guarani and Tupi Indians, including stories of vast, regenerative cataclysms that lead the way to paradise, or the 'land without evil'. Clastres also emphasized the fact that sixteenth-century writers associated such indigenous myths with the biblical deluge.[14]

Indeed, the Bible is full of myths about large bodies of water, which, combined with Brazil's native mythology, left an indelible mark on the nation's imaginary. The historian Sérgio Buarque de Holanda describes the ways in which beliefs in the earthly paradise have been linked to water since the book of Genesis. In it, the Garden of Eden is the cradle from which springs a large river, which splits into four branches, forming the earth's main rivers. He writes:

> Paradise motifs, inseparable from that myth [of Eldorado], have acquired new consistency here [in Brazil] with the parallel drawn by some authors between the rivers São Francisco and Plate, on the one hand, and the Nile, on the other, whose waters, according to an old tradition, found their true sources in Eden.[15]

Pero Vaz de Caminha's letter, Jean de Léry's and André Thevet's books, letters written by Jesuit missionaries and many other documents left behind by Europeans who visited Brazil in the sixteenth century fuelled the myth of an Eden-like country which was perpetuated in the Brazilian imaginary. This amalgam of legends, corroborated by the specific geography of a country rich in an immense coastline and abundant rivers, were skilfully combined by Glauber, in *Black God, White Devil*, with stories of popular uprisings in the backlands, such as those of Canudos and Pedra Bonita.

In the film, although the sea is the main utopian figure, utopia itself is represented by 'the island', a realm of fantasy, lacking graphic representation, announced by preacher Sebastião thus: 'God separated Heaven and Earth, but it went wrong. When he separates them again we will see the island' ('*Deus separou o céu e a Terra, mas tava errado. Quando separar de novo, a gente vê a ilha*'). According to Sebastião, in the island, 'Horses feed on flowers and children drink milk from rivers. Men eat bread made from stone, and dust of the earth turns to flour. There is water and food in abundance as in heaven' ('*Os cavalos se alimentam de flores e os meninos bebem leite nos rios. Os home come o pão feito de pedra e poeira da terra vira farinha, tem água e comida, tem a fartura do céu*'). Such lines are again inspired by the prophecies transcribed in *Rebellion in the Backlands*, which forecast a 'promised land, where milk flows in rivers through banks of corn cakes' ('*terra da promissão, onde corre um rio de leite e são de cuscuz de milho as barrancas*').[16] But Glauber is drawing even further back on an inaugural moment in Brazilian imaginary, which gives these prophecies both historic and mythical resonances.

'The island' is a constant feature of legends relating to paradise regained in the New World. It is usually depicted as a distant, steep mountain, access to which is invariably obstructed by rough seas or deep rivers. Christopher Columbus, whom Buarque de Holanda described as a man fearless of the impossible, preferred to compare the paradise island to 'a woman's breast, or the pointed half of a pear, rather than to any rough mountain'.[17] The most famous of all mythical islands is Utopia itself, described by the Renaissance English writer Thomas More in his book *Utopia*. Here, the island's paradisiacal qualities are well protected by all sorts of barriers. Surrounding More's island,

> other rocks lie under water, and are very dangerous. The channel is known only to the natives, so that if any stranger should enter into the bay, without one of [the Utopian] pilots, he would run great danger of shipwreck; for even they themselves could not pass it safe, if some marks that are on the coast did not direct their way; and if these should be but a little shifted, any fleet that might come against them, how great soever it were, would be certainly lost.[18]

A curious detail of this fictitious island, home to the perfect society, is that its origins are associated with Brazil. In the classic book *O índio brasileiro e a Revolução Francesa* (*The Brazilian Indian and the French Revolution*), Afonso Arinos de Melo Franco defends the thesis that More's Utopia is a fictionalized account of the island of Fernando de Noronha, in the northeast of Brazil, which the English author had found out about in Amerigo Vespucci's letters.[19] Vespucci, in his turn, describes it as 'blessed with abundant fresh water, infinite trees and countless marine as well as terrestrial birds ... so gentle that they fear not being held in one's hands'.[20] Arinos completes his hypothesis:

> The English philosopher needed a vague land like this in which to place his perfect human beings. A land he could turn into the birthplace of social peace and justice, into a fortunate island rising high above a rough sea of cruelty, misery and oppression, which was the world he lived in.[21]

An essential aspect of Utopia is its impossibility. The word, invented by More, brings together the Greek term *topos*, or 'place', and the combination of two prefixes, *ou*, which is negation, and *eu*, meaning 'good quality'. Thus 'utopia' signifies both 'good place' and 'no place', an ambiguity aimed at camouflaging More's plans of social change designed for his own country, England. Originally a practical project, Utopia was eventually universalized with the meaning of the impossible dream of an ideal society, whose very perfection makes it unfeasible.

A similar dialectic construct, which simultaneously confirms and denies Eden, lies at the core of *Black God, White Devil*'s maritime utopia. From the top of Monte Santo, Manuel and the preacher Sebastião look out on to the endless scorched backlands before them, dreaming of the island of plenty, which never appears to the camera. 'The island doesn't exist, but it lives in our soul!' ('A ilha não existe, a gente traz ela dentro da alma!'), murmurs Sebastião, confirming that utopia is nothing but a manifestation of faith. Glauber's mythic backlands–sea formula expresses the harrowing feeling of this utopian country that could have turned out right but was fated not to from the day it was discovered. This is how Sebastião's truncated speech, echoed in the film's discontinuous editing, summarizes the history of Brazil: 'Dom Pedro Alves discovered Brazil and made the stairs of stone and blood [of Monte Santo]' ('Foi dom Pedro Alves que descobriu o Brasil e fez a escada de pedra e de sangue [de Monte Santo]'). This synthetic account mixes Dom Pedro, the emperor, with Pedro Álvares Cabral, the discoverer, in a succession of trials and disasters that continue to the present. The aim of Glauber's dialectics is, thus, to restore the utopian myth in order to prove that its antithesis rules the day.

**Aesthetic matrices**

Although conceptually tied to Brazil's history, Glauber's sea imagery drew its aesthetic inspiration from a foreign model, François Truffaut's *The 400 Blows*. In the final sequence of this *nouvelle vague* milestone, young Antoine Doinel, played by Jean-Pierre Léaud, runs headlong towards the sea he has never seen before.

The maritime utopia here translates liberation, and it is indeed the search for freedom that drives the plot. The film's original title was *La fugue d'Antoine*, drawing on the musical form of the fugue to signify the protagonist's flights. Indeed, Antoine manages to flee his school, his family and, in the end, the reformatory where he is doing time for petty misdemeanours. In the end, unlike Manuel in *Black God*, he actually meets the utopian sea and touches it with his feet before immediately recoiling. The

The sea at the end of *The 400 Blows* is reduced to a blur behind the hero's frozen close-up, which asserts the supremacy of the individual over objective reality.

camera then closes in on him to capture his puzzled look in freeze-frame, while the sea is reduced to a blurred background.

Filmed on location around Villers-sur-Mer in the Pays d'Auge, the sequence is remarkable for its realism, in vogue in Europe since Italian neo-realism. The use of sequence-shots brings to the fore the physical exertion of Jean-Pierre Léaud, forced to run long stretches without breaks, while the wintry, inhospitable set further torments him. Even the climactic encounter with the sea is a let down. It does not correspond to a project of cosmic inversion, as in Glauber's film, nor does it offer an end to the hero's afflictions. The sea that gently ripples along this fenced-in, domesticated beach is monotonous, cold and uninviting in its vastness. Unsurprisingly, the boy immediately rejects it after a brief touch with his feet still in socks and shoes. The context and, in particular, nature appear devoid of interest for a character who had previously shown a predilection for secretive, sealed spaces, such as his friend's bedroom where he could smoke and drink, or the dark cinema auditorium. The frozen close-up of his face thus confirms the supremacy of the individual's psychological drama over the objective reality.

Doinel's final enigmatic expression suits the film's general ironic atmosphere, corroborated by the self-reflexive actor that Léaud has been from childhood. In *The 400 Blows*, there is no room for any serious political discourse such as Glauber's, and yet *Black God's* final sequence bears a number of resemblances to that of its French predecessor and is an undeniable citation: the protagonist who runs towards the utopian sea he had

never seen before; the use of sequence-shots to emphasize the actor's physical strain; the individual's heroic battle against everything and everyone, including Manuel's wife, who falls over and is left behind by him in his desperate race.

But the differences are just as striking. *Black God's* sea, rather than presenting a cold, placid geometry as in the French film, is a dynamic mass, as noted by Ismail Xavier:

> The moving camera shows us the sea from above, in such a way as to avoid the composition of a smooth surface, delimited by the horizon's stable line. The sea affirms itself as a living mass, with the ebb and flow of the waves.[22]

Rather than being the focus of interest, the hero is summarily abandoned in a brusque cut, while the *sertão* miraculously turns to sea by the editor's sleight of hand. The filmmaker, who a while ago was keen to free his hero from the influences of god and the devil, becomes God himself, imposing a solution through editing and provoking revolution through art.

Coherently, throughout the film, Manuel had proven his determination to endure all measures of sacrifice to realize the backlands–sea prophecy. His final dash makes actor Geraldo Del Rey's real suffering under the location's blazing sun all too apparent, echoing other passages of the film, such as his climb up Monte Santo's hundreds of steps on his knees with a heavy rock on his head. The blood that trickles down his head at the end of this feat looks, and is, real, a fact confirmed by testimonies of crew and

The sea at the end of *Black God, White Devil* causes the hero to disappear under the waves of revolution.

cast members.[23] His complete disappearance under the agitated sea thus consummates the immolation of the individual for the sake of social transformation.

The way in which Glauber cites an auteurist, personal film, such as *The 400 Blows*, in a film which champions rebellion and violence against class oppression, actually inverts its meaning. In the early 1960s, Glauber was fascinated by the *politique des auteurs*, idealized by Truffaut and his colleagues of the *Cahiers du Cinéma* in the 1950s, to give directors maximum power. But he interpreted it according to his own convenience, that is to say, as the revolutionary action of a leader who is at once an artist and a politician. Dismissing his French colleagues' devotion to American cinema, Glauber defined auteur cinema as non-commercial cinema and the film director as a revolutionary leader, as he proclaimed in his early writings:

> The politics of a modern auteur is revolutionary: nowadays one needn't even qualify an auteur as revolutionary, because the word auteur is a totalizing noun. To say that an auteur is reactionary, in cinema, is the same as saying he is a commercial director: this is situating him as craftsman: as non-auteur.[24]

Truffaut's and Glauber's sea images thus present two opposite poles of the individual and the social utopia. But these will merge together in Brazilian recent cinema's reinterpretation of the maritime utopia.

## The anti-utopian matrix

*Black God, White Devil*, filmed in 1963, at a time when there was great political hope in Brazil, draws a progressive hero who finally frees himself from the country's retrograde and anti-republican influences. The film presents a true utopian agenda, much in the style of Thomas More, 'who was a progressive, an evolutionist and even a revolutionary in the legitimate sense of the word', according to Afonso Arinos.[25] In its turn, *Land in Anguish*, made after the 1964 military coup, is a post-utopian film, which speculates on the errors that led to the demise of the revolutionary project, blaming the very formulators of the Brazilian Eden myth for its failure.

*Land in Anguish* is about the mythic sea that transported the European discoverers to an Eldorado of privileges, which bears little resemblance to More's socialist Utopia. The beginning of the film is a long and slow aerial sequence-shot of the sea occupying the totality of the frame, with a *candomblé* song[26] in the background suggesting a mystic trance. The camera that slides from left to right captures the sea's rounded surface as if it were the globe itself illuminated by the sun's metallic glow. Credits are superimposed on the images, while the camera glides away over mountains covered with dense forest, followed by a valley through which a river winds its way. There are no signs of human presence in this pristine scenery, over which appears the title in parentheses: 'Eldorado, inner country, Atlantic'.

This majestic, placid opening, enacting paradise regained, bears striking similarities to the opening of *I Am Cuba* (*Soy Cuba*), a Russo-Cuban production directed by Mikhail Kalatozov in 1964.[27] Reinterpreting

The composition of the sacrificial hero includes the actor's real physical strain (Manuel, in *Black God, White Devil*).

Cuban revolutionary utopia, *I Am Cuba* begins with long, smooth aerial shots of the sea, leading to the Caribbean island's immaculate hills and palm-tree forests. In the black and white photography the sea presents a metallic glow, while the palm trees acquire a white shine under the sun – an effect achieved with the use of negative sensitive to infrared rays.[28] The camera eventually stops before a white wooden cross at the sea shore, bearing an inscription which marks Christopher Columbus's visit to the island. 'Cuba's' female voice-over recites:

> Once, Christopher Columbus landed here. He wrote in his diary: 'This is the most beautiful land ever seen by human eyes.' Thank you, Señor Columbus. When you saw me for the first time, I was singing and laughing. I waved the fronds of my palms to greet your sails. I thought your ships brought happiness.

This is followed by a narrative of miseries and tears at the time of colonial exploitation.[29]

In *Land in Anguish*, Eldorado allegorizes Brazil as much as all other Latin American countries, connected with each other through their colonial history. As in *I Am Cuba*, paradise regained is presented only to be immediately denied. The solemn arrival in Eldorado is abruptly interrupted by the insertion of various sequences of action and violence. We are now on the terrace of a palace, where the populist leader, Vieira, surrounded by assessors and press agents, prepares his resignation speech. Loud, extradiegetic jazz drumming clashes with the overlapping voices in the diegesis. Machine gun in hand, journalist and poet Paulo Martins calls for a revolutionary stand, but is rejected and flees in his car accompanied by Sara. Two policemen chase after them and wound him. Throughout his long agony on the sand dunes, Paulo Martins delivers a monologue that forms the basis for the flashback of his story.

Sea imagery again fills the screen, with more extradiegetic *candomblé* drumming and singing, given new meaning by the dramatic scenes of defeat just shown. A character alights on the beach as if he were the first European to do so and presides over an inaugural Mass with three other figures representing the clergy, the Indians and the kingdom; the last two are wearing carnival costumes. The newly arrived leader is Porfírio Díaz, a name borrowed from the famous Mexican dictator and applied to a Brazilian character to indicate historical similarities across Latin America. The blank expression on the faces of all of them, the enormous black flag stuck in the sand by Díaz and the deserted beach where only the representatives of the elite can be seen create a funereal atmosphere. The utopian sea, tied to the genesis of Brazil and the Americas, is then revealed as the very

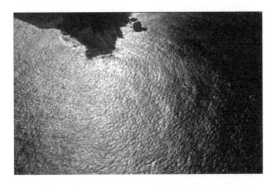

The European discoverers' mythical sea leads to a post-utopian Eldorado, in *Land in Anguish*.

The discovery mythology in *I Am Cuba*: as in *Land in Anguish*, images of the sea introduce a tale of misery.

origin of the continent's anti-popular authoritarianism and class struggle.

*Land in Anguish*'s carnivalized theatre of the discovery stages the end of the dream of paradise for the oppressed poor like the cowherd Manuel in *Black God*. The desperate trance of most characters, and of Paulo Martins in particular, who finds no outlet other than poetry for his revolutionary fury, dissolves all constructive action into multiple vicious circles, exemplified by strident popular rituals and the ruling classes' hysterical sex orgies. Thus, in the successive political disasters the film presents, utopia dissociates itself from the myth of Eden, in an Eldorado turned into the stage of bourgeois decadence.

## Nostalgia

Both *Black God, White Devil* and *Land in Anguish* were produced in the 1960s, a historical moment when the national project lay at the centre of political debate. This concern fell off Brazilian cinema's agenda a long time ago. National concerns and political themes withered throughout the 1970s and 1980s. Embrafilme, the Brazilian government's film-funding agency, started its downturn at the end of the 1980s, culminating in its shut-down by the Collor government in 1990. During the short Collor period, baleful cultural policies delivered a fatal blow to the film industry, forcing many filmmakers to leave the country and work elsewhere or give up filmmaking altogether. It was a time when the myth of the promised land could not be further from Brazilian imagination. But less than two years later, in 1992, Collor was impeached and, with the instalment of a new government, cinema began a slow recovery.

This short period of artistic hiatus is reflected in the film with the suggestive title *Foreign Land* (Walter Salles and Daniela Thomas, 1995), a typically transitional work, released just after the crisis. Using the same word 'land' (*terra*) recurrent in the titles of Glauber's films,[30] *Foreign Land* travels the inverse route of the discoverers, describing the loss of the paradise regained five centuries ago, while taking its Brazilian characters back to their European fatherland, Portugal. Walter Salles reveals that the idea for the film came from Jean-Pierre Favreau's photograph of a ship run aground next to a beach. The image struck him and his collaborators, Daniela Thomas and Marcos Bernstein, as an 'emblem of exile', as they explain:

> No longer a political exile as in the dictatorship years, but a new, economic exile that has turned the Brazil of the 90s into a country of emigration for the first time in 500 years. The image of a foreign land is offered as a solution, albeit an idealized one, for the absence of perspective, self-image, identity.[31]

Scenes of action and violence disrupt
the configuration of the utopian sea in
*Land in Anguish*.

The carnivalized theatre of the discovery puts an end to the dream of paradise for the oppressed in *Land in Anguish*.


This programmatic statement shows how conscious Salles was of his intention to reconnect with a certain strand of Brazilian cinema, which had been left behind with the suppression of the national agenda. His search for an 'identity', however, asked for a detour abroad, through which he could establish a dialogue with other international tendencies and conquer a share in the global market. Let us see how it happened.

The image of a sea unable to take a ship to its final destination is indeed central in *Foreign Land*, functioning as a metaphor for the loss of identity. Salles travelled to Cape Verde in search of the wrecked ship in Favreau's photograph, and there he shot emblematic scenes of a couple gone astray against the backdrop of the sea and the ship that never found its course. The lack of ties and the lack of direction are the film's main themes, through which the directors join a certain international current preoccupied with modern uprootedness. A particularly relevant influence is Wim Wenders and his films of the 1970s, such as *Kings of the Road* (*Im Lauf der Zeit*, 1976), whose characters are permanently in search of their lost homeland. Salles and Thomas borrowed from Wenders not only these characters of modern eternal foreigners, but also the Portuguese locations, where the German filmmaker had previously shot *The State of Things* (*Der Stand der Dinge*, 1982) and *Lisbon Story* (1994).

Shot in sophisticated black and white, reminiscent of the American film noir, *Foreign Land* is in every respect a cinephile's work, marked by nostalgia. Nostalgia also characterizes Wenders's independent productions such as *The State of Things*, a film which reflects on Wenders's own problems with *Hammett* (1978–92), which he was directing in the USA at the same time. *Hammett* is another homage to film noir, and, had Wenders's wish prevailed, it would have been shot in black and white, but this was not allowed by its American producer, Francis Ford Coppola.

*Foreign Land* is full of citations and references which will not be dealt with here. But the parallel with Glauber is illuminating of the utopian myth's trajectory in Brazilian cinema. In *Land in Anguish* the anti-utopian movement is represented by Díaz's rise to power, allegorizing the 1964 military coup. Similarly, in *Foreign Land*, utopia is disrupted by the televised image of the newly appointed finance minister, Zélia Cardoso de Melo, announcing the plan to freeze all bank accounts in Brazil, in March 1990. This documentary footage is then linked up to the fictional story: on hearing about the confiscation of her paltry savings, a widow who dreamed of visiting her native land, the Basque country, has a stroke and dies. Her only child, Paco, gets mixed up with diamond smugglers who send him on a clandestine mission to Portugal. There he meets Alex, an older Brazilian girl who finds herself equally disorientated after the death of her partner, a drug addict also involved in smuggling precious stones.

Although political facts are constantly referred to, politics never becomes a theme in the film. The focus is on the individual destinies of middle-class characters, affected by the economic recession but not by class struggle. While in *Land in Anguish* the utopian Eldorado is flawed from the outset because it is a project of the ruling classes for their own benefit, in *Foreign Land* it responds to a positive belief of the middle classes, endorsed (as a loss) by the enunciation. Glauber's symbolic characters, driven by the urge to change the world, are thus replaced by common individuals, moved by personal aspirations. In keeping with this, 'fatherland' is substituted by 'father', and politics by religion.

It is typical of Walter Salles, an intellectual filmmaker entirely aware of the concepts he manipulates, to express his choices in didactic dialogues. Paco's mother dies murmuring the word 'father' in Basque. Prior to that, she had compared Paco to her own father, whom she longed to see again in her homeland. The metaphor of the holy Trinity is further elaborated when Paco is called 'Christ the Redeemer' by a neighbour, when he stretches his arms out in a Christ-like fashion while trying on a shirt made by his mother, a sewing lady, a detail that suggests his final sacri-

The shipwreck stands for the loss of identity in *Foreign Land*.

The sea in *Foreign Land* represents nostalgia for the discovery utopia.

fice. Paco is also described as a descendant of the old Conquistadors, who once thought they had discovered paradise in the Americas. It is in this role that he gets tied up with smuggling the same precious stones that the first colonizers so desperately sought. This reference is made explicit by his name, 'Eizaguirre', exaggeratedly pronounced as 'Ex-Aguirre' by theatre actor Luiz Melo in the role of Igor, the Mephistophelean dealer who gets him into smuggling. Igor laughingly compares Paco to Lope de Aguirre, the Spanish Conquistador who famously sailed to South America in search of Eldorado.

Such nostalgic allusions to a past of great deeds, or great hopes, typically culminate with a sea scene. Alex and Paco find themselves in Cabo Espichel, Europe's farthest westerly point, seated at the edge of a precipice beyond which lies the vast open sea. For a moment the sea fills the frame, before the camera drifts back to capture Alex and Paco from behind, looking out to the sea before them. The explicative dialogue that follows relates to the discovery mythology and the maritime utopia.

> Alex: You have no idea of where you are, do you? This is the tip of Europe (*flinging her arms open*). This is the end! What courage, don't you think? To cross this sea 500 years ago. ... Just because they thought paradise was there. (*She points left towards the horizon.*) Poor Portuguese ... they ended up discovering Brazil.
> *Paco laughs. Alex remains serious.*
> Alex: What are you laughing about?

The derisory joke about Brazil shows the frustration of a generation that has been prevented from climbing up the social scale and must find solace in the personal sphere, that is to say, in a love affair. Within the plot, the sea in *Foreign Land* is nothing but nostalgia for the utopia of a paradisiacal country that once really existed for the middle classes, who are now

reduced to exiles. And on an aesthetic level, the sea works as homage to a cinema in which it still had a political meaning. It is not with anti-colonial rebellion, but with nostalgia that the film looks back to these lost fathers and fatherlands – Portugal, Spain, Paco's grandfather – and to past cinematic fathers. The resulting utopia, even though stemming from politics or a politicized period, is not enough to define a political proposition (as Jameson observes, 'utopian visions are not yet themselves a politics').[32]

Reduced to a pre-political stage, the protagonists derive their charm from occasional displays of their artistic gifts, frustrated by the economic coup. Before his mother's death, Paco was studying Goethe and wanted to be a theatre actor. Alex's boyfriend was a saxophonist and composer. Even Alex proves to be a singer at the end of the film: at the wheel of the car in which Paco lies in agony on her lap, she delivers the song 'Vapor Barato' by Luís Melodia and Waly Salomão, whose lyrics typically talk about a flight 'aboard an old ship'.

These sensitive beings, forced by their new immigrant status into inappropriate jobs like waitressing or smuggling, deserve another chance, the film indicates. And that is exactly what happened in real life in Brazil a few years after the period depicted in the film. With the change in government, life instantly became better for the middle classes, as well as for artists, with clear reflections on film.

### The backlands that turned to sea

A new era was ushered in by the Real Plan, launched during Itamar Franco's provisional government (1992–94) by the then finance minister, Fernando Henrique Cardoso, which brought new hope to Brazil's political scenario. In January 1995, Cardoso took office as president and was thus able to complete his economic reform.

The backlands turn to sea in *Corisco and Dadá*.

The year 1993 saw the release of the Brazilian Cinema Recovery Award (*Prêmio Resgate do Cinema Brasileiro*), which reallocated the assets of Embrafilme, awarding 90 film projects, 56 of them for long feature films. That same year the Audiovisual Law was passed, through which private companies were given fiscal incentives to invest in film production. As a result, Brazilian annual feature-film output, which had been reduced to near zero in the early 1990s, rose to 20 titles in 1995 and to an average of 30 titles in the following years. This small and short-lived economic improvement lifted the country, all of a sudden, out of its limbo of underdevelopment to the illusion of economic strength, as the new currency, the *real*, was level with the dollar. The middle classes felt empowered as they could even afford trips abroad. To be a tourist in Europe, rather than the immigrant of the Collor period, constituted a considerable change of status for middle-class youths like those portrayed in *Foreign Land*. And this had important consequences for a cinema that was being revived in the wake of the country's new cultural policies.

The shame of being Brazilian, as depicted in *Foreign Land*, saw a turnaround in films released only a couple of years later, entailing a rebirth of the national consciousness. Filmmakers felt an urge to film Brazil. Films such as *Corisco and Dadá*, *Perfumed Ball* and *Believe Me*, all released between 1996 and 1997, exude a passionate curiosity for Brazil's landscapes, physiognomies, language, regional accents, habits and beliefs. In 1998, Walter Salles made a film with the suggestive title of *Central do Brasil* (literally, 'the centre of Brazil'), to be discussed in detail in the next chapter, which sent him back to the heart of his native country after a disillusioned trip to the foreign land.

With the trend towards a 'rediscovery' comes the recycling of the

utopian sea. This reappears attached to the arid backlands, with implicit and explicit references to the Glauberian backlands-sea formula. *Corisco and Dadá* (1996) makes direct allusions to Glauber. Its director, Rosemberg Cariry, from an intermediary generation between Cinema Novo and the new cinema of the 1990s, confirms his main source:

> I decided to make films when I saw Glauber's *Antonio das Mortes* [*O dragão da maldade contra o santo guerreiro*, 1969]. We have many things in common, the *sertão*, the same imaginary and archetypes, and the same epic drive.[33]

*Corisco and Dadá* reveals from the outset that its main conceptual source is Glauber's *Black God, White Devil*. The initial credits are followed by a sequence of images of a wide sea, basking in the suave light of both dusk and dawn. Here, as well as in the nostalgic *Foreign Land*, the sea's utopian vocation is made explicit in the dialogue. A female storyteller tells a group of fishermen gathered around her on the beach the story of the *cangaceiro* Corisco and his companion Dadá. She starts by saying, 'The backlands is the sea', and then the story unfolds in flashback.

The opening maritime scene, replayed at regular intervals throughout the film, gives indeed the impression that the backlands have become the sea. The story is told in the form of a past full of horrors in the backlands, in which Corisco has to face nature's adversities, police persecution, the merciless sun, the death of his newborn children, solitude. But in the present everything seems calm, pacified. The seascape is tranquil and pretty, even bearing a touch of advertising *kitsch*, recalling the 'glossy' superficiality Jameson attributes to the nostalgia film.[34] The storyteller offers cakes and coffee to those around her and everyone eats and listens peacefully to the story of their forefathers. Glauber's tempestuous sea has

Images of the sea combine with the account of the biblical Genesis in *Believe Me.*

moved on to a more advanced, Eden-like stage, as if utopia had come true, without the need of any aesthetic or political revolution. Cariry does not hesitate to compare his sea to paradise lost and regained:

> I open up to the cosmos. The indigenous myths – of the land without evil, which is actually the sea – are also evoked by me. The sea as a symbol of paradise, the backlands that turns to sea, the Tapuia water myths from the northeast. I work with the backlands–sea duality, the endless *sertão* that somehow resembles the sea. As Guimarães Rosa says, 'the backlands lacks a lock'. Corisco's story is told by the sea, to balance out the film's dramatic construction and its look.[35]

*Perfumed Ball* (1997) deals with the same themes as *Corisco and Dadá*, even including the same documentary footage of *cangaço* made by the Lebanese peddler Benjamin Abraão in the 1930s and utilized by Cariry in his film. In *Perfumed Ball*, it becomes even clearer that the conflict between backlands and sea, as it had been formulated by Glauber, has now been overcome. The scrubland where the *cangaceiro* Lampião hides out is lush (the film was shot after a rare rainy period), and water, from rivers or the sea, appears with more frequency than the backlands themselves. In one of the initial sequences, the camera, pulling away from Lampião, rides on a long aerial shot over the arid *sertão* until it encounters the abundant, agitated waters of the São Francisco river. A sense of continuity, even identity, is thus produced between the backlands and the sea, both dominated by the figure of Lampião.

In his turn, the *cangaceiro* no longer appears as the coarse bandit formed by northeastern poverty. Lampião has become a kind of dandy who is given to dancing, dressing up, using perfume, drinking whisky and even going to the movies in town. Backlands and sea, as well as town and country, have become part of the same universe. Ismail Xavier thus

describes the difference between this vision and Glauber's backlands–sea conception:

> The universe of the *sertão* [in Glauber] has a dignity and a wholeness that depends on isolation and scarcity. ... Backlands and littoral belong to separate worlds. ... *Perfumed Ball* takes the opposite direction. The backlands are no longer a sealed cosmos, a place of isolation. Everything circulates and is inserted in a circuit of exchange. The connection between backlands and littoral is signalled by a variety of products, from the perfume to the whisky bottle in Lampião and Maria Bonita's camp, from the dark cinema auditorium in the city to the filmmaker who films the *cangaceiros* in the middle of the backlands.[36]

*Perfumed Ball* breaks free from Glauber's insular utopia to create an atmosphere suggesting a globalized co-fraternization, in which a Lebanese man is drawn to a Brazilian *cangaceiro* and vice-versa. The film's music, of a genre called 'mangue-beat', by Chico Science and Fred Zero Quatro, creates the same mix, by fusing northeastern rhythms like the *baião* with American pop. The film founds a new genre in Brazilian cinema, the 'árido movie', another blend of things, that proposes to approach Brazil through internationalized means and tools which are quite foreign to the purism of the national project that fed the early Cinema Novo.

Another film shot in the northeastern backlands during this period is *Believe Me* (1997). It also opens with images of a large expanse of water, with a long tracking shot over the sea. At first, it cannot be precisely defined, suggesting the primordial chaos from which God created the world. From this image, which fills the frame with light blue undulations, emerges in fade the hand of an old man who is narrating the biblical Genesis. His speech lends an almost matter-of-fact tone to God and his miracles:

The sea in *Behind the Sun* is nostalgia for a cinematic utopia.

And there's a page that goes like this: When God Almighty created the skies, with the planets ... Now, on the second day He made Earth and on the third day He created all the little animals that live on the face of the Earth. And there's a page that goes like this: God made us in His own image and likeness and He grabbed a rib and made woman. Ah, you, my lady, are the bone from my bones, the flesh from my flesh - Eve! He was the one that called her Eve.

The mention of the Garden of Eden, where Adam and Eve were created, merges with the sea imagery to transform the backlands, yet again, into paradise regained.

Directors Bia Lessa and Dany Roland are clearly fascinated with the rediscovery of the northeastern backlands, with their colour, popular festivals, music and religion. This is a far cry from the Cinema Novo films, in which these elements appear in the tragic setting of drought and poverty. These backlands turned into sea reflect another mixture that resembles the blend of international pop and regional northeastern music of *Perfumed Ball*. Lessa and Roland's background in theatre came into play in the series of workshops they coordinated with amateur actors from the interior of Ceará state, in which they reworked excerpts from Thomas Mann's novel *The Holy Sinner*. The end result combines erudite and popular cultures, as the actors' improvisations, in a way, restore the origins of the medieval oral tale of Mann's cultivated text. Thus high and low cultures fuse together in a popular celebration where there are no oppressors or oppressed, victims or defendants, in an Eden-like northeast where the backlands have merged with the sea.

## Virtual utopia

These three films - *Corisco and Dadá*, *Perfumed Ball* and *Believe Me* - belong to a recent, but short phase in Brazilian cinema, which includes other films such as *Landscapes of Memory*, with its waters penetrating the arid backlands, and *Bocage, the Triumph of Love*, with its opening sequence of a stunning sea that carries the Portuguese poet to his libertine paradise. A euphoric impetus animated these productions during a brief optimistic phase of the Brazilian economy, reflecting an initial belief in the benefits of neo-liberalism and globalization.

However, this enthusiasm over the rediscovery of Brazil soon cooled off, giving way to a new realistic trend which acknowledged the permanence of the country's same old social problems. Many of the more recent films feature *favelas*, or shanty towns (especially in Rio, but also in other locations), drug and arms dealing, migration from the northeast and the gulf that separates social classes. A significant example among these is *Midnight* (1999), in which a northeastern migrant turned bandit in a Rio *favela* finally reaches the sea, only to be murdered on the beach. (For a full analysis of this film, see Chapter 2.)

A similar destiny is given to the protagonist of a music video, made in the same period, for the song 'My Soul' ('A minha alma') by rap group O Rappa. In it, a *favela* boy decides to go to the beach on a Sunday but, before he can, he is murdered by the police that raid the *favela* hill. Once again, the utopian sea is refused to the poor. The video was directed by Kátia Lund (a member of the Salles brothers production company) and Paulo Lins, the author of the celebrated novel *City of God*. This book alone has inspired a whole series of films about shanty towns in Rio, where disenchantment and criticism of public institutions predominate. In all these films, as well as in the award-winning *City of God* (*Cidade de Deus*, Fernando Meirelles and Kátia Lund, 2002, the theme of Chapter 5), the access to the maritime paradise remains a privilege of the upper classes.

As it has become increasingly distant, Brazilian cinema's utopian sea has finally re-encountered Truffaut. In the closing scene of *Behind the Sun* (*Abril despedaçado*), directed in 2001 by Walter Salles, Tonho, a *sertanejo* caught up in a feud between two families over land, walks through the arid backlands until he reaches a sea that cannot be justified in terms of geography or storyline. It is a magical event, originating from citation, and as such it dispenses with the realistic techniques used in *The 400 Blows* and *Black God, White Devil*. Here, the hero, played by leading man of the moment, Rodrigo Santoro, does not run in the long sequence-shots used in the old films to accentuate spatial continuity and the actor's real physical exertion. Instead, he walks calmly in a series of short takes across the scrubland before finally appearing, thanks to the editing, on top of some sand dunes by the sea.

Reverse-shot editing shows that the character is deeply moved by the sea's grandeur, while Antônio Pinto's music in the background and the waves' thundering sound reinforce the melodramatic atmosphere. Towards the end, the camera zooms in on his face to show that he is holding back his tears. Another shot shows the hero from behind, centre frame, looking out to the sea as the waves tumble at his feet. Sentimental and inexplicable, this finale is pure nostalgia for Truffaut's individualistic cinematic utopia, combined with Glauber's social dream. The northeast's poverty-stricken protagonist, a descendant of Manuel, seems to have finally reached Antoine Doinel's sea of liberation. But this is a virtual utopia that does not belong to society or the individual, but to cinema only.

CHAPTER TWO

# THE CENTRE, THE ZERO AND THE EMPTY UTOPIA

**Films**

*Central Station* (*Central do Brasil*, Walter Salles, 1998)
*Midnight* (*O primeiro dia*, Walter Salles and Daniela Thomas, 1999)
*Latitude Zero* (*Latitude Zero*, Toni Venturi, 2000)

# THE CENTRE, THE ZERO AND THE EMPTY UTOPIA

In this chapter, I look at three Brazilian films, shot at the turn of the millennium, in which utopian gestures and inaugural desires with relation to the nation are expressed in their own titles. They are: *Central do Brasil* (literally, 'the centre of Brazil', or *Central Station*, Walter Salles, 1998); *O primeiro dia* (literally, 'the first day', or *Midnight*, Walter Salles and Daniela Thomas, 1999) and *Latitude zero* (*Latitude Zero*, Toni Venturi, 2000). All three seem to revolve around the idea of an overcrowded or empty centre in a country trapped between past and future, in which the zero stands for both the announcement and the negation of utopia.

As I have observed elsewhere,[1] the reconstruction of a national utopian imaginary during the film revival from the mid-1990s onwards included the geographical exploration of the country with renewed curiosity about the human element and its typicality. Behaving like Brazil's first discoverers, several filmmakers undertook journeys aimed at mapping the national territory. For a few years, Brazil became an obsessive object of research, in films devoted to a passionate scrutiny of its peculiarities, such as *Central Station*, or a bitter criticism of them, such as *Chronically Unfeasible* (*Cronicamente inviável*, Sérgio Bianchi, 1999), both set in locations from north to south of the country. Brazil offered sumptuous scenarios in films such as *Bocage, the Triumph of Love* (*Bocage – o triunfo do amor*, 1998), shot in seven different states, and *The Oyster and the Wind* (*A ostra e o vento*, Walter Lima Jr, 1997), set on paradisiacal beaches in the states of Ceará and Paraná. In these exploratory expeditions, particularly attractive for those directors who were returning from sojourns abroad, such as Walter Salles, the search for a 'centre' and a 'point zero' became a recurrent gesture.

As was the case in previous new waves, the filmmakers invested with the mission of reviving Brazilian cinema also felt the urge to be novel. This was not an easy task, since the return to zero was not meant to turn film history into a *tabula rasa*, but, on the contrary, to reconnect with old cinematic traditions. This seemed to be the only way in which to reformulate utopian projects and reach a coveted state of 'Brazilianness', a term Walter Salles picked up from Hélio Pellegrino's comments on Glauber and turned into the very definition of *Central Station*.[2]

The new zero meant, therefore, to recycle previous zeros, such as Glauber's, who once called Brazilian culture a 'culture year zero', adding, 'From zero, like Lumière, Cinema Novo restarts at every film, stammering a brutal alphabet which tragically means "underdeveloped civilization".'[3] 'To start from zero' had been a favourite slogan of many new waves of the world, reaching extremes of romanticism, for example, in the case of Werner Herzog, who in the early days of the New German Cinema used to define filmmaking as an 'art of illiterates', which should start from zero 'as if film history did not exist'.[4]

On the other hand, the Brazilian film revival was reacting against the negative period immediately before it, the late 1980s and early 1990s, when the zero had made a return to express the 'end of history' and postmodern scepticism. Both meanings are symbolically encapsulated in a film made by the master of puns Jean-Luc Godard, precisely in 1990, whose title is a real treasure: *Allemagne 90 neuf zéro* (*Germany Year 90 Nine Zero*). Here the French word *neuf* means both 'nine' and 'new' and refers to the fall of the Berlin Wall as well as to the film *Germany, Year Zero* (*Germania anno zero*), shot by Roberto Rossellini in 1947 in a Berlin razed to the ground after the Second World War. The revival directors obviously felt closer to Rossellini's zero, that suggested negation but also inauguration. On the one hand, it allegorized a devastated country and Europe, where desperate children committed suicide. On the other, it created the *tabula rasa* where young filmmakers from Germany and other countries – such as Godard and his *nouvelle vague* colleagues – could inscribe a new film aesthetics, free from the taints of a brutal past that had turned to dust.

In an insightful essay on Rossellini, Sandro Bernardi quotes Walter Benjamin with reference to *Germany, Year Zero*, saying:

> With death, what had been part of history falls back into the domain of nature; what had been natural falls back into the domain of history.

*Germany, Year Zero*, writes Bernardi, 'constitutes a journey into the world of death and of ruins'. But, he continues,

*Germany, Year Zero*: a new cinema arises from the rubble of war.

the war and the catastrophe of ideologies have brought the world back to
its starting point and have plunged the space that once was a city back
into the state of nature.

As an illustration, Bernardi observes that, in the documentary footage that
opens the film, grass grows amid the ruins of Berlin. Rossellini himself
had once identified utopia with autopsy, saying that the discovery of the
new could only be achieved through an archaeological study of the dead
under the rubble.[5]

More than 40 years later, Godard, in *Allemagne 90 neuf zéro*, returns to
Berlin to collect the debris of history amid the rubble of another ideologi-
cal catastrophe, the end of the socialist utopia, thus updating Rossellini's
worldview for contemporary filmmakers. The film stars Hans Zischler,
who had featured alongside Rüdiger Vogler in *Kings of the Road* (*Im Lauf
der Zeit*, 1976), in which two *flâneurs* travel along the border between West
and East Germany on a romantic search for the lost link between history
and a homeland torn apart by war. Throughout the 1970s and 1980s, Wim
Wenders patiently applied himself to the reconstruction of the narrative
structure and the fable, bombarded by his idol Godard. His road movies,
whose characters are endlessly searching for a story and a home, left their
mark and created a school of which Brazilian filmmaker Walter Salles is a
keen pupil. For his part, Godard enjoys nothing more than deconstruct-
ing his own followers by means of parody precisely when they quote him,
and producing gems of self-reflexive humour, such as these lines in *Allemagne 90 neuf zéro*:

Pieces of history for sale! Parts of the wall for ten cents. Books, flags, shirts, buttons, come closer, ladies and gentlemen and buy![6]

A film made up of citation and deconstruction, with references ranging from Goethe to Conrad in the best postmodern style, *Allemagne 90 neuf zéro* blends Second World War ruins from the 1940s with the destruction of the Wall in the present, thus reducing history to random fragments of time and space and denying existence to the nation and its narrative potential. Laura Mulvey observes in Godard the recurrent return to zero, which acquires at each time a different meaning, referring both to the origin of cinema and the feminine myths created by the American classical cinema.[7] At each return, the utopian gesture is interrupted by the deviations of history and the cyclical death of cinema itself.

Looking at the same themes as Godard did in *Allemagne 90 neuf zéro*, the films analysed here take an opposite route and offer some sort of happy ending to Wenders's nostalgic searches. While focusing on the zeros of nation, history and film history, they adopt the utopian gesture as a way to recover their integrity. Rejecting postmodern deconstruction, they take a step forward which, in fact, implies a return to certain conventions of genres such as melodrama. Although none of them are aesthetically radical, they all refer to moments of radicalism in Brazilian cinema, in particular, films by Nelson Pereira dos Santos, Ruy Guerra and Glauber Rocha. The dry backlands, once the focus of attention of these three filmmakers, become the cradle of 'Brazilianness' in *Central Station*, in which the move-

The ruins of the Berlin Wall turn into 'pieces of history' in *Allemagne 90 neuf zéro*.

ment towards the sea, undertaken by Glauber's characters in *Black God, White Devil*, is reversed, with characters who return from the littoral to the *sertão* animated by the curious utopia of paradise in the backlands. *Midnight*, in its turn, re-enacts Glauber's backlands–sea prophecy in Rio, in the zero hour of the new millennium, presenting the daily sea of Rio's upper classes as unattainable for the poor northeasterner. Finally, *Latitude Zero* depicts an emptied, 'zeroed' Eldorado at an abandoned goldmine in the heart of Brazil as the end of the macho utopia and the installation of the feminine principle.

## The utopian backlands

*Central Station* epitomizes the passionate rediscovery of Brazil, and was celebrated internationally as the landmark of the Brazilian Film Revival, coincidentally in the symbolic city of Berlin, where it won the Golden Bear at the 1998 film festival. Back in his native land after his adventure with *High Art* (*A grande arte*,1991), an international production in English, and *Foreign Land* (*Terra estrangeira*, 1995), filmed in Brazil, Portugal and Cape Verde, about Brazilians in exile, Walter Salles and his co-scriptwriters found in Wim Wenders (already a strong influence in *Foreign Land*) a good road to the journey back home. The chosen model for the storyline was *Alice in the Cities* (*Alice in den Städten*, Wim Wenders, 1974), a transnational plot about a German pre-adolescent girl who lives in Holland, is abandoned by her mother in a New York airport and falls into the hands of a German journalist suffering from writer's block, who takes her back to Germany to look for her grandmother. In *Central Station*, it is the young boy Josué who finds himself abandoned in Rio's central station when his mother is run over by a bus. He then falls into the hands of Dora, a former primary school teacher now degraded to writing letters for the illiterate. At first she sells him to a gang that deals in human organs, but subsequently regrets her decision and takes him on a long journey through the northeast to search for his father.

Both films revolve around improbable encounters[8] between a lost child and a solitary adult, both of whom, after a long period of estrangement and rejection, regain the feeling of family. Clear though the connection with Wenders may seem, it is just part of a wider strategy. Marcos Bernstein and João Emanuel Carneiro's minutely elaborated script actually contains a number of incidents aimed at accommodating references to Brazil's cinematic past as a means to legitimize their current approach to the nation and draw the film towards its conciliatory ending. Wenders had also gone back to his cinematic fathers, such as Fritz Lang, Godard and John Ford, to forge a style entirely based on homage. But for Salles, going back to Brazil meant, above all, re-enacting Cinema Novo's national project, structured by two poles of poverty: the rural backlands in the northeast and the urban *favelas* in Rio.

And so the film's journey begins in Rio, whose slums and train station, Central do Brasil, had once been the locations of Nelson Pereira dos Santos's *Rio, Northern Zone* (*Rio, Zona Norte*, 1957), and it culminates in the northeast in such locations as Milagres, already utilized by Ruy Guerra in *The Guns* (*Os fuzis*, 1963) and Glauber Rocha in *Antonio das Mortes* (*O dragão da maldade contra o santo guerreiro*, 1969). Salles even managed to insert a reference to Glauber's birthplace, Vitória da Conquista, through the actor Othon Bastos, a Cinema Novo icon, who, in *Central Station*, plays a Protestant lorry driver (Glauber also had a Protestant background) born in that town.

Thus the romantic nostalgia for an undefined homeland, typical of Wenders's characters, is substituted by the euphoria of the re-discovered fatherland. In the process, the written word is also recovered: instead of a blocked journalist, we have a professional scribe whose pen, at the end of the film, flows freely in a letter that details her own story. The restoration of the narrative gift is intimately tied to the retrieving of 'Brazilianness' and the effusive enthusiasm for the rediscovered homeland, something totally absent in *Alice in the Cities* and other Wenders films, in which the theme is precisely the impossibility of a nation or a fatherland. The allegorical title of *Central do Brasil* asserts a belief both in the country's wholeness and its point zero, its core, which is the Rio station where migrants from all over the country converge.

The film begins with location shots focusing on a series of illiterate Brazilians, chosen from Central do Brasil's real-life passengers, who dictate letters to the scribe Dora (Fernanda Montenegro, whose performance won her the Silver Bear in the 1998 Berlin Festival). The emphasis on illiteracy, a recurrent theme among new-wave directors such as Glauber and Herzog, here receives humanist overtones. The illiterate speakers are first shown in shot–reverse shot montage, but they soon monopolize the camera's attention, which closes in on their faces, while their speeches are reduced to the names of the towns and states they come from. A young woman, unable to properly address her letter, is from Mimoso, Pernambuco. The following speakers, taken in frontal close-ups, simply say: Cansanção, Bahia; Carangola, Minas Gerais; municipality of Reriutaba, Ceará; Muzambinho, Minas Gerais. Beyond the curious names of these towns, pronounced with naive pride, there is the specific geography established by the states,

The gallery of faces at the opening of *Central Station* composes a portrait of Brazil.

all located north of Minas Gerais, that is to say, in the Brazilian northeast. The choice is clear: there are no southerners among the illiterates.

This gallery of faces is so striking and became so famous because the eye that looks at them through the camera is clearly fascinated by their peculiar racial features, ranging from white European to black African. It thus suggests, even before its physical discovery later in the film, a northeast full of colour. The characters' speeches, marked by their original accents and slang, are recorded with enhanced clarity, as if captured by an innocent ear that had never heard such a tongue before. Old and young fraternize in the moving simplicity of poverty, and their speeches are invariably closed with a calm, tolerant smile.

This array of common people plays an important role in the configuration of a realist, documentary-style backdrop. The first person to dictate a letter, addressed to her husband in prison, is a tearful Socorro Nobre, an ex-convict in real life who had previously been the subject of a documentary by Walter Salles himself. Hers is the most touching speech, if not for the echoes of her personal tragedy, certainly for her exceptional talent as an amateur actress. In this sequence, the image and sound editing reproduces verbal metaphors, such as 'I'll remain locked outside here, waiting for you'. The camera is placed behind rows of bars and columns to create a station full of fences, while the sound of gates slamming suggests a prison that finds no support in the diegesis. The purpose is to smoothly blend the film's realist base with the fiction superimposed on it, without alienating the audience. Two of the protagonists, the northeastern Ana and her son Josué, emerge from this array of faces as the prototype of the common Brazilian, and are given, as if naturally, more time, heavier make-up and longer dialogues.

The way the Brazilian people are presented in this opening of documentary intention seems to echo at least two aspects of what Marilena Chauí calls 'Brazil's foundational myths', which, she says, obstruct political action: (1) Brazil has a peaceful, orderly, generous, cheerful and sensual people, albeit one that suffers a great deal; (2) Brazil is a country devoid of all prejudices including those of race and creed, and practises the mingling of races as a means of strengthening its character.[9] Indeed, these smiling, well-groomed, gentle illiterate people, exhibiting a colourful racial mix that includes details of comic simplicity, such as the boy who calls his beloved 'hot pussy' in the letter he dictates to Dora, seem at one with life, irrespective of their poverty.

The problem, as it were, is not with them, but with the station itself, which the film, in its totalizing impetus, portrays as the concentration of all evil. In the station, among unemployed people degraded to informal vendors, and abandoned children turned to shoplifters, circulate at large murderers and human organ dealers, while outside the station chaotic traffic kills innocent pedestrians, like Josué's mother. Because reality is adapted to fiction, and not vice-versa, the logical causality is replaced by fate. Ana's death is not attributed to a breach of traffic regulations, but to the spinning toy Josué carries with him as a memento of his carpenter father. When he stops to pick up the toy he had dropped on the asphalt, his mother turns back to call him and is hit by an oncoming bus. Thus Josué, who seems to have no other relatives or friends, instantly joins the legions of abandoned children in the big city which remains oblivious of him.

The cause of these ills is not investigated, since class conflict, as well as a hypothetical, if at all existing, ruling class, remains outside the filmic space, hence outside the central station and beyond what is recognized as Brazil. Fiction becomes natural thanks to the use of the document, and the central station itself turns into wild, adverse nature. As such, it gives shelter to the villain Pedrão, a security guard hired by the station vendors, who murders pickpockets and operates a scheme of organ trafficking. Devoid of class or background, Pedrão is a mere representation of evil that disappears without a trace as the story develops.

The lack of an oppressive power allows for the action to be transferred from the collective to the individual realm. What draws Josué and Dora together is not the economic hardship they face, but their biographical coincidences: she was also abandoned by her alcoholic father and lost her mother when she was the same age as the boy. The solution, then, is to find the father and not, as suggested by Gilberto Vasconcellos in a bout of humour, to enrol Josué in a Rio Ciep (or a free boarding school), with which deed Fernanda Montenegro's character 'would have gained ethical density'.[10]

The search for the father, in the diegesis, is equivalent, on a meta-linguistic level, to the search for the home country lost in the Cinema Novo past, where the filmmaker of the present hopes to find historical affiliation. Needless to say, nostalgia for the fatherland and father figures had never been an issue for the Cinema Novo, whose filmmakers never doubted the land they belonged to and turned their backs on preceding filmmaking traditions. This was typical of most new-wave directors, from the 1950s to the 1970s, determined as they were to negate their predecessors, referred to as *cinéma du papa* in France, or *Papas Kino*, in Germany. In the Brazilian *Cinema Marginal* (or Underground Cinema), at the end of the 1960s, the assassination of the father, represented by Cinema Novo, acquired Oedipal proportions, as described by Jean-Claude Bernardet in *O vôo dos anjos*.[11]

In *Central Station*, the need to recognize the homeland and the search for the reassurance of an affiliation indicate the narrator's external position in relation to the narrated object. In the second part of the film, in which Dora and Josué journey through the arid northeast by bus, truck and *pau de arara* (back of trucks), the stunning images of Brazil's poor areas, captured in glorious colour by the celebrated director of photography Walter Carvalho, have something strange, even uncanny about them. Their advertising chic prompted Ivana Bentes to develop, with reference to the New Brazilian Cinema, the concept of 'cosmetics of hunger', as opposed to Glauber Rocha's 'aesthetics of hunger'.[12] Though he draws on his experience as a documentarist to render the lives of common people, Salles's poverty is so clean and aestheticized that one immediately senses the narrator's remoteness.

Fernão Ramos has already observed the recurrence in recent Brazilian cinema of characters of foreigners who embody a kind of superior conscience to the native Brazilian plagued by an inferiority complex.[13] Indeed, the revival filmmakers, all of them from the upper classes, seem torn between an affinity with the foreigner, who is also the former colonizer, and their sincere compassion for, and sympathy with, the poor and oppressed native. They still seem to be tormented by the syndrome of Antônio das Mortes, a prophetic character in Glauber Rocha's films, who, according to Jean-Claude Bernardet in his classic book *Brasil em tempo de cinema*, represents the middle classes in perennial hesitation between the perks of the ruling class and the real needs of the poor.[14] By approaching a class other than his or her own, the filmmaker becomes the guilt-ridden ethnographer in search of redemption through a benevolent, idealized representation of the other.[15]

The drought and poverty of the northeastern homeland are shown as picturesque details that have no consequences for the lives of its inhabitants and require no intervention. Actually the film, as a typical example of its period, rather than retrieving the nation, makes clear, through its detached stance and citation structure, that the re-enactment of the national project is no longer possible. Utopia can only be realized as an absence, a hypothetical reunion with a father called Jesus who never materializes and is only conceivable as fiction or myth. In order to make this unlikely father and fatherland credible, the narrative moves towards melodrama and the characters migrate from the modern universe full of such threats as the central station to the secure and comfortable isolation of archaic Brazil, and, in so doing, they take the inverse route to that followed by real northeastern migrants.

Justification for such a conservative solution, which goes against the logic of rural exodus, is found in religious faith. The journey back home corresponds to the retrieval of Christian dogmas, reiterated in the film's iconography. Icons of the Madonna with the baby Jesus abound in the decorations of houses in both Rio and the backlands, and serve as counterpoints to Josué's expressions of yearning for his mother. Alone in the station after Ana's death, he kneels before an altar of the Virgin Mary with child. His prayers are answered when he meets his surrogate mother, Dora, who helps him fulfil his destiny. In Dora's Rio apartment, the boy sees a cottage in the countryside painted on a china plate on the wall. A shot of the plate is followed by a reverse shot of Josué who smiles, and then the camera focuses on an icon of the Madonna with child. The utopian triangulation of home–Virgin–boy is set into motion, and it is up to Dora to make it happen.

Though she starts off as cruel and insensitive, Dora gradually reveals her good side thanks to Josué's influence. This process culminates in

The Virgin Mary with Child is a central element in the configuration of home in *Central Station*.

Dora's trance amid the fireworks, candles and hymns of a religious procession. The spinning camera during Dora's trance is another citation of Glauber, who used similar techniques to portray popular trances, but in his case with a critical view of the alienated masses, who were easily manipulated by 'a cross or a sword'. In this reading of Glauber against the grain, the result is the miracle of revelation: the cynical scribe who used to destroy the letters dictated to her becomes aware of her sins, regrets them and decides, from then on, to post the letters. At the end of the trance Dora awakens on Josué's lap, in an inverted Pietà composition purposely idealized by Salles,[16] through which the son is identified with the father called Jesus, just as in the Christian myth. Subsequently, Dora and Josué have their photographs taken with a cardboard figure between them representing Father Cícero, a religious and political leader of the early twentieth century and still revered as a major paternal figure in the northeast. The photo becomes each one's prize possession and guarantees the film a happy ending when they separate and are left alone, choking back the tears as they independently smile at the photo.

Ismail Xavier has already observed the affinity between the concept of the nation, in its totalizing reach, and the meaning of the sacred.[17] In *Central Station*, the promise of the Madonna and Pietà icons finally comes true through the photographs that reconstitute the sacred family, reuniting and identifying homeland and home. The photograph, described by Charles S. Peirce as the icon par excellence owing to its resemblance to the object,[18] is a constant in Wim Wenders's films, in which the characters keep trying and always failing to obtain proof of the real. In *Central Station*, the enunciation sanctions popular religion as Cinema Novo had never done. The family is portrayed as equivalent to the homeland in its symbolic wholeness in a similar way to that of the American hegemonic cinema. This is how it recovers the fable, though not social history, turned superfluous with the internalization of the drama. Though the film flirts with the postmodern citation cinema and Wenders's romantic modernity, it ends up playing by the rules of the domestic melodrama.

With the insertion of Father Cícero's image, the homeland is confirmed as the iconography of the past, exerting a pacifying influence on the present. Just like the photograph, the backlands are also frozen in a utopian, archaic territory, immune to time and the ills of modernity, which have been left behind in central station.

Dora's trance culminates in the tableau of the inverted *Pietà* in *Central Station*.

Nation and family come into being under the sign of the sacred, represented by Father
Cicero in *Central Station*.


## The zero and the empty utopia

Such an interpretation of Brazil was obviously not unanimous in the
late 1990s, which marks the peak of the film revival. In *Midnight*, again
directed by Walter Salles, in partnership with Daniela Thomas, just a year
after *Central Station*, Brazilian society becomes the stage for injustices that
find no solution in the archaic *sertão*, but are perpetuated in the urban
violence of the present. The inaugural myth is formulated in a tone of
hope within the film title, *O primeiro dia*, which refers to the first day of
the millennium. But it is then denied by the storyline: of the four main
characters, three die violently between New Year's Eve and the year's first
day, and the fourth survives a suicide attempt.

*Midnight* is one of a series of films about *favelas*, supported by the
production company VideoFilmes, which includes directors such as Kátia
Lund, Eduardo Coutinho, João Moreira Salles and even writer Paulo Lins,
as part of a project of social intervention through which the filmmakers
become involved with the communities in focus. The documentarist João
Moreira Salles, Walter's brother and director of the remarkable documentary about drug and arms dealing in Rio, *News from a Private War* (*Notícias
de uma guerra particular*, 1998), won notoriety for financing the autobiog-
raphy of Marcinho VP, a drug dealer wanted by the police and eventually
murdered. Paulo Lins wrote his famous book *Cidade de Deus* (*City of God*),
which was turned into a film directed by Fernando Meirelles and Kátia
Lund, based on anthropological research carried out in a *favela*. Finally,
Eduardo Coutinho has been for decades documenting and discussing
Brazil's social inequality from the *sertão* to the *favelas* in an entirely political and self-committed way.

Though deriving from an essentially Brazilian project, *Midnight* originated abroad. It was financed by French television channel ARTE, which commissioned films about the turn of the millennium from new filmmakers from ten different countries: Germany, Belgium, Brazil, the United States, Spain, France, Hungary, Mali and Taiwan, resulting in the series '2000 vu par ...'. Its production structure does not differ greatly from that of *Central Station*, which was financed by both national and international producers. However, the target audiences of *Midnight* could be seen as potentially more sophisticated, since the ARTE series included markedly auteurist directors such as Tsai Ming Liang (Malaysia/Taiwan) and Abderrahmane Sissako (Mauritania/Mali).

As in *Central Station*, documentary techniques and materials are largely employed to construct the backdrop to the fictional story. But in spite, or rather because, of the scarcity of means and the mere three weeks in which it was made, the film conveys a sense of urgency which is more favourable to the expression of the real. Problems with police corruption, subhuman prison conditions, arms dealing, tensions between social classes and Rio's generalized violence are expressed in a tone of denunciation, often through location shots. Sets which had already been used in *News from a Private War*, such as the Kafkaesque corridors of a confiscated arms depot, lend the film a revelatory quality which cannot be found in *Central Station*'s scenic essays of the *sertão*.

Necessarily synthetic, as it needed to summarize the millennium in little more than an hour, *Midnight* has gaps which were incorporated into the plot. The characters have no past history and barely constitute individuals. As a result, the film tends to produce stereotypes through which the poor are associated with the good, and the powerful with the evil. Even the blackmailer Chico, from the *favela*, extorts money from the police for a noble cause, which is to finance his wife and son's New Year's Eve commemorations. The protagonists are called João and Maria (John and Mary), blatantly fictitious names, like 'everyman', or a certain man and a woman, who are nothing but exemplary social figures. The secondary characters also remain undefined as individuals and thus follow the same pattern of social types.

An effective resource used to lend credibility to such precarious protagonists was to envelop them in silence. João is a convict who is privileged enough to have his own cell in a crowded prison, until another prisoner, Vovô (Grandpa), is transferred there. Even when urged to talk by his new companion, João says that he 'only wants to sleep' and remains silent. Maria, a young middle-class woman, is more eloquent, but she has the

peculiar job of teaching sign language, which also lends her an aura of
living with silence. Other script devices complete this composition: when
Pedro, Maria's partner, abandons her, she breaks the phone in a fit of rage,
ruling out any further possibility of communicating with her beloved,
who incidentally is the film's most laconic character. Later, on the verge
of suicide, Maria refuses to talk to her rescuer, João, saying, just like him,
that she 'only wants to sleep'.

As an exemplary character, João, played by Luís Carlos Vasconcelos,
is reminiscent of other moments in Brazilian cinema. He is the typical
heroic cowherd/*cangaceiro* who has migrated to a Rio *favela*. Such a reference is discernible not just for those who had seen him two years earlier
as *cangaceiro* Lampião in *Perfumed Ball*: he is betrayed by the typical laconi-
cism of the dry backlands, the markedly northeastern accent of his few
lines and his foreign, superior attitude inside the *favela*. His friend Chico
calls him 'the man of silence' and 'samurai', emphasizing his character of
noble warrior in contrast to the ordinary *favela* inhabitants.

This bandit, notable for his strong hand and shooting skills, is a kind
of updated version of the northeastern cowboy of *The Big City* (*A grande
cidade*, Carlos Diegues, 1966). Played by the emblematic actor Leon-
ardo Villar of *The Given Word* (*O pagador de promessas*, Anselmo Duarte,
1962), Diegues's hero leaves the *sertão* to try his luck in Rio and ends up a
*favela* thug. João's foreignness brings him close to yet another emblematic
character of Glauber's films, Antônio das Mortes. In the same way that
Antônio takes money from the 'colonels' (land owners) and the church to
kill the preacher Sebastião and *cangaceiro* Corisco, João buys his freedom
in exchange for murdering a friend. And he lets himself fall for Maria,
a middle-class character, from whom he gets a brief glance of liberation,
and who, thanks to him, experiences revelation. His arrangement with the
ruling class combined with his sympathy for the oppressed turns him into
a tortured, solitary being, just like Antônio das Mortes, and condemned
to a tragic ending.

But it would perhaps be inaccurate to classify such characters as allegorical. In their incompleteness they are rather nostalgic reminiscences of
past allegories, of a time when starting from zero was possible, cinema
was really new and the characters, in their revolutionary impulses, dragged
the masses with them. Such a nostalgic charge can be felt, for example, in
Pedro, played by Carlos Vereza, famous for his role as the writer Graciliano Ramos in *Memories of Prison* (*Memórias do cárcere*, Nelson Pereira dos
Santos, 1984). Pedro is so fragmentary and inexplicable that he seems to
have stepped into the wrong film. In one of his scanty lines he reacts to

Maria's remark that he is old by saying, 'And you are such a young girl ...'.
In fact Pedro does not seem to belong in Maria's contemporary reality. His
work as a solitary writer does not fit there, but is trapped in the time of
*Memories of Prison*, from 14 years before. In the end, he and his computer
disappear mysteriously, leaving Maria perplexed. Pedro's presence in the
film is so ephemeral that Maria's overblown reaction would hardly be credible were it not for Fernanda Torres's convincing performance.

Another nostalgic character is the old prisoner Vovô, played by
seasoned samba composer Nelson Sargento, who at a certain point delivers
the chorus of one of his famous songs: 'Samba, you agonise but never die/
A rescuer always comes by/ Before your last sigh ...'. Though essentially
a homage to the real composer, the character of Vovô ends up playing a
central role. His endless gibbering, typical of the *'samba do crioulo doido'*
('the mad black's samba'), is presented as a mysterious prophecy. While he
awaits his amnesty, he repeats:

> It will turn, nine will turn to zero, the other nine will turn to zero, yet
> another will turn to zero and one will turn to two. The year 2000 is the
> year of freedom!

But then, realizing that he will merely be transferred to another cell, he
shouts:

> It will all turn to zero, nobody will remain to tell the story, you damned
> guards!

Later, when he is dying, he pleads: 'João, it'll turn to zero, you'll do what
has to be done, won't you?'

One cannot but associate these utterances with the prophecy repeated
in *Black God, White Devil*: 'The backlands will turn to sea, and the sea will
turn into backlands.' However, in *Midnight*, the prophecy is not connected
with promises of riches in a paradisiacal island, or with revolutionary
hopes of the oppressed classes. The change refers only to the coming of
the new millennium, expressed as a 'turn to zero', that is to say, as an
empty utopia.

The film's ending guarantees its fulfilment. After killing his friend,
João takes refuge on the roof of a high-rise where he finds Maria, who
is preparing to commit suicide. When she opens out her arms, imitating
the statue of Christ the Redeemer on the distant Corcovado, and gets
ready to jump, she is held back by João. They end up making love at the
millennium's zero hour to the light and sound of the fireworks. At this
climactic moment, reinforced by Antônio Pinto's dramatic music, the
Glauberian backlands–sea utopia and the zero metaphor are re-elaborated.

The 'turning to zero' in *Midnight* recycles Glauber's backlands-sea prophecy.

The camera, turning in the opposite direction to that of the spinning couple, who dance in each other's arms, reminds us of Dora's trance in *Central Station*, as well as other trances suggested by spinning cameras in Glauber's films. Meanwhile, João shouts the prophetic announcement he had learned from Vovô:

> It will turn, nine will turn to zero, another nine will turn to zero, yet another will turn to zero and one will turn to two. Everything is going to

Maria's night of love with the bandit in *Midnight* is reminiscent of Rosa and Corisco's adulterous encounter in *Black God, White Devil*.

turn around. Right will turn wrong, wrong will turn right and those who killed will now save.

This ballet of camera and actors accompanying the 'turn to zero' reveals itself as an insightful solution, as it turns around the surface of Glauber's backlands–sea prophecy and the northeast millennarian beliefs without actually formulating them. At the same time, it cites the trance of Rosa and Corisco, in *Black God, White Devil*, who spin in each other's arms to the sound of Villa-Lobos in their adulterous transgression. But the announcement of a social revolution is replaced by the conquest of a vague individual freedom, and the year turning to round numbers suggests nothing more than numerological superstition. Thus the hour zero turns around itself in a kind of empty prophecy, exhausting itself in the nostalgic citation of a past utopia and negating the very inauguration of the millennium the film's title announces. Purposely configured as citation, the zero in *Midnight*, unlike Rossellini's, does not aspire to change the world or pave the way for new cinematic languages, but only to express the desire – devoid of a project – for communication between different social classes. Indeed, its messenger is finally reduced to the nothing he himself called for: he is shot dead in a moment of distraction when admiring his middle-class lover as she, and only she, bathes in the paradisiacal sea.

The backlands man almost reaches the sea, but dies on the beach. The everyday sea of the Brazilian wealthy classes, there for their sole entertainment, remains out of the reach of the poor northeastener. Accordingly, two different concepts of sea are presented in the montage. At first the frame is entirely filled by the sea where Maria bathes; in the next shot, João is sitting on the sand, watching her from a distance. These two shots, edited together, are striking for their discrepancy. The first, from João's point of view, is a dream-like image, the sea is green, calm, too clean to be true. The second, from Maria's point of view, is the realistic sight of a man sitting on a dirty beach the day after a New Year celebration, surrounded by the party's sleepy stragglers.

Whereas in *Black God, White Devil* the straight-line tracking shot of the character running towards a hypothetical sea expresses the teleology that breaks the vicious circle of the religious trance,[19] in *Midnight* it is João's gunshot fired into the sky and mixing with the fireworks at the millennium's zero hour that unleashes a revelation to the middle-class character. But its content remains unexplained. When she opens the window on the year's first day and comes face to face with the shacks cramming the *favela's* hillside, Maria is bathed by a light that suggests some kind of religious illumination which finds no backing in the story and is reduced

The utopian sea of the oppressed contrasts with the ordinary beach of the middle classes in *Midnight*.

to a rhetorical effect. The fact remains that the *favela* is now part of the bourgeois experience, in a country that still has no inclination to change.

## The empty centre and the twilight of the male

*Latitude Zero* is set in the actual as well as metaphorical centre of Brazil: Poconé, state of Mato Grosso, close to the Equator, hence the reference to the zero latitude. It derives from a project of low-budget cinema designed by its director, Toni Venturi, together with a group of São Paulo filmmakers, which resulted in the launching of a low-budget film financing line by Brazil's federal government. By way of cost reduction, but also as an aesthetic option, the film has only two actors. They rehearsed their parts exhaustively before moving to the locations, in order to reduce shooting time and material. The cast's state of readiness allowed for a great number of long takes, aimed both at saving money and emphasizing the performances' theatrical style.

Venturi's purpose was to inaugurate a viable production system for the Brazilian cinema while preserving its auteurist vocation. But *Latitude Zero*, in its drive for originality, can be seen as a 'film of *auteurs*', for it carries different fingerprints through which the interaction between the director and his collaborators can be observed. First of all, the film is marked by the presence of Débora Duboc, a stage actress and Venturi's wife, who is the object of a fascinated camera gaze that sets her free to develop her own conception of acting and confer a feminist perspective on the entire film. Cláudio Jaborandy, in his first important role on the screen, was also granted freedom to develop his own performance, which makes use of a wide palette of emotional states between sanity and madness.

The playwright Fernando Bonassi is a central figure within this São Paulo group, which has been working across boundaries between film and theatre since *Starry Sky* (*Um céu de estrelas*, Tata Amaral, 1997), a violent drama about a couple which anticipates several elements of *Latitude Zero*. Bonassi is the author of the play *The Evil Things in Our Minds* (*As coisas ruins de nossas cabeças*), turned into a film script by Di Moretti, Venturi's collaborator since his first short films. His is the idea of the synthetic title that suggests the centre of Brazil, the earth's point zero and the annihilated characters who restart from scratch. The composer Lívio Tragtenberg, who wrote the film score, is another important name within the São Paulo cinematic revival. From film to film he has been exploring the thin line between 'symphony and cacophony', as expressed in the title of Jean-Claude Bernardet's film about São Paulo (*São Paulo, Symphony and Cacophony/São Paulo, sinfonia e cacofonia*, 1994), also with music by Tragtenberg, which has set the tone for a number of recent São Paulo productions.

Regional characteristics aside, the title is a clear national allegory. But, in keeping with the need for cutting costs, rather than the crowds that make the country's bustling centre in *Central Station*, the option was to stage an empty, post-utopian centre. The location is an abandoned goldmine where the only remaining inhabitant is Lena (Duboc), in an advanced state of pregnancy, who runs a bar devoid of patrons. In the monumental natural scenery, the pocked walls of red earth are reminiscent of the hundreds of busy hands that once worked there. Now they are the Eldorado that has fallen apart, the ruined utopia, the paradise once dreamed of by the discoverers, now lost; the sea that turned into backlands.

Roughness is suggested from the outset, as the opening credits appear to the sound of nails being hammered. We then see Lena who, in the dark interior of her bar (later revealed as the *Dama de Ouro* or 'Queen of Diamonds'), is banging nails into boards to seal its door. We begin at the end: a bar is being closed by its grotesquely dirty, dishevelled owner, who

The ruins of Eldorado in *Latitude Zero*.

is getting ready to abandon ship. Once the door has been sealed and the packing done, Lena devotes a few moments to relics of the past she keeps in a little box, together with the money for the trip: a chain with crucifix, which she kisses, and her picture with Matos, later revealed as the man responsible for her pregnancy. But she soon sets these objects aside and stretches out on a chair where she starts to massage her own tired body, in gestures that culminate in masturbation.

Her solitary sex, in the present, is thus the negation of religion and the man, shown in the form of a dead past inside a box. The long take of the camera spinning around her while her moans increase produces an opposite effect to that of Dora's religious trance in *Central Station*, or that of Maria's explosive ecstasy in *Midnight*. Here it is a solitary woman who climaxes with a primal, beastly scream, without the attenuating effect of music, thus overcoming everything with her own physique and no metaphysics.

Laura Mulvey, in her analysis of *Hail Mary* (*Je vous salue Marie*, Jean-Luc Godard, 1982), comments on how Godard equates female dissimulation with cinematic illusionism through the religious symbol. She says:

> Belief in God depends on belief in the woman's impossible virginity which represents her 'wholeness', an evisceration of the psychologically threatening and physically disgusting 'inside'. It is only as 'whole' that woman can drop the mask of artifice with which she both deceives man and conceals the truth of her body.[20]

Still with reference to *Hail Mary*, Mulvey comments on the meaning of the netball Maria plays with, which is 'round and complete, the circle of the feminine once again, but impenetrable, with no *hole*', thus constituting 'a denial of the wound, the open vagina, the hole'.[21] *Latitude Zero*, on the contrary, stresses the carnal aspect of the pregnant woman who thus becomes the reverse of the Hollywood feminine revered, and criticized, by Godard. Her main attribute is precisely the obscene orifice which is constantly about to expose itself to the camera. Instead of negating sexual activity in order to sanctify the foetus, the film reiterates Lena's sex drive in the present, thus eliminating the possibility of the sacred.

In contrast to the present-time female carnality, a male idealism gone stale is presented in the person of Vilela (Jaborandy), a fugitive soldier who comes to stay at Dama de Ouro following 'Colonel' Matos's directions (the grade of 'colonel' referring to both militarism and an oligarchic, archaic Brazil). Vilela interferes with Lena's departure and convinces her to re-open the bar. She finally gives in, but retains her typical pragmatism. While refurbishing the restaurant she brings an intact wedding

The wedding imaginary among poor women in *Black God, White Devil* and *Latitude Zero*.

dress and bridal wreath out of a box, tries on the wreath and admires the dress for a minute before tearing it in half and using it as a curtain. This scene is reminiscent of other strong moments in Brazilian cinema featuring the imaginary of unrealized weddings among poor women: the solitary bride on the banks of the Tietê river in *The Margin* (*A margem*, Ozualdo Candeias, 1967), and, again, Rosa, in *Black God, White Devil*, who dances through the scrubland wearing the wreath of the bride who has just been violated by Corisco.

The parallel between Lena and Rosa could go further, as far as the clash between female pragmatism and male idealism is concerned: Rosa gives no credit to Manuel's account of Sebastião's miracles and carries on pounding manioc flour; Lena also grounds manioc, while suspiciously listening to Vilela's impossible plan to reactivate the gold fields. In Glauber's film, male idealism finally leads to political revolution, at least on the artistic level, when the sea floods the backlands through an editing effect. In *Latitude Zero*, the man is not even granted the gift of art, since the deserted land is a result of his past projects.

Lena and Vilela's relationship develops on the basis of misunderstandings. Their dialogues are rather parallel monologues (which expose the artificiality of the film's theatrical staging). The utterances from both sides are connected by association of terms, rather than meaning. Vilela says, for example, that his obsession with his ex-wife is a 'disease', and Lena replies that you can always tell someone's life story by the 'diseases they've had'. This dialogue of the deaf, similar to the famous dialogue of the couple in *Barren Lives* (*Vidas secas*, Nelson Pereira dos Santos, 1963), blocks, by means of its artifice, any possibility of melodrama. The fleeting moments of tenderness between the two, resulting from pure physical urge, also reinforce the opposition between masculine and feminine projects, leading to Lena's inevitable repulsion that causes Vilela to rape her.

Indeed, Vilela, who is a throwback to Brazil's dictatorial past as much as his boss Matos, knows no other than the predatory way. His frantic activity is obviously doomed to failure as it echoes the reasons for the current devastation, namely, the extractivist mentality, formerly applied to gold and now to wood. Meanwhile Lena just wants to rid herself of all male oppression, both past and present. Her battle is bolstered by the feminine attribute of maternity. Against the macho utopia that resulted in an excavated, hollow land, she sets her round, full belly. To photograph her is tantamount to showing her concrete, physiological needs, and in this sense the film is like an immersion into the female womb, whose boiling state is indicated by images of the sun, the burning forests, the red earth, as well as her own explosions. The pregnant woman thus acquires a threatening, proto-revolutionary character, which culminates with the birth scene in which she sits with her legs wide open facing the camera, surrounded by hundreds of burning candles.

Reduced to the toughness of the survival and reproduction instincts,

The pregnant woman acquires a proto-revolutionary character in *Latitude Zero*.

Lena evades the typical Christian dilemma between the Virgin mother and the prostitute, which Godard regularly revisits in his different year zeroes. *Latitude Zero* also lambasts the dream of the father and the father-land, fixed, in *Central Station*, on the *tableau* of the inverted Pietà, in which the son becomes both father and hero. Brazilian foundational myths in this case are conspicuous by their absence: the rich land, as well as the multi-racial people that exploited it, have evaporated, leaving behind nothing but a vast desert.

The story, then, starts from zero, with the first encounter between man and woman, correcting the previous error of male domination. Unlike *Midnight*, in which the man is eliminated by alien forces and the woman is inexplicably redeemed, in this film it is the woman who eventually kills the man, sets fire to the useless home and the false hopes of the family trinity, and leaves on the back of a truck with her son on her lap. Instead of *Central Station*'s inverted Pietà *tableau*, *Latitude Zero* offers a portrait of the Madonna in which the woman is the protective and providing figure for the man-child, thus configuring the twilight of the male. The new Brazilian utopia seems to be, in this auteurist, independent cinema, the country of the Amazons.

## CHAPTER THREE

# TO BE OR NOT TO BE A CANNIBAL

**Films**

*Hans Staden* (Luiz Alberto Pereira, 1999)

*How Tasty Was My Little Frenchman* (*Como era gostoso o meu francês*, Nelson Pereira dos Santos, 1970–72)

*Macunaíma* (Joaquim Pedro de Andrade, 1969)

# TO BE OR NOT TO BE A CANNIBAL

The ability to look at oneself as the Other – a point of view from which
one arguably obtains the ideal view of oneself – seems to me to be the
key for Tupi–Guarani anthropophagy.
Eduardo Viveiros de Castro, A inconstância da alma selvagem[1]

The film *Hans Staden* (1999) opens with a grandiose image of the sea on
which travels a caravel, framed in aerial shot. The location is actually
the river Tagus, a convenient choice, as Portugal was one of the film's
co-producers and had a replica of Vasco da Gama's caravel. But the large
water expanse filling the frame stands for the great sea once crossed by the
discoverers. It thus reproduces the utopian sea, which this time serves as
an introduction to another important aspect of the discovery mythology,
cannibalism.

The film's protagonist is the famous adventurer from Hessen, Hans
Staden, who in 1554 was held captive by the Brazilian Tupinambá Indians. His story is recorded in a book he wrote which became an invaluable
document of one of Brazilian history's foundational moments.[2] The book's
greatest attraction is the detailed description of the Tupis' cannibalistic
customs, of which Staden himself, according to his account, was a victim
who miraculously escaped alive.

Pereira's decision to focus on the cannibal as part of Brazil's foundational mythology situates him within a tradition in Brazilian art launched
by the modernist movement in the 1920s and theorized by Oswald
de Andrade, the formulator of the 'Anthropophagic Utopia'. As to his
aesthetic references, the main source was the film *How Tasty Was My Little
Frenchman*, directed by Nelson Pereira dos Santos in 1970 and released in
1972. Nelson had also extracted elements from Staden's book to express

The maritime opening of *Hans Staden*.

his vision of Oswald's anthropophagy, which he combined with political and social utopias of the late 1960s. Proving its enduring centrality in the national imaginary, the figure of the cannibal reappears in the globalized context of the 1990s, albeit devoid of the utopian features which, in the past, had turned it into an art object. Though reduced to a relic of the past, it still carries the sensationalist features which have been responsible for its popularity since the sixteenth century.

The cannibal's trajectory in Brazilian cinema reflects an interesting migration of the national identity through Brazilian society's different ethnic components. In this chapter, I will first investigate the origins of the cannibal myth, then move on to a brief review of *Macunaíma* (Joaquim Pedro de Andrade, 1969) and its cannibalistic allegories, followed by more detailed analyses of *How Tasty Was My Little Frenchman* and *Hans Staden*, which discuss the place of cannibalism in the national imaginary.

## The good and the bad cannibal

The cannibal, both as a real and imaginary figure, has been associated with the New World from the outset. As observed by Afonso Arinos, some maritime maps of the time of the great discoveries referred to the country as 'Brésil Cannibale', that is, the dwelling of a monster with a dog's face.[3] Like other fantastic creatures believed to inhabit the lands overseas, it was not originally associated with human beings and much less with noble savages. Even the sixteenth-century Huguenot travellers, such as André Thevet and Jean de Léry, who were frequently deferential towards the Indians and admired some aspects of their social organization, found it hard to forgive their anthropophagic practices. It was Montaigne, an important source of Oswald de Andrade's utopia, who for the first time linked cannibalism to the idea of the noble savage. His main sources were the accounts by Staden, Thevet and Léry, and interviews he himself conducted with three Tupinambá Indians taken to France probably in the year 1566.[4] In his famous essay 'Of the Cannibals', in which the society of native Brazilians is described as a true paradise, he concludes:

> I conceive there is more barbarity in eating a man alive, than when he is dead; in tearing a body limb from limb by racks and torments, that is yet in perfect sense; in roasting it by degrees; in causing it to be bitten and worried by dogs and swine (as we have not only read, but lately seen, not among inveterate and mortal enemies, but among neighbours and fellow-citizens, and, which is worse, under colour of piety and religion), than to roast and eat him after he is dead.[5]

This commentary, which became widely known and provided the basis for the Enlightenment theory of natural goodness, allows for different readings. Frank Lestringant questions the degree of seriousness contained in such 'unexpected praise of naked, anthropophagic peoples', given the blatant amount of irony and humour it contains.[6] In fact, Montaigne's intention, in 'Of the Cannibals', was to criticize the society of his time rather than to understand the Brazilian Indians' behaviour. For this reason, he often resorted to what Christian Marouby termed a 'negative rhetoric',[7] a technique in vogue at his time and apparent, for example, in the following passage:

> I should tell Plato, that it is a nation wherein there is no manner of traffic, no knowledge of letters, no science of numbers, no name of magistrate or political superiority; no use of service, riches or poverty, no contracts, no successions, no dividends, no properties, no employments, but those of leisure, no respect of kindred, but common, no clothing, no agriculture, no metal, no use of corn or wine.[8]

Rather than to the savages, this definition applies, through negation, to Montaigne's own society. The Indians themselves remain entirely idealized and their social structure ignored, for their occupations, agricultural activities, kin relations and laws are summarily dismissed as nonexistent. '[His] positive evaluation [of the Indians],' says Todorov about Montaigne's relativism, 'derives from a misunderstanding, the projection on the other of an image of oneself – or, more precisely, of an ideal of oneself, which, for Montaigne, was incarnated by classical civilisation.'[9]

These are the ideas that, filtered by the eighteenth-century illuminists, inspired the Brazilian modernists in the 1920s. They provided the basis for the Anthropophagic Movement, whose principles are detailed in Oswald de Andrade's famous 'Anthropophagic Manifesto', first published in the *Revista de Antropofagia* in May 1928. The great novelty introduced by the modernists is a reversal of perspective, through which the idealized other becomes the anthropophagic self, who devours the colonizer in order to incorporate his power. Building on the defence of the native formulated in his 'Brazil-Wood Poetry Manifesto' in 1924, Oswald de Andrade championed the devouring of cultural and artistic techniques imported from the developed countries to turn them into export products. To that end, he preached the return to an indigenous primitivism free from the constraints of civilized society. In a poetic pun, Oswald expressed the need to recover the creative 'idleness' (*ócio*, in Portuguese) which had got lost somewhere between 'priesthood' (*sacerdócio*, literally 'holy idleness') and 'business' (*negócio*, literally the 'negation of idleness'), brought in by the European. 'Tupi or not Tupi, that is the question,' he exclaimed in his 'Anthropophagic Manifesto', which elects the Indian as the keeper of the national identity.[10]

The basic sources for the Oswaldian utopia are the Renaissance ideal of paradise regained in the land of Brazil and the Enlightenment theory of natural goodness. Montaigne, Léry and Thevet's writings, Caminha's famous letter reporting on the discovery of Brazil, as well as Rousseau and the French illuminists are objects of constant citation. As for modern references, Oswald borrows from Engels, Freud and Nietzsche to condemn all messianic cultures founded on paternal authority, private property and the state, and to reassert the belief in a classless, matriarchal society which would emerge from technological progress. Echoing the primitivist vogue launched by Francis Picabia's 'Manifeste Cannibale Dada' (1920) and cultivated by the French avant-garde, Oswald's utopia is a combination of primitivism and futurism, according to which the 'man of the primeval hordes', free from social and sexual oppression, would incarnate the 'man of the future' with all 'the phallic power of the Brazil-wood'.[11]

The revolution caused by Oswald's utopia is primarily due to the identification of the Brazilian with the anthropophagic Indian in a subaltern society, eager to forget its origins and imitate the European colonizer. It was obviously a metaphorical cannibalism he defended, which, far from the actual devouring of human flesh, contented itself with the absorption and digestion of abstract concepts and techniques. Even with relation to the Indians from the time of the discovery, Oswald's view of anthropophagy was highly idealized. He did not conceive of anything other than ritual cannibalism, motivated by noble reasons and practised against the enemy as an extreme act of revenge. In a dignifying note, he observes that 'the Anthropophagic ritual among the Greeks had already been annotated by Homer', and continues:

> Seen as *Weltanschauung*, [anthropophagy] can hardly lend itself to materialist and immoral interpretations such as those rendered by the Jesuits and the colonizers. Rather it belongs, as a religious act, to the primitive man's rich spiritual world.[12]

Hence the choice of the word 'anthropophagy', which, for him, carried a ritual and communal connotation, as opposed to cannibalism, which 'means anthropophagy for greed and also anthropophagy for hunger, as registered in chronicles of besieged cities and lost voyagers'. Drawing on Freud, Oswald proposes to turn taboo back into totem 'through a metaphysical operation connected to the anthropophagic rite'.[13] Once removed from cannibalism's physical needs, anthropophagy is purified and invested with a romantic character which is entirely attuned to the theory of natural goodness.

Roberto Schwarz observes that Oswald's primitivist euphoria was due greatly to the coffee prosperity in São Paulo state at that time, and could only have stemmed from an intellectual of the economic elite. For Schwarz, the basis of Oswald's poetics were to be found in

> the future coffee was projecting ahead. The universe of quasi-colonial relations it produced did not appear to him as an obstacle, but as an element of life and progress, and, as it were, of a progress which was more picturesque and humane than others, as none of the parties would be doomed to disappearance.[14]

With the development of anthropological and archaeological studies, the sources have multiplied and today there is a rich bibliography on the Brazilian Indian's cannibalistic habits in all their variations, which are certainly more complex than they are described in Oswald's noble anthropophagy. Eduardo Viveiros de Castro, for example, defines cannibalism as the Amerindian's primordial way of connecting with the world, which is a 'relation of cannibalistic predation and incorporation'. In such a system, oppositional terms such as 'subject' and 'object', or the 'self' and the 'other' give way to a set of relations between variable terms. This view is the basis of Viveiros de Castro's 'perspectivism' theory:

The basic idea behind the term 'perspectivism', which I have borrowed from the Western philosophical vocabulary and applied to Amerindian thought, is that the relation precedes the substance. Thus subjects and objects are before anything else the effect of the relations in which they are located. They are thus defined and redefined, produced and destroyed according to the changes in the relations through which they were constituted.[15]

Suggestive though they are, such ideas have had no artistic repercussion so far. The formulators of the Brazilian anthropophagic utopia, even the more recent ones, do not seem to have taken an interest in scientific researches on the Brazilian Indians' true customs. When the native cannibal re-emerges in the late Cinema Novo, and again in the New Brazilian Cinema, it is still the idealized noble native, extracted from the Renaissance literature and Brazil's foundational myths, which had inspired an intellectual and economic elite in the 1920s. The problem of a split identity between the native savage and a civilized foreigner still seems to occupy an essential part of the national imaginary.

### Consumer cannibalism

In the 1960s, Brazilian cinema seemed to define itself by the stomach – to use a phrase with modernist overtones. In the early years of the decade, it was animated by the 'Aesthetics of Hunger', as expressed in the title of Glauber Rocha's famous manifesto and translated into images in his classic *Black God, White Devil* of 1964, which expressed the revolutionary hopes that the 'backlands would turn to sea' and the oppressed would come to power (see Chapter 1). In the same year, the Brazilian left wing's revolutionary hopes were frustrated by the military coup and buried forever by Institutional Act number 5 (AI-5), decreed at the end of 1968. At this point, the Aesthetics of Hunger gives way to anthropophagy, which finds expression in two exceptional films: *Macunaíma* and *How Tasty Was My Little Frenchman*.

Macunaíma was conceived at the height of the Tropicalist movement, which was particularly strong in the field of popular music. Tropicalism proposed cannibalization in every sense: between popular and high cultures, fine art and *kitsch*, good and bad tastes, all the while keeping its distance from left-wing political correctness. Similar features can be observed in *Macunaíma*, in which Oswaldian anthropophagy appears reinvigorated but charged with destructive power. Based on Mário de Andrade's modernist novel *Macunaíma*, published in 1928 (the same year as Oswald's 'Anthropophagic Manifesto'), the film presents anthropophagy as a general rule of a self-devouring humanity. Anthropophagites are both underdeveloped peoples and capitalist imperialism. In a bitter manifesto, written shortly after the passing of the AI-5, Joaquim Pedro describes cannibalism as the basic mechanism of all consumerism:

> Every consumer is reducible, in the last analysis, to cannibalism. The present work relationships, as well as the relationships between people – social, political, and economic – are still basically cannibalistic. Those who can, 'eat' others through their consumption of products, or even more directly in sexual relationships. ... The Left, while being devoured by the Right, tries to discipline and purify itself by eating itself – a practice that is simply the cannibalism of the weak.[16]

Anthropophagy, for Joaquim Pedro, is moreover

> an exemplary mode of consumerism adopted by underdeveloped peoples. In particular, the Brazilian indians, immediately after having been 'discovered' by the first colonisers, had the rare opportunity of selecting their Portuguese-supplied Bishop, Dom Pedro Fernandes Sardinha, whom they devoured in a memorable meal.[17]

Although based on the modernist proposal, Joaquim Pedro's vision of anthropophagy carries a dose of disillusionment that disqualifies it as a utopia. The film bears similarities with other anti-utopian films of the period, such as *Pigsty* (*Porcile*, Pier Paolo Pasolini, 1969) and *Week-end* (Jean-Luc Godard, 1967), both featuring scenes of cannibalism, which Joaquim Pedro himself considered akin to his film.

Anthropophagy as a social rule, in the film *Macunaíma*, is far removed from the libertarian, cheerful carnivalization of the book at its origin and closer to a 'mechanism of predatory appropriation', in Ismail Xavier's words.[18] Randal Johnson goes as far as asserting that in the film the protagonist Macunaíma is shown in an exclusively negative light.[19] Despite the remarkable sense of humour with which the adventures of Macunaíma, 'the hero without any character', are narrated, and despite his seductive personality, anthropophagy is seen, in the last analysis, as the country's structural vice. Industry owners devour their subordinates, the oppressed devour each other and in the end the hero himself is allegorically devoured by Brazil.

As a syncretic character, Macunaíma brings together the basic ethnic elements which form the Brazilian: he is black by birth, lives in an Indian hut in the jungle and, as the story unfolds, becomes European white. Conceived as Brazil's representative par excellence, he embarks on a journey through the country in which cannibalism is a frequent event. In various moments, he eats or tries to eat human flesh, for example, when he tastes a bit of Currupira's leg.[20] Macunaíma himself is almost cooked and devoured by the wife of Piaimã, the industrialist giant, whom he finally manages to throw into a human *feijoada*.[21] Macunaíma nearly experiences autophagy when he crushes and tries to eat his own testicles. His relocation from the jungle to the city introduces him to unrestrained consumerism, and he becomes an avid buyer of all sorts of useless products and gadgets. His melancholic end could only be an anthropophagic apotheosis: he is devoured in the river by Uiara, who turns his green and yellow Brazilian flag jacket into a pool of blood.

The film, in short, rather than limiting anthropophagy to the primitive, turns it into a general rule for the rich and poor, oppressors and oppressed, condemning society as a whole to cannibalistic self-destruction.

## Amorous cannibalism

*How Tasty Was My Little Frenchman* takes the opposite route to *Macunaíma*. Rather than an allegorical updating of inaugural myths, it provides an allegory of contemporary Brazil by sending it back to the sixteenth century and the anthropophagic Tupis. The film recounts the adventures of Jean, a Frenchman under the command of the Calvinist Villegagnon, who in the mid-sixteenth century set foot in the area which is today Rio de Janeiro in an attempt to occupy Brazil. To protect the region, called 'Antarctic France' by the French, he built the Fort of Coligny. While fleeing from Villegagnon's forced labour and austerity, Jean is captured by the Tupiniquims, Portuguese allies, and fights on their behalf. He then falls into the hands of the Tupinambás, French allies and enemies of the Portuguese, who take him for a Portuguese and hold him captive while they prepare for his ritual killing and devouring.

The basic storyline was extracted from Hans Staden's book, but the main character was turned into a Frenchman, and excerpts from a number of other sixteenth-century accounts were added, such as those by Jean de Léry, André Thevet, Villegagnon, Father José de Anchieta, Father Manoel da Nóbrega, Pero de Magalhães Gandavo, Gabriel Soares de Souza and Mem de Sá. Nelson's intention, as he declared in an interview with Helena Salem – although this is not necessarily the point the film itself makes – was to render a cinematic translation of Oswald's utopia by adopting, like him, the notion of noble anthropophagy:

> The [film's] plot tries to recover that bit of Brazilian culture, which has been colonized for centuries. The theory of anthropophagy is one whereby the Brazilian (and the Indian) assimilates foreign culture. The Indian ate

his enemy to acquire his strength, not to feed himself physically. It was a ritual. The more powerful the enemy, the tastier he was thought to be.[22]

Still in his interview with Salem, Nelson explained that he first had the idea for the film in the early 1960s when he was shooting *Barren Lives* (*Vidas secas*, 1963), based on a Graciliano Ramos novel, in the state of Alagoas, on the site where Bishop Sardinha was devoured by the Caeté Indians. This event is at the origin of another Ramos novel, *Caetés*. Nelson says:

> Ramos wrote his novel in an attempt to recover Brazilianness, as if he were screaming: 'We are all Indians!' He was trying to establish an internal point of view and find within himself what could have survived from Brazil's early Indians – an Indian capable of devouring a bishop – and make him feel as 'a man of his time'. I found this starting point interesting, although I did not draw on Ramos's story, which is psychological.[23]

Nelson's intention to identify the main point of view with that of the anthropophagic Indian is already indicated in the title of the film, *How Tasty Was My Little Frenchman*, formulated in the first person, from the perspective of Seboipepe, a Tupinambá Indian woman. The content of the title is validated by the fact that, at the end of the film, she devours the Frenchman, thus fulfilling Oswald de Andrade's utopian and metaphorical proposal of devouring the European dominator. Whether Seboipepe is representing the Brazilian in general, and whether her point of view is the one which actually prevails in the film, is another matter. The fact is that the film makes use of a number of alienating and distancing techniques, typical of 1960s self-reflexive cinemas, and, as a result, the production of spectatorial identification becomes a rather complex process. Let us start by examining the use of language.

Two main languages, French and Tupi, both of them foreign to present-day Brazilians, are spoken in the film, entailing the need for subtitles even in its original version. The use of Tupi could be seen as a radical search for national identity, harking back to indigenist and patriotic currents from the early twentieth century, which defended the adoption of Tupi as Brazil's official language. The choice can also be seen as a homage to Humberto Mauro, the patriotic director of *The Discovery of Brazil* (*Descobrimento do Brasil*, 1937), in which the Indians also express themselves in Tupi, although they readily accept the European catechism. The Tupi dialogues of *How Tasty Was My Little Frenchman* were translated by Mauro himself. However, the foreign-language dialogues work primarily as an alienation effect, which is accentuated by their association with humour.

An example is the scene in which the Tupinambás are trying to establish the nationalities of Jean and two other Portuguese men they have just captured. The Indians point to their own tongues and summon the foreigners to speak. Jean recites a strophe of Etienne Jodelle's poem, 'Ode on the singularities of André Thevet's Antarctic France' ('Ode sur les singularitez de la France Antarctique d'André Thevet'):

> Ces barbares marchent tous nuds,
> Et nous nous marchons incognus,
> Fardez, masquez.
> (Those barbarians walk about quite naked,/ Whereas we walk about incognito,/ Powdered and masked.)

The Portuguese, in their turn, recite a recipe of lamprey stew, in an unequivocal allusion to the Indian cannibalistic rituals.[24] The comic effect of these speeches derives from the fact that they are delivered in an automatic, detached manner by the speakers, who offer ironic comments about themselves alluding to the end they will meet as a gastronomic treat. As for the ode by Jodelle, a member of the Pléiade group, which is dedicated to Thevet, it compares, in its following verses, 'the savage and the civilized man in a manner largely favourable to the former'.[25] Here is some more of it:

> Celuy là fait beaucoup pour soy
> Qui fait en France comme moy,
> Cachant sa vertu la plus rare,
> Et croy veu ce temps vicieux,
> Qu'encore ton livre seroit mieux
> En ton Amerique barbare,
> Car qui voudroit un peu blasmer
> Le pays qu'il nous faut aymer
> Il trouveroit la France Arctique
> Avoir plus de monstres, je croy
> Et plus de barbarie en soy
> Que n'a pas la France Antarctique.
> Ces barbares marchent tous nuds,
> Et nous nous marchons incognus,
> Fardez, masquez. Ce peuple estrange
> A la pieté ne se range.
> Nous la nostre nous mesprisons,
> Pipons, vendons et deguisons.
> Ces barbares pour se conduire
> N'ont pas tant que nous de raison,
> Mais qui ne voit que la foison
> N'en sert que pour nous entrenuire?[26]

These verses are another interesting instance of negative rhetoric by a poet who criticizes his own society through an idealized description of the other.

Such use of self-commentary has already prompted Richard Peña to say that the film 'declares its independence from the point of view of any character'.[27] Indeed, irony and self-reflexivity contradict the title's suggestion that Seboipepe is the first-person narrator. The story is actually told by a combination of various verbal and visual texts, enunciated by different subjects, including Seboipepe and the Frenchman Jean. Contradictory testimonies by Léry, Thevet and Villegagnon are set side by side and illustrated with images and dialogues which are also in disagreement with them. Before the opening credits, a voice-over announces: 'Latest news of Antarctic France sent by Admiral Villegagnon'. This voice-over is the only speech in current Brazilian Portuguese in the whole film and refers to Villegagnon's letter to Calvin dated 31 March 1557. The letter was partly reproduced in Jean de Léry's book *History of a Voyage to the Land of Brazil* (*Histoire d'un voyage faict en la Terre du Brésil*), first published in 1576.[28] The voice-over then renders the letter:

> The country is deserted and uncultivated, there are no houses, no roofs, nor any country accommodations. On the contrary, there is much unfriendly and savage company, lacking in courtesy and humanity. So very different from us in their habits and education. With no religion and no knowledge of truth, virtue, justice or injustice, true animals in human bodies.

The style of this initial paragraph is once again reminiscent of Montaigne's negative rhetoric, now directed against the Indian, the abject 'other' in need of redressing. Voice-overs usually impart a third-person, omniscient point of view, which sets up the perspective for the entire film. But, in this case, irony brings the voice-over's authority into question, as the speaker imitates the typical style of official newsreels produced at the time of the dictatorship, which reported on governmental achievements. The background music is another ironic comment, as it stems from the French newsreels ('Actualités françaises') shown in Brazilian cinemas in the 1960s.

The clash between the voice-over and the images results in parodic effects. While in his letter Villegagnon complains about his subjects' lack of discipline, the images show them suffering like slaves under his rule.[29] Towards the end of the letter, the voice-over describes the rebels being released to defend themselves, while the images show the opposite: Jean, in chains and tied to an iron ball, is hurled into the sea in a summary execution (from which he eventually manages to escape).

Among the film's different narrative materials are prints extracted from the books by Hans Staden, Thevet and Léry; written texts by various authors presented in the form of intertitles; and diegetic and extradiegetic music, ranging from authentic Indian war chants to Zé Rodrix's experimental exercises. Dib Lutfi's camera work further obstructs the formation of a unified point of view, with its long shots, unexpected zooms on secondary or indistinct objects and focus on empty spaces, not to mention the montage based on *faux raccords* and jump cuts. This, however, is nothing but the film's strategy to convey an opinion on its subject. The contradictory narrative materials and the discontinuous editing are meant to disavow the testimonies given by the European discoverers, as well as, reaching the present time, the supposed neutrality of the dictatorship's official documentaries.

Echoes of Oswald de Andrade's libertarian ideas are noticeable when, behind the back of Calvinist Villegagnon's puritanical repression, natives and Frenchmen rejoice in the exercise of communal meals and sex. Sexual freedom is a central element and permeates the entire film, turning historical facts into allegories of the present. The Indian women who ostentatiously rid themselves of the gowns imposed by the French are reminiscent of the young Parisians who burned their bras in May 1968. The freedom and impudence with which the camera frames the cast's frontal nudity, including that of the Frenchman, hints at the climate of sexual liberty typical of the 1960s communes (unsurprisingly, the film faced many problems with censorship both in Brazil and abroad). Nelson himself, together with his team, lived in a community during the shooting of *How Tasty Was My Little Frenchman*, a method he adopted for the several films he shot in the area of Parati on the southern coast of Rio de Janeiro state.

In a way, *How Tasty Was My Little Frenchman* can be seen as a celebration of the communion of bodies that occurs both in cannibalism and the sexual act, two activities the film treats as libertarian and anti-authoritarian. The Portuguese title, *Como era gostoso o meu francês*, contains a pun on this double meaning, as *gostoso* means both 'tasty' and 'sexy'. The film as a whole plays with the verb *comer* (to eat), which also means to have sex. To be sure, the convergence of cannibalism and eroticism is a fact that has been exploited since the discovery. Already Amerigo Vespucci described the native Brazilian women as 'well shaped, solid, meaty, with firm breasts; unfortunate ones who exhibit them flaccid or drooping are not to be found',[30] only to subsequently turn these beauties into cannibal monsters.

Amerigo Vespucci's arrival in the New World, in a Renaissance print. Fully dressed and carrying the symbols of European technology, Vespucci meets a naked beauty whose raised forefinger is both an invitation to sex and an indication of the European visitor's end in a cannibalistic feast, like the one shown in the background.

In the film's pivotal scene, between Jean and Seboipepe, these two paths cross. Romantic as much as realist, the scene shows Seboipepe explaining to Jean, in a body language which soon evolves into caresses, the way in which he should behave during the ceremony of his killing and devouring. The brunette Ana Maria Magalhães and the blond Arduíno Colassanti, both at the peak of their youth and beauty, run naked over a large boulder in the idyllic landscape of sea and forest. Seboipepe pretends to pull her lover on an invisible rope tied to his neck, then lies on top of him to show how each of his limbs will be severed, finally reaching his neck, the part she is going to eat. The lesson on ritual cannibalism ends in sex, a moment in which cannibalism and eroticism become synonymous.

Sexual cannibalism, in the film, has a further meaning of racial integration, which is also fulfilled in the realms of languages and customs. Reciprocal learning and a playful mix of tongues take place between natives and foreigners. Seboipepe keeps muttering French words, while the Europeans communicate in Tupi. Rather than being shocked, the French seem comfortable with the Indian lifestyle, delivering their enemies to cannibalistic banquets (a fact which draws on historical documents) and using hoes, just like the Indians use their *ibirapema*, to knock down, with a single blow on their heads, their untrustworthy compatriots.

The final ceremony of Jean's execution is an apotheosis of racial integration. Jean reacts according to Seboipepe's instructions. Only, at the end, he utters the vindictive phrase in French, not in Tupi as he had been told: 'My friends will avenge my death, and there will be none of you left on this earth.' At this point, there is no difference between the French and the Portuguese (Jean has been killed as a Portuguese), or between Tupinambás and Tupiniquims (he had been captured by both). There is only the order of the devourers and the devoured, in a combat where not just the Indians but the insubordinate Europeans will be defeated.

The last image is a text plate quoting Mem de Sá, the governor general of Brazil, who announces the annihilation of all Tupiniquim Indians, the Portuguese allies, by official decree. As is known, both Tupinambás and Tupiniquims, the largest Indian populations in Brazil at the time of the discovery, were exterminated by wars and diseases brought in by the Europeans. In *How Tasty Was My Little Frenchman*, this annihilation happens at the very moment when the utopian alliance between colonizers and colonized, preached by Oswald de Andrade, could have taken place. But this is prevented by the oppressive powers on both sides, represented by such figures as Villegagnon and Mem de Sá. The anthropophagic utopia fails in much the same way as, in 1960s Brazil, revolutionary hopes that united an intellectual elite with peasants and workers were crushed by the military coup.

As in *Macunaíma*, the intention is to convey a synthesis of Brazil capable of allegorizing the country's current political situation. In *How Tasty Was My Little Frenchman*, the fault is found at the very foundation of the country, a moment in which the Brazilian identifies with both the native cannibal and the European adventurer. Together, they could have experienced an idyllic communion, but their projected paradise was destroyed by repressive powers on both sides.

### The other cannibal

The 500-year anniversary of Brazil's discovery, celebrated in 2000, prompted a series of historical events and constituted the ideal occasion in which to rethink the country and its Indians at the time of the arrival of the Europeans. The film *Hans Staden* was born in connection with these events, corroborated by the fact that its director and scriptwriter, Luiz Alberto Pereira, comes from Taubaté, near Ubatuba (in the north coast of São Paulo state), and was therefore familiar with the region where the historical events portrayed in the film took place.[31]

Various aspects of *Hans Staden* point to both Staden's book and the film *How Tasty Was My Little Frenchman* as its primary sources. The Tupari song at the opening, collected and reworked by Marlui Miranda, echoes the title of Nelson's film, saying 'You are good [*gostoso*/tasty], I am going to eat you.'[32] This war chant provides the background for the opening credits, as in Nelson's film, which opens to the sound of a similar song. And as in Nelson's film all characters speak their own tongues (or modern versions of their mother tongues), entailing the need for subtitles.

Although a clear homage to *How Tasty Was My Little Frenchman*, *Hans Staden* also betrays an intention to 'correct' the historical and visual infidelities of its model. Luiz Alberto Pereira has declared in several interviews that, as far as the film's concept is concerned, he tried to remain as faithful as possible to Hans Staden's account, searching for historical foundation for locations, music, dance, body paint and Indian customs in general. 'Nelson used painted chicken feathers, whereas I obtained the authentic ones,' he once stated.[33] This well-intentioned striving for precision and faithfulness has prompted Robert Stam's ironic comment that 'Pereira seems to be the last person alive who actually believes it possible to show "exactly what Brazil in the sixteenth century was like"'.[34] To be sure, both films share the purpose of discussing this formative moment of the Brazilian people, when contact (and conflict) first takes place between the 'civilized' European and the 'savage native', raising the question of national identity. However, the answers they come up with are opposed to each other.

To begin with, the option for a faithful depiction of Hans Staden's account leads to the establishment of a single narrative point of view. The story is told in the first person by the actor Carlos Evelyn, who plays Staden, in voice-over commentary (betraying a slight São Paulo accent behind his fluent German). The images appear as a faithful illustration of his narrative, as opposed to the conflictive narrative layers of *How Tasty Was My Little Frenchman*. As a result, the Brazilian Indian (the Tupinambá in this case) is presented from the outset as the exotic 'other', since its image derives from the narrator's suspicious and defensive look. The classical shot–reverse shot editing is used to reinforce the hero's subjective point of view, who, again in contrast to *How Tasty Was My Little Frenchman*'s detached camera work, is granted repeated close-ups.

Because they are seen through foreign eyes, the Indians' 'authentic' features are exaggerated to the point of expressionist deformation. When they sing and dance, everything about them is menacing: the whites of their eyes stand out against the red of their body paint; their singing mouths are like grimaces; their gestures, their chants, all is uncanny. Marlui Miranda and Lelo Nazário's music, based on research with indigenous peoples and

Hans Staden takes centre stage as the holder of the voice of reason, in Luiz Alberto Pereira's film. The compositions are clearly inspired by the Renaissance prints that illustrate Hans Staden's and Jean de Léry's accounts, in which balance is attained by placing the European character in the centre of the frame.

combined with atonal instruments and effects, contributes to the general atmosphere of exoticism even when it is diegetic.

Rather than being based on ethnographic research or any real indigenous choreography, the circles of dancing Indians are actually reminiscent of the Renaissance prints that illustrate Léry and Staden's books, with their respect for classical equilibrium and geometry. The reduced behavioural repertoire of the Indians, who seem incapable of any reaction other than chanting and dancing at each new event, turns the film into a sort of jungle musical which offers little enlightenment on their true habits. The Indians are thus excluded from the configuration of the point of view, as opposed to *How Tasty Was My Little Frenchman*, in which room for the native's view is made by the conflicting versions of the official history.

The decision to follow Staden's account literally caused *Hans Staden* to turn its back on the document and plunge into fiction and the genre film, in this case, the narrative of adventures. It is common knowledge that the accounts provided by the first travellers to the Americas contained a high degree of fantasy. Mythological creatures, such as dog-faced men (the cannibals), feature in accounts as early as Columbus's letters. Impressed by the New World's novelties and secure in the knowledge that hardly any witnesses would come forward to contradict them, travellers felt free to vent their fantasy, often resorting to Greek and Latin mythologies, which were fashionable at the time, as well as to biblical legends. This is the reason why Staden insists on the veracity of his account so as to avoid being taken for yet another impostor. He writes:

> Certainly many an honourable man in Castilla, Portugal, France or even Antwerp, in Brabant, who has been in America, will testify that things were indeed as I described them. Before those unfamiliar with such foreign lands, I call for these witnesses and God above all.

Staden then draws up a list of names of potential witnesses.[35] However, the lines that follow soon reveal a considerable degree of imagination. In order to attach credibility to his entire account, one would need to believe in miracles, for, according to Staden, it was God who inspired and saved him from the perils he faced. Thanks to this divine intervention, he acquired the power to summon or halt rain when necessary and to cure sick Indians with a mere touch of his fingers or blow of his breath, among other feats, thus impressing the Tupinambás and managing to escape their cannibalistic intentions. The end of the book summarizes the miraculous nature of his whole adventure:

Dear reader! I only briefly recounted my voyages over land and sea, as all I wanted was to describe their beginning, when I was in the hands of a cruel and savage people. I only wished to show how the Saviour of all evil, Our Lord and God, with His powers, freed me when I least expected from the hands of the savages.[36]

In its fidelity to the book, the film also becomes a narrative of miracles, realized or partially faked by a clever European, who was bound to get the upper hand over uncultivated and naive Indians. In tune with Staden's account, the Indians are portrayed in an infantile manner, starting with the women's shrill, childish chanting. Pereira's satirical verve, already apparent in his previous films, such as the comedy *Man in the Box* (*O efeito ilha*, 1994), contributes to the caricature of the Indians, who are constantly in clownish situations, making faces, crying or drunk. Despite the film's good intentions, the indigenous customs, including cannibalism, appear, just as in genre films, as barbarian acts perpetrated by an uneducated people, a condition that fully justifies the good hero Staden's struggle to rid himself of them and reach the happy ending.

The differences with Nelson's film are striking. In *How Tasty Was My Little Frenchman*, the subject is a war in which both parties are fighting to win. Chief Cunhambebe urges the French to give him gunpowder and cannons, dismissing traditional gifts such as scissors and mirrors, which the Europeans offer in exchange for pepper and Brazil wood. Conversely, *Hans Staden's* infantilized Indians cannot think of anything beyond the toys of European technology. At a certain point, Staden's Indian lover asks the French tradesman for 'many cannons' in exchange for her parrot. Her request, made in the film's prevailing infantile tone, is shown as a joke that sparks off the Frenchman's laugh, as much as it should do to the spectator.

The Indian's otherness is crystallized in the key scene of cannibalism, when a Maracajá prisoner is killed and devoured by the Tupinambás. The ritual is shown in minute detail, as in Staden's book, in its several stages: the dances, the painting of the *ibirapema*, the painting of the prisoner's body, his vengeful replies to the executioner's insults, the fatal blow, the general screaming, the preparation of the feast and its swallowing. The cannibalistic details had been omitted from *How Tasty Was My Little Frenchman*, which merely shows Seboipepe administering a short bite on what one presumes is her dead lover's neck, followed by a close-up of her indifferent eyes. But in *Hans Staden*, the meticulous and sensationalist description of the cannibalistic meal is even more graphic than in the book, with details such as the pair of ears that float to the top of the stew.

At this point, Staden, who was at first out of focus in the back of the frame, comes into focus shaking his head in disgust, while the other Indians blur in the background to the sound of their chewing mouths. Thus Staden is configured as the superior conscience, at the centre of the frame, supported by the camera's attention, which defines the enunciation's point of view. His figure in such moments reclaims the same central position it enjoys in the Renaissance prints that illustrate Staden's book, where it functions as the point of equilibrium in a chaotic and convulsive world.

*Hans Staden* offers an updated version of the national identity, in tune with the globalized spirit and commercial cinema, rather than with the utopian propositions typical of the 1960s and 1970s, while focusing on the same foundational moment of the Brazilian nation. Its uncritical adoption of a single character's point of view, depicted in a book which is undoubtedly a valuable historical document, but necessarily partial, fails to include precisely that of the Indian. Cannibalism appears as a curiosity of a people gone extinct in a remote past, leaving no traces behind, and now only useful as a source of black humour.

The present-day Brazilian, the film seems to suggest, prefers to identify with Hans Staden, a European like so many who still live in the country and characterize its cultivated classes. The narrator seems to endorse the dream achieved by this heroic foreigner of returning to a civilized Europe which has been duly cleansed from the anthropophagic, libertarian and erotic threats that so fascinated the modernists in the 1920s and cinema at the end of the 1960s. Instead of utopia, the film offers a mere happy ending.

## CHAPTER FOUR

# THE BLACK PARADISE

**Films**

*Orfeu* (Carlos Diegues, 1999)
*Black Orpheus* (*Orfeu negro/Orfeu do carnaval/Orphée noir*, Marcel Camus, 1959)

**Play**

*Orfeu da Conceição* (Vinicius de Moraes, 1955)

# THE BLACK PARADISE

noir messager d'espoir
... tu connais tous les chants du monde
'Bois-d'Ébène', Jacques Roumain

The black theme, a frequent political banner in Brazilian cinema between the mid-1950s and the late 1970s, practically disappeared from the screen after the early 1980s , with the decline of the left and the progressive depoliticizing of the arts. *Orfeu*, directed by Carlos Diegues in 1999, could be seen as a step towards reviving the race issue. The film is primarily based on the play *Orfeu da Conceição* (published in 1955 and performed for the first time in 1956), Vinicius de Moraes's daring proposal for turning *favela* characters into heroes of Greek mythology, to be played by an all-black cast.[1] *Orfeu* is also a re-interpretation of the film *Black Orpheus*, directed in 1959 by Marcel Camus and based on Vinicius's play. The title 'Black Orpheus' harks back to Jean-Paul Sartre's famous 'Orphée noir', a celebratory preface to Negritude, written for an anthology of black and Madagascan poetry which was edited by the Senegalese poet and political leader Léopold Sédar Senghor.[2]

Diegues's *Orfeu* contains, furthermore, some echoes of *Orpheus* (*Orphée*), shot in 1949 by Jean Cocteau, in whose oeuvre, including poetry and theatre, Orpheus is a recurrent theme. One of the first films to take the Orphic myth to the screen, *Orpheus* stars Jean Marais in the role of a hero who travels through the mirror and inhabits both the land of the living and the dead. The film provides a sequel to *The Blood of a Poet* (*Le sang d'un poète*, 1929), a surrealist film akin to *An Andalusian Dog* (*Un chien andalou*, Luis Buñuel, 1929) and *The Golden Age* (*L'âge d'or*, Luis Buñuel and Salvador Dalí, 1930), in which the poet bridges two worlds. Cocteau only drew the theme to a close in his film-testament, *The Testament of Orpheus* (*Le testament d'Orphée, ou ne me demandez pas pourquoi!*), released, like *Black Orpheus*, in 1959.

Jean Marais' marble beauty in *Orphée* is reflected in the Greek statues at the opening of
*Black Orpheus*, which explode to make room for Orpheus, played by Breno Mello. Toni
Garrido in Diegues's *Orfeu* has already overcome all problems of race.

Unlike previous Brazilian interpretations of Orpheus, which focused
on the black, and like Cocteau's *Orpheus*, which explores Marais' marmo-
real beauty and classical profile, Diegues's Orpheus has no additional
names; he is simply Orfeu, albeit played by a black actor. The reason for
this is clear from the opening images. They present a well-off and well-
adapted hero, whose problems with class and race seem nonexistent, or at
least already resolved. With a house in the most privileged spot on a *favela*
hillside, with a picture-perfect view of Rio de Janeiro, Orfeu is a kind of
dandy, who sports a collection of designer shirts and suits, his hair carefully styled in tiny braids, reading spectacles which give him an intellectual
air, a mobile phone always at the ready like a businessman, and a latest-
generation laptop on which he types his musical scores. He is surrounded
by children of all shades of colour, from blond (one of them is referred to
by the name of Russo, or 'Russian') to dark black, a multi-coloured palette
also reflected on the tiles on the front of his house, his shirts and the
exuberant carnival costumes under preparation around him. Orfeu, with
his immaculate chocolate skin, is only one among so many colours.

In Camus' *Black Orpheus*, which opens with images of Greek statues
as does Cocteau's 1949 *Orpheus*, the static white marble of the statues
explodes to give way to black men dancing samba to the sound of drumming in the *favela*. In Diegues's *Orfeu*, the Greek myth is no longer used
as a term of comparison; the hero is presented as if the myth itself had
always referred to a black man from the Brazilian *favela*. His skin colour
and social status are naturalized in order to rule out any suggestions of
protest.

This is somewhat curious, as *Orfeu* is part of a wave of *favela* films

launched in the wake of Paulo Lins's book *City of God* (*Cidade de Deus*), in which the racial issue is explosive and lies behind all conflicts. Lins, who is black, contributed personally to the dialogues of *Orfeu*, and Carlos Diegues's own cinematic past is that of a militant for the black cause. He had been dealing with *favela* and black-related themes from his very early works, such as 'Escola de Samba Alegria de Viver' ('Alegria de Viver Samba School'), a segment he contributed to the film *Favela Five Times* (*Cinco vezes favela*), produced by the Centre for Popular Culture (CPC) in 1962. Later, at the height of Cinema Novo, he directed *Ganga Zumba* (1964), a film about the rebel slave who became the leader of the Quilombo dos Palmares (a famous hiding camp for fugitive slaves), a historical drama set in the seventeenth century, with an all-black cast, which allegorized the problems faced by African-Brazilians in the present.

*Xica* (*Xica da Silva*, 1976) and *Quilombo* (1984) are his further incursions into the slave period, which allegorize situations of oppression and rebellion in the present. Many black Brazilian actors owe their celebrity to these films, such as actress Zezé Motta, who was introduced in *Xica* and since then has been directing an NGO which recruits and finds placements for black actors. In *Orfeu*, a new black actor was revealed, Toni Garrido, the Cidade Negra band leader, who plays the title role, alongside an older generation, including again Zezé Motta, in the role of Conceição, the protagonist's mother, and Milton Gonçalves, as Inácio, his father.

However, recent Brazilian cinema, which is still predominantly in the hands of white directors, shows no signs of interest in racial questions, even when it comes to *favela* films. Mentions of the oppression of blacks are occasionally to be found, for example, in Eduardo Coutinho's documentaries such as *The Mighty Spirit* (*Santo forte*, 1999) and *Babilônia 2000* (2000), but they rarely interfere with the main plot. Also the *favela's* ethnic profile varies from film to film, from predominantly black, as in *City of God* (2002), to mostly white, as in *Midnight* (1999). The casting for the inhabitants of the *favela* in *Orfeu* shows a concern for ethnic variety that is reminiscent of the multi-racial style of contemporary American cinema. Good and evil are unrelated to skin colour: Lucinho (Murilo Benício), the top drug dealer on the *favela* hill, is white, whereas his right-hand man is black, and there is even a girl, the character of Be Happy, in command of the gang, an uncommon event in *favela* books and films. The black woman in *Orfeu* has indeed been emancipated: Mira, Orfeu's girlfriend before Eurydice's arrival, is a *Playboy* cover girl, quite an achievement if you consider the real status of black Brazilian women. Even Eurydice, who arrives by boat in *Black Orpheus*, arrives in *Orfeu* by plane, a considerable progress which prompts, in the story, Conceição's remark that in her time it took 'almost three days by bus' to travel from Bahia to Rio.[3]

The characters' new status shows how *Orfeu* is removed from the Brazilian social films of the 1950s, in particular from an inaugural Orphic character, such as the black composer Espírito da Luz, played by Grande Otelo in the classic film *Rio, Northern Zone* (*Rio, Zona Norte*, Nelson Pereira dos Santos, 1957). An undeniable influence on *Black Orpheus*, Nelson's film tells the story of an illiterate, destitute, short, black, but musically gifted man, who has his songs stolen by a bunch of smart white guys. This plot establishes a clear division between good and evil, the former on the side of the poor, endowed with artistic talent, and the latter with the white characters, who become rich by exploiting the poor.

In the era that ushers in the new Orpheus, such a division has become outdated. Good guys can also be winners, as is the case with the protagonist, who could easily be living away from the *favela*, as he is constantly reminded by the other characters in the film. But, in order to become a hero, Orfeu first needs to rid his community of its bad elements. His struggle faces no racial obstacles, though a few mentions of race are made, such as the policeman called 'Paraíba' (indicating someone coming from the mostly white, though poor countryside of the northeast) and the designation of Eurydice as an 'Indian', even though the actress who plays her, Patrícia França, displays a mix of African and Portuguese features. Eurydice can even be seen as the personification of the myth of the three races (Indian, African and European), whose blend configures Brazil as a supra-racial paradise, governed by love and music. If such a paradise fails to come to fruition, it is solely due to the fatal interference of chance.

Nevertheless, the configuration of this utopian island, which is the *favela* in the new *Orfeu*, includes the challenges it is constantly facing, portrayed in another, 'realist', dimension of the film. This comprises the hill's negative side, absent from both Camus' and Nelson's films, where drug dealers and murderers terrorize a population who only mean well as they merrily go about the preparations for carnival. It is among these criminals that the question of social exclusion, so crucial in Paulo Lins's writings, finally comes to light. Take, for example, this dialogue between Orfeu and Lucinho:

> Orfeu: Go away, Lucinho, leave this hill while you still can. Get out of this life.
> Lucinho: And do what? Become a road sweep or a cleaner, which is what the people down there want us to be? Spend my life cleaning other people's toilets and die in the shit just like that loser of my father did? At my age I've already given my mother and siblings a house to live in.
> Orfeu: You won't live long, Lucinho.
> Lucinho: The little I live I'll live well.

In this case, social exclusion is unrelated to racial issues, as opposed to what occurs in Paulo Lins's *City of God*, in which similar exchanges cannot be separated from the colour factor. As this dialogue progresses, we are informed that Lucinho had to engage in crime because he lacked Orfeu's musical gifts, as if artistic talent were enough to define social status. Let us examine how the film develops such a view.

## The reinvention of Orpheus

Ever since the first Western opera, *Orfeo* (Claudio Monteverdi, 1607), the myth of Orpheus has been revisited by all kinds of writers, painters, poets, musicians and artists, confirming its inaugural vocation. It comes as no surprise that cinema, as much as other arts, should continue to revisit the myth, which contains foundational narrative motifs. It is primarily the story of creation itself, in which Orpheus, god of Thrace, son (or disciple) of Apollo and the Muse Calliope (or, in Vinicius's version, Clio), invents the lyre, which he uses to enchant all creatures, including trees, rocks, animals, children and, above all else, women. In short, Orpheus is the one who breathes life into things.

The myth also contains the matrix of romantic love, which is the exclusive and eternal love he feels for the nymph Eurydice. This love, in its turn, unleashes the basic feelings of envy and jealousy which cause the story's 'sudden change' (*peripeteia* in Greek). According to the legend, Eurydice is also coveted by the envious Aristaeus, and when she tries to flee from him she steps on a venomous serpent and dies of its bite. After losing Eurydice, Orpheus becomes mute and silences his lyre, showing the identity between love and art. He then undertakes a trip to the underworld (interpreted as 'hell' in Christian cultures) to recover his beloved. Once again he plays his lyre and enchants Charon, the ferryman who transports the dead, and Cerberus, guard dog of the underworld, as well as Hades (or Pluto), god of the dead, and Persephone, his wife. They let him recover Eurydice on condition that he never looks back on his way out from the underworld.

This is the temptation, similar to the one in the legend of Sodom and Gomorrah, that Orpheus succumbs to when, on reaching the daylight, he anxiously turns round to see Eurydice and she instantly disappears. He then becomes a recluse and decides to avoid women forever, thus incurring the jealousy and wrath of the Maenads (or Bacchantes), used to a life of orgies. They kill him, tear him apart and throw his head and lyre into the river. These reach the island of Lesbos, which thenceforth becomes the capital of lyrical poetry.

Though revisiting such an over-exploited theme, Vinicius de Moraes's approach is nonetheless innovative in several senses. The Black Experimental Theatre (Teatro Experimental do Negro) was in full swing at the time, and plays featuring all-black casts were not novel. And yet, as Vinicius himself emphasized, it was the first time an all-black cast ascended to the stage of Rio's Municipal Theatre, gaining unprecedented press coverage owing to the author's prestige.[4] *Orfeu da Conceição* also inaugurated one of the most celebrated musical partnerships, both in Brazil and the rest of the world, between Vinicius and the then young conductor Antônio Carlos Jobim. The songs they wrote for the play, with the addition of those later composed for Camus' film, have become worldwide classics. The staging of the play, as well as bringing celebrity to its black actors, such as Haroldo Costa (who later became a filmmaker), Abdias Nascimento (a writer and political activist) and Lea Garcia, featured a set designed by the architect Oscar Niemeyer, whose first theatrical design this was.

But the foremost pioneering aspect of Vinicius's play was the adaptation of the myth to the black universe. According to the poet, the idea behind the black Orpheus dated back to 1942, and preceded not only the African Negritude movement but also Sartre's 'Orphée noir', written in 1948. This is how Vinicius describes his invention:

> It was in 1942, at a dinner with my friend, the American writer Waldo Frank, that something one could call the embryo took shape from which, a few months later, was born the idea of *Orfeu da Conceição*. At the time I was accompanying the author of *America Hispana* on all his visits to *favelas*,

*macumba* [African-Brazilian] rituals, black clubs and festivals in Rio, and felt particularly imbued with the spirit of the race. In one of our chats, we suddenly became aware, through a series of random associations, of the feeling that all those celebrations and festivities we had been witnessing were somehow related to ancient Greece; as if the black, in this case the black from Rio de Janeiro, were a Greek in rough stone – a Greek still deprived of culture and of the Apollonian cult of beauty, but no less affected by the Dionysian lust for life.[5]

The first act of the play, which would later be called *Orfeu da Conceição – tragédia carioca* (*Orfeu da Conceição: A Rio Tragedy*) was written in this period. However, the final and full version would only come to light 13 years later, according to a chronology published at the end of the play and included in the volume *Theatre in Verse* (*Teatro em versos*), which specifies: 'Niterói, 1942; Los Angeles, 1948; Rio, 1953; Final version for publication: Paris, 19 October 1955'.[6] By the time of the last version, Negritude, Sartre and Cocteau had already been and gone, and Camus' *Black Orpheus* was being made with a title taken from Sartre.

Vinicius's position in this historical context is interesting. Even though overcome with admiration for black music, he saw it as a rough diamond that needed cutting, like 'a Greek in rough stone', in his words, who although 'deprived of culture and the Apollonian cult to beauty', possessed 'a Dionysian lust for life'. His play points in both these directions: on the one hand, there is Orpheus's music, stemming from the heights of the *favela* hill and inspired by a spiritualized Eurydice; on the other, there is the unconstrained, sensual carnival, played in the lower city, which stands for the hell where the hero loses his Eurydice.

The perception of black culture as a spontaneous expression of nature resonated with the world's left wing at the time, which was beginning to wake up to the cause of Africans and African descendants. In his famous preface, Sartre praises the black poet's proximity to the forces of nature and myth, both already far removed from the European:

> the black is closer than us to the great time when, as Mallarmé says, 'the word created the Gods'. It is almost impossible for our poets to reconnect with popular traditions: ten centuries of cultivated poetry separate both and, moreover, the folklore inspiration has dried out: we could, at most, imitate its simplicity from the outside. The blacks from Africa, on the contrary, are still in the great period of mythical fecundity, and the black poets of the French language do not go about their myths as we go about our songs: they let themselves be enveloped by them so that at the end of the incantation, magnificently evoked, Negritude emerges. This is the reason why I call *magic* or incantation this method of 'objective poetry'.[7]

The mention of a period that is 'still' mythical in which the blacks live reveals an evolutionist vision of culture, similar to Vinicius's, which would find no resonance nowadays. For Robert Stam – whose factual chronology is slightly mistaken here, given that the idea of a Brazilian Black Orpheus, as we saw, precedes Sartre's article on Negritude – Vinicius leads on from 'the tradition of European primitivism and of the Negritude movement, which posited Greece as reason and Africa as emotion'. For him, 'de Moraes saw Afro-Brazilian performances as bringing a Dionysian dimension to an Apollonian theme'.[8]

The play's first staging was not devoid of conflicts and setbacks, and led, at one point, to an actors' revolt for lack of remuneration.[9] Some of them, such as Abdias Nascimento, later turned against the poet's mythological project:

> Black-faced white actors, Black Christ, Black Orpheus: in the last analysis they all conspire in the historical rape of my people. African religious culture is rich and alive in our religious communities all over Brazil. We have no need to invoke Greece or the Bible in order to raise it to the status of mythology. On the other hand, Greece and Europe owe to Africa a great deal of what they call 'Western Civilization'.[10]

Meanwhile, the recourse to classical mythology allowed Vinicius to reverse perspective: by making black the universal colour, the black was removed from the customary role of passive object of the white's gaze, and transformed into the subject of action, free of all stigmatizing difference. Sartre sought the same role reversal when he resorted to the Orphic myth to define the new black poets:

> Here are black men who stand up and look at us, and I invite [the reader] to feel with me the emotion of being looked at. For the white enjoyed for three thousand years the privilege of seeing without being seen.[11]

Sartre characterizes the black poet as author of the 'only great revolutionary poetry' in the French language, at that time,[12] a poetry he calls 'Orphic',

> because the black's tireless descent into himself makes me think of Orpheus going to Pluto to reclaim his Eurydice. It is thanks to an exceptional poetic felicity, delivering himself to trances, rolling on the ground as possessed by his own self, singing his wrath, regrets and hatred, exposing his wounds, his life torn between 'civilisation' and the old black depths, in short, becoming more lyrical, that the black poet reaches with more certainty the great collective poetry.[13]

*Orfeu da Conceição*, even though set in the *favela* and spoken in popular language, was conceived in such a way as to avoid all realism, so that the universality of the myth could flourish. Vinicius specifically warns against turning the 'myth of Orpheus into a realist tragedy'.[14] His interest in setting the story at carnival time was due precisely to the inversion that takes place during this period, which allowed 'the blacks to free themselves of their poverty in the luxury of costumes bought with an entire year's savings'.[15] Another of Vinicius's anti-realist demands was the exclusive use of black actors. He justified this by saying, 'It seems to me that it would be, so to say, to go against [the play's] Hellenic spirit to cast racially mixed actors.'[16]

This purism, while favouring the exaltation of African descendants, paved the way, with its rejection of realism, for folkloric readings such as Marcel Camus'. And indeed *Black Orpheus* simply returned the theatrical drama back to its real locations, on the streets and hills of Rio de Janeiro, without adding any realist basis to them, thus reducing the black Olympus idealized by Vinicius to naive primitivism. The blacks, in Camus' film, constitute a poor and yet happy population, sensual yet innocent, leading a life with no conflicts but those of love and dancing samba all day long, even when they have to cart water on their heads up the hill. Stam observes, with humour, that *Black Orpheus*,

> offers a highly idealised view of life in the *favelas*: spacious, cheerfully painted, rustic cabins, complete with coloured curtains, metal bed and menagerie, offering the best views in Rio. Indeed, the film's treatment of the *favelas* at times resembles a real-estate ad; anyone would love to live there.[17]

Two points of view result from the above, which are intertwined and yet divergent: that of Vinicius, providing an all-black universe in which African descendants transcend their condition to become equal to gods; and that of Camus, which provides the black with an idealized life of perfect happiness. The new *Orfeu* seems to have sought to unite and overcome these two visions by combining the Greek myth with a vision of the black's real life in the *favela*. Diegues and his co-writers' endeavour was to establish a realist dimension without losing sight of the myth and the tragedy, a complicated equation to solve.

### The realist dimension

In the *Orfeu* pressbook, Diegues tells about his long-held desire to shoot a new version of *Orfeu da Conceição* which would 'correct' Marcel Camus' interpretation of the play in the film *Black Orpheus*. This film had generated an international perception of Brazil as a black and musical paradise, which was furthermore sanctioned with the awards of the Golden Palm at Cannes and the Oscar for Best Foreign Film in 1959. Vinicius himself was famously dissatisfied not only with the cinematic version of the play but also with the way his music, written in partnership with Tom Jobim and Luiz Bonfá, was utilized. Despite the film's international accolade and the fact that it continues to attract legions of viewers throughout the world, a section of Brazil's film critics, especially a young generation which would later launch the Cinema Novo, rejected it categorically. Diegues recalls his own disappointment:

> In 1959, with a few shorts behind me, and immersed in the primal soup of people and ideas that would later spawn Cinema Novo, I felt a wave of disappointment as I watched *Black Orpheus*, a French production directed by Marcel Camus and based on *Orfeu da Conceição*. Despite its sincere sympathy for Rio de Janeiro's geographic and human scenery, and even a certain affection it demonstrated for its subject matter, the film went down the way of a touristy and exotic view which betrayed the meaning of the play and missed all of its fundamental qualities. I felt, to tell the truth, personally offended, and from then on I started to dream of the film which has become our *Orfeu*.[18]

In 1980 Diegues presented his *Orfeu* project to Vinicius de Moraes, who offered him the copyrights for the screen and volunteered to write the screenplay with him. His death in July of that year brought the project to a halt. After American producers took a momentary interest in it around 1991, it was in Brazil, in 1998, that an entirely new version of the script eventually managed to raise funds, and the film was finally released in 1999.

There is no doubt that *Orfeu* was true to the 'spirit of the play', as far as Vinicius's demands are concerned, as it maintains its black protagonist and many of its original dialogues, poems and songs. However, the decision to have a mixed-race cast interferes with 'the myth's integrity' or 'the Hellenic spirit' Vinicius talks about. This seemed to be a necessary step in order to update the story according to the *favela*'s current profile in real life. Sérgio Augusto summarizes Diegues's thoughts, according to which,

> the *favelas* are currently undergoing their third historical phase. Until the 1950s, representations of the *favela* hill, in samba songs, on stage and on the screen, were mostly lyrical. This was the way with *Favela of My Loves* (*Favela dos meus amores*), directed by Humberto Mauro in 1935, in *Tudo azul* (by Moacyr Fenelon, 1951), *Orfeu da Conceição*, *Rio, 40 Degrees* (*Rio, 40 graus*, Nelson Pereira dos Santos, 1956) and *Black Orpheus*. In the past, notions of purity and even privilege with relation to *favela* were widespread, for it was believed that 'those who lived up on the hill were

near to heaven' (*quem mora lá no morro vive pertinho do céu*), as proclaimed Herivelto Martins's samba song. Today such a view would be unacceptable, for the *favelas* have become a far cry from the peaceful, bucolic and scarcely populated places they used to be. Urban growth and disorganised migration turned them into overcrowded spaces and paved the way for violence and criminality, giving rise to what Diegues calls the 'plaintive phase', when living up on the hill became like living close to hell. A new phase would take over in the 1990s: that of the fight for affirmation, of pride of being a *favela* inhabitant, despite all its adversities. *Orfeu* attempts to provide a faithful portrayal of this phase.[19]

The obvious aim of this description is to convey a positive view of the *favela*. Vinicius's intention was no different, when he found in the legend of the 'Greek Orpheus or Black Orpheus ... a perfectly positive story, which represents man's struggle ... to promote, through music, his total integration into the lives of his fellow creatures'.[20] Such a view corresponds to an emphasis on one's 'pride in being a *favela* inhabitant', even though problems of overcrowding, criminality and drug trafficking are still far from any solution in Brazil's real *favelas*. A director who is not averse to popular appeal, Diegues placed particular emphasis on the spectacular aspect of *favela* life, especially during carnival time, and went on to stage and partly document a carnival parade in all its details.

But the film's most innovative aspect is its focus on the modern aspect of the present-day *favela* as a reflex of its dwellers' expectations of ascending the social scale. The concern with fashion is reflected in the way Orfeu dresses and styles his hair, the clothes and accessories the drug dealers wear, the slang they use, the up-to-the-minute trainers sported by kids like Máicol (a misspelling of 'Michael' Jackson), who are still dithering between the paths of good and evil. The attachment to gadgets such as Orfeu's mobile phone and laptop completes the configuration of this technological *favela*, through which the black is given access to the imaginary of consumerism.

This is the *favela* which, duly updated and idealized through unrestrained sympathy, is intended to provide a realist basis for the myth. From its opening sequences, aerial shots of a stunning Rio de Janeiro are interspersed with shots of a mass of shacks buried deep in the heart of the city, revealing the contrast between social classes. These introductory images are reminiscent of the famous opening of *Rio, 40 Degrees* (1956), in which the city is presented as 'the name before the title', or, as it were, the leading actor. A realist technique par excellence, it contextualizes the drama and offers a social backdrop for individual relations. But the shots of the hill that follow are cut together in the fast pace typical of music videos, and accompanied by the sound of a rap beat mixed with the voice-over of a speaker from Voz do Morro (The Voice from the Hill), a pirate radio station. The use of music video, which is essentially a commercial product, though a place of integration between cinema and music, plays a double role: on the one hand it brings to the fore the aggressive aspect of the hill, with quick cuts between shots that bring the *favela* closer and closer, as if they were being 'shot' at the viewers' eyes; on the other, it celebrates the creativity of a community, which, despite its poverty, is capable of dictating musical trends. Throughout the film, rap music is used to create a contrast to the samba played in smooth *bossa nova* style, setting an aggressive novelty against a well-established, passive rhythm.

A rap song disrupts the trance of the carnival parade, in the middle of the *samba-enredo*[21] composed by Caetano Veloso for the fictitious samba school Unidos da Carioca (Carioca United).[22] Composed by Gabriel o Pensador, the rap song evolves in an abrupt rhythm that mimics the shot fired at Eurydice at the very moment when Orfeu is presenting his number at the carnival. Though an imported musical form, rap is shown in this scene as an evolution of Brazilian samba, whose past phases are carefully outlined in Caetano's *samba-enredo*. The chorus sings: 'When Hilário left/ Pedra do Sal/ Rei de Ouro emerged/at carnival'. These lyrics refer to Hilário Jovino Ferreira, one of the thousands of African descendants from the state of Bahia who migrated to Rio de Janeiro in the nineteenth century and who was the founder of the *rancho* Rei de Ouro (King of Diamonds), drawing on Catholic and *nago* (yoruba) traditions of Bahia and a precursor of the present-day carnival *blocos* of Rio.[23]

Alongside such self-reflexive musical commentaries, meta-cinema is utilized to produce a realist effect. An example is the brief insert of a famous scene from the *chanchada* (musical comedy) *Carnaval Atlântida* (José Carlos Burle, 1952), shown on the television set in the room where the samba school's women try on their costumes. In the scene, black actor Grande Otelo, disguised as a Greek, dances carnival steps with Helen of Troy. Given that this is the same comic Grande Otelo who plays the Orphic character in *Rio, Northern Zone*, this completes the reconstruction, in the background, of the humble origins of the successful present-day Orfeu of Diegues's film.

Indeed, references to real and cinematic characters from the past provide the new Orfeu with a historical backdrop. The current musical trend, which breaks free from the 'Brazilian authenticity' of *favelas* and samba rhythms of the past by absorbing international and pop influences, includes a homage to old musical traditions and is sanctioned by a series of real celebrities who make special appearances in the film. Among them are the veteran samba composer Nelson Sargento, Caetano Veloso, who performs one of his songs in an entirely extradiegetic scene, the samba school leader Joãozinho Trinta, and the filmmaker Carlos Diegues himself, who makes a brief appearance as a barman.

Orfeu's perfection being inevitably idealized, his 'realist' counterpart is the white Lucinho, who stands for Aristaeus in the myth. In an age when black people and black music have supposedly conquered the world and the charts, the white man has become frustrated and bitter, though not for reasons of social or racial oppression. Lucinho's bitterness, both in the tale and in Vinicius's play, derives from personal reasons. In love with Eurydice in the mythical version, Lucinho, in this case, is more interested in Orfeu, his childhood friend, for whom he nurtures a homosexual crush, which comes to the fore in the scene where the two kiss on the mouth, when Orfeu kills him.

Because such characters, fictitious as they are, are meant to provide *Orfeu* with a realist picture of contemporary life on a *favela* hill in Rio de Janeiro, special care was taken with the language they speak, something that corresponds to one of Vinicius's few realist recommendations: 'because this is a play where popular slang plays a very important part, and because popular speech is extremely prone to change, current [linguistic] conditions should be taken into consideration when it comes to restaging this play'.[24] The dialogues in *Orfeu*, to which Paulo Lins personally contributed, capture in minute detail the slang used by drug traffickers, policemen, young artists, evangelical Christians, samba performers and other sectors of the *favela*. Finally, the bloodbath, which draws the curtain on Eurydice, Lucinho and Orfeu, in a typical Greek tragic style, finds resonance in the drama of real *favelas*, where violence is the daily bread, a fact made explicit in the scene where a boy is exterminated by a drug gang just because he had sex, by mutual consent, with an adolescent.

These elements, conceived to produce realist effects, are not meant to affect the positive and idealized vision of the *favela*. Though the aerial shots render images of real *favelas*, *Orfeu*'s plot is staged on an artificial film set, built to showcase and stylize local colour, shown in the literal sense of the coloured graffiti, clothes, homes and skin tones, as well as sordid details. The labyrinthine stairs, the filthy sewers and rubbish heaps also add colour, in a certain way, to the 'Brazilian mix' which constitutes the *favela* world. Everything there is familiar, homely and trustworthy, like the cosy bars where the old samba players gather, or the small evangelical temples where people hide from drink or the temptations of the flesh.

Even the shots from the drug wars, which fill in for the fireworks set off by watchers who warn the criminals when the police arrive, acquire a daily life tone.

## Myth and transcendence

Sex and temptations of the flesh are central to all the works analysed here. In Cocteau's and Sartre's depictions, Orpheus is a transgressive character. In Cocteau's *Orpheus*, the hero scorns his puritanical and domestic Eurydice, who carries a child of his, in order to cross to the other side of the mirror by means of a diabolical pact, and meet Death, a *femme fatale* played by Maria Casares, with whom he falls madly in love. Sartre's black poets turned into Orpheuses resuscitate the power of the earth and the flesh in a 'sexual pantheism' which unites them with 'black Africans' phallic dances and rites'.[25]

Conversely, Vinicius's couple, Orpheus and Eurydice, are punished after a sexual encounter in which she loses her virginity and, on her way back home, is knifed by Aristaeus. In Diegues's version, the puritanical nature of sublime love is even more accentuated. The beautiful erotic scene that opens the film, in which Orfeu makes love to his girlfriend Mira, immediately points to the carnal dimension he must overcome to become a hero. Mira, the sultry and 'easy' woman, is quickly dispatched with a 'get out' which Orfeu flashes across his computer screen. The only night of sex he manages to enjoy with the, until then, virgin Eurydice is not shown, indicating the spiritual bond between them, which is presented as better suited to the myth – but which actually is conservative and typical of the melodrama.

In keeping with this, Eurydice, who is already in her carnival costume, does not attend carnival, choosing instead to visit the evangelical temple where Inácio, Orfeu's father, a former alcoholic and samba player, tries to put his bohemian past behind him. Orpheus's 'descent into hell' is linked, in Sartre as well as in Vinicius and Camus, to African or African-Brazilian religious trances and magic, as experienced in *umbanda* and *macumba*.[26] Diegues turned his back on the usual use of *umbanda*, which is a widespread cultural expression in the *favelas* and provided *Black Orpheus* with its most powerful, phantasmagorical scenes. His Orfeu seems far removed from his African cultural roots and too cultivated to adhere to such popular beliefs. The trance is thus transferred to the carnival parade itself, which includes images of an actual parade of the samba school Viradouro, from Niterói, headed by Joãozinho Trinta, who had coincidentally chosen 'Orpheus' as the theme for the 1998 carnival.

The trance-like atmosphere, configured by the thunderous drumming and the repetitive chorus of the *samba-enredo*, sets the tone for the final events: the death of Eurydice, who is accidentally shot by Lucinho, the recovery of her body by Orfeu in a rubbish dump below a precipice, Orfeu's murder of Lucinho, and the murder of Orfeu by the jealous Maenads. The general tragedy is then turned into music by both Máicol, the boy painter, fan of Michael Jackson, and Mr Inácio, the renovated samba player who, in the thick of the moment, regains his musical vocation. The former with his rhythmic shouts and the latter with his whistle create a new musical form, a samba-rap that fuses old and new, the ideal and the real.

As the film draws to a close, the *favela* hill returns to its everyday violence after the 'great illusion of carnival' is over, as sung in 'Felicidade', a song by Jobim and Vinicius, delivered with innocent simplicity by Jobim's adolescent daughter, Maria Luiza Jobim, who plays a minor role in the film. The Orphic paradise lasts no longer than the three days of carnival. Nevertheless, the last image of the film shows Orfeu and Eurydice dancing samba together in the carnival parade, denying the film's realist dimension and reaffirming, to the benefit of a positive vision of the black and the *favela*, the reality of the myth.

## CHAPTER FIVE

# AN INTERRUPTED UTOPIA

**Film**

*City of God* (*Cidade de Deus*, Fernando Meirelles and Kátia Lund, 2002)

**Book**

*Cidade de Deus* (Paulo Lins. São Paulo: Companhia das Letras, 1997)

# AN INTERRUPTED UTOPIA

Words fail. Bullets talk.
Paulo Lins, *Cidade de Deus*

In both the book and the film *City of God* the degree of 'realism' is strik-ing. It is impossible not to be impressed by the 'insider's point of view', as identified by Roberto Schwarz,[1] through which an intellectual from the *favela* as well as the characters drawn from this location speak in their own voices, from both the page and the screen. In this chapter, the film and the book *City of God* will be looked at as outstanding examples of recent works on the *favela*, whose realism interrupts the utopian gesture. The analysis will identify the elements that give the novel and the film what I would term their 'realist aspect' and reveal the laborious process through which this is produced. As I will endeavour to show, the creation of the apparent 'spontaneity' which predominates in both works requires a considerable dose of artifice.

Since its publication in 1997, the novel *City of God* has made its mark, raising its author, Paulo Lins, to the status of one of Brazil's greatest writ-ers.[2] It has given literary expression to an issue that is today central to Brazilian society and politics, namely the 'favelization' (spread of *favela* communities) and the war on drug dealing. This topic, as approached by Lins, has subsequently provided rich pickings for Brazilian cinema (within which, furthermore, the *favela* represents a traditional genre). Several films about *favelas* were made in the wake of this novel's publication, such as *Midnight* and *News from a Private War* (see Chapter 2), and some of them, like *Orfeu* , even called on the skills of Paulo Lins when it came to writing the dialogues (see Chapter 4). Lins even co-directed music videos for the rap group O Rappa on the same subject (see Chapter 1). But, naturally, adapting the novel itself for the screen was a far greater challenge in view of its extraordinary quality.

Nevertheless, it is fair to say that in various ways the film *City of God*, directed by Fernando Meirelles with the collaboration of Kátia Lund, proved to be a worthy match for the novel on which it is based. Consequently critics are faced with the difficult task of identifying, within the intersemiotic translation, the corresponding and equally successful techniques in both of the works. I would suggest that a good place to start such a study is the most original aspect of the book, that is to say, its use of language. The thing that first strikes you about *City of God* is the revelation that a vast number of Brazilians speak a language that not only differs from educated Portuguese, but is totally unknown among the upper classes. The inventive use of slang, that verges on a dialect in its own right, results in an agile, precise, synthetic and quick-fire language, which is highly expressive of contemporary Brazil. In my view this language constitutes the main source of the realism of the novel, and, through indirect ways, also of the film.

**Murdered words**

When someone refers to the 'insider's point of view' in relation to the novel *City of God*, you immediately think of the background of its author, who was born and brought up in a *favela*, managing against all odds to break out of the lifestyle predestined for him and to bridge the gulf between the social classes. His entrance into the world of literary fiction came about as a result of an ethnographical research project, coordinated by Alba Zaluar, entitled 'Crime and Criminality among the Popular Classes', which was intended to give a voice to a community that never appears in the media, unless through the mouthpiece of the ruling classes. But the origins of the author and his previous research do not adequately account for the realism of the novel. Lins's writing is far removed from the spontaneous testimony of popular writers, who, unfamiliar with erudite conventions, 'write like they speak'. It is true that the narrator of the novel insists on maintaining the narrow insider's vision of someone who is ignorant of 'life outside' and the causes of his misfortunes. However, the extreme linguistic sophistication that is obvious from even the opening lines of the novel leads us to reject the idea that Lins is using direct register.

The Brazilian critic Antonio Candido, in his famous essay 'A Dialectic of *Malandragem*', used the term 'structural reduction' to refer to how realist writers used to manipulate non-literary material in order to make it 'part of an aesthetic order ruled by its own rules, not the rules of nature, society or the individual'. However, according to Candido, 'nature, society and the individual seem to be present on every page'.[3] Something similar happens with the manipulation of language in *City of God*, which seems to contain in its own structure the materiality extracted from the facts.

Let us take as an example the first ten pages of the book, written in a deliberately poetic way, full of alliterations, rhymes and figures of speech. The first paragraph contains a series of alliterations of the letter 'b': '*Barbantinho e Buscapé fumavam um baseado à beira rio, na altura do bosque de Eucaliptos*' (meaning 'Stringy and Rocket were smoking a joint by the riverside, near the Eucalyptus wood'). This is a reference to two secondary characters who, in the present day within the story that is dominated by a war between drug gangs, are enjoying a moment of contemplation. Although they are still young, they are recalling their own childhood and what the City of God was like in the past, as if it were way back in time. The soft consonant 'b' continues to feature in the words *bagana* (joint), *braçadas* (strokes), *arrebentação* (surf), *boiando* (floating) and *brincar* (playing), words that introduce a description of a Golden Age, when the City of God was still 'one big farm'. Before the encroachment, according to the narrator speaking in the third person, of that 'such a modern world', with its property speculation and factories, the characters enjoyed a rural childhood, when they used to buy fresh milk, dig up vegetables, pick fruit in the fields, ride horses on the hills, go fishing and hunting for rodents and sparrows to eat with manioc flour. In those days, herds of cattle passed by 'in the tranquillity of those unaware of death'.

That tranquil river, on the banks of which the characters recollect a past crushed underneath houses and the other buildings of a new *favela*, then begins to turn red, a colour that precedes the appearance of human bodies – corpses from the war that is now being waged. At that point, the narrator stops dead, in order to make a comment in the first person, the only time that he does so in the whole novel: 'Poetry, my benefactor, illuminate ... the shades of my words', he pleads, before plunging headlong into a prose that will have 'bullets flying into phonemes'. This abrupt cut occurs in a kind of mini-chapter of just 13 lines, that is entirely poetic in its format, containing metre, cadence and rhyme, and which ends with two phrases that announce the nature of the prose that is to follow: 'Words fail. Bullets talk.'

From that point on, the narrator in the third person takes the reins of the plot, and we witness the evolution of a language that, through onomatopoeia, synthesis and aggression, attempts to materialize gun shots, the cut and death. The prose that follows is radically different from the opening pages of the novel, although it continues to draw on similar poetic techniques. The initial introspection gives way to action, leaving no room for description or reflection. The words themselves cease to be passive signifiers to become active referents. The initial softness of the letter 'b' is replaced by the percussive 'p' of *rapá* (man or bro), the obsessive vocative that marks the end of many of the conversation lines and punctuates the whole novel.

The noun *rapá* is a shortened form of the word *rapaz* (boy), derived from the term *rapace*, a word with a curious etymology: *rapace* in Latin means 'a person who steals' and in the Middle Ages it was used to refer to servants or lackeys. When transformed by the inhabitants of the *favela* into the form of *rapá*, an oxytone that eats up the resting end syllable of the usually paroxytone Portuguese words, the final 'pá' produces an onomatopoeic effect that evokes the aggression of a gun shot. The 'ra', in turn, brings to mind the repetition of machine gun fire, or at the very least, repetitive percussion rhythms, as captured in the word 'rap', a music that articulates the protests of American blacks as well as other marginalized groups throughout the world. Thus you could say that the single word *rapá* encapsulates the essence of the entire novel, since it single-handedly evokes virility, bullets, high speed and abrupt halt, which is death.

This technique, which dictates the choice of the words used throughout the novel, gives language an almost absolute power, enhanced by the sense of speed, repetition, accumulation and massification. Writer Guimarães Rosa, who elevated the uneducated language of Brazil's backlands to the status of erudite literature, unearthed from it a universalizing ethics charged with mythical power. Paulo Lins's achievement, although similar, has the peculiarity of showing the appropriateness of the language spoken by deglamorized criminals, children who are enslaved by a logic that they neither know of nor can control, and which ultimately annihilates them. In Lins's hands this quick-fire language of shortened words and phrases acquires an interesting poetic quality, like a poem that before attaining philosophical status comes to an abrupt halt, as the 'bullets penetrate the phonemes', and that ends up being nothing more than a collection of clichés and prejudices. The characters tend to express themselves in proverbial forms, but because these are not preceded by any explanatory discourse, the result is often nonsense or black humour, as in these examples: 'When one Brazilian pees, all the others pee', or 'The blond child was the son of God, the white one God brought up, the dark child was his bastard son and the black one was shit by the Devil.'

The language of *City of God* is so authoritarian that it manipulates the very characters who speak it. If you just think of the names of the characters, practically all of them are known by nicknames, which in just one or two words sum up the life story of each individual and imprison them in certain characteristics. There is no shortage of examples: the name Cabeção (translated as 'Melonhead' in the film), which is given to a policeman, instantly reveals that he is from Brazil's northeast, where people supposedly have 'flat heads', and also reflects the prejudice against northeasterners, which he also suffers and which, to a certain extent, justifies his violent and vindictive behaviour towards blacks. The 'good guy' is called Mané Galinha (translated as Knockout Ned in the film), from which we deduce that, despite being black, he is 'Mané', an abbreviation of the name Manuel, a very common name in the Portuguese community and which became in Brazil synonymous with the unintelligent. (The Portuguese have traditionally been the butt of jokes in Brazil for their legendary stupidity.) 'Galinha', on the other hand, refers to this character's ability to attract women.

Thus the language of the novel reveals the prejudiced nature of a culture that has neither time nor space for reflection. In this land of tough guys who kill and die like flies, life is described in ready-made phrases that are loaded with conservative morality, such as the following: 'Women are like dogs. They soon get used to new owners.' Such discrimination is directed at gays, the Portuguese, blacks, northeasterners, whites, in a word: all the characters who, in the narrative, are slaves to their linguistic labels.

In the novel City of God, words also die young, like the characters, children who are turned into adults and then die before they are 20 years old. Given this context, pre-formed ideas are not only natural but essential, since there is no time to hesitate or to choose. In gang warfare whenever a character is about to 'unwrap an idea' he is killed by his interlocutor, or he kills the latter before any dialogue can take place. Repentance is also offset by more deaths, with the result that everything is reduced to the indifference of mass production or, to put it more accurately, mass annihilation. The speed of the bullets interrupts and remedies the slow pace of the speech.

In order to guarantee some kind of existence, however ephemeral, nouns need to be concise and radical, reducing, for example, workers to idiots (otário or 'sucker/mug') and criminals to animals (bicho-solto – 'wild beast'), qualifications that often correspond to their death sentences. The murdered phoneme is also a murderer, in a world dominated by speed and ephemerality. In fact, the verb matar ('to kill'), among the gang members, is replaced with passar (literally 'to pass' or 'waste'). 'Pass him, pass him!' shouts over and over again Li'l Zé, the most prolific and quick-working criminal, who does not sleep or relax, but compulsively snorts cocaine, which keeps him both desensitized and yet alert enough to 'waste' anyone who crosses his path. Death is just an incidental occurrence in the vicious circle of life.

## Concentration

Unlike the novel, the film adaptation was not tied to words, and could rework the linguistic devices into other aspects of the film, such as the performance of the actors, the photography, the editing, the dialogues, the music and so on. Not to mention the script, written by Bráulio Mantovani, who brilliantly performed the arduous task of eliminating countless characters and incidents, as well as merging together many others. As far as the realism is concerned, what perhaps stands out most of all is the cast. Audiences in Brazil and all over the world have been fascinated by the 'authenticity' of the children and teenagers whose faces bear witness to their own origins, as well as those of the characters they are portraying, namely the *favela*. The appearance on screen of real-life *favela* inhabitants, with their varying shades of dark skin, their frequently semi-naked, raw beauty, seems to emphasize the characters' veracity and restore the reality that gave rise to this fictitious story. Without a shadow of a doubt, the film has the revelatory quality of a 'hidden reality' that previously characterized neo-realist films that depicted the ravages of war, or the films of the Brazilian Cinema Novo movement that depicted the misery of the Brazilian backlands. However, given that the film is not a documentary and that the actors are not nor could ever be the gangsters they portray, its realist aspect is clearly not due to a mere attempt at copying reality.

We know from press releases and interviews given by the filmmaking team that the casting was a laborious and costly process, which took a whole year to complete. In several *favelas* (or communities, to use the team's politically correct terminology), amateur theatre schools and young people's associations, 2,000 people were interviewed, from which 400 youngsters were chosen to take part in a theatre workshop. The workshop, which concentrated on improvisation exercises, was directed by Guti Fraga, the founder of the Nós do Morro group, an acclaimed amateur theatre group composed of *favela* inhabitants. As a result of these improvisation exercises, which were observed and reported on by the directors and other members of the team, the 60 main actors and 150 supporting cast of the film were selected.

But the training given to the cast was still not over. Each actor was then coached by Fátima Toledo, and a short film was made, entitled *Palace*

Visual rhyme and suggestions of cutting in *City of God*: the knife, Li'l Ze's teeth and the chicken's beak and claws.

*II*, which acted as a screen test but also as a run-through for the directing, set design, camera work and editing of the feature film *City of God*. During this process radical changes were made to the script, the dialogues and the performances, all with the intention of 'naturalizing' what was believed to be the 'reality' of the *favela*. It was via this intense and prolonged period of coaching that the filmmakers managed to achieve shockingly and almost unbearably realistic scenes, such as the one featuring the two children tortured by Li'l Zé, who end up shot, one of them lying dead. Given the energy that was channelled into achieving this level of technical mastery, it is clearly inadequate to attribute the film's realist aspect simply to the physical appearance and origins of the cast. The film's realism must, therefore, stem from its form.

Let us take as an example the opening scene of the film. It adapts the poetic style of the first pages of Paulo Lins's novel, combining it with an incident when a chicken is chased through the *favela*, that takes place almost at the end of the book. The images and the editing aim to create a visual rhyme, in the style of Eisenstein. The film opens with the preparation of food for a meal, adopting the metaphor of the knife (you could say that at the beginning of the film 'knives do the talking') and other cutting objects: the blade being sharpened alternates with the beak of a live chicken, the claws on the feet of other dead chickens and a close-up of the protruding, snarling teeth of Li'l Zé (the most feared gangster in the *favela*, as we subsequently discover). The sound of the knife being sharpened on the stone disrupts the samba rhythm – a forewarning of the violence that will bring an end to the Golden Age of the community, which is described in the following scenes to the sound of old samba songs. Then we hear the first phrase shouted by Li'l Zé, that ends with the synthetic word *rapá*: 'Grab the chicken, *rapá*!' Both the escaped chicken and the people who are chasing it are in danger of taking a bullet.

In this brief prologue, the virile nature of the story is established, a story that is composed essentially of male characters (a story of 'rapazes'/ 'boys'), and that is conveniently full of phallic imagery: the chicken (the 'cock'), the knife, the carrot being peeled, and the gun itself. Here it is worth remarking on the visual/linguistic pun with 'chicken' and 'carrot', words used as nicknames of Li'l Zé's two enemies whom he wants to kill and eat, as he jokingly says later in the film. In this sequence, the personality of Li'l Zé is also established, as is his relationship with the other residents of the *favela*, and the spatial and temporal setting of the film, all scanned by the fast pace of a diegetic samba percussion. This is how cinema can translate the rules of synthesis, metre and rhyme, incorporating into its form the features of its subject-matter. The violence of the language used here becomes as palpable as, or even more so than, the violence of the action on screen. Incidentally, it is important to remember that explicit scenes of violence are rare in the film. Virtually no blood is shown, and you do not see the customary severed limbs of Hollywood thrillers. The violence is contained in the form of the film, especially in the editing, and for this reason is all the more powerful.

But now we are touching on a more complex question. Eisenstein defined his montage of attractions by the degree of aggression contained in the images and by their capacity to elicit an emotional response from the audience. In the film *City of God* the aggression is conveyed not only via the imagery and signs of cutting and death, but also by the abrupt cuts in the editing. Cuts, as we know, are traditionally seen as contravening the conventions of realist cinema. The great theorist of film realism, André Bazin, writing after the Great War and appalled by violence, defended the sequence-shot and the deep-focus cinematography, techniques that, according to him, respected the integrity of the time and space of phenomenological reality. Eisenstein, in his revolutionary, combative films – rejected by Bazin – championed cuts, aggression and shock treatment.

Obviously, the film *City of God* is also in tune with the precepts of classic editing, the objective of which is not to achieve realism but a 'reality effect'. The violence, whether contained in the plot or the language, cannot fail to produce the same effect desired by American commercial cinema, namely, the illusionistic catharsis. The frenetic rhythm of the novel is translated into the quick-fire cuts of the digital editing, in the style of an advertisement or music video. In truth, the film could easily have gone down the route of the postmodern language of a cinema of citation, such as that of Tarantino, who only 'surfs' on the surface of reality. The film could equally have reproduced the easy gimmick of contemporary American cinema, infinitely repeating attractions that relegate the narrative to a secondary place.[4] But the film, just like the novel, avoids such schemes via the importance it gives to the narrative. Paulo Lins's great achievement was precisely to find a language with which to portray the encounter between the most violent modernity and the narrative power of the myth. As a consequence of the bullets and the brusque cuts, the tale is not fragmented but rather is shrunk and condensed.

One line in the film, adapted from the novel, exemplifies this process. The words are spoken by a boy of just eight years of age, called Steak 'n' Fries, who works as a look-out for Li'l Zé's gang. The following is how he responds when he is dismissed as a 'child' by Knockout Ned: 'Who are

you calling a child? I smoke, I sniff, I've killed, I've robbed. I'm a man.'
During his brief existence so far, this character, who considers himself an
adult, has not missed any stage of his life but radically shortened all of
them. Already an experienced man of the world, this eight-year-old adult
is not only ready to kill but also ready to die, which is predictably what
happens to him soon after.

### The weight of history

The three-part structure of both the book and the film reflects the desire
to create a sense of balance and completeness. The novel is deliberately
divided into three 'stories': (1) Shaggy's story, (2) Benny's story, (3) Li'l Zé's
story. The emphasis placed on the word 'story' (história, in Portuguese,
means both 'story' and 'history') is not incidental or unwitting: on the
contrary, it indicates that the life stories of these criminals – who in real
life are only known for their crimes – are urgently crying out to be told.
By foregrounding story and history, the novel continually reinforces the
importance of its connection with reality.

The same is true of the film, the three-part structure of which hinges
on the characters of Shaggy, Benny and Knockout Ned (three 'good' gangsters) and on three different timeframes: the end of the 1960s, the 1970s
and the beginning of the 1980s, each with their respective costumes, fashions and music. The development of the mythical structure is made even
more apparent with the references to 'Paradise', 'Purgatory' and 'Hell' in
relation to the three different phases in the history of the City of God
shanty town. In the novel, the passage from one phase (or story) to the
next is marked by a speeding up of the narrative, which in the final part
ends up summarizing entire life destinies (invariably tragic) in just a few,
frantically paced lines. In the film, the editing gives this sense of increasing speed, together with the lighting and sound effects, use of colour and
camera work.

In the first part of the film, which I referred to earlier as the Golden
Age of the community, we are conveniently confronted with golden
sunlight and the orange hues of the unpaved roads of the City of God
favela. Exterior shots from a static camera predominate, as well as long
dialogues. In the second part of the film the number of interior and night-
time shots increases. As the number of dead bodies pile up, the camera
frees itself from the tripod, and when Benny is murdered the images
become confused owing to the unprivileged position of the camera and
the fragmentation caused by the strobe lighting at the disco where the
scene takes place. The final part of the film, that deals with Knockout

Ned's revenge on Li'l Zé, who raped the former's girlfriend and killed members of his family, is the darkest. The camera, frequently hand-held, becomes unsteady as it goes in search of objects that hide in badly lit locations. The cuts become ultra-fast and abrupt. The close of the film, as in the novel, shows the Runts (a group of very young delinquent children) taking the place of Li'l Zé and planning a series of murders. Thus their own premature deaths and the even shorter lives of future generations are implicitly predicted.

This structure, which begins in paradise and ends in hell, suggests a romantic nostalgia for the past. As we know, the myth of the Golden Age or of Paradise Lost differs from the utopian myth. The former consists of a past that is lost and now unattainable, whereas utopia, the ideal place conceived of not by the gods but by man, shapes up the *telos*, reaffirming faith in reason and the possibility of a better future.[5] Nostalgia, more easily identified in the novel than in the film, refers to a vision of the *favela* as a rural space, although implanted in an urban context.[6] The utopian *telos* is disrupted by modernization, represented by the arrival of guns – which again takes us back to the real and symbolic rupture caused by bullets. This rupture corresponds in the novel to the establishment of the 'neofavela' that buries alive the previous rural world.

As I have already commented in the previous chapters, several recent Brazilian films articulate a nostalgia for a past when utopian thoughts were possible. In particular, some of the films that deal with *favelas*, like the previously mentioned *News from a Private War*, *Midnight* and *Orfeu* (all of which tellingly involved Kátia Lund and/or Paulo Lins), attest to the changes caused by the appearance of guns, which marks a dividing line between two separate historical periods. Carlos Diegues, when he conceived of his film *Orfeu*, was also convinced of the radical changes that drug dealing and firearms brought with them to *favela* communities. As explained in Chapter 4, he divides the *favela* history into three phases: (1) the phase of the lyrical samba, up to the end of the 1950s, when 'those who lived up on the hill were near to heaven'; (2) the 'plaintive' phase, which started with the waves of chaotic migration that brought overcrowding and criminality to the *favelas*, making them closer to hell; (3) the phase of the pride of being a *favela* inhabitant, despite all its adversities.[7]

In the film *City of God* the lyrical samba of the time when the *favela* was synonymous with being close to heaven is used to recreate the mood of what I referred to as the community's Golden Age. This first part of the film opens to the strains of the samba 'Alvorada' ('Dawn') by Cartola and Carlos Cachaça, which goes:

Dawn up there on the hill
How beautiful!
Nobody is crying, there's no sadness
Nobody is unhappy
The colourful sun is so pretty, so pretty

Another samba by Cartola, 'Let Me Go', brings this section of the film to a close, accompanying the death of Benny:

Let me go, I need to leave
I'm off to try
To laugh so as not to cry[8]

It is also worthy of note that the criminals in the *favela* during this Golden Age were still a kind of social bandit, who shared out the fruits of their robberies among the poor population, such as when they hold up the gas delivery truck. The emergence of drug dealing, particularly involving cocaine, marks the transition to crime on an industrial scale, which ceases to have a social function and is motivated by purely personal issues of rivalry and revenge. As Ismail Xavier has stated in an excellent essay, recent Brazilian cinema is full of characters whose discomfort stems from the fact that they are stuck in the past and obsessed with the desire for revenge.[9] Now that the political motivations that previously inspired social bandits, as portrayed in Cinema Novo, have been exhausted, the criminals in New Brazilian Cinema only act out of resentment, and their aggressive behaviour is turned against their own kind, when not against themselves.

**An interrupted utopia**

Aggression for trivial reasons, as practised by Li'l Zé and the other gang members in *City of God*, who kill someone because 'he's a pain in the ass', interrupts the utopian trajectory that was beginning to emerge in several different ways: via religion, work and studying. However, it does not hinder the full development of the several short stories that make up the narrative of *City of God*. In Chapter 1, I considered the utopia of the sea in Brazilian cinema, which from Glauber Rocha's films onwards has promised the poor a share in the wealth of the coast. In *City of God* the picture-postcard Rio de Janeiro, with its coastline and beautiful scenery, remains a privilege of the rich, attainable only as a 'vision' for the inhabitants of the *favela* (as in the case of the character Clipper who, after having a 'vision', chooses religion as his way out). As an image, the beautiful Rio is merely a hazy silhouette on the horizon in the film. The sea is only attainable for Rocket, the social climber who has to get close to the 'groovies', that is, the white inhabitants of the City of God.

Rio de Janeiro is thus presented as a divided city (to use Zuenir Ventura's term),[10] containing, on the one hand, the sea of the rich and, on the other, the *favela* of the poor. However, this division, which interrupts the utopia and destroys young lives, does not lead to an 'interrupted spectacle', to use Robert Stam's term with regard to anti-illusionistic techniques.[11] Consequently, none of the self-reflexive techniques used in the film create a distancing effect, the most obvious one being the alter-ego of the film-maker personified by the character Rocket, the omniscient narrator of the film. Devised as a middle-man, with access to the middle classes, he is also the film's conscience, suggesting an identification with the editor himself sitting at his editing table. Behaving as the truth keeper, he organizes, with his voice-over, the facts that make up the narrative, dictating at whim the freeze-frames, flashbacks and fast forwards, zooms and long shots, thus exposing the mechanics of digital editing.

Several times, after a flashback, the story, under the control of the narrator's voice-over, returns to the same point, showing the identical scene from a different point of view. This is the case, for example, when Li'l Zé takes Blacky's 'mouth' (drug-selling turf). Explaining the story of each of the characters involved, Rocket's commentary takes the narrative back to the beginning three times, as if the editor is testing the different points of view offered by three different cameras. At no time, however, is the story called into question, and thus the repetition of the scene from different angles does not ultimately discredit the narrator, unlike, for example, in Sérgio Bianchi's film *Chronically Unfeasible* (*Cronicamente inviável*, 1999), which uses a similar technique.

Rocket can still be interpreted as a reference to filmmakers/photographers of the past, when he takes a photograph of Li'l Zé and his gang, just as in the 1930s Benjamin Abraão famously photographed and filmed the bandit Lampião and his followers, unwittingly leading to his capture and subsequent death. This subject has been repeatedly exploited by filmmakers in Brazil as a form of self-reflexive commentary, in such works as *Memories of Banditry* (*Memórias do cangaço*, Paulo Gil Soares, 1965), *Corisco and Dadá* (*Corisco e Dadá*, Rosemberg Cariry, 1996) and *Perfumed Ball* (*Baile perfumado*, Paulo Caldas and Lírio Ferreira, 1997). Likewise in *City of God* the publication of the photograph of Li'l Zé and his gang on the front page of the *Jornal do Brasil* newspaper prompts the police to begin to hunt them down. The police do not kill Li'l Zé but they force him into an extortion racket and take his money, making him vulnerable to the gang of Runts, who shoot him dead in a 'Soviet attack'. Thus, indirectly, the camera becomes the murderer of the object that it captures, analogous to a gun, as has been extensively studied in film theory.[12]

The self-reflexive position of Rocket is what in fact guarantees the real-ist quality of the performances of the actors. Indeed, the highly polished, exquisite dialogues in the film, which draw on the very best of the novel, would not be possible if the narrator did not take on the didactic function of presenting and explaining the characters and their stories. Stripped to the bare essentials, the speech has none of the superfluous information common in film dialogues, which is intended to contextualize the speak-ers. Rocket, who, unlike the other characters, is not in a hurry, has all the time in the world to explain, in voice-overs, how drug dealing is organized in the *favela*, even providing a glossary of the hierarchy of the drug busi-ness, from the 'look out' to the 'manager'. This is an example of didactic, ironic and good-humoured self-reflexivity, as created by Jorge Furtado, in his short film *Island of Flowers* (*Ilha das Flores*, 1989), which led to an entire school and today is regularly used in TV series such as *City of Men* (*Cidade dos homens*), inspired by the film *City of God*.

The essential speech of the characters, resulting from their ignorance of educated norms and the creative lack of awareness with which they express prejudices and clichés, brings to the fore the childlike innocence of these serial murderers, rapists and mutilators. This for me is the most moving reality that emanates from *City of God*. The extreme skill in the use of linguistic devices in the novel, and cinematic techniques in the film, is directed towards avoiding an interruption of the utopia that would put an end to history. Although aimless, these armed children, who were born to kill many people and die young, are the essence of Brazil's contemporary history, and probably that of many other countries.

CHAPTER SIX

# THE URBAN DYSTOPIA

**Film**

*The Trespasser* (O *invasor*, Beto Brant, 2002)

# THE URBAN DYSTOPIA

'The Trespasser is ... the portrait ... of Brazil trapped in a moral and social cul-de-sac.' This phrase, extracted from Neusa Barbosa's essay in the press release for The Trespasser, summarizes the film's intention to reveal a 'chronically unfeasible' country, to cite the title of Sérgio Bianchi's film (Chronically Unfeasible/Cronicamente inviável, 1999). It is easy to verify the effectiveness of such a proposal through the reactions of the critics. Acknowledging The Trespasser, as I do myself, as one of the best recent Brazilian productions, most of them were ready to confirm its power to reveal a national situation. Walter Salles, for example, wrote that The Trespasser shows the 'Brazilian social structure upside down. Wherever you look it is Brazil, unveiled by a camera held in a radical, organic way by director of photography Toca Seabra.'[1] Mario Sergio Conti, in turn, identified the very structure of the film with that of Brazilian society, stating that:

> The script follows a general idea with a long tradition in Brazilian art: the tension between centre and periphery, captured in the heart of underdevelopment. This tension, in the film, leads to the investigation of an increasingly visible aspect of contemporary Brazil, which is the extra-legality of capitalism.[2]

Luiz Zanin Oricchio also considered the film's main revelation to be 'the predatory character of capitalism Brazilian style'.[3] My purpose here is not to evaluate the judgement that the film supposedly conveys about Brazil, but rather to ask: What does The Trespasser actually reveal about the country? How far can a fiction film be taken as evidence of the ethical condition of a real place? And is the country in the film really Brazil?

Document and fiction, conflicting elements as well as basic prerogatives of cinema, constitute the main problem in relation to this film as much as its key. Let us begin with the subject-matter, which seems so convincing as a denunciation of Brazil's moral decadence. Although set in a scenario entirely recognizable as contemporary Brazil, the film is not based on a real story but on a fictional idea by Beto Brant's faithful collaborator, novelist Marçal Aquino, and turned into a screenplay by Aquino, Brant and Renato Ciasca. Two of the protagonists, the engineers Ivan and Gilberto, are presented as prominent figures of the São Paulo business class. Some of their actions, such as the payment of a bribe to a government officer – a transaction vaguely mentioned, the aim of which is not explained – are easily identifiable with similar events that proliferate in Brazilian political life. Others, such as keeping a deluxe brothel and hiring a professional killer to eliminate their third partner, Estêvão, cannot be immediately connected with specific facts, and their accumulation on the character of Gilberto suggests the usual devices used to shape a villain in a fiction film.

A third protagonist interacts with Ivan and Gilberto, Anísio, the professional killer and the 'trespasser' of the film's title, brilliantly performed by singer and composer Paulo Miklos. His 'trespassing' derives from his being a man from the *favela* who, after carrying out his contract killing, decides to mingle with the men who commissioned him, blackmailing them until he succeeds in being upgraded to their social class. What could be deemed 'realist' about such a character? Marcelo Coelho made an interesting observation in this respect:

> If I am associating [the character of Anísio] with ETs and animation characters, this is because in some way Paulo Miklos's performance, pitch and style are not really a caricature, but intentionally unrealistic. No, unrealistic is also not the word. Anísio looks real, but real like a pop painting, like an Andy Warhol work; it is as if he were lit by a fluorescent light.[4]

In my view, it is not Miklos's performance that is unrealistic, but the very character he plays. As we know, capitalist societies in general, and the Brazilian one in particular, are structured on exclusion. The poor in these societies, even if they succeed in becoming rich through drug dealing and other crimes, are prevented from climbing the social ladder by the sophisticated defence mechanisms of the ruling classes, which include the support of the police and the army. Even *favela* artists, who come to prominence through the legitimate exercise of their talent, are confronted with barriers within their own communities, ravaged by gang wars. An eloquent example here is the rapper Sabotage, the great revelation in the cast of *The Trespasser*, who was murdered soon after the opening of the film as a result of an ongoing gang war. Characters like Anísio are, therefore, very rare beyond the fictional universe, and I will attempt to demonstrate that his origins are to be found in genre cinema rather than in the crime chronicle.

In addition, it is worth mentioning a fourth more discreet, but equally central character in the film: Marina, the daughter of Estêvão, the major shareholder of the construction company, who is murdered together with his wife on the orders of his two other partners. Marina is young, attractive, but alienated to the point of automatism, thus becoming easy prey to her parents' murderer, who seduces her and takes her on a continuous round of bars, drugs and clubs. Fictitious though her character may seem, her relationship with the murderer proved to be a kind of premonition of a new social phenomenon (or disease). Soon after the film was released, a rich businessman and his wife were murdered in São Paulo by the delinquent boyfriend of their daughter. A similar case occurred more recently in Rio de Janeiro involving a Shell executive and his wife, turning this kind of crime into a symptom of our times. Nevertheless, besides the astonishing similarities between Marina's story and those two subsequent real cases, such as the daughters' attending parties just after the double murders and their involvement with drugs, there are also significant differences. A notable one is the fact that the real-life crime, at least in the São Paulo case, was commissioned by the daughter herself, confirming her active role in opposition to Marina's passivity in *The Trespasser*. Another difference is that the murderer in the real São Paulo case, a young man of poor origin, was immediately imprisoned and removed from society, in contrast to the film's trespasser, a winner who takes possession of his victims' property and their daughter.

The importance of such details will be examined below. Meanwhile, let us summarize the three basic types of material contained in the film's subject-matter. First, the allegorical example extracted from the real political scene, garnished with fictitious elaboration. Second, the imaginary situation of a *favela* criminal allowed to ascend the social scale. Finally, the social analysis later confirmed by real-life events.

Now let us examine the modes through which these different types of narrative material, which include the contemporary political scene, the fiction and the critique, can produce not only the usual illusionist reality effect but also the impression of revealing the reality of a country. Even though the fictional material predominates, it does not impair the documentary effect, suggesting that this derives not from the story but from the way it is told. A closer look at the narrative technique of *The Trespasser* may therefore offer the key to the film's impact.

Snapshots of the four-minute sequence-shot in which the logic of capitalist exploitation is explained in *The Trespasser*. In the background we can see the nanny Gilberto is furtively flirting with, and building foreman Cicero.

### The document

In the film, the most effective way in which fiction is given the status of reality is, obviously, the use of real locations. From the first image to the last the set is insistently characterized as the city of São Paulo. Phrases like 'Take the 23' (or the 23 de Maio Avenue, an important São Paulo artery) are duly accompanied by long tracking shots through the Anhangabaú and Ibirapuera tunnels, along the Dr Arnaldo flyover, Paulista Avenue, the several *marginais* (or riverside expressways) and Águas Espraiadas Avenue (a newly constructed road which dissected a huge *favela*, the remains of which are still visible on either side of it).[5] These are geographically coherent itineraries, which link the different city zones and are easily recognizable to those who are familiar with São Paulo and plausible to the foreign viewer. The contextualization of the plot in the city of São Paulo is reinforced by multiple tracking shots through the city suburbs, capturing the populace in their daily activities in front of their houses, shops and bars.

The locations are also emphatically real even in the interior shots. Bars, nightclubs and even a leisure centre (such as Body One, in the Vila Madalena district, which appears here in a case of discreet product placement) are real, identifiable premises, into which the camera, often in sequence-shots, penetrates from the outside to indicate the spatial continuity. This is what happens, for example, in the scene in the Liberdade district, in which the camera, coming from the nocturnal street with its typical Japanese lanterns, enters a karaoke bar with East Asian customers and an amateur singer, reproducing a typical São Paulo scene.

The sequence-shots and the deep-focus cinematography, with their obedience to real time and space, as well as natural lighting and the hand-held camera used to create the spontaneity of the newsreel, are employed

in various moments to bind cast and locations together and give the impression that the fiction emerges spontaneously from a real context. An example is the long four-minute sequence-shot in which, in a discussion, Gilberto outlines his worldview to Ivan. During the conversation the camera turns rapidly, as if following the character's unexpected movements, to catch in the background a nanny that Gilberto is furtively flirting with, and then, in a reversing pan, building foreman Cícero at the door of the construction site. Gilberto says:

> This is how the world is, old man. Cícero may have a stupid face. But if need be he becomes a beast. ... In reality, these folks want your car, your position, your money, your clothes. They want to fuck your wife, Ivan. They are just waiting for a chance. This is what we are going to do to Estêvão: we will take advantage of our opportunity before he does the same.

The sexy nanny and the oppressed building foreman, although obviously played by actors, are shown as integral parts of the real city in the background, upon which the protagonists from the upper class are superimposed in the foreground. The logic of capitalist exploitation in the fictional plot is thus presented as the logic of the real city.

An element that characterizes the cast as an extension of the documentary cityscape is the use of the accent and vocabulary of the São Paulo middle classes, as well as those of the drug and crime gangs from the *favelas*. These details are aptly combined with the rap, rock and hip-hop music of local artists Paulo Miklos, Sabotage, Pavilhão 9 and Tolerância Zero. The construction of Miklos's vocabulary, which included the contribution of Sabotage himself, was particularly effective as a realist reproduction of *favela* slang.

These contextualizing elements bring to the fore the ugly, dirty, inhar-
monious and awkward aspects of the city, confirming *The Trespasser* as the
recent chapter in a certain current of São Paulo cinema, which emerged
with the so-called 'Marginal Cinema' of Rogério Sganzerla in the 1960s
and continued with Carlos Reichenbach's films in the 1970s. Interestingly enough, this cinema, identified as it always has been with a specific
geography and aesthetics (or anti-aesthetics), was always divided into
two strands, both stemming from the São Paulo Boca do Lixo (literally,
'Garbage Mouth', the red-light district where film production companies
were located): the semi-documentary production of filmmakers such as
Ozualdo Candeias and the outspokenly fantastic strand of a primitivist
such as José Mojica Marins, aka Coffin Joe. And since Sganzerla's time this
production has taken the form of a self-reflexive, citation cinema, resulting
in the 1980s in a certain postmodern current, also derived from the Boca
do Lixo cinema, but more akin to artifice, studio, cartoon and cinephilia,
such as the films by Guilherme de Almeida Prado, Wilson Barros and
Chico Botelho.

Beto Brant and his team's output is a combination of these elements,
and we will see how, in *The Trespasser*, documentary images of the disorderly, polluted, ugly city become the source of horror fantasies.

### The rotten side

*The Trespasser* is the product of a recent trend in Brazilian literature intimately connected with the cinema, to which novelist Marçal Aquino
belongs. This literature, the most influential precursor of which is arguably
the work of Rubem Fonseca, specializes in crime-genre narrative. As well
as for *The Trespasser*, Beto Brant turned to the crime thriller for his two
previous feature films, both also based on Aquino's novels and eloquently
entitled *The Killers* (*Os matadores*, 1997) and *Friendly Fire* (*Ação entre amigos*,
1998). Thus *The Trespasser* is connected to genre from the outset.

It is recognized that genre, both in literature and cinema, is an expression of the *Zeitgeist*. Even though made up of rules that are repeated from
work to work, a genre's boundaries are fluid, being constantly reshaped
according to contemporary phenomena, thus ensuring its survival through
time. São Paulo, as a peripheral, chaotic metropolis, typical of late capitalism, provides the ideal setting for the updating of the crime thriller, with
its typical mixture of blackmail, conspiracy, greed, murder and general
pessimism.

The German abstract-expressionist artist Anselm Kiefer gave the title
of 'Lilith' to his series of huge paintings based on photos of São Paulo city,

seen in all its monstrosity from its highest skyscraper, the Itália building. The title refers to the demonic goddess of Hebrew mythology, Adam's first wife, whose occupation was to ruin men and slaughter new-born babies. *The Trespasser* also leans towards the expressionist style, as far as expressionism, with its exaggerations, deformations, paroxysms and contrasts, favours the development of the crime-thriller genre. Originating in the periods of crisis around the First World War, European expressionism instituted urban chaos as the epicentre of fear, a feature later re-elaborated by the film noir, which reflected the influence of European immigrants in the United States during the Second World War.

The expressionist city, with its crowds of anonymous, solitary souls, is the home of automata or 'docile subjects', to use Jonathan Crary's terminology, typical of modernity. The epitome of expressionist modernity in cinema is the somnambulist Cesare, the protagonist of *The Cabinet of Dr Caligari* (*Das Kabinett des Doktor Caligari*, Robert Wiene, 1920), who, under Caligari's diabolic spell, becomes a murderer. In *The Trespasser*, the 'docile subject' is Marina, hypnotized by the repetitive rhythm of techno music and sedated by drink and drugs, who becomes a body devoid of 'political force', to use Crary's words once more, falling under the spell of her parents' assassin.[6] The proof that this character, although echoing Brazilian reality, also incorporates genre elements, is precisely her automatism. In the real story that occurred in São Paulo, as pointed out above, the woman was the crime's originator, while in the film she is reduced to a passive role. She thus acquires the features both of the expressionist automaton and of the misogyny prevailing in the crime genre, where the mind and the action are male attributes.

Music, combined with music-video techniques, is the element of fashion employed to update the genre. In a typical music video, images do not have their own meaning, but are also 'automata' in as much as they follow the hypnotic pulsation of the music, thus preventing concentration and comprehension and favouring diversion, distraction and dispersion. In *The Trespasser*, the combination of quick cut, artificial lighting, cold colours (especially green), grainy exposure and shock montage, accompanying songs of an often frenetic beat, is aimed at deforming and fragmenting the object and ultimately negating the objective real.

São Paulo, with its social contradictions apparent even in its wealthy quarters, the awkwardness of which betrays the misery that inhabits their fringes, provides the ideal set for the destabilizing intervention of the music video, which reduces the documentary surface to fragments. Such a technique resembles the structure of the romantic fantastic tale, in which the apparently stable bourgeois reality is disrupted by the sudden emergence of a ghostly, supernatural dimension, i.e. a hidden reality. Here the sequence-shot, usually so faithful to reality, acquires an opposite function with the camera mimicking the protagonist's trespassing movements. The violence with which the camera, coming from the exterior, penetrates private, intimate realms, unveiling the characters' inner reality, causes the vertigo of fear typical of suspense, while destabilizing the documentary settings. The often nocturnal ambience of this other dimension, in contrast to the daylight bathing the world of appearances, is a clear element of genre inherited from the noir and expressionist styles.

The unexpected appearance of Anísio in the bourgeois universe causes the crack on the surface of the illusory real, through which emerges that other, chaotic, cruel dimension, presented as 'truer' in the film. 'Welcome to the rotten side of life,' Gilberto tells Ivan after they hire the killer, thus evidencing the bi-dimensional conception of the world which governs the film. Finding no exact parallel in the real universe of a São Paulo *favela*, which he supposedly represents, Anísio bears more resemblance to a Mephistophelean demon. He is short, acne-scarred, hoarse, with a big nose, in short, the embodiment of the grotesque. However, just like Mephistopheles, he casts a spell over people through his cunning. Anísio could be seen as a kind of 'return of the repressed', which, for Freud, may occur in the individual as well as in the social sphere. His grotesque figure could be translated as the underdeveloped portion which Third World ruling classes do their best to hide, but which springs up when least expected through the 'scars of repression' on the thin crust of their world.[7]

Although the documentary techniques in The Trespasser aim to naturalize the actions of this diabolic character, they would be hardly conceivable in a real-life context. Anísio, odd as he is, invades a private company without identifying himself and, instead of being stopped, he inspires respectful behaviour among all the staff and even the Rottweiler dog trained to attack intruders like him. His immediate familiarity with this Cerberus, which lets itself be petted like a lamb, suggests an affinity between him and the canine race, as if Anísio himself were 'the dog', a synonym of the devil in Portuguese and other languages. The metaphor is developed into a symbol when Anísio gives Marina a little dog to be the girl's guard in her constant trance of drugs and clubbing. Thus Anísio's beastly nature becomes apparent, as usual in the horror tale, in which malign characters are often identified with vampires, hyenas, spiders, and so on – not to mention the literary versions in which Mephisto displays a 'dog's face'.[8]

Anísio, the Mephistophelean character who identifies with the Rottweiler dog and manipulates Marina through his cunning in *The Trespasser*.

In an article about Guimarães Rosa's novel *The Devil to Pay in the Backlands*, Davi Arrigucci Jr notes the kinship between the devil and animals
such as the horse and the python, and their power of 'mixing themselves
in everything', which, in the novel, results in 'inversions, mixtures and
reversibilities of various kinds'.[9] In *The Trespasser*, Anísio, the diabolic
keeper of the knowledge, penetrates and disorganizes the bourgeois world,
mixing up the public and the private, rulers and subjects, the rich and the
poor.

As has been the case since Goethe, the spectator is led to identify and
sympathize with the Faustian character, namely Ivan. This is achieved
through the skilful manipulation of the point of view. In the novel *The
Trespasser*, Ivan is the first-person narrator, which facilitates his configuration as a hero ruined by a fault of character. But in the film, thanks to the
possibilities of the medium, there are multiple points of view, which vary

according to the alternation between documentary and genre techniques. Let us consider the example of the opening sequence, in which the pact with the devil takes place.

Ivan and Gilberto enter a bar in the poor periphery of São Paulo and face the camera, positioned in Anísio's subjective point of view. Anísio is thus not visible; we only hear his voice asking for payment for the murder he has been commissioned to carry out. Ivan's face, looking mutely at the camera, is the sheer expression of horror. The dark make-up around his eyelashes enhances his wide-open eyes on his serious face, his low chin forcing his look upwards and creating a contrast between his red cheeks and the whiteness of the sides of his face. At this moment, as in many others in the film, he is the pure expressionist man, who 'does not look, but sees', in the famous definition by Kasimir Edschmidt.[10] As in the old expressionist films, in which big wide-open eyes obsessively occupy the centre of the screen, Ivan's deep eyes seem to reach beyond the object they are looking at, producing a 'metaphysical vision', which is the exteriorization of his inner world. Ivan's visions of horror, provoked by his feelings of guilt and regret, will contaminate the whole narrative from the beginning. After signing the pact with Mephisto, the Faustian character will spend the rest of his days contorting in 'pain, affliction, moans, tears and tremors', as the Faustian state of mind has been described.[11]

Ivan's trance, which alternates with moments of clairvoyance of an equally expressionist kind, begins in the next sequence when Gilberto drags him to a luxurious brothel, which is later revealed to be his own property. The music-video technique is then put into action, in a quick editing of crooked, grainy shots, bombarded by green and red lights.[12] Ivan, pushed into the arms of a prostitute, is led into a bedroom and at this point the shots, in a temporal zigzag, alternate past, present and future images, including one of him arriving home and finding his wife asleep, a fact which will only occur later when he actually returns home. This is a

Ivan's expressionist look in *The Trespasser*.

kind of premonitory flash-forward both of Ivan and the film itself, conferring on Ivan's expression of his inner world the status of reality.

Madness and a persecution complex, typical ingredients of the expressionist *Weltanschauung*, are recycled here through this visionary character who suddenly 'discovers the truth' about his partner and friend and is convinced that he will be the next victim. Thus the sequences in which Ivan is present are often the representation of a disorderly world, with quick, discontinuous shots, cold, artificial lighting, an unstable camera and grainy images, reinforcing the character's absolute isolation in the city. An example is the scene in which Ivan, after buying a gun, rolls and groans in a hotel bed, devoured by fear and guilt, conveniently bathed in green light. Near the end of the film, the scene in which he walks along the deserted, nocturnal avenue, again enveloped in green light and flanked by shapes of shacks, is reminiscent of the famous picture 'The Scream' by Edvard Munch. This foundational expressionist work portrays a solitary human being, crossing a straight bridge through the meandering landscape, his thin body like a flame, his head reduced to a skull and dominated by the orifices of the eyes and the mouth forming an 'Oh!' of sheer terror.

Thus fear and death, extrapolating the supposed attributes of a decadent Brazil, fuse into a mythic master narrative, of which *The Trespasser* is only a recent version.

### The mixture and the modern

One of the best and most original devices employed in the film for the updating of the crime-thriller genre is to combine the trespasser's hypnotic power over people and animals with the lysergic effect of the music-video montage. Thus the grotesque figure of the demon becomes the complete expression of late capitalism, and the union between Anísio and Marina a merging between archaic and modern.

As befits his Mephistophelean character, Anísio takes Marina on hallucinogenic tours through the impoverished São Paulo suburbs. But instead of a magic carpet flying over exotic countries, we have tracking shots on land, collecting documentary snapshots in sequences which are nothing but music videos of Sabotage's songs about the miserable Southern Zone and its 'difficult daily life'. At this point, thanks to the jump cuts, the *favela* appears as a natural continuation of the rich centre. The breaking of geographic boundaries caused by the brusque cuts results in striking and entirely recognizable evidence of the state of aesthetic communion among Brazilian urban social classes, although, of course, they still remain economically apart. Marina just smiles at this mixed universe where everything seems equivalent and all is diversion.

As a form of closure to his revenge, the trespasser finally parks the car on a deserted hilltop in the poor periphery. A very similar, if not the same, location is presented earlier in the film, in a scene showing Gilberto, Ivan and Estêvão's father examining the car where the bodies of Estêvão and his wife have been found and from where they have just been carried away by the mortuary van; in the background, a song by Tolerância Zero screams: 'Welcome to the nightmare of reality.' Marina, arriving at the same place, feels slightly frightened and asks whether it is dangerous. Anísio replies, 'No, this is the *favela*'s paradise', pointing to the landscape below which is no more than a few pale blinking lights. Being thus reassured, and after snorting cocaine, she delivers herself to sex with the trespasser.

This horrific scene, in which a murderer plays with his victim's total alienation, summarizes the dystopia to which the metropolis's 'paradise' is finally reduced. Anísio here could almost be seen as a representative of the oppressed who, through cunning, seizes the power from his oppressors. He does indeed seem at times to demonstrate awareness of his social class's political position, for example, in the brilliant and most documentary-like scene of the film in which he imposes on Ivan and Gilberto the inventive and political art of rapper Sabotage. A black, tall, skinny, gap-toothed young man, singing a rap in an engineering office, Sabotage is the irruption of nocturnal reality into the illusory daylight. However, Anísio is for the most part acting single-handedly and in his own interest, with no profit for his peers, being no more than one of those resentful characters described by Ismail Xavier as the successors, in contemporary Brazilian cinema, of the social bandits of the past.[13]

Ivan, persecuted and swallowed up by the monstrous metropolis, where betrayal lurks in every corner, regrets the loss of the utopian dream. In a scene at the seaside, succeeding the one of Anísio and Marina in the *favela* 'paradise', he enjoys a provisional peace with his lover, who soon after will be unmasked as Gilberto's spy. He then tells her that this Edenic sea was once the site of the pleasures of his youth, in a mythical past now definitively buried.

At the end of the film, Marina sleeps with the pet dog given to her by the demon, after a night of clubbing, group sex and drugs. Meanwhile, Anísio and Gilberto, who have become partners and are conspiring at Marina's place, receive Ivan who arrives handcuffed in a police car, his face even more startled when he realizes that he has been delivered into the hands of those he was escaping from. It is the end of the Faustian utopia and the dystopia come true, in a city and a country dominated by evil.

Ivan, haunted by paranoia and a persecution complex, is reminiscent of the character in Edvard Munch's 'The Scream'.

## Conclusion

At this point, we may perhaps return to the initial questions about the
revelatory character of the film, its value as a document and its references
to Brazil, and suggest some answers.

The revelatory character of *The Trespasser* does not seem to lie where
it is normally found, that is in the main plot. Although suspicious deals
between construction companies and the government are customary in
Brazil, such an event is only vaguely mentioned in the film, being nothing
more than a pretext for the main action of the double homicide. Realist
fiction privileges the detail, while the generality observed in *The Trespasser*
is typical, precisely, of the generic art. Murders by commission, treach-
ery, blackmail and Mephistophelean characters are equally typical of the
generic art and cannot be read as revealing of a real, single country. Therefore, in my view, the pessimistic conclusion that Brazil is an 'unfeasible
country', to return to Sérgio Bianchi's term, on the basis of this storyline,
is not justified.

Nevertheless, the way in which the critics as well as the publicists themselves immediately qualify the film's atmosphere of amorality as typically
Brazilian calls for further reflection. Indeed, it could be argued that the
impact caused by the film indicates a revelatory quality. However, I tend
to believe that the novelty here is of an aesthetic kind: the representation
of the protected universe of the ruling classes permeated by the ugliness
and abjection that surround it. The fact that, in the film, the aesthetic
contamination passes for an ethical diagnosis of Brazil as a whole is due,
in my view, to the skill with which genre elements are articulated with the
document. As to the city's periphery invading and taking over the rich
centre, be it individually or collectively, this is for the moment a highly
improbable scenario in Brazil. Thus the trespasser himself appears as the
least realist and most genre-like character of the film.

The abundance of documentary images enables the audience to
recognize a country and, more specifically, a city. Scenes like the musical intervention by the rapper Sabotage constitute precious documentary
evidence, on celluloid, of a key moment in São Paulo's cultural history.
But the organization of these documentary images and songs by means of
the fashion element of music video, far from a condemnation *in toto* of the
country, tends to insert contemporary Brazil into a globalized culture. A
part of this cultural output, including the political raps by Sabotage and
others played in the film, is shown from an entirely positive perspective.
Globalization is indeed the very content of Sabotage's lyrics, which say, for
example: 'I don't know what kills more/ the hunger, the gun or Ebola/

The rapper Sabotage makes an impressive appearance in *The Trespasser*.

who suffers more/ the blacks from here or from Angola.' The element of fashion contributed greatly to the film's success, and it is not just a coincidence that the rap 'Quem que caguetou?' ('Who's the Squealer?'), by Tejo, Black Alien and Speed, included in the film's soundtrack, was turned into a music-video advertisement for the Japanese car Nissan, recently shown in several European countries.

Finally, *The Trespasser* is a fiction film, but fiction can be even more revealing than documentary through critical analysis. This is what happens on the level of the film form, which updates the crime thriller with the introduction of music-video language as a privileged space for the representation of contemporary alienation. In this sense, the character of Marina, living exclusively for entertainment and fuelled by drugs and clubbing, in a time devoid of political proposals, is probably the main revelation of a symptom of late capitalism. However, this is of course a transnational situation.

'There is a collective therapy to be performed on the victims of depoliticization,' says Fredric Jameson in relation to our post-utopian era.[14] This is one possible message conveyed by *The Trespasser*. Another is that the devil is part of a universal imaginary from which cinema can still extract good profit.

# NOTES

## Foreword

1. An effect of extreme realism, obtained, paradoxically, via symbolic means in opposition to the realistic treatment of external reality, was the object of a famous analysis by Erich Auerbach of the work of Baudelaire. See 'Les fleurs du mal di Baudelaire e il sublime', in Erich Auerbach, Da Montaigne a Proust, trans Giorgio Alberti (Bari: De Donato, 1970), pp 192–221.

## Introduction

1. Francis Fukuyama, The End of History and the Last Man (London: Penguin, 1992).
2. Fredric Jameson, The Seeds of Time (New York: Columbia University Press, 1994).
3. Fredric Jameson, Postmodernism, or, the Cultural Logic of Late Capitalism (London/New York: Verso, 1991).
4. Jameson, 'Nostalgia for the Present', in Postmodernism, or, the Cultural Logic of Late Capitalism, p 287.
5. 'Diversões eletrônicas' (or 'electronic pleasures') is the title of one of Arrigo Barnabé's famous songs of that time.
6. Glauber Rocha has directed a so-called trilogia da terra (or 'land trilogy'), composed of Deus e o diabo na terra do sol (Black God, White Devil, 1964), Terra em transe (Land in Anguish, 1967) and A idade da terra (The Age of the Earth, 1981).
7. Cf. Lúcia Nagib, 'Going Global: The Brazilian Scripted Film', in Sylvia Harvey (ed), Trading Culture: Global Traffic and Local Cultures in Film and Television (Eastleigh: John Libbey, 2006).

## Chapter 1. Images of the Sea

1. Sertão: the dry and poverty-stricken hinterlands of the Brazilian northeast.
2. Cordel literature is a kind of popular poetry from the northeast of Brazil,

often illustrated with wood-block prints and sold in pamphlet form.

3.  A *cangaceiro* was a kind of social bandit from the Brazilian northeast, active mainly during the first half of the twentieth century. The activity of the *cangaceiros* is called *cangaço*. Corisco was a notorious member of the gang led by Lampião, the most legendary *cangaceiro* of all time.

4.  Fredric Jameson, *The Geopolitical Aesthetic: Cinema and Space in the World System* (Bloomington and Indianapolis: Indiana University Press; London: BFI, 1995), p 118.

5.  Cf. Ismail Xavier, *Sertão-mar: Glauber Rocha e a estética da fome* (São Paulo: Brasiliense, 1983), and, by the same author, *Allegories of Underdevelopment: Aesthetics and Politics in Modern Brazilian Cinema* (Minneapolis and London: University of Minnesota Press, 1997).

6.  Ismail Xavier, 'Eldorado as Hell: Appropriations of the Imaginary of the Discovery', in John King, Ana López and Manuel Alvarado (eds), *Mediating Two Worlds: Cinematic Encounters in the Americas* (London: BFI Publishing, 1993), pp 192–203.

7.  *Sertanejo*: the *sertão* man.

8.  '1964 – Glauber Rocha, Walter Lima Jr, David Neves, Leon Hirszman – *Deus e o diabo na terra do sol*', in Alex Viany, *O processo do Cinema Novo* (Rio de Janeiro: Aeroplano, 1999), p 62.

9.  Euclides da Cunha, *Rebellion in the Backlands*, trans Samuel Putnam (London: Picador, 1995; first edition, University of Chicago Press, 1944), p 193.

10. Roberto Ventura, *Folha explica Os sertões* (São Paulo: Publifolha, 2002), p 46.

11. Euclides da Cunha, *Rebellion in the Backlands*, p 20.

12. Interview with Rosemberg Cariry in the press release of the film *Juazeiro – The New Jerusalem* (*Juazeiro – a nova Jerusalém*, 2004).

13. *Ibid.*

14. Hélène Clastres, *Terra sem mal*, trans Renato Janine Ribeiro (São Paulo: Brasiliense, 1978), pp 24ff.

15. Sérgio Buarque de Holanda, *Visão do paraíso* (São Paulo: Nacional, 1977), p 61.

16. Euclides da Cunha, *Rebellion in the Backlands*, p 243.

17. Sérgio Buarque de Holanda, *Visão do paraíso*, pp 156–7.

18. Thomas More, *Utopia*. Accessible on the Internet at http://www.d-holliday.com/tmore/utopia002.htm.

19. Afonso Arinos de Melo Franco, *O índio brasileiro e a Revolução Francesa* (Rio de Janeiro: Topbooks, 2000), pp 135–51.

20. Américo Vespúcio, *Novo Mundo – as cartas que batizaram a América*. Presentation and notes by Eduardo Bueno (São Paulo: Planeta, 2003), p 116.

21. Afonso Arinos de Melo Franco, *O índio brasileiro e a Revolução Francesa*, p 139.

22. Ismail Xavier, *Sertão Mar – Glauber Rocha e a estética da fome*, p 73.

23. Cf. Interviews in the extras of the DVD of *Deus e o diabo na terra do sol*, Prefeitura do Rio/Seleções DVD.

24. Glauber Rocha, 'Introdução', in *Revisão crítica do cinema brasileiro* (São Paulo: Cosac Naify, edição do Espólio Glauber Rocha, 2003), p 36.
25. Afonso Arinos de Melo Franco, *O índio brasileiro e a Revolução Francesa*, p 150.
26. *Candomblé*: African-Brazilian religion, which worships deities called *orixás*.
27. *I Am Cuba* was shelved for decades and only relaunched in the early 1990s.
28. The negative stock utilized by the director of photography, Sergei Urusevsky, was provided by the Russian army, according to information given in the film *Soy Cuba – the Siberian Mammoth* (*Soy Cuba – o mamute siberiano*), a 2005 Brazilian documentary directed by Vicente Ferraz.
29. Besides this opening, there are other astonishing similarities between *Land in Anguish* and *I Am Cuba*, suggesting that Glauber might have seen this film in the period between *Black God, White Devil* and *Land in Anguish*, although I have not been able to confirm this hypothesis.
30. I am referring to Glauber's *trilogia da terra*, or 'land trilogy', which includes *Deus e o diabo na terra do sol*, *Terra em transe* and *A idade da terra*.
31. For this and the film's dialogue quoted here, see Daniela Thomas, Marcos Bernstein and Walter Salles, *Terra estrangeira* (Rio de Janeiro: Rocco, 1996).
32. Jameson, *Postmodernism, or, the Cultural Logic of Late Capitalism*, p 159.
33. Interview conducted by Helena Salem, in *O Estado de S. Paulo*, 7 March 1996, p D1.
34. Jameson, *Postmodernism*, pp 181ff.
35. Interview conducted by Helena Salem.
36. 'O cinema brasileiro dos anos 90', interview with Ismail Xavier, in *Praga*, no. 9 (São Paulo: Hucitec), p 144.

## Chapter 2. The Centre, the Zero and the Empty Utopia

1. See, for example, 'Tendências do cinema brasileiro atual', in *Studies in Latin American Popular Culture*, no. 18 (1999), pp 19-32.
2. On the desire for 'Brazilianness', see Walter Salles's interview with Jurandir Freire Costa, 'Um filme contra o Brasil indiferente', in *Folha de S. Paulo*, *Mais!*, 29 March 1998, pp 5-7.
3. Glauber Rocha, *Revolução do Cinema Novo* (São Paulo: Cosac Naify, 2004), p 133.
4. Quoted in Lúcia Nagib, *Werner Herzog: o cinema como realidade* (São Paulo: Estação Liberdade, 1991), p 136.
5. Sandro Bernardi, 'Rossellini's Landscapes: Nature, Myth, History', in David Forgacs, Sarah Lutton and Geoffrey Nowell-Smith (eds), *Roberto Rossellini: Magician of the Real* (London: BFI Publishing, 2001), p 51.
6. In the original, in German, in lower cases, without punctuation and in verse: 'hier stück geschichte/nur zehn pfennige/mauersteine aus Berlin/koppeln/bücher/fahnen/hemden, knöpfe/kommen sie heran/meine herrschaften, kaufen sie'. Cf. Jean-Luc Godard, *Allemagne neuf zéro: phrases (sorties d'un film)* (Paris: P.O.L., 1998), no page numbers.

7. Cf. Laura Mulvey, 'The Hole and the Zero: Godard's Visions of Femininity', in Laura Mulvey, *Fetishism and Curiosity* (Bloomington, Indianapolis and London: Indiana University Press/BFI, 1996).

8. Ismail Xavier uses the expression 'unexpected encounter' for similar events, in his chapter 'Brazilian Cinema in the 1990s: The Unexpected Encounter and the Resentful Character', in Lúcia Nagib (ed), *The New Brazilian Cinema* (London and New York: I.B.Tauris, 2003).

9. Marilena Chauí, *Brasil: mito fundador e sociedade autoritária* (São Paulo: Fundação Perseu Abramo, 2001), p 8.

10. Gilberto Felisberto Vasconcellos, 'Capitalismo popular e privatização do imaginário', in *Folha de S. Paulo, Ilustrada*, 2 May 1998, pp 4–6.

11. Jean-Claude Bernardet, *O vôo dos anjos: Bressane, Sganzerla* (São Paulo: Brasiliense, 1991).

12. Cf. Ivana Bentes, 'The *sertão* and the *favela* in Contemporary Brazilian Film', in Lúcia Nagib (ed), *The New Brazilian Cinema*.

13. Cf. Fernão Pessoa Ramos, 'Humility, Guilt and Narcissism Turned Inside Out in Brazil's Film Revival', in Lúcia Nagib (ed), *The New Brazilian Cinema*.

14. Jean-Claude Bernardet, *Brasil em tempo de cinema* (Rio de Janeiro: Civilização Brasileira, 1967).

15. See, in this sense, Michael Renov, 'Domestic Ethnography and the Construction of the "Other" Self', in Jane M. Gaines and Michael Renov (eds), *Collecting Visible Evidence* (Minneapolis and London: University of Minnesota Press, 1999).

16. See Walter Salles's comments in the extras of the DVD of *Central Station* (Buena Vista Home Entertainment, 2002).

17. Cf. Ismail Xavier, 'Historical Allegory', in Toby Miller and Robert Stam (eds), *A Companion to Film Theory* (Oxford: Blackwell, 1999).

18. Cf. Charles S. Peirce, *Peirce on Signs: Writings on Semiotic*, ed James Hoopes (Chapel Hill: University of North Carolina Press, 1991).

19. Cf. Ismail Xavier, *Sertão mar: Glauber Rocha e a estética da fome*.

20. Mulvey, *Fetishism and Curiosity*, p 85.

21. *Ibid.*, p 92.

## Chapter 3. To Be or Not To Be a Cannibal

1. In the original: '*Essa capacidade de se ver como Outro – ponto de vista que é, talvez, o ângulo ideal de visão de si mesmo – parece-me a chave da antropofagia tupi-guarani.*' Eduardo Viveiros de Castro, *A inconstância da alma selvagem e outros ensaios de antropologia* (São Paulo: Cosac Naify, 2002), p 281.

2. The original title of Hans Staden's book reads: *True story and description of a land of naked, cruel savages, who eat human flesh, situated in the New World of America, which was unknown before and after Jesus Christ in the lands of Hessen, until the last two years, given that Hans Staden, from Homberg, Hessen, made its acquaintance through his own experience, and he now brings it to public knowledge through this printed work.* I used here the Brazilian edition: Mary Lou Paris and

Ricadro Ohtake (eds), *Hans Staden: Primeiros registros escritos e ilustrados sobre o Brasil e seus habitantes*, trans Angel Bojadsen (São Paulo: Terceiro Nome, 1999).

3.  Afonso Arinos de Melo Franco, *O índio brasileiro e a Revolução Francesa* (Rio de Janeiro: Topbooks, 2000), p 38.

4.  *Ibid.*, pp 92ff.

5.  Michel de Montaigne, *Os ensaios: livro I* (São Paulo: Martins Fontes, 2000), chapter xxxi, p 313. English version available at www.orst.edu/instruct/phl302/texts/montaigne/montaigne-essays–2.html.

6.  Frank Lestringant, *O canibal: grandeza e decadência* (Brasília: UnB, 1997), p 142.

7.  Cf. Christian Marouby, *Utopie et primitivisme: Essai sur l'imaginaire anthropologique à l'âge classique* (Paris: Seuil, 1990), pp 115ff.

8.  Montaigne, *Os ensaios: livro I*, p 309.

9.  Tzvetan Todorov, *Nous et les autres: la réflexion française sur la diversité humaine* (Paris: Seuil, 1989), p 70.

10. Oswald de Andrade, *A utopia antropofágica* (Rio de Janeiro: Globo, 1990), pp 10-11.

11. An excellent analysis of Oswald's ideas can be found in Benedito Nunes, 'Antropofagia ao alcance de todos', in Oswald de Andrade, *A utopia antropofágica*.

12. Oswald de Andrade, 'A crise da filosofia messiânica', *ibid.*, p 101.

13. *Ibid.*

14. Cf. Roberto Schwarz, 'A carroça, o bonde e o poeta modernista', in *Que horas são?* (São Paulo: Companhia das Letras, 1987), p 24.

15. See 'A filosofia canibal', Eduardo Viveiros de Castro interviewed by Rafael Cariello, in *Folha de S. Paulo, Mais!*, 21 August 2005, pp 5ff.

16. Joaquim Pedro de Andrade, 'Cannibalism and Self-Cannibalism', in Randal Johnson and Robert Stam (eds), *Brazilian Cinema* (expanded edition) (New York: Columbia University Press, 1995), pp 82-3.

17. *Ibid.*

18. Cf. Ismail Xavier, *Allegories of Underdevelopment: Aesthetics and Politics in Modern Brazilian Cinema* (Minneapolis and London: University of Minnesota Press, 1997), p 144.

19. Cf. Randal Johnson, 'Cinema Novo and Cannibalism: *Macunaíma*', in Johnson and Stam (eds), *Brazilian Cinema*, p 181.

20. Currupira: a legendary forest dwarf, whose feet point backwards.

21. *Feijoada*: black bean and pork stew.

22. Quoted in Helena Salem, *Nelson Pereira dos Santos: o sonho possível do cinema brasileiro* (Rio de Janeiro: Nova Fronteira, 1987), p 261.

23. *Ibid.*, pp 257-8.

24. A lamprey is an eel-like jawless fish, with a sucker mouth, horny teeth and a rasping tongue.

25. Afonso Arinos de Melo Franco, *O índio brasileiro e a Revolução Francesa*, p 159.

26. 'He who behaves as I do in France/ does much to his own advantage/ Hiding his most precious virtue/ And in view of these corrupt times, I think/ That your book would be even better/ In your barbarian America/ For whoever would criticize a little/The country we should love/ Would find that Arctic France/ Has more monsters, I believe/ And is itself more uncivilized/ Than Antarctic France./ Those barbarians walk about quite naked,/ Whereas we walk about incognito,/ Powdered and masked. That strange nation/ Does not adopt an air of piety./ We scorn ours,/ We trick, sell and disguise it./ In their conduct, those barbarians/ Do not show as much intelligence as we do,/ But he who / whoever sees only the crowd/ Uses it merely to harm us.' Translation generously provided by Honor Aldred. For more comments on this poem, see Luís Madureira, 'Lapses in Taste: "Cannibal-Tropicalist" Cinema and the Brazilian Aesthetic of Underdevelopment', in Francis Barker, Peter Hulme and Margaret Iversen (eds), *Cannibalism and the Colonial World* (Cambridge: Cambridge University Press, 1998), p 122.

27. Richard Peña, 'How Tasty Was My Little Frenchman', in Johnson and Stam (eds), *Brazilian Cinema*, p 193.

28. Edition used here is Jean de Léry, *Viagem à terra do Brasil*, trans and notes by Sérgio Milliet (Belo Horizonte/São Paulo: Itatiaia/Edusp, 1980).

29. The images of the French's suffering under Villegagnon are clearly inspired by Jean de Léry's account.

30. Quoted in Afonso Arinos de Melo Franco, *O índio brasileiro e a Revolução Francesa*, pp 53ff.

31. This information was obtained through a private talk with the director.

32. This information was obtained through a private talk with the singer and composer.

33. Luiz Alberto Pereira's statement was made in a seminar at the Centre for Cinema Studies, Pontifícia Universidade Católica de São Paulo, 27 September 2000.

34. Cf. Robert Stam, 'Cabral and the Indians: Filmic Representations of Brazil's 500 years', in Lúcia Nagib (ed), *The New Brazilian Cinema*, pp 224-5. Stam is drawing on Luiz Alberto Pereira's interview with Paulo Santos Lima, 'Hans Staden mostra os dentes no cinema', *Folha de S. Paulo*, 17 March 2000.

35. Paris and Ohtake (eds), *Hans Staden*, pp 115-16.

36. *Ibid.*, p 115.

## Chapter 4. The Black Paradise

1. The edition used here is Vinicius de Moraes, *Teatro em versos*, ed Carlos Augusto Calil (São Paulo: Companhia das Letras, 1995).

2. The edition used here is Jean-Paul Sartre, 'Orphée noir', in Léopold Sédar Senghor, *Anthologie de la nouvelle poésie nègre et malgache de langue française* (Paris: Quadrige/PUF, 1998; first edition, 1948).

3. This detail was introduced, according to the film's pressbook, as a homage to Godard, who once said, about Camus' film, that Eurydice should have arrived in Rio by plane rather than boat, so she could see one of the world's most astonishing landscapes.
4. Cf. 'Vinicius de Moraes pede para fazer o seguinte comunicado aos artistas', in Vinicius de Moraes, *Teatro em versos*, p 113.
5. Vinicius de Moraes, 'Radar da batucada', in *Teatro em versos*, p 47.
6. *Ibid.*, p 109.
7. Jean-Paul Sartre, 'Orphée noir', p xxiv.
8. Robert Stam. *Tropical Multiculturalism: A Comparative History of Race in Brazilian Cinema and Culture* (Durham and London: Duke University Press, 1997), p 168.
9. See 'Vinicius de Moraes pede para fazer o seguinte comunicado aos artistas', in Vinicius de Moraes, *Teatro em versos*.
10. Quoted in Stam, *Tropical Multiculturalism*, p 169.
11. Jean-Paul Sartre, 'Orphée noir', p ix.
12. *Ibid.*, p xii.
13. *Ibid.*, p xvii.
14. Quoted in José Castello, *Vinicius de Moraes: O poeta da paixão* (São Paulo: Companhia das Letras, 1994), p 182.
15. *Ibid.*
16. *Ibid.*, p 49.
17. Stam, *Tropical Multiculturalism*, p 174.
18. *Orfeu Pressbook.*
19. *Ibid.*, pp 22–3.
20. Vinicius de Moraes, 'Radar da batucada', in *Teatro em versos*, p 48.
21. *Samba-enredo*: a narrative samba song performed by a samba school during carnival.
22. *Carioca* is applied to the natives of Rio de Janeiro.
23. *Rancho*: a group of people who parade during Epiphany. *Bloco*: a group of people in costume who dance and sing to the sound of carnival music. For the story of Hilário Jovino dos Santos, see Roberto Moura, *Tia Ciata e a Pequena África no Rio de Janeiro* (Rio de Janeiro: Biblioteca Carioca, 1995), p 88.
24. Vinicius de Moraes, 'Radar da batucada', in *Teatro em versos*, p 54.
25. Jean-Paul Sartre, 'Orphée noir', p xxxii.
26. *Umbanda* and *macumba*: two syncretic African-Brazilian religious forms, combining several African religions with Catholic and spiritualist rites.

## Chapter 5. An Interrupted Utopia

1. Roberto Schwarz, 'City of God', in *New Left Review* 12, November–December 2001, pp 102–12.
2. I have used here the first edition of the book: Paulo Lins, *Cidade de Deus* (São Paulo: Companhia das Letras, 1997).

3. Antonio Candido, 'Dialética da malandragem', in O discurso e a cidade (São Paulo: Duas Cidades, 1993), p 9.
4. See Linda Williams, 'Discipline and Fun: Psycho and Postmodern Cinema', in Christine Gledhill and Linda Williams (eds), Reinventing Film Studies (London: Arnold, 2000), pp 351-78.
5. See the chapter 'A Utopia de Thomas Morus', especially p 151, in Afonso Arinos de Melo Franco, O índio brasileiro e a Revolução Francesa (Rio de Janeiro: Topbooks, 1976).
6. On the favela as a rural space, see Jane Souto de Oliveira and Maria Hortense Marcier, 'A palavra é: favela', in Alba Zaluar and Marcos Alvito (eds), Um século de favela (Rio de Janeiro: Fundação Getúlio Vargas, 1998), p 90.
7. Cf. Orfeu Pressbook, pp 22-3.
8. Fernando Meirells told me an interesting detail about this song: it was written on the death of the composer's daughter, who was a cocaine addict.
9. Cf. Ismail Xavier, 'Brazilian Cinema in the 1990s: The Unexpected Encounter and the Resentful Character', in Lúcia Nagib (ed), The New Brazilian Cinema, p 56.
10. Zuenir Ventura, Cidade partida (São Paulo: Companhia das Letras, 1997).
11. Robert Stam, O espetáculo interrompido (Rio de Janeiro: Paz e Terra, 1981).
12. See, for example, Paul Virillio, Guerre et cinéma (Paris: l'Etoile/Cahiers du Cinéma, 1991).

## Chapter 6. The Urban Dystopia

1. Walter Salles, 'Centro e periferia se misturam em O invasor', Folha de S. Paulo, Ilustrada, 16 February 2002, p E10.
2. Mario Sergio Conti, 'Estilhaços viram um todo multifacetado', Folha de S. Paulo, Ilustrada, 5 April 2002, p E10.
3. Luiz Zanin Oricchio, Cinema de novo: um balanço crítico da retomada (São Paulo: Estação Liberdade, 2003), p 181.
4. Marcelo Coelho, 'A história do bandido que roubou o filme inteiro', Folha de S. Paulo, Ilustrada, 14 April 2002, p E6.
5. This road was subsequently renamed Jornalista Roberto Marinho.
6. Cf. Jonathan Crary, Suspensions of Perception: Attention, Spectacle, and Modern Culture (Cambridge, MA, and London: The MIT Press, 2000), p 74.
7. Cf. Sigmund Freud, 'The Return of the Repressed', in Moses and Monotheism: An Outline of Psycho-Analysis and Other Works (London: Vintage, 2001).
8. J.W. Smeed, Faust in Literature (London, New York and Toronto: Oxford University Press, 1975), p 34.
9. Davi Arrigucci Jr, 'O jagunço cansado', in Ana Pizarro (ed), América Latina: palavra, literatura e cultura. Vanguarda e Modernidade, vol. 3 (Campinas: Editora da Unicamp, 1995), p 449.
10. Quoted in Rudolf Kurz, Expressionismus und Film (Zurich: Hans Rohr, 1965).
11. Smeed, Faust in Literature.
12. Beto Brant has revealed to me that here the lighting is an effect produced in

the lab.

13. Cf. Ismail Xavier, 'Brazilian Cinema in the 1990s', in Lúcia Nagib (ed), *The New Brazilian Cinema*.
14. Fredric Jameson, 'Utopianism and Anti-Utopianism', in *The Seeds of Time* (New York: Columbia University Press, 1994).

# FILMOGRAPHY

## CHAPTER ONE

*Deus e o diabo na terra do sol (Black God, White Devil)*
Brazil, 1964
DIRECTOR: Glauber Rocha
PRODUCER: Luiz Augusto Mendes
ASSOCIATE PRODUCERS: Jarbas Barbosa and Glauber Rocha
DIRECTOR OF PRODUCTION: Agnaldo Azevedo
ASSISTANT DIRECTORS: Paulo Gil Soares and Walter Lima Júnior
ORIGINAL STORY: Glauber Rocha
SCRIPT: Glauber Rocha and Walter Lima Júnior
ART DIRECTORS: Glauber Rocha and Paulo Gil Soares
PHOTOGRAPHY: Waldemar Lima
SET AND COSTUME DESIGN: Paulo Gil Soares
TITLES: Lygia Pape
SOUND DESIGN: Agnaldo Azevedo and Geraldo José
WOOD-BLOCK PRINTS: Calazans Neto
POSTER: Rogério Duarte
CONTINUITY: Walter Lima Júnior
EDITING: Rafael Justo Valverde
MUSIC: Heitor Villa-Lobos
SONGS: Sérgio Ricardo and Glauber Rocha
LOCATIONS: Monte Santo, Feira de Santana, Salvador, Canché (Cocorobó) and
   Canudos, in Bahia
PRODUCTION AND DISTRIBUTION COMPANY: Copacabana Filmes
BW, 35mm, 125 mins
CAST: Othon Bastos (Corisco), Maurício do Valle (Antônio das Mortes), Geraldo
   del Rey (Manuel), Yoná Magalhães (Rosa), Lídio Silva (Sebastião), Sônia dos
   Humildes (Dadá), Maria Olívia Rebouças, Marrom (Cego Júlio), João Gama
   (the priest), Roque Santos, Regina Rosemburgo, Billy Davis, Antônio Pinto
   (the 'colonel'), Milton Rosa (Moraes), Mário Gusmão and inhabitants of
   Monte Santo.

*Terra em transe* (*Land in Anguish*)
Brazil, 1967
DIRECTOR: Glauber Rocha
EXECUTIVE PRODUCER: Zelito Vianna
ASSOCIATE PRODUCERS: Luiz Carlos Barreto, Carlos Diegues, Raimundo Wanderley
   and Glauber Rocha
ORIGINAL STORY AND SCRIPT: Glauber Rocha
ASSISTANT DIRECTORS: Antônio Calmon and Moisés Kendler
MANAGER: Tácito Al Quintas
DIRECTOR OF PHOTOGRAPHY: Luiz Carlos Barreto
CAMERA: Dib Lutfi
CAMERA ASSISTANT: José Ventura
STILLS: Luiz Carlos Barreto and Lauro Escorel Filho
PHOTOGRAPHIC WORK: José Medeiros
ELECTRICIANS: Sandoval Dória and Vitalino Muratori
ENGINEERING: Aloysio Vianna
SET AND COSTUME DESIGN: Paulo Gil Soares
PERIOD COSTUMES: Clóvis Bornay
WARDROBE: Danusa Leão and Guilherme Guimarães
EDITING: Eduardo Escorel
EDITING ASSISTANT AND TITLES: Mair Tavares
NEGATIVE EDITING: Paula Gracel
SOUND EDITING: Sérgio Ricardo
CONDUCTOR: Carlos Monteiro de Souza
SINGERS: Gal Costa and Sérgio Ricardo
MUSIC: *O guarani*, by Carlos Gomes; *Bachianas 3 and 6*, by Heitor Villa-Lobos;
   overture of *Otello*, by Verdi; *Canto negro Alué* of Bahia Candomblé; *Samba de
   favela* of Rio de Janeiro
LOCATIONS: Rio de Janeiro and Duque de Caxias, Rio de Janeiro state
CO-PRODUCTION: Mapa Filmes and Difilm
DISTRIBUTION: Difilm
LAB: Líder Cinematográfica
SOUND STUDIO: Cinematográficas Herbert Richers
BW, 35mm, 115 mins
CAST: Paulo Autran (Porfírio Díaz), Glauce Rocha (Sara), Jardel Filho (Paulo
   Martins), José Lewgoy (Felipe Vieira), Paulo Gracindo (Julio Fuentes), Paulo
   César Pereio (student), Hugo Carvana (Álvaro), Danuza Leão (Sílvia), Modesto
   de Souza (senator), Mário Lago (capitão), Flávio Migliaccio (a common man),
   Thelma Reston (Felício's wife), José Marinho (Jerônimo), Francisco Milani
   (Aldo), Emanuel Cavalcanti (Felício), Zózimo Bulbul, Antônio Carnera,
   Ecchio Reis, Maurício do Valle, Rafael de Carvalho, Darlene Glória, Ivan
   de Souza, Elizabeth Gasper, Irma Alvarez, Sônia Clara, Jofre Soares, Clóvis
   Bornay, Guido Vasconcelos

*Les quatre cents coups* (*The 400 Blows*)
France, 1959
DIRECTOR: François Truffaut
ORIGINAL STORY: François Truffaut
SCRIPT: François Truffaut and Marcel Moussy
PRODUCER: François Truffaut
ORIGINAL SCORE: Jean Constantin
CAMERA: Henri Decaë
EDITING: Marie-Josèphe Yoyotte
SET DESIGN: Bernard Evein
DIRECTOR OF PRODUCTION: Georges Charlot
MANAGER: Jean Lavie
ASSISTANT MANAGER: Robert Lachenay
ASSISTANT DIRECTOR: Philippe de Broca
SECOND ASSISTANT DIRECTORS: Robert Bober, Francis Cognany and Alain Jeannel
SOUND: Jean-Claude Marchetti
SOUND ASSISTANT: Jean Labussière
EDITING ASSISTANTS: Cécile Decugis and Michèle de Possel
PHOTOGRAPHY ASSISTANTS: Alain Levent
OPERATOR: Jean Rabier
BW, 35mm, 94 mins
CAST: Jean-Pierre Léaud (Antonine Doinel), Claire Maurier (Gilberte Doinel,
    the mother), Albert Rémy (Julien Doinel, the father), Guy Decomble ('Petite
    Feuille', the French teacher), Georges Flamant (Mr Bigey), Patrick Aufray (René),
    Daniel Couturier, François Nocher, Richard Kanayan, Renaud Fontanarosa,
    Michel Girard, Henry Moati, Bernard Abbou, Jean-François Bergouignan,
    Michel Lesignor, Luc Andrieux, Robert Beauvais (the headteacher), Bouchon,
    Christian Brocard, Yvonne Claudie (Mrs Bigey), Marius Laurey, Claude
    Mansard, Jacques Monod, Pierre Repp (the English teacher), Simone Jolivet,
    Laura Paillette, Jean-Claude Brialy (man on the street), Jacques Demy (a
    policeman), Jean Douchet (the lover), Jeanne Moreau (a woman with a dog),
    François Truffaut (a man in the fairground)

*Terra estrangeira* (*Foreign Land*)
Brazil and Portugal, 1995
DIRECTORS: Walter Salles and Daniela Thomas
PRODUCER: Flávio R. Tambellini
CO-PRODUCERS: Paulo Dantas (Brazil) and Antônio da Cunha Telles and Maria João
    Mayer (Portugal)
SCRIPT: Daniela Thomas, Walter Salles and Marcos Bernstein
ADDITIONAL DIALOGUE: Millôr Fernandes
DIRECTOR OF PHOTOGRAPHY: Walter Carvalho
SOUND DIRECTOR: Geraldo Ribeiro
ART DIRECTOR: Daniela Thomas

COSTUME DESIGN: Cristina Camargo
EDITING: Walter Salles and Felipe Lacerda
MUSIC: José Miguel Wisnik
PRODUCTION COMPANIES: VideoFilmes and Animatógrafo
DISTRIBUTION: Riofilme
BW, 35mm, 100 mins
CAST: Fernanda Torres (Alex), Fernando Alves Pinto (Paco), Alexandre Borges (Miguel), Laura Cardoso (Manuela, mother), Tcheky Karyo (Kraft), João Lagarto (Pedro), Luís Melo (Igor), Beth Coelho, Gerald Thomas

*Corisco e Dadá* (*Corisco and Dadá*)
Brazil, 1996
DIRECTOR AND PRODUCER: Rosemberg Cariry
EXECUTIVE PRODUCERS: Jefferson de Albuquerque Júnior and Maria Juruena de Moura
ORIGINAL STORY AND SCRIPT: Rosemberg Cariry
DIRECTOR OF PHOTOGRAPHY: Ronaldo Nunes
SOUND DESIGN: Márcio Câmara
ART DIRECTORS: Jefferson de Albuquerque Júnior and Rosemberg Cariry
SET DESIGN: Walmir Paiva, Zé Tarcísio and Fábio Vasconcelos
COSTUME DESIGN: Renato Dantas
MAKE-UP: Antônio Pacheco
EDITING: Severino Dadá
MUSIC: Maestro Toinho Alves and Quinteto Dantas
PRODUCTION COMPANY: Cariry Produções Artísticas
DISTRIBUTION: Riofilme
COLOUR, 35mm, 103 mins
CAST: Chico Diaz (Corisco), Dira Paes (Dadá), Antônio Leite, Abidoral Jamacaru, Chico Chaves, Denise Milfont, Luiz Carlos Salatiel, Virgínia Cavendish, Regina Dourado, B. de Paiva, Teta Maia, Maira Cariry

*Crede-mi* (*Believe Me*)
Brazil, 1997
DIRECTORS: Bia Lessa and Dany Roland
SCRIPT: Bia Lessa and Dany Roland, loosely based on *The Holy Sinner* by Thomas Mann
CONSULTANT: Violeta Arraes
TECHNICAL CONSULTANTS: Carlos Klachquin and Marcello Dantas
VISUAL DESIGN AND TITLES: Fernando Zarif and Dora Levy
EDITING: Sérgio Mekler
EDITING ASSISTANTS: Tiago Borba and Eduardo Quintino
FINISHING: Helgi Thor and Cia. de Imagem
SOUND MIXING: Rob Filmes
PRODUCTION COMPANY: Bia Lessa Produções Artísticas

DISTRIBUTION: Riofilme
COLOUR, Beta/35mm, 75 mins

*Baile Perfumado* (*Perfumed Ball*)
Brazil, 1997
DIRECTORS: Paulo Caldas and Lírio Ferreira
EXECUTIVE PRODUCERS: Marcelo Pinheiro, Aramis Trindade, Lírio Ferreira, Paulo Caldas and Germano Coelho Filho
SCRIPT: Hilton Lacerda, Paulo Caldas and Lírio Ferreira
DIRECTOR OF PHOTOGRAPHY: Paulo Jacinto dos Reis
SOUND: Geraldo José
DIRECTOR OF PRODUCTION: Cláudio Assis
ART DIRECTOR: Adão Pinheiro
SOUND DIRECTORS: Valéria Ferro and Renato Calaça
SOUND EDITING: Virgínia Flores, César Migliorin and Fernando Ariani
EDITING: Vânia Debs
MUSIC DIRECTION: Chico Science, Fred Zero Quatro, Sérgio 'Siba' Veloso, Lúcio Maia and Paulo Rafael
HISTORY CONSULTANT: Frederico Pernambucano de Mello
PRODUCTION COMPANY: Saci Filmes
DISTRIBUTION: Riofilme
COLOUR/BW, 35mm, 93 mins
CAST: Duda Mamberti (Benjamin Abraão), Luiz Carlos Vasconcelos (Lampião), Aramis Trindade (Tenente Lindalvo Rosa), Chico Diaz (Cel. Zé de Zito), Jofre Soares (Padre Cícero), Cláudio Mamberti (Cel. João Libório), Germano Haiut (Ademar Albuquerque), Manoel Constantino, John Donovan (boy), Giovanna Gold (Jacobina), Daniela Mastroiani (woman in Recife), Rutílio Oliveira, Roger de Renor, Geninha da Rosa Borges (Arminda)

*Abril despedaçado* (*Behind the Sun*)
Brazil/France, 2001
DIRECTOR: Walter Salles
PRODUCER: Arthur Cohn
ASSISTANT PRODUCER: Jean Labadie
EXECUTIVE PRODUCERS: Mauricio Andrade Ramos, Lilian Birnbaum and Walter Salles
SCRIPT: Walter Salles, Sérgio Machado and Karim Aïnouz, based on the book *Froides fleurs d'avril* by Ismail Kadaré
ADDITIONAL DIALOGUE: João Moreira Salles and Daniela Thomas
ASSISTANT DIRECTOR: Sérgio Machado
DIRECTOR OF PRODUCTION: Marcelo Torres
ASSISTANT PRODUCER: Andrea Wiemann
DIRECTOR OF PHOTOGRAPHY: Walter Carvalho
SECOND-UNIT PHOTOGRAPHY: Toca Seabra

ART DIRECTOR: Cássio Amarante
COSTUME DESIGN: Caio Albuquerque
EDITING: Isabelle Rathery
LOCATIONS: States of Bahia and Tocantins
PRODUCTION COMPANIES: VideoFilmes (Brazil) and Bac Filmes (France)
COLOUR, 35mm, 99 mins
CAST: Rodrigo Santoro (Tonho), José Dumont (father), Ravi Ramos Lacerda (Pacu), Rita Assemany (mother), Luiz Carlos Vasconcelos (Salustiano), Flavia Marco Antonio (Clara), Caio Junqueira (Inácio), Everaldo de Souza Pontes (Isaías's grandfather), Mariana Loureiro (Isaías's wife), Servílio de Holanda (Isaías), Wagner Moura (Mateus), Gero Camilo (Reginaldo); special appearances: Othon Bastos (Lourenço), Vinícius de Oliveira (Ferreira family), Sôia Lira (Ferreira family), Maria do Socorro Nobre (Ferreira family)

CHAPTER TWO

*Central do Brasil* (*Central Station*)
Brazil/France, 1998
DIRECTOR: Walter Salles
ORIGINAL STORY: Walter Salles
SCRIPT: Marcos Bernstein and João Emanuel Carneiro
EXECUTIVE PRODUCERS: Elisa Tolomelli, Lilliam Birnbaum, Thomas Garvin and Donald Ranvaud
DIRECTORS OF PRODUCTION: Marcelo Torres and Afonso Coaracy
PRODUCERS: Martine de Clermont-Tonnerre and Arthur Cohn
DIRECTOR OF PHOTOGRAPHY: Walter Carvalho
EDITING: Felipe Lacerda and Isabelle Rathery
ART DIRECTORS: Cassio Amarante and Carla Caffé
COSTUME DESIGN: Cristina Camargo
CASTING: Sérgio Machado
MAKE-UP: Antoine Garabedian
ORIGINAL SCORE: Antônio Pinto and Jacques Morelenbaum
ASSISTANT DIRECTOR: Kátia Lund
SET DESIGN: Mônica Costa
SOUND: Jean-Claude Brisson, François Groult and Mark A. van der Willigen
SOUND MIXING: Bruno Barrière
PRODUCTION COMPANIES: VideoFilmes, Riofilme and MACT
DISTRIBUTION: Riofilme
COLOUR, 35mm, 112 mins
CAST: Fernanda Montenegro (Dora), Marília Pêra (Irene), Vinícius de Oliveira (Josué), Sôia Lira (Ana), Othon Bastos (César), Otávio Augusto (Pedrão), Stela Freitas (Yolanda), Matheus Nachtergaele (Isaías), Caio Junqueira (Moisés), Socorro Nobre, Manoel Gomes, Roberto Andrade, Sheyla Kenia, Malcon Soares, Maria Fernandes, Maria Marlene, Chrisanto Camargo, Jorseba

Sebastiano Oliveira, Andréa Albuquerque, Sidney Antunes, Rita Assemany, Parícia Brás, João Braz, Marcelo Carneiro, Telma Cunha, José Pedro da Costa Filho, Estelinha Moreira da Silva

*O primeiro dia* (*Midnight*)
France/Brazil, 1999
DIRECTORS: Walter Salles and Daniela Thomas
PRODUCER: Elisa Tolomelli
EXECUTIVE PRODUCER: Beth Pessoa
DIRECTOR OF PRODUCTION: Maria Carlota Fernandes
SCRIPT: Daniela Thomas, João Emanuel Carneiro, Walter Salles and José de Carvalho
PHOTOGRAPHY: Walter Carvalho
DIRECT SOUND: Heron de Alencar
SOUND EDITING: Luiz Adelmo
DIALOGUE EDITING: Ana Chiarini
ART DIRECTOR: Carla Caffé
COSTUME DESIGN: Verônica Julian and Cristina Camargo
EDITING: Felipe Lacerda and Isabelle Rathery
MUSIC: Antônio Pinto, Eduardo Bid and Naná Vasconcelos
PRODUCTION COMPANIES: VideoFilmes, Riofilme and Haut et Court
DISTRIBUTION: Lumière and Riofilme
COLOUR, 35mm, 75 mins
CAST: Fernanda Torres (Maria), Luiz Carlos Vasconcelos (João), Matheus Nachtergaele (Francisco), Nelson Sargento (Vovô), Tonico Pereira (prison warder), Áulio Ribeiro (José), Luciana Bezerra (Rosa), Antônio Gomes (Antônio), Nelson Dantas (the chemist), Carlos Vereza (Pedro), José Dumont

*Latitude Zero*
Brazil, 2000
DIRECTOR: Toni Venturi
PRODUCER: Toni Venturi
EXECUTIVE PRODUCERS: Daniel Santiago and Lilian Sola Santiago
SCRIPT: Di Moretti, based on the play *As coisas ruins de nossas cabeças* by Fernando Bonassi
DIRECTOR OF PHOTOGRAPHY: Jacob Solitrenick
CAST-COACH: Marcio Aurelio
SET DESIGN: Helcio Pugliese
DIRECT SOUND: Miguel Angelo
SOUND EDITING: Eduardo Santos Mendes
ASSISTANT DIRECTOR: Amilcar Claro
ART DIRECTOR: Andréa Velloso
MUSIC: Lívio Tragtemberg
EDITING: Idê Lacreta

PRODUCTION COMPANY: Olhar Imaginário
DISTRIBUTION: Riofilme
COLOUR, 35mm, 85 mins
CAST: Débora Duboc (Lena) and Cláudio Jaborandy (Vilela)

## CHAPTER THREE

*Hans Staden*
Brazil/Portugal, 1999
DIRECTOR: Luiz Alberto Pereira
PRODUCER: Luiz Alberto Pereira
EXECUTIVE PRODUCERS: Jorge Neves and Henrique Espírito Santo
DIRECTORS OF PRODUCTION: Ivan Teixeira and Henrique Espírito Santo
SCRIPT: Luiz Alberto Pereira, based on the book *Duas viagens ao Brasil* by Hans
    Staden
CAST-COACH: Walderez Cardoso
CAST TRAINING: Fátima Toledo and Marlui Miranda
DIRECTOR OF PHOTOGRAPHY: Uli Burtin
ORIGINAL SCORE: Marlui Miranda and Lelo Nazário
SOUND ENGINEER AND DIRECT SOUND: Jorge Vaz
ART DIRECTOR: Chico de Andrade
SET DESIGN: Zeca Nolf and Clíssia Moraes
COSTUME DESIGN: Cleide Fayad
MAKE-UP: Sônia Silva and Uirandê de Hollanda
SOUND EDITING: Nério Barbéris
EDITING: Verônica Kovensky
SOUNDTRACK: Nério Barbéris
PRODUCTION COMPANIES: Lapfilme Produções (Brazil) and Jorge Neves Produções
    Audiovisuais (Portugal)
DISTRIBUTION: Riofilme
COLOUR, 35mm, 92 mins
CAST: Carlos Evelyn (Hans Staden), Beto Simas (Nhaêpepô-oaçu), Stênio Garcia
    (Pajé), Sérgio Mamberti (Jacó), Cláudia Liz (Marabá), Darci Figueiredo (Ipiru-
    guaçu), Milton de Almeida (Alkindar-miri), Ariana Messias (Nairá), Walter
    Portela (Abati-poçanga), Reynaldo Puebla (Guaratinga-açu), Luiza Albuquerque,
    Teresa Convá, Olga da Silva, Maria de Oliveira, Hissa de Urkola, Francisco
    di Franco, Darci Figueiredo (Ipiru), Cíntia Grillo, Mário Jacques (captain),
    Macsuara Kadiweu (Cunhambebe), Carol Li (Joacy), Daniel Minduruku,
    Adelino Neves, Alfredo Penteado (Caruatá), Antônio Peyr (Perot), Daniel
    Portela (cacique, tribe chief), Jefferson Primo (Paraguá), Valdir Raimundo,
    Valdir Ramos, Sônia Ribeiro, Lena Sá, Jurandir Siridiwê

*Como era gostoso o meu francês* (*How Tasty Was My Little Frenchman*)
Brazil, 1970–72
DIRECTOR: Nelson Pereira dos Santos
PRODUCERS: Luiz Carlos Barreto, Nelson Pereira dos Santos, César Thedim and K.M. Eckstein
ORIGINAL STORY AND SCRIPT: Nelson Pereira dos Santos
TUPI DIALOGUE: Humberto Mauro
ASSISTANT DIRECTOR: Luiz Carlos Lacerda de Freitas
PRODUCTION MANAGERS: Irênio Marques Filho and Pedro Aurélio Gentil
ASSISTANT PRODUCER: Carlos A. Diniz
ETHNOGRAPHIC RESEARCH: Luiz Carlos Rippermera and Ronaldo Nunes
SOUND DESIGN: Nelson Ribeiro
SOUND ASSISTANT: Geraldo José
SPECIAL EFFECTS: Geraldo José and Antônio César
SET DESIGN: Régis Monteiro
COSTUME DESIGN: Mara Chaves
MAKE-UP: Janira Santiago, José Soares, Ren Boechat, Nilde Goebel, Hélio Fernando and Ana Correia da Silva
EDITING: Carlos Alberto Camuyrano
CONTINUITY: Raimundo Bandeira de Mello
TITLES: Waldir Surtan
VOICE-OVER: Célio Moreira
MUSIC: Guilherme Magalhães Vaz and Zé Rodrix
PRODUCTION COMPANIES: Produções Cinematográficas L.C. Barreto and Condor Filmes
DISTRIBUTION: Condor Filmes
COLOUR, 35mm, 83 mins
CAST: Arduino Colassanti (Jean, the Frenchman), Ana Maria Magalhães (Seboipepe), Eduardo Imbassahy Filho (Cunhambebe), Manfredo Colassanti (French merchant), Ana Maria Miranda, Gabriel Arcanjo, José Kleber, Gabriel Araújo, Luiz Carlos Lacerda de Freitas, Janira Santiago, João Amaro Batista, José Soares, Hélio Fernando, Ital Natur, Maria de Souza Lima, Wilson Manlio, Ana Batista

*Macunaíma*
Brazil, 1969
DIRECTOR: Joaquim Pedro de Andrade
PRODUCERS: K.M. Eckstein and Joaquim Pedro de Andrade
SCRIPT: Joaquim Pedro de Andrade, based on the novel *Macunaíma* by Mário de Andrade
ASSISTANT DIRECTOR: Carlos Alberto Prates Correa
PRODUCTION MANAGER: Chris Rodrigues
PHOTOGRAPHY: Guido Consulich and Affonso Beato
CAMERA: Ricardo Stein

GUIDE-SOUND: Juarez Dagoberto da Costa
SOUND EFFECTS: Walter Goulart
SET AND COSTUME DESIGN: Anísio Medeiros
MAKE-UP: Rubens Abreu
EDITING: Eduardo Escorel
VOICE-OVER: Tite de Lemos
MUSIC: Antônio Maria, Carlos Gomes, Geraldo Nunes, Sady Cabral, Macalé, Lamartine Babo, Heitor Villa-Lobos and Orestes Barbosa
PRODUCTION COMPANIES: Filmes do Serro, Grupo Filme, INC-Instituto Nacional de Cinema and Condor Filmes
DISTRIBUTION: Difilm
COLOUR, 35mm, 108 mins
CAST: Grande Otelo (black Macunaíma), Paulo José (white Macunaíma), Dina Sfat (Ci), Milton Gonçalves (Jiguê, Macunaíma's brother), Rodolfo Arena (Manaape, Macunaíma's brother), Jardel Filho (Giant Wenceslau Pietro Pietra), Joana Fomm (Sofará), Maria do Rosário (Iquiri), Maria Lúcia Dahl (Iara), Miriam Muniz (Caapora), Edi Siqueira (Filhinha), Carmen Palhares (Filhona), Rafael Carvalho (Currupira), Carolina Whitaker (princess), Hugo Carvana (swindler), Zezé Macedo (the Thin Woman), Wilza Carla (the Fat Woman), Maria Clara Pellegrino, Maria Letícia, Valdir Onofre, Guaraci Rodrigues, Nazareth Ohana, Tânia Márcia

### CHAPTER FOUR

*Orfeu*
Brazil, 1999
DIRECTOR: Carlos Diegues
PRODUCERS: Renata de Almeida Magalhães and Paula Lavigne
DELEGATE PRODUCER: Flávio R. Tambellini
ASSOCIATE PRODUCER: Daniel Filho
SCRIPT: Carlos Diegues, in collaboration with Hermano Vianna, Hamilton Vaz Pereira, Paulo Lins and João Emanuel Carneiro, based on the play *Orfeu da Conceição* by Vinicius de Moraes
PHOTOGRAPHY: Affonso Beato
CAMERA: Gustavo Hadba
ASSISTANT DIRECTOR: Vicente Amorim
EDITING: Sérgio Mekler
ART DIRECTOR: Clóvis Bueno
COSTUME DESIGN: Emília Duncan
SAMBA SCHOOL DIRECTOR: Joãozinho Trinta
MUSIC: Caetano Veloso
SOUND: Mark van der Willigen
PRODUCTION COMPANY: Rio Vermelho Filmes
CO-PRODUCTION: Globo Filmes

DISTRIBUTION: Warner

COLOUR, 35mm, 115 mins

CAST: Toni Garrido (Orfeu), Patrícia França (Eurídice), Murilo Benício (Lucinho), Zezé Motta (Conceição), Milton Gonçalves (Inácio), Isabel Fillardis (Mira), Maria Ceiça (Carmen), Stepan Nercessian (Pacheco), Maurício Gonçalves (Pecê), Lucio Andrey (Piaba), Eliezer Motta (Stalone), Sérgio Loroza (Coice), Silvio Guindane (Máicol), Castinho (Oswaldo), Gustavo Gasparini (Mano), Paula Assunção (Deise), Patrícia Costa (Lurdes), Andréa Marques (Sheila), Cássio Gabus Mendes (Pedro), Ivan de Albuquerque (He-Man), Léa Garcia (Máicol's mother), Maria Ribeiro (Joana), Nelson Sargento, Caetano Veloso, samba school Unidos do Viradouro

*Orfeu negro* (or *Orfeu do carnaval; Black Orpheus*)

Brazil/France/Italy, 1959

DIRECTOR: Marcel Camus

PRODUCER: Sacha Gordine

SCRIPT: Marcel Camus and Jacques Viot, based on the play *Orfeu da Conceição* by Vinicius de Moraes

ASSISTANT DIRECTORS: Robert Mazoyer and Bartolomeu Andrade

DIALOGUE: Vinicius de Moraes and Marcel Camus

PHOTOGRAPHY: Jean Bourgoin

SOUND DESIGN: Amaury Leenhardt

ORIGINAL SET DESIGN: Jacques Viot

SET DESIGN: Loup Bonin

EDITING: Andrée Félix

EDITING ASSISTANT: Geneviève Wilding

MUSIC: Antônio Carlos Jobim, Luís Bonfá, Antônio Maria and Vinicius de Moraes

PRODUCTION COMPANIES: Dispat Film (Paris), Genna Film (Roma) and Tupã Filmes (São Paulo)

DISTRIBUTION: Rank Filmes

COLOUR, 35mm, 100 mins

CAST: Breno Mello (Orfeu), Marpessa Dawn (Eurídice), Lourdes de Oliveira (Mira), Léa Garcia (Serafina), Adhemar Ferreira da Silva (Death), Alexandro Constantino (Hermes), Waldemar de Souza (Chico), Jorge dos Santos (Benedito), Aurino Cassiano (Zeca), Maria Alice, Ana Amélia, Afonso Marinho, Arlete Costa, Dinorah Miranda, Esther Mellinger, Eunice Mendes, Jackson Costa, Maria de Lourdes, Teresa Santos, Zeni Pereira, Agostinho dos Santos, Eliseth Cardoso, samba schools Portela, Mangueira, Acadêmicos do Salgueiro, Império Serrano and Unidos da Capela

## CHAPTER FIVE

*Cidade de Deus* (*City of God*)
Brazil/France/USA, 2002
DIRECTORS: Fernando Meirelles and Kátia Lund
PRODUCERS: Andrea Barata Ribeiro and Mauricio de Andrade Ramos
EXECUTIVE PRODUCER: Elisa Tolomelli
CO-PRODUCERS: Marc Beauchamps, Daniel Filho, Hank Levine, Vincent Maraval, Donald Ranvaud, Juliette Renaud and Walter Salles
SCRIPT: Bráulio Mantovani, based on the novel *Cidade de Deus* by Paulo Lins
DIRECTOR OF PHOTOGRAPHY: César Charlone
CAMERA ASSISTANT: Breno Cunha
ORIGINAL SCORE: Ed Côrtes and Antônio Pinto
EDITING: Daniel Rezende
EDITING ASSISTANT: Fred Ricci
ART DIRECTOR: Tulé Peak
COSTUME DESIGN: Bia Salgado and Inês Salgado
MAKE-UP: Anna van Steen
PRODUCTION MANAGER: Claudine Franco
ASSISTANT DIRECTORS: Lamartine Ferreira, Malu Miranda and Isabella Teixeira
SOUND DESIGN: Martin Hernandez
SOUND: Guilherme Ayrosa, Carlos Honc, Alessandro Laroca, Paulo Ricardo Nunes, Alejandro Quevedo and Adam Sawelson
SOUND RECORDING AND EDITING: Rudy Pi, Unsun Song and Roland N. Thai
VISUAL EFFECTS: Renato Batata
PRODUCTION COMPANIES: O2 Filmes and VideoFilmes
CO-PRODUCERS: Globo Filmes, Lumière and Wild Bunch
DISTRIBUTION: Lumière
COLOUR, 35mm, 130 mins
CAST: Alexandre Rodrigues (Buscapé/Rocket), Leandro Firmino da Hora (Zé Pequeno/Li'l Zé), Phellipe Haagensen (Bené/Benny), Douglas Silva (Dadinho/ Li'l Dice), Jonathan Haagensen (Cabeleira/Shaggy), Matheus Nachtergaele (Sandro Cenoura/Carrot), Seu Jorge (Mané Galinha/Knockout Ned), Jefechander Suplino (Alicate/Clipper), Alice Braga (Angélica), Emerson Gomes (Barbantinho/Stringy), Edson Oliveira (older Barbantinho), Michel de Souza Gomes (younger Bené), Roberta Rodrigues (Berenice), Luís Otávio (younger Buscapé), Maurício Marques (Cabeção/Melonhead), Gustavo Engracia (newspaper chief editor), Darlan Cunha (Filé-com-fritas/Steak 'n' Fries), Robson Rocha (Gelson), Thiago Martins (Lampião), Leandra Miranda (Lúcia Maracanã), Graziela Moretto (Marina Cintra), Renato de Souza (Marreco), Karina Falcão (Paraíba's wife), Sabrina Rosa (Galinha's girlfriend), Rubens Sabino (Neguinho), Marcos 'Kikito' Junqueira (Otávio), Edson Montenegro (Buscapé's father), Gero Camilo (Paraíba), Felipe Silva (Rafael), Daniel Zettel (Thiago), Charles Paraventi (Tio Sam), Luiz Carlos Ribeiro Seixas (Touro), Paulo 'Jacaré' César (Tuba), Danielle Ornelas (Paraíba's neighbour)

CHAPTER SIX

*O invasor* (*The Trespasser*)
Brazil, 2002
DIRECTOR: Beto Brant
PRODUCERS: Renato Ciasca and Bianca Villar
ASSOCIATE PRODUCERS: Alexandre Borges, Malu Mader, Paulo Miklos, Marco Ricca and Mariana Ximenes
SCRIPT: Beto Brant, Marçal Aquino and Renato Ciasca, based on the novel *O invasor* by Marçal Aquino
MUSIC: Rica Amabis, Daniel Ganjaman, Paulo Miklos, Sabotage and Tejo
PHOTOGRAPHY: Toca Seabra
EDITING: Manga Campion
CASTING: Deborah Carvalho
ART DIRECTOR: Yukio Sato
COSTUME DESIGN: Juliana Prysthon
MAKE-UP: Gabi Moraes
ASSISTANT DIRECTORS: Lígia Feliciano and Cláudia Gama
SOUND DESIGN: Roberto Ferraz and Louis Robin
SOUND EDITING: Roberto Ferraz and André Pozzano
AVID OPERATOR: Fred Ricci
PRODUCTION COMPANY: Drama Filmes
COLOUR, 35mm, 97 mins
CAST: Marco Ricca (Ivan), Alexandre Borges (Gilberto), Paulo Miklos (Anísio), Mariana Ximenes (Marina), Malu Mader (Cláudia/Fernanda), Chris Couto (Cecília), George Freire (Estêvão), Tanah Correa (Dr Araújo), Jayme del Cueto (Norberto), Sabotage (Sabotage), Marina Franco (Marina's friend), Daniela Tramujas (Luísa), Thavyne Ferrari (Giba's daughter), Priscila Luz (Lúcia), Marcos Azevedo (nightclub manager), Sílvio Luz (Rangel), Amanda Santos (Alessandra), Ida Sztamfater (Silvana), Tom Curti (Dr Luchesi), Manoel Freitas (Romão), Joel Pimentel (Leo), Andreia Regina (Debi), Piero Sarjentelli (Jaime), Arthur Marsan (Alê), Mario Bortolotto (detective)

# INDEX

*complete*

# DOG

# Complete DOG

Helen Digby and Maria Costantino

Published by SILVERDALE BOOKS
An imprint of Bookmart Ltd
Registered number 2372865
Trading as Bookmart Ltd
Blaby Road
Wigston
Leicester LE18 4SE

D&S Books Ltd
Kerswell,
Parkham Ash, Bideford
Devon, England
EX39 5PR

e-mail us at:- enquiries@d-sbooks.co.uk

This edition printed 2006

ISBN 1-84509-2953

DS0074. Complete Dog

Creative Director: Sarah King
Editor: Clare Haworth-Maden
Project editor: Judith Millidge
Designer: Debbie Fisher & Co.
Photographer: Paul Forrester

Fonts: Futura and Times New Roman

Material from this book previously appeared in The Dog Care Handbook and The Handbook of Dog Breeds.

Printed in Thailand

1 3 5 7 9 10 8 6 4 2

# CONTENTS

# INTRODUCTION

'Ah! You should keep dogs – fine animals – sagacious creatures ...' as Mr Winkle advised Mr Pickwick in Charles Dickens' **The Pickwick Papers,** and it is a piece of advice that has been followed by millions of us for centuries. It is a cliché to remark that a dog is man's best friend, but it is a statement that has been reinforced over thousands of years. Human beings and dogs share a symbiotic relationship in many ways: people adopt dogs as pets and care for them in return for companionship, protection and unquestioning devotion. Man and dog have evolved a unique, inseparable partnership over the centuries. Owning a dog is a privilege and a responsibility, but canine devotion must be repaid with practical care, security and respect. Dogs have provided humans with support and protection – both physical and psychological – for thousands of years, and the least that the human race can do after such a long relationship is to ensure that their domestic animals are happy and fulfilled.

*SENSITIVE AND GENTLE, LABRADORS ARE POPULAR FAMILY PETS.*

*INTRODUCE YOUR DOG TO OTHER PETS GRADUALLY.*

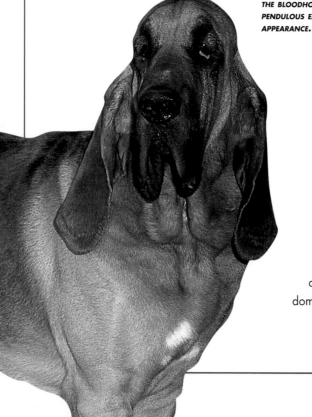

*THE BLOODHOUND'S LONG MUZZLE AND PENDULOUS EARS GIVE IT A DOLOROUS APPEARANCE.*

There are more than four hundred distinct breeds of dog, and their diverse appearances are entirely the result of human intervention. Dogs have been bred to suit the whims of their owners, and the variety of their looks is reflected in their many talents and characters. The steady Saint Bernard, which exudes calm, has been trained as a mountain-rescue animal; the exceptional sense of smell of bloodhounds, Labrador retrievers and German shepherd dogs is utilised by law-enforcement agencies to uncover drugs; while innumerable breeds make wonderful companions, providing their owners with unlimited affection and devotion. Dogs are one of the two most popular domestic animals in the world – the other is the cat.

Most humans have a basic instinct to care for living things and, for many people, dogs fulfill this need. Dogs are pack animals and will obey the person whom they regard as their pack leader – usually their owner. They are essentially uncomplicated animals, grateful for a warm home, regular supply of food and a small amount of territory to defend. They are unquestioningly loyal, fiercely protective and do not criticise us – few humans are so amenable!

*LARGE AND IMMENSELY STRONG, SAINT BERNARDS REQUIRE LOTS OF SPACE.*

Owning a happy and healthy dog is a rewarding occupation, but this can only be achieved through proper care. This book provides a comprehensive introduction to caring for dogs; it attempts to explain certain aspects of doggy behaviour and provides details of how to keep your dog in the best-possible health.

It also offers some solutions for common problems that can occur, even in the best-regulated kennels.

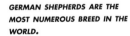

*GERMAN SHEPHERDS ARE THE MOST NUMEROUS BREED IN THE WORLD.*

*MAN'S BEST FRIEND HAS BEEN IMMORTALISED IN ART FOR CENTURIES.*

# THE ORIGIN OF THE SPECIES

Although a brief review of the dog's ancient forbears may not seem entirely relevant to a twenty-first-century book on dog care, careful study of the dog's evolution provides answers to many aspects of canine behaviour.

No animal family on earth, wild or domestic, is as varied as that of the dog. Sizes range from the 70 kg (154 lb) Saint Bernard to the 2.5 kg (5.5 lb) Chihuahua; looks are as diverse as the shaggy, dreadlocked komondor or the completely hairless Xoloizcuintle; the Irish wolfhound has exceptionally long legs, whereas, at the other end of the spectrum, the dachshund's short legs barely raise its body off the ground.

*THE SAINT BERNARD AND THE CHIHUAHUA OCCUPY OPPOSITE ENDS OF THE CANINE SPECTRUM IN TERMS OF SIZE.*

*DOGS ARE DESCENDED FROM WOLVES, WHICH WERE DOMESTICATED IN PALEOLITHIC TIMES.*

The dog family, Canidae, contains about thirty-five species grouped into fourteen genera. They include the domestic dog (*Canis familiaris*), the wolf (*Canis lupus*), fourteen species of fox and four species of jackal. They are native to almost every part of the world and clearly belong to an adaptable family, living across a diversity of habitats, from tropical rainforests to frozen northern woods, from deserts to icy tundra.

Fossil evidence suggests that dogs evolved from a small, weasel-like mammal called Miacis that lived about 60 million years ago. The first canids, the Cynodictis, evolved from Miacis and appeared during the Miocene era, between thirty and forty million years ago; they were medium-sized animals, longer than they were tall, with a long tail and fairly thick coat. Two branches descended from Cynodictis, Cynodesmus in Africa and Tomarctus in Eurasia, the ancestor of wolves, dogs and foxes.

It is hard to believe that such diverse animals are descended from a single common ancestor. Charles Darwin was so overwhelmed by the sheer number of different dog breeds that he propounded the theory of mixed descent from two wild species, the wolf (*Canis lupus*) and the golden jackal (*Canis aureus*). Over recent years, experts have agreed that the domestic dog is probably descended from the wolf: its bone structure, especially that of the skull and teeth, is nearly identical to small wolves, and

people were probably as susceptible as their modern descendants to small, cuddly, furry animals. Like dogs, wolf cubs can be trained if they are adopted by humans at around three to seven weeks of age, and demonstrate as much affection as dogs towards their human masters.

Palaeolithic wolves and humans shared a number of common habits. Both were primarily active during the daytime, hunting and foraging. Wolves are intelligent creatures which are emotionally responsive and able to convey a wide array of non-verbal messages through changes in posture, attitude and facial expression. A great deal of human communication is similarly non-verbal, so it is possible that Palaeolithic people built a co-operative relationship with their adopted wolves. Both humans and wolves live in 'packs'. Palaeolithic man inhabited a social group of family members numbering approximately ten to twenty individuals, who survived by co-operative hunting of game, and wolves behave in the same way.

So the domestication of wolves came about because they shared a number of habits and needs with humans and, as cubs, pandered to the human need to tend to small, helpless creatures. As wolves and humans lived closer together, they developed a mutual understanding. Wolves became more sociable and relaxed around human beings, learning to respond to commands; while, over time, humans exploited wolf behaviour, using wolves to assist in hunting and to guard their homes.

**DOGS AND WOLVES SHARE MANY BEHAVIOURAL TRAITS.**

its behavioural patterns reinforce this evidence. One study recorded ninety different behavioural traits in domestic dogs, and all except for nineteen minor characteristics were shared by wolves. By contrast, the behavioural patterns observed in wolves which were not shared by dogs related to hunting in situations rarely encountered by domestic dogs. When dogs have mated with wolves, they have usually produced fertile offspring, which suggests very strongly that dogs and wolves are part of the same family.

It is likely that wolves were first domesticated during the Stone Age or, more properly, Palaeolithic times, approximately fourteen thousand years ago. Archaeological remains of canine jawbone fragments show that Palaeolithic dogs had a short jaw compared to the wolf, which probably evolved as a result of changes in diet. Human beings lived by hunting and foraging for food every day, and, having observed the hunting techniques of wolves, may have decided to befriend them with a view to utilising their skills. It is more likely, however, that the relationship between man and wolf, and subsequently dog, was accidental. Wolf cubs may have been adopted as pets – Palaeolithic

**THE MASTIFF IS ONE OF THE OLDEST DOG BREEDS.**

Climate change and the emergence of settled, rather than nomadic, societies were also important factors in wolf domestication. Wolf cubs are reliant on their mother until they are four or five months old. They live in semi-permanent dens and their mother must commute between the cubs and sources of food during this time. A nomadic lifestyle thus being out of the question for wolves, domestication can be pinpointed reasonably accurately to around fourteen thousand years ago, when humans ceased to be nomadic.

So how did the domesticated wolf produce the bewildering variety of dog breeds in existence today? The answer lies simply in inbreeding. Deprived of the chance to roam and thus mate with a wide genetic mix, pet wolves living in small, isolated societies could only mate with related individuals. Humans helped by favouring wolves with useful characteristics and killing or driving away those with undesirable features. Some communities may have preferred small dogs, others large ones; one hamlet may have liked long-haired animals, the one across the river, short-haired ones. Gradually, over many generations, local varieties of dogs emerged, each a distinct product of the culture from which it had originated. As people began to live in permanent settlements and to benefit from the relative prosperity and security of this lifestyle, they could afford to keep dogs as companions, not simply as working animals. They quickly saw that they could keep dogs just for their looks or temperament; the business of dog-breeding had begun.

It is clear from the images of dogs in the earliest-surviving examples of art, from ancient Assyria, Babylon and Egypt, that they had been bred to serve different purposes. Frescoes and wall-paintings dating from 4000 BC illustrate animals that are recognisable as greyhounds, Salukis and mastiffs, proof that distinct breeds of dogs had emerged, each with a different function. Archaeological excavations at Avebury, in Wiltshire, have revealed the five-thousand-year-old remains of a small, long-legged, short-backed dog, a complete contrast to the great Babylonian mastiff. These remains are also evidence that as humans became more fond of dogs in life, they chose to be buried near to them in death.

*ABOVE: LONG-LIMBED AND ELEGANT, SALUKI HOUNDS ORIGINATED IN THE MIDDLE EAST.*

*LEFT: LIKE HUMANS, WOLVES NUTURE THEIR YOUNG, A HABIT WHICH MADE THEM PRIME CANDIDATES FOR DOMESTICATION.*

# WORKING DOGS

Human beings began to breed a variety of types of dog suited to widely differing tasks, not all of which were utilitarian. Dogs were also bred for aesthetic purposes, or to accentuate certain attractive or novel physical features. People tried to develop existing aggressive canine traits by breeding pugnacious dogs to fight either each other or other animals, such as bears or bulls. Charles Darwin explained the principles of breeding to enhance genetic characteristics in *The Origin of Species*:

'Thus it is known that a cross with a bulldog has affected for many generations the courage and obstinacy of greyhounds; and a cross with a greyhound has given a whole family of sheep-dogs a tendency to hunt hares. These domestic instincts, when thus tested by crossing resemble natural instincts, which in a like manner become curiously blended together, and for a long period exhibit traces of the instincts of either parent...'

**ALTHOUGH PUGNACIOUS IN APPEARANCE, BULLDOGS ARE EXTREMELY GOOD-NATURED.**

**BORZOIS WERE BRED IN RUSSIA FOR WOLF-HUNTING.**

**DEERHOUNDS ORIGINATED IN SCOTLAND.**

## HUNTERS

Wolves and humans hunted similar prey, and Palaeolithic man may well have followed hunting wolves and then intercepted them as they captured their game. However, this would have been a time-consuming method of hunting, and although even today Aboriginals in Australia exploit dingoes' hunting skills, it is an occasional, opportunistic means of acquiring food. The earliest evidence of dogs assisting in human hunting comes from ancient Egypt, with reliefs and wall-paintings showing dogs virtually identical to the modern basenji, a hunting breed widely prevalent in Africa today. The ancient Egyptians, or their forebears, had obviously bred a dog specifically for hunting, and the dog's superior natural abilities to find and retrieve game became increasingly important.

Dogs have accompanied human hunters for centuries, and require little training in what, for them, is a natural inclination. Hunting for pleasure was adopted by the aristocracies of ancient China, India, Persia and Egypt and spread throughout medieval Europe. It continues to be popular among the leisured classes today, although it has become a matter of some controversy in Britain. Dogs' highly developed sense of smell enables them to sniff out game for their masters to trap, spear or shoot. Canine hunting skills evolved and altered as humans adopted different weapons: the introduction of guns, for example, meant that dogs were trained in setting and retrieving techniques.

# TRACKERS

Dogs possess a sense of smell that is far more efficient than that in humans. Rescue dogs can be trained to track a scent on the ground and others can follow a scent in the air; hunting dogs, such as retrievers and pointers, can not only track birds, but can distinguish one type from another. Bloodhounds are the archetypal 'sniffer dogs' and have the ability to follow a trail tenaciously for hours. The Red Cross still uses dogs to sniff out injured people on battlefields or in disaster zones. In recent times, dogs such as German shepherds and Labrador retrievers have been trained to sniff out drugs and explosives and to track missing persons, often with great success.

LABRADOR RETRIEVERS ARE EASY TO TRAIN.

# GUARD DOGS

THE DOBERMAN MAKES AN EXCELLENT GUARD DOG.

The dog's pack mentality means that if it senses the arrival of strangers – human or otherwise – it will alert the other members of the pack. When they are alarmed or excited, domestic dogs react by barking, which is a distinct difference from their vulpine counterparts, who bark only in moments of extreme alarm. It is evident from Babylonian art that mastiffs were very popular as criminal deterrents. They were reportedly given intimidating names, such as 'Expeller of the Sinful' and 'Hesitate Not', monikers which are not so very different from the modern habit of naming fierce-looking dogs 'Tyson', after the renowned boxer.

The dog's natural ability as a runner prompted people to use dogs to run alongside their carriages during the eighteenth and

nineteenth centuries – when the carriage stopped, the dogs were present to protect the travellers. Two hundred years ago, Dalmatians were bred specifically for this purpose, their black-and-white coats usefully merging with the shadows at night, making them invisible to footmen and highwaymen.

Dogs continue to prove their value as guards. Police forces in a number of countries train Dobermans, which are excellent patrol dogs, and German shepherds, which can learn to guard, attack and 'arrest' suspects, gripping a subject firmly, but without injury, until law-enforcement personnel arrive. Well-trained dogs are immensely valuable to the police, the prison service or any authority seeking to control big crowds. They are very useful in guarding large areas, such as airfields, because they are fast runners, while their agility means that they can squeeze into inaccessible places and their powers of scenting and hearing are infinitely superior to those of their human masters.

INTELLIGENT GERMAN SHEPHERDS MAKE GOOD GUARD DOGS.

**DALMATIANS ARE ENERGETIC AND AFFECTIONATE.**

**STURDY ROTTWEILERS ARE BRAVE GUARD DOGS.**

# DOGS OF WAR

Dogs have performed valiant service in times of war. Man's inhumanity to man looms large from the pages of history, so it is not surprising that this inhumanity has been inflicted on humankind's closest animal companion, too. The dog's natural inclination to protect and guard was exploited in large dogs, and the more ferocious were used as dogs of war, to harass enemies and protect armies. During the Peloponnesian War (431–404 bc), the barking of a dog named Sorter alerted Corinth to a stealth attack, and the grateful citizens later erected a monument to this vigilant animal.

The Spanish Conquistadors travelled to the New World with mastiffs with which to intimidate and hunt down the native people, dogs furthermore playing a critical part in many campaigns because they were adept at breaking up ambushes in dense forests. First employed by the Spanish as early as 1493, dogs proved horribly effective. Among the most famous was Becerrillo ('Little Calf'), who reputedly killed so many men that he earned an additional share of the booty for his master, Juan Ponce de León. Other Conquistadors, including Hernando Cortés, executed their prisoners by turning the 'dogs of war' on them.

Dogs continue to be trained to perform a variety of wartime tasks, some more acceptable than others. During the Second World War, for example, the Soviet Red Army strapped anti-tank mines to its dogs' backs and trained them to seek out German tanks. Unfortunately, the dogs had not been trained in the finer points of tank recognition and, when released on to the battlefield, indiscriminately aimed for the Soviet tanks as well.

**THE TIBETAN MASTIFF IS A FIERCE DEFENDER.**

# HERDERS

Dogs were probably used as guardians of cattle and sheep very early on in their relationship with people. In Sumerian scrolls dating from 5000 bc, the dog-headed goddess Bau was described as a protector of flocks; it also seems likely that the name of the goddess was derived from the sound of a dog's bark. The earliest sheepdogs were probably valued more for their ferocity in scaring away predators and thieves than for their capacity to herd livestock. The Roman writer Marcus Tarentius Varo noted in 10 bc in De Re Rustica that, 'There are two kinds [of dog,] one for hunting connected with the wild beasts of the woods, the other trained for purposes of defence, and used by shepherds'.

**POPULAR DOGS, BRIARDS WERE FRENCH SHEEPDOGS.**

Smaller than most of the European herding breeds, collies are probably the most commonly used sheepdogs in Britain, particularly the highly intelligent Border collie, which has succeeded its cousin, the Rough collie (immortalised on film as Lassie during the 1950s). Formal sheepdog training begins when a dog is six months old, and the dog is encouraged to get used to being around sheep before actually herding them. The Old English sheepdog was more often used to drive sheep and cattle to market than to herd them. Australia has produced the kelpie, an energetic working dog tough enough to cope with the demands of rough terrain and extremes of temperature.

**AIREDALES ARE THE LARGEST TERRIERS.**

Herding breeds vary across the world according to geographical location: because they have to deal with different animals in every type of terrain, herding dogs are the product of local breeding in order to meet the needs of a particular area. Ancient breeds of flock-guarding sheepdogs are still employed in parts of Europe and Asia, such as the savage Tibetan mastiff, the Komondor and Kuvasz from Hungary, and the Pyrenean mountain dog, none of whom appear as reliable and steady as the Old English sheepdog, for example.

**TOUGH AND HARDY, THE KELPIE IS AN AUSTRALIAN SHEEPDOG.**

# CENTURIES OF WORK

Many dogs demonstrate a desire to please their human masters, and over the years this desire has been exploited by training dogs to do an amazing range of tasks. 'Comforters' were small lapdogs that were once used to attract the fleas and lice that would otherwise have infested their owners, while 'turnspits' were dogs trained to turn the great roasting spit over an open fire. However, as society changes, so, too, do the uses of dogs, and today guide dogs, sniffer dogs and working dogs are indispensable.

Motorised transport has diminished the use of dogs as beasts of burden and transport, but in some areas of the world dogs are still used for this purpose by people, such as the North American Inuit, who traditionally employ sled dogs. Characterised by a sharply pointed muzzle, broad skull and pointed ears, sled dogs like Siberian huskies have powerful bodies and thick, rough coats. In the harsh environment of the Arctic Circle, teams of huskies often prove more reliable than mechanical transport, which may break down in the extreme cold.

Laws have been passed either to control dogs or to prohibit certain classes of society from owning them. During the eleventh century, for example, King Canute banned greyhounds from the game-packed royal forests to prevent poaching. The Tudors and

*SIBERIAN HUSKIES ARE TOUGH WORKING DOGS.*

Stuarts used heavy fines to control dog ownership, and during the Great Plague of 1665 over forty thousand dogs were slaughtered to halt the spread of the disease (which was spread by fleas living on rats, and presumably also on dogs, although, ironically, the dogs could have assisted in killing the rats). More recently, in 1991 the British government passed the Dangerous Dogs Act, making it a criminal offence for a dog to be out of control in a public place.

# SOCIAL WORK

One of the most famous roles of the working dog is as a guide dog for blind people. It is likely that dogs have accompanied blind people for centuries – Charles Dickens remarks on one such case during the mid-nineteenth century – but properly trained dogs were first used after the First World War, when German soldiers, blinded in the hostilities in France, were given specially trained dogs as companions to help them return to civilian life.

*OWNING A DOG CAN BE THERAPEUTIC.*

Golden and black Labrador retrievers are today most commonly used as guide dogs, along with German shepherds. In Britain, such dogs are bred by the Guide Dogs for the Blind charity from bitches specially chosen for their intelligence and equable temperament. The average working life of a guide dog is eight or nine years, and its training is rigorous, beginning when the dog is six weeks old. Puppies begin their training with a sighted 'puppy-walker', who accustoms the dog to buses, trains, urban scenes and crowds – everyday situations encountered by a blind person.

*GOLDEN RETRIEVERS ARE EQUABLE DOGS, IDEAL FOR FAMILIES.*

When the dog is a year old, it begins the next phase of its training at a guide-dog centre, where it learns how to deal with crossing roads and coping with traffic and to judge height and width so that its owner does not bump into obstacles.

Dogs have also been trained to support deaf people, for instance, to alert their owners to an important sound, such as a boiling kettle or a telephone, by touching them and leading them to the source of the noise. Research has proved that elderly, lonely or distressed people benefit from the companionship of a dog, and charities like Pets as Therapy (PAT) provide friendly, reliable dogs to visit hospices or residential homes to cheer people of all ages.

*TOY POODLES ARE INTELLIGENT AND LONG-LIVED.*

The Far East, however, is an exception. Here dogs are more often seen on menus than with their owners. Dogs were once farmed as a food source in parts of China, Polynesia and Central America, a custom which was probably a means of coping with chronic shortages of any other animal protein. (It may be significant that cannibalism was also prevalent in the same areas, possibly for the same reason.) Domestic dogs treat humans as members of their own species, and people in return endow their dogs with human characteristics, real or imagined, which is probably why dog-eating is regarded with extreme distaste in many cultures.

## RACING AND COMPETITION DOGS

It is in the nature of dogs to run around, and dog-racing began in Roman times as hare-coursing, a sport that is still practised today using greyhounds, whippets and lurchers. Greyhound-racing using a fake hare first occurred in Britain in 1876, but the sport died out because the runners simply finished too closely together. After the First World War, however, an Oklahoma farmer discovered a patent for a mechanical hare and built a circular track, after which greyhound-racing quickly became popular and was reintroduced to Britain in 1924.

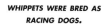

Competitive sled-racing began in Alaska during the 1880s, using teams of Siberian huskies and Eskimo malamutes. It remains an exceptionally popular sport in North America and northern Europe, to the extent that racing continues after the snow has melted with sleds mounted on rollerblades.

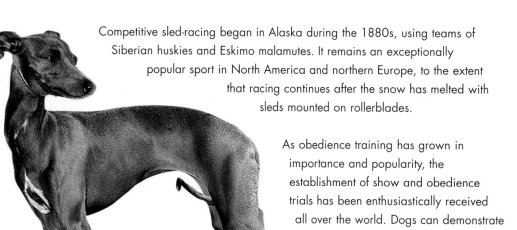

*ITALIAN GREYHOUNDS LOVE TO CHASE.*

As obedience training has grown in importance and popularity, the establishment of show and obedience trials has been enthusiastically received all over the world. Dogs can demonstrate their achievement of a certain level of training in these and, if they are really good, can win extra awards and titles.

*WHIPPETS WERE BRED AS RACING DOGS.*

The initial level emphasises basic training, with a dog showing that it can walk at heel and obey simple spoken commands. At the highest level, dogs demonstrate their skills in tracking and scenting tests.

*HUSKY RACING IS A POPULAR SPORT IN NORTHERN CLIMES.*

*LARGE ELEGANT DOGS, GREYHOUNDS LIKE TO INHABIT A SPECIAL CORNER OF THEIR HOME.*

# DOGS IN MYTH AND LEGEND

The importance of dogs to humans is underlined by the fact that dogs feature in the mythology and legends of just about every culture, from Celtic through Native American to ancient Greek. Certain characteristics stand out in canine mythology: dogs are invariably loyal, faithful and steadfast helpers of people; it is only if they appear in an unusual form (such as the three-headed Cerberus) that they pose a serious threat.

The ancient Egyptians believed that dogs possessed supernatural qualities and pampered them by giving them servants and the finest food. Only royalty could own pedigree dogs, and when the pharaoh died, his dog was often buried with him to provide him with protection in the afterlife. Just as the ancient Egyptians believed that dogs followed their owners into the afterlife, many cultures regarded dogs as mediators between the realms of the living and the dead: the Egyptian underworld god Anubis was depicted with a jackal's head, for example, while Cerberus, the three-headed dog, was said to guard Hades, the underworld of ancient Greek mythology. In the Zoroastrian religion, corpses are quickly removed to sacred ground, where a priest prays and a dog and a sacred fire keep evil forces at bay.

The Celts believed that dogs had curative powers, as did the Greeks, who linked them to Aesclepius, the god of healing. Dogs were kept at Epidaurus, the shrine of Aesclepius, and the god was sometimes shown accompanied by a dog who could reputedly cure illness by licking the afflicted person.

*DOGS WERE IMPORTANT TO THE ANCIENT EGYPTIANS, WHO BELIEVED THEY POSSESSED SUPERNATURAL ABILITIES.*

Dogs recur throughout classical literature. In *The Odyssey*, Homer says that Ulysses' faithful dog, Argus, recognised his master on his return from Troy when no one else could – and then died of joy. Horace mentions that the sight of a black dog with its pups was considered unlucky.

*complete DOG*

Many Roman legends recount tales of dogs' fidelity, but the Romans also sacrificed dogs at the annual festival of Robigalia, which was intended to protect cornfields from too much heat or blight during the summer. The Romans clearly linked dogs with great heat, calling the six or eight hottest days of summer *caniculares dies,* 'dog days', and believing that Sirius, the 'Dog Star', rose with the sun and added to its heat, the 'dog days' thus combining the heat of the sun with the apparent warmth of the exceptionally bright Dog Star. In Graeco-Roman mythology, the dog Sirius was sacred to the messenger god Hermes (Mercury) and Artemis (Diana), the goddess of the hunt; he also accompanied Hekate (Hecate), signifying war, and Orion the hunter.

**ANUBIS, THE EGYPTIAN GOD OF THE UNDERWORLD, WAS DEPICTED WITH A JACKAL'S HEAD.**

**THE CELTS BELIEVED IN THE CURATIVE POWER OF DOGS.**

The dog was important in Chinese folklore and was regarded in much the same way as black cats in European superstition. In China, the 'Fu Dog', a symbol of good luck and happiness, is traditionally placed at the front door to ward off evil spirits.

The three great monotheistic religions are, at best, indifferent to dogs. In Judaeo-Christian tradition, dogs rarely receive a good word, while Islam regards them as unclean creatures and requires its adherents to cleanse themselves after coming into contact with them. Like many Islamic laws, however, this one is based on common sense: rabies has long been prevalent throughout the Near and Middle East, so it is prudent to ensure that one does not become contaminated with it through an infected dog's saliva.

# DOGS IN ART AND LITERATURE

Writers as illustrious as Homer and Horace, Sir Thomas More, Alexander Pope, Mark Twain and James Thurber have all proffered advice about dog care, expressed their affection for their pets and noted their habits and foibles.

One of the best-loved dogs appears in J M Barrie's *Peter Pan*. The Darling children's nurse is Nana, a Newfoundland, hired because the family was too poor to afford a human nanny, but who 'proved to be quite a treasure of a nurse … It was a lesson in propriety to see her escorting the children to school, walking sedately by their side when they were well behaved, and butting them back into line if they strayed'.

Dog-owners have been keen to immortalise their pets virtually since the animal was first domesticated, and dogs can be seen in Palaeolithic paintings and are also represented in ancient Egyptian art, their stylised images appearing in classical Greek sculpture, too. In medieval art, a dog symbolises fidelity, and in many

**THE NEWFOUNDLAND HAS A WELL-DESERVED REPUTATION AS A RELIABLE AND FRIENDLY BREED.**

*A BLOODHOUND IMMORTALISED HUSH PUPPY SHOES.*

Dogs appeared in both hunting and formal portraits of the great men and women of the sixteenth and seventeenth centuries. The nobility of Europe wished to be recorded for posterity surrounded by items of value, or possessions that lent them status, and small lapdogs often appear in the court portraits of Velásquez and Van Dyck, as do long-limbed hunting dogs beside their beautifully clad masters. By the eighteenth century, fashions had changed, and dogs were illustrated in their own right. The works of notable artists such as George Stubbs, famed for his animal portraits, are testimony to the esteem in which pet dogs were held by their wealthy owners.

By the nineteenth and early twentieth centuries, dogs were being depicted on magazine covers and postcards, as china figurines and in cartoons. They were also popular choices for advertisements: Hush Puppy shoes adopted a bloodhound, Dulux paint employs an Old English sheepdog, while Andrex toilet paper uses an impossibly cute Labrador puppy, but the longest-lived must surely be Nipper, a terrier shown faithfully listening to a gramophone in the logo for HMV records (HMV stands for 'His Master's Voice').

medieval funerary monuments a dog is placed at the feet of a woman's effigy to represent affection and fidelity. Although male funerary effigies often had a lion at their feet to represent the manly virtues of courage and valour, some Crusaders are shown with their feet resting on dogs, symbolising the fact that they followed the standard of Christ as faithfully as a dog follows his master. Dogs appeared in miniature in medieval illuminated manuscripts and tapestries, too, most famously the Bayeaux Tapestry, in which King Harold is shown out hawking with five dogs.

By the time of the Renaissance, dogs were featuring in many different styles of picture. They added a pleasing sense of normality both to formal portraits, such as Jan van Eyck's *Arnolfini Wedding* (1434), and to depictions of great religious scenes. A greyhound can be seen hunting in the background of Benozzo Gozzoli's *The Journey of the Magi* to Bethlehem (c. 1459–63), for example, seemingly unaware of the great men passing a few feet away as it rushes onwards. In the same picture, the Magi's military escort is accompanied by a black-and-tan hound, who has the alert air of a guard dog.

*A SHEEPDOG IS A FAMILIAR ADVERTISING STAR.*

# CELLULOID CANINES

As Hollywood turned a giant mirror on the world and reflected life back at us as entertainment, dogs inevitably had a large role to play. The first great canine star of the silver screen was Rin Tin Tin, a German shepherd dog who starred in twenty-two silent movies. Rescued by an American airman in France in 1918, Rin Tin Tin was, by all accounts, an exceptional dog. He excelled at stunts, would stand still for thirty minutes so that the studio lighting could be adjusted and had an excellent relationship with his owner, Lee Duncan, who said, 'We simply understand each other, and until you understand your dog you can never hope to teach him anything'. In 1947, fifteen years after his death, Rin Tin Tin was 'revived' for a television series that was just as popular as the original films.

**DOBERMANS ARE OFTEN SEEN AS FIERCE DEFENDERS.**

Dobermans are invariably portrayed as savage, extravagantly clipped poodles as slightly ridiculous, while Labradors are brave and beloved by children. Anthropomorphism plays its part, too. Films like *The Incredible Journey* (1963), also known as 'two dogs and a cat' to many toddlers) endow the dogs with very different characters: the old Labrador retriever is eminently sensible and trusts his human masters; the young bull terrier is impulsive, cocky and excitable. The third animal star, the cat, is simply too cool for words. This characterisation of dogs and cats is taken to extremes in *Cats and Dogs* (2001), a film whose central feature is the enjoyable conceit that the world is ruled by, yes, cats and dogs, who con humans into thinking that they are pliable companions. How ridiculous is that?

**A POODLE WITH A SMART CONTINENTAL CUT.**

Lassie, a Rough collie with a luxurious coat and super-canine intelligence, was the other great canine cinematic success story. Pal, the dog who played Lassie, lived an enviably pampered life in his own apartment and had stunt doubles to stand in for him during the dangerous scenes.

Dogs have peppered every genre of film, from Dorothy's feisty terrier, Toto, in *The Wizard of Oz* (1939) to the narcotics cop's German shepherd in *K9* (1988). Because they embody faithfulness, companionship and utter reliability, dogs tend to be typecast:

**DALMATIANS – ONE IS SUFFICIENT FOR MOST HOMES.**

## CHAPTER 2

# THE CANINE WORLD

No species on earth is more diverse than the dog. Originally intended to be reasonably fast hunting animals, many breeds now struggle to work up much of a pace and prefer a gentle walk around the block rather than a vigorous run. Human intervention rather than natural selection has worked to produce the huge range of shapes and sizes that exist today. Indeed, many breeds would die out extremely quickly if left to themselves; the respiratory problems and whelping difficulties among bulldogs provide just one example. Human tinkering, however, is unable to replace the basic genetic characteristics that form the building blocks of canine physiology and psychology, and all dogs, regardless of their breed share a number of fundamental characteristics.

They have efficient cardiovascular systems designed for running, with deep rib cages to protect their vital organs. They have highly developed sensory organs to underline their role as natural hunters and defenders of territory. With efficient, sensitive hearing, and a highly refined sense of smell, even the smallest dog will bark as a warning when strangers approach. All dogs, like their vulpine ancestors, are pack animals, genetically programmed to respect the hierarchy of their pack or family. They feel secure knowing their place in the pack, which explains why dogs readily accept the dominance of their human owners.

# CANINE PHYSIOLOGY

*THE POWERFULLY BUILT ELKHOUND (ABOVE, LEFT) HAS A DENSE WEATHER-PROOF COAT, QUITE UNLIKE THE LOOSE FOLDS OF SKIN AND EXTREMELY SHORT, STRAIGHT COAT OF THE SHAR PEI (ABOVE RIGHT).*

Despite their great range of shapes and sizes, all dogs share the same genetic and physical specification. Dogs are quadruped mammals, with a musculature, limb structure and cardiovascular system designed for running. They have thirty-nine pairs of chromosomes (compared to humans' twenty-three pairs), a skeleton consisting of three-hundred-and-nineteen bones and forty-two adult teeth, which are perfectly designed for shredding flesh and tearing food. The structure of their limbs and muscles is intended to enable them (or their ancestral wild dogs) to run on their toes for long periods without tiring. Their heart and lungs are large in order to cope with the need to supply blood and oxygen to an energetic body. In short, nature intended dogs to be hunters.

Dog sizes vary tremendously: the Irish wolfhound, for example, measures 1 m (about 32 in) at the withers, whereas the Chihuahua stands at 12 cm (5 in). The colour and thickness of coats vary from the gloriously coiffed Afghan hound to the less than hirsute Mexican hairless dog. The shape of a dog is determined primarily by its head, body and legs, and the size of these differs considerably from breed to breed.

*THE CHINESE CRESTED IS ENTIRELY HAIRLESS APART FROM THE EXTRAVAGANT TUFT OF HAIR ON THE HEAD.*

THE AFGHAN HOUND HAS A DISTINCTIVE SHAGGY COAT.

IRISH WOLFHOUNDS ARE THE TALLEST DOGS.

BULLDOGS ARE AFFECTIONATE AND
GOOD-NATURED.

Humans have altered various canine characteristics through selective breeding. The German shepherd dog, the breed closest to the dog's vulpine ancestor, possesses all of the characteristics of a well-balanced dog: a long-haired coat, well-muscled limbs to power prolonged bursts of running and a long muzzle enclosing a range of teeth for gripping and shredding. Other breeds are less fortunate, however. Although selective breeding can accentuate useful characteristics, such as the ability to run faster, it can also produce breeds with shorter life expectancies and hereditary disorders. Bulldogs, for example, have bandy legs and squashed faces and may experience breathing difficulties; Irish setters are prone to an incurable, inherited, eye disease; while King Charles spaniels are 50 per cent more likely than other breeds to be suffering from heart defects by the age of five.

CHIHUAHUAS ARE THE WORLD'S
SMALLEST DOGS.

THE GERMAN SHEPHERD HAS A LONG MUZZLE.

THE SHORT-NOSED CAVALIER KING CHARLES
SPANIEL.

# THE SKIN AND COAT

With a few exceptions, dogs are covered in hair, which may be straight or wavy. The hair follicles are attached to tiny muscles that cause the hairs to bristle at times of stress. In addition, sensitive whiskers are sited near the nose.

Coats vary a great deal in dogs – more so than in any other species of domestic animal – and the type is a good indication of the geographical origin of a breed. Dogs have two textures of hair, the top coat or guard hair and the undercoat or down, and the relative thickness and distribution of these hair textures governs the style of coat. The density of both types of hair varies tremendously between breeds, too. Long, warm coats are

*THE COAT OF THE WIRE-HAIRED FOX TERRIER IS DENSE.*

*PEKINGESE HAVE PROFUSE, THICK COATS.*

common in breeds originating from northern Asia, such as the Pekingese, whose appearance is in complete contrast to the sleek, short-haired Rhodesian ridgeback, an African dog. Dogs from warm climates often possess short coats, with a high

density of almost waterproof hair that provides good insulation. Wire-haired breeds have coats with thick guard hairs, which provide an excellent all-weather barrier, as well as protection against bites from other animals.

Many breeds shed their hairs seasonally, although this cycle depends to some extent on temperature, length of daylight hours, hormonal factors, nutrition and genetic predisposition. In autumn, as the days become shorter, dogs' coats usually become thicker and the hairs longer; hairs are then shed in the spring, when the dense winter undercoat becomes redundant. Growth is slowest during the summer months.

Dogs' paws are covered by an extra-tough epidermis, with a tough, protective epidermal layer on the footpads. Sweat-producing glands help maintain the footpads' suppleness, although the footpads are not sensitive to heat or cold.

# THE SKELETON

Canine skeletons are robust structures that provide an excellent framework for the body. A strong skull incorporates protective pockets for the eyes and ears, and the neck vertebrae have extensions attached to powerful muscles. The shoulder blades are attached to the rest of the skeleton only by muscle, which allows enormous flexibility for running. Long ribs form a protective cage around the vital organs and the shoulders and hips act as pivots, allowing the limbs to move gracefully and accurately. The weight distribution between the front and hind legs is relatively equal.

*LONG-LEGGED GREYHOUNDS ARE EXTREMELY FAST.*

GUNDOGS LIKE THE GERMAN LONG-HAIRED POINTER
GENERALLY HAVE WIDE HEADS
AND LONG MUZZLES.

SALUKI HOUNDS HAVE NARROW SKULLS.

MASTIFFS HAVE BROAD SKULLS AND
WIDE-SET EYES.

BOXERS HAVE POWERFUL, WIDE HEADS.

The bones are anchored together by ligaments, while tendons attach muscles to the skeleton. Canine tendons are well developed and tendon injuries are rare, although excessive weight can cause some ligaments to tear. The weakest link is often a hind knee, which may be the source of trouble in a limping, overweight, middle-aged dog.

There are three basic head shapes: a narrow skull with a long face (the dolichocephalic skull of the Saluki, for example); a wide skull with a long face (like the mesocephalic head of the pointer); and a wide head and short muzzle (such as the boxer's brachycephalic skull, which is taken to its extreme in the short-nosed pug, which has virtually no muzzle at all).

PUGS ARE PRIZED FOR THEIR SHORT NOSES.

The earliest dogs were probably about the same size as dingoes, and finished growing at the age of ten months. Mastiffs, which were first bred about five-and-a-half thousand years ago, did not mature until the age of eighteen months. Today, larger breeds reach maturity later than smaller ones.

Most dogs are well equipped to run over long distances. The configuration of their shoulder and pelvic bones, and the articulation of their leg bones and spine, allow most breeds to move fast with ease. Some breeds have been bred to emphasise a specific gait: the German shepherd, for example, is known for its 'flying trot', which makes it look as though it is soaring through the air, although one foot always remains in contact with the ground. Greyhounds, which have been bred for speed, are most comfortable when galloping. Their spines are exceptionally flexible, allowing them to extend all four legs at once, with all four paws off the ground.

Despite their size, Afghan hounds, which were bred to chase game over rocky terrain, are able to turn in extremely small spaces because of the flexibility of their hip joints and lower back. Short-legged dachshunds were bred to hunt badgers underground, and their sausage-like shape enables them to dive down narrow tunnels in search of prey.

DACHSHUNDS STAND 13–25 CM (5–10 IN.) HIGH.

# THE MUSCULAR SYSTEM

Healthy dogs display co-ordinated movement and a smooth, flexible gait controlled by the three muscle groups: smooth muscle, which controls movement of the viscera; cardiac muscle, which governs the heart tissue; and skeletal muscle, which the dog can control and which enables it to move.

**HEALTHY DOGS HAVE POWERFUL THIGHS TO AID RUNNING.**

The most powerful skeletal muscles are sited in the jaw, giving a dog the strength to bite or hold firmly, and in the thighs, providing instant propulsive energy for running. The neck muscles allow the head to turn more than 220 degrees, and both the ears and the tail are well muscled to enable social signalling.

Muscle shrinkage occurs either through underuse or, more rarely, if the nerve supply is damaged. Regular daily exercise is therefore vital to ensure fluid muscular movement, especially for young dogs, who require two periods of exercise per day. Jumping is excellent exercise for lean dogs, but note that heavier, older animals could damage their spinal cord if they land awkwardly.

**ABOVE: GERMAN POINTERS HAVE STRONG JAWS AND NECKS.**

**ALL DOGS NEED EXERCISE. JUMPING IS ESPECIALLY GOOD FOR YOUNGER ANIMALS.**

# THE CARDIOVASCULAR SYSTEM

*DOGS ARE NATURAL AND HEALTHY-RUNNERS.*

Dogs are natural runners, and their highly efficient cardiovascular system is both adept at producing vast amounts of oxygen during exercise and at dealing with the resulting waste products.

Different parts of the body require varying amounts of nourishment at different times, and the heart pumps oxygen-bearing blood around the body in response to its needs. The dog's brain receives anything from 10 to 20 per cent of the blood pumped by the heart, and this figure remains constant whatever the dog is doing. During exercise, up to 90 per cent of the blood pumped by the heart can be diverted to the muscles to provide the animal with extra stamina.

Blood cells collect waste products as they circulate around the body and carry them to the liver for detoxification. They are then carried to the lungs, where carbon dioxide is expelled and replaced by nourishing oxygen. Fresh red blood cells travel through the arteries to release this oxygen into the tissue cells.

# THE DIGESTION

The canine mouth is typical of a carnivorous scavenger. Six pairs of incisor teeth are positioned at the front of the mouth for nibbling, cutting and grooming, flanked by two pairs of canines, which are used for biting and tearing at food (or prey). The canines have extremely long roots and are very sturdy teeth. The remaining teeth are premolars, used for shredding and cutting, and molars, for chewing and grinding.

The canine tongue is comparatively thin and is mainly used for the processing of food, for cleaning the coat and for perspiring. (Hot dogs cool down by letting their tongues hang out and panting. Panting causes moisture to evaporate from the tongue, which cools the skin. Dogs also sweat through the pads on their paws.)

Dogs' gastrointestinal systems are designed to deal with large amounts of food received infrequently and irregularly – although most domestic animals today enjoy regular meals. Dogs rarely chew their food, instead gulping or swallowing it so that it passes directly through the oesophagus and into the stomach, where it is broken down by digestive enzymes. The food then leaves the stomach through the pyloric sphincter and moves into the small intestine. Most of the digestion and absorption of food occurs in the small intestine, aided by the pancreas and the liver. The

*UNABLE TO SWEAT EXCEPT THROUGH THEIR PAW PADS, DOGS PANT TO HELP THEM COOL DOWN.*

pancreas regulates the digestive process by secreting enzymes, as well as insulin and glucagons to regulate glucose levels. As in humans, the liver is the largest internal organ in the dog's body. It has six lobes (compared to humans' two) and produces bile to help the absorption of fat, as well as metabolising proteins and carbohydrates. It excretes toxins from the blood and manufactures blood-clotting agents. These are all vitally important functions, and liver disease can be a major problem in dogs.

From the small intestine, any remaining food shifts to the large intestine, which contains large numbers of bacteria. These guard against infection, break down waste material and process vitamins. Once digestion is complete, waste matter is defaecated.

# THE URINARY AND REPRODUCTIVE SYSTEMS

Further waste matter is dealt with by the kidneys, which hang from the roof of the abdomen and are protected by the dog's bottom ribs. The kidneys filter toxic substances from the blood, clear waste then passing into the renal pelvis through two ureters to the bladder. The urethra discharges urine from the penis or through the vulva.

Dogs reach sexual maturity between six and twelve months of age, although emotional maturity is not achieved until about eighteen months. A female dog who has puppies very young may not have the emotional resources to cope with being a good mother, so it is important to ensure that she does not mate during her first oestrus cycle.

Male dogs are always sexually active, constantly on the lookout for a willing mate, to whom they are attracted by scent. Females ovulate only twice a year. During the pro-oestrus cycle, lasting about twelve days, a female dog's vulva swells and produces a discharge. This is followed by five days of oestrus, when eggs are released into the Fallopian tubes, and it is at this point that she chooses a mate. The ovaries remain active for life. (See also the section on breeding, pages 113 to 116.)

# THE SENSES

A dog's five senses are attuned very differently to those of humans. The canine sense of smell is sensitive, sophisticated and the dog's most acute sense. It is for this reason that dogs are employed to track missing persons or to sniff out contraband drugs or explosives. Some breeds have a more highly developed olfactory sense than others: that of German shepherds and bloodhounds, for example, is far more efficient than that of short-nosed breeds, such as pugs.

It is estimated that dogs' sense of smell is at least a hundred times better than humans' (and may be as high as 100 million times more efficient). The average dog possesses over 200 million scent receptors (humans have 5 million), and the area of the brain devoted to smell is correspondingly larger.

Dogs famously have damp noses, and the moisture helps to capture scent and transmit it to the nasal membranes sited on the thin turbinate bones within the nose. Convoluted folds within these bones trap the scent and send messages to the olfactory-bulb region of the brain. The vomeronasal organ, situated in the roof of a dog's mouth, is devoted entirely to sex-scenting, enabling a dog to identify a suitable mate.

Body odours are produced by a number of secretions and glands in the dog's body, from saliva, ear secretions, vaginal and

*BLOODHOUNDS HAVE THE BEST SENSE OF SMELL.*

*PUGS HAVE SHORT, WRINKLED NOSES.*

preputial discharges and from glands around the anus and on top of the tail. All provide information about the sexual status of the animal and are used to scent-mark territory. The anal-sac glands deposit a drop of pheromone-enriched liquid on top of faeces, which is as distinct to each individual as fingerprints in humans.

By contrast, the canine sense of taste is quite poor. Humans have six times as many tastebuds as dogs, and the tongues of dogs appear almost rough because the surface is covered with lumpy papillae, which house the taste receptors. If left to their own devices and forced to scavenge for food, dogs will eat almost anything. They are initially attracted to food by smell, after which taste and texture receptors take over. Dogs can taste sour or acid foods over the whole tongue, sweet tastes at the sides, salt along the sides and at the base, but water only at the tip.

*DOGS HAVE A HIGHLY DEVELOPED SENSE OF SMELL.*

Hearing in dogs is very acute. They are able to hear sounds well beyond the range of the human ear, often from a great distance. Many aboriginal breeds possessed large, erect ears, and canine ears are generally mobile, enabling them to detect sounds four times further away than humans can hear. Dogs are also capable of shutting off their inner ear in order to filter out distracting noises.

More than any other body part, the shape of dogs' ears has been modified by selective breeding. The natural shape is erect and mobile, like wolves' ears, and some breeds retain this, giving them an air of alertness. At the other extreme, however, are the pendulous ears of ground-scenting dogs like the bloodhound. Some breeds, such as the greyhound, have 'rose' ears, which can be raised or folded back when running.

*DOGS USE BODY LANGUAGE TO COMMUNICATE.*

Dogs are sensitive to touch. Whiskers (known as vibrissae) around the muzzle, which can be moved voluntarily, are equipped with many nerve fibres and can sense air flow. Dogs use touch and smell to communicate with one another, and touch plays an important part in bonding with a dog. Dogs huddle together for warmth and use licking and pawing as a means of establishing dominance.

Canine vision is less acute than dogs' sense of smell. They have proportionately larger corneas than humans, which means that their night vision is highly efficient, but the mixture of rods and cones in the central area of their retinas allows only poor colour definition and generally less acute eyesight. The position of dogs' eyes varies among breeds. Many hunting dogs, such as whippets and greyhounds, have eyes set at the sides of their heads, giving them excellent peripheral vision that is ideal for hunting and chasing. The eyes of other breeds, such as bloodhounds and boxers, for example, are positioned more frontally, giving them good binocular vision.

*GREYHOUNDS HAVE GOOD PERIPHERAL VISION.*

The dog possesses a 'third' eyelid, a membrane layer at the inner angle of the eyelid which generally protects the eye from irritants. It cannot be moved voluntarily, but shifts across the eye when the eye is pulled deeper into the socket by muscle action.

Many animals are credited with a sixth sense that enables them to know when natural disasters are about to occur or, more prosaically, when a member of the family is approaching. Dogs are intelligent creatures, and many dog-owners believe that their pets can judge their moods or that they try to tell them when something is wrong. Scientific studies have revealed that dogs possess an electromagnetic sense that makes them aware of earth tremors and vibrations and that may enable them to travel great distances to find their way home.

*BOXERS' EYES ARE FRONT-SET.*

*complete DOG*

# CANINE BEHAVIOUR

Canine behaviour results from a combination of nature and nurture. Dogs are sociable creatures, who prefer the company of other dogs and people to living alone, while canine logic is very simple, being governed by the needs of survival and comfort. Because survival means food, tasty snacks become an important bargaining counter when training a dog. Certain behaviour, such as jumping up to lick a person's face, is governed by the basic instinct to beg for food. (Licking a mother wolf's face stimulates the regurgitation of food for the cub.)

The genetic make-up of dogs provides them with a number of basic survival instincts based on the behaviour of the pack animal. These basic instincts are modified during the dog's life, most critically during the early weeks of life. Born with a number of genetically pre-programmed characteristics, from the age of about three weeks puppies will socialise with their littermates, learning to interact with them and with people. Puppies learn by watching their mothers and, until they are twelve weeks old, absorb everything that they see, hear, taste, smell and feel. The more it learns during these vital early weeks, the more adaptable the puppy will be as an adult dog.

*THIS SMALL DOG HAS LEARNT TO BEG.*

*ALL DOGS BEGIN LIFE IN A CANINE PACK.*

Pack animals exist in a close-knit hierarchy dominated by a leader – usually a male – who controls pack activity. Fortunately, most dogs are happy to follow a dominant male, secure in the knowledge that someone else is in charge. Domestic dogs regard their owners as pack leaders and will follow them and defend their territory. Dog-owners must establish themselves as the dominant partner within the home by training their dog to follow human, rather than canine, behavioural cues. Exposure to humans when a puppy is under six weeks old will help to ensure that it will be accustomed to people and be able to learn from them.

*PUPPIES SHOULD BECOME ACCUSTOMED TO BEING HANDLED BY HUMANS WHEN THEY ARE VERY YOUNG.*

Pack animals are sophisticated creatures who have learnt a number of rules about co-existing successfully. Wolves hunt together, share food and huddle together for warmth, increasing the chances of their own, and the pack's, survival. Puppies begin their lives in a natural pack until they leave their mother and become part of a human pack. At first, the mother is pack leader simply because she controls the food source and provides warmth and security. By the age of three weeks, puppies are strong enough to play, to experiment with making physical contact with each other and to learn to test their bodies. Puppies initially learn about pack hierarchy through play. Once a puppy is removed from the mother to the care of a human, the dog owner – the controller of food, warmth and security – becomes pack leader.

By the time a dog has matured emotionally, at about eighteen months of age, it has usually established its status within the pack (generally a human family). A dominant dog may challenge its allocated position by refusing to obey commands or picking on the weakest member of the pack to assert itself (because this may be a child in a family household, early training to establish control over a dog is crucially important).

Dogs are extremely territorial, and within a pack each member is responsible for defending the pack's territory. Dogs respond quickly when they sense something new or strange approaching their territory, and will alert the rest of the pack (or household) by barking. Dogs may become aggressive when defending their territory, but for many owners this is desirable, security being one of the main reasons for dog-ownership.

*MOTHERS TEACH THEIR YOUNG HOW TO BEHAVE AND OFTEN NIP THEM TO CONTROL BEHAVIOUR.*

*complete DOG*

*THIS DOG DEFENDS WHAT IS CONSIDERS TO BE ITS TERRITORY BY CHASING A CAR AWAY.*

Canine aggression takes several forms, each with different causes. Maternal aggression is the natural response of a mother trying to protect her pups. Predatory aggression is seen when a dog is catching prey, such as a rabbit or bird, or even when chasing a cat or car.

Dogs that have been trained to catch people demonstrate trained aggression, which is usually only sparked by a verbal command. Territorial aggression is a natural canine characteristic, although problems may arise if a dog actually attacks someone. Dogs usually try to intimidate opponents with a display of aggressive behaviour, but will try to avoid full-blown conflict (hence the phrase 'his bark is worse than his bite').

Dogs will defend their territory against other dogs, as well as humans, and this behaviour is more common among dogs whose owners are absent, when the dog becomes extra-protective of its territory. Frightened dogs often become aggressive, while dogs being harassed by small children may

*WHEN TWO DOGS MEET, ONE OF THEM WILL USUALLY TRY TO ESTABLISH A DOMINANT POSITION.*

bite because they misunderstand their behaviour. Males around the age of two years will often fight to establish dominance, and other dogs will defend their toys or food bowls. Persistent aggression in adult males can be solved by castration.

All dogs love playing, but less dominant dogs play more willingly and more frequently. Play is vital for dogs because it provides stimulation, exercise, encourages dexterity and reinforces the bonds of affection between owner and pet. Play should also emphasise status: dogs must be submissive to their owners, so humans should dominate play activity.

*DOGS ARE NATURALLY ALERT, FRIENDLY AND CURIOUS ANIMALS.*

Dogs demonstrate attachment to their human owners by bringing them 'gifts' of toys or sticks or by rolling over, asking to be tickled. People interpret these types of behaviour as affection, and although they are certainly signs that a dog is feeling relaxed and happy, animal behaviourists disagree about the emotional depth of dogs' feelings.

*ROLLING OVER IS A PLEA FOR TICKLING AND PLAY.*

# UNDERSTANDING CANINE BODY LANGUAGE

Dogs have evolved a complex range of non-verbal communication based upon body language and communication by scent. Their interaction is based upon the simple logic of pack animals and is intended to ascertain rank and establish dominance or submissiveness within the pack. The meaning of some actions is clear to humans, but others are more complicated and are still not fully understood by animal behaviourists. Dogs use their ears, faces, mouths, tails and bodies, either independently or in combination, to convey messages to each other and to humans. Dogs are extremely expressive social creatures and there is usually enough common ground between dogs and their owners for mutual understanding. People often interpret canine communication in human terms.

*THIS HAPPY DOG'S EXPRESSION IS EASY TO READ!*

Dogs' facial expressions are reasonably clear, and eye contact is an important factor. Although dogs have fewer facial muscles than humans, the mouth is a good indicator of mood: bared teeth are a sign of aggression, while the 'submissive grin' is the sign of a subservient dog. Dominant dogs will stare at other individuals to establish rank, while submissive dogs will look away. Aggressive dogs exhibit erect ears, bared teeth and a hard stare, whereas submissive animals have flattened ears and a closed mouth. Erect ears are a sign of confidence and alertness in both friendly and aggressive dogs, and ears flattened against the head usually indicate fear or submission. Another obvious indicator is tail carriage: a tail held down, between the legs, is the sign of a fearful and submissive dog, but when held high, it indicates confidence and excitement.

A dog's posture also provides clues as to its mood, and subtle gestures are used for communication, although canine expression is limited by dogs' bodies. Dogs are restricted by their need to stand on all four legs most of the time, and they have forelegs rather than arms, so cannot demonstrate fine gestures. They can alter their centre of gravity to lean forwards or backwards by lowering their back legs; they can stand up, lie down, crouch or roll over; they can make themselves look larger or smaller by raising or lowering the hairs on the back of their neck; or they can vary their posture by turning sideways or facing another animal. These postures are used in conjunction with facial expressions, scenting and tail carriage.

*MAKING EYE CONTACT IS IMPORTANT TO DOGS.*

An aggressive or frightened dog will raise its hackles in an attempt to appear bigger and, when on the verge of attack, will take up a forward stance with its ears raised. Frightened dogs assume a backward stance, leaning back, tail down, lips bared and ears back, although, if cornered, the dog may become more aggressive. A submissive dog almost crouches, with its eyes averted, ears back and tail down and, if really overwhelmed, it will lie on its back, belly exposed.

A number of ritual forms of behaviour are common to all dogs, particularly during courtship and among dogs at play. Mating rituals are usually triggered by the scent of the female and advance with the male trying to attract the female's attention by leaping around. If he is successful, the dogs will first spar with their front legs before the female will allow the male to mount her. Dogs play as much as humans, perhaps to rehearse situations and to provide exercise. An invitation to play begins with the 'play bow', when one dog drops on to its forelimbs, with its hindquarters raised, showing that it is about to play rather than engage in full combat. This is followed by tail-wagging and small leaps, with the mouth open, until the 'opponent' takes up the chase, which usually ends with a mock fight. Some younger dogs can become over-excited, and owners must try to ensure that the games do not spiral out of control.

*WITH ERECT EARS AND A PERKY TAIL, THIS DOG IS CONFIDENT AND ALERT.*

Given the highly efficient canine sense of smell, it is not surprising that scent is an important factor in dog behaviour. When two dogs meet, they immediately sniff each other's muzzle, inguinal and anal areas to establish sex and status. Pheromones, present in saliva, urine, faeces and vaginal and preputial secretions, provide a wealth of information to other dogs about the reproductive state of females and the dominance of males. Scent-marking – usually by urinating – is used by male dogs to establish territory and to communicate with other dogs.

*THIS POINTER IS POISED FOR ACTION WITH WEIGHT LEANING FORWARDS AND TAIL EXTENDED.*

*TWO SMALL DOGS PRACTISE FIGHTING.*

There are four main groups of canine sound, each with distinct meanings and uses: barking, howling, growling and whining. Barking is the sound most commonly associated with dogs, and usually indicates excitement and a state of alertness; it is used as a warning signal if a dog's territory is being threatened. Howling is less common, but is the noise of pack animals. A communal sound, once one dog starts, its howling is quickly copied by other dogs within earshot. Growling dogs are obviously aggressive and on the verge of attacking or fighting, whereas whining or whimpering dogs are crying for attention. Puppies whimper as a sign of distress, while adult dogs do it to invoke sympathy. Interestingly, dogs rarely whine in the presence of other dogs unless they are trying to appease a dominant dog.

A male dog may mark as many as eighty distinct sites with his urine within a four-hour period, and urban dogs who share their territory with many other animals mark more frequently than rural dogs. Female dogs also scent-mark, although their behaviour is more cyclical and restricted to one phase of the oestrus cycle. The urine of a female dog is extremely attractive to male dogs during her receptive phase. Dogs persistently sniff the ground when being walked, probably to ascertain which of their canine neighbours has preceded them.

Dogs also communicate vocally (although the basenji, a hunting dog from central Africa, has no bark, it emits a yodel-like cry when it is happy). Canine hearing is well developed and dogs can hear sounds at much higher frequencies than humans.

*DOG SNIFFING: AN IMPORTANT METHOD OF FINDING INFORMATION.*

# CANINE BODY LANGUAGE

| MOOD | EARS | EYES | MOUTH/TEETH | BODY | TAIL | NOISE |
|---|---|---|---|---|---|---|
| Aggressive. | Close to head. | Staring forcefully. | Teeth bared in snarl. | Tense, dominant position. Poised for action. | Held straight out from body. | Growl or loud bark. |
| Alert. | Erect. Moving to catch sounds. | Open normally. | Closed or slightly open, with teeth covered. | Slightly dominant position, possibly on tiptoes. | Up. Maybe wagging. | None. Possibly a low bark. |
| Anxious. | Slightly laid back. | Narrowed, avoiding gaze. | Closed – possibly in 'grin'. | Tense, forelegs lowered | Down, in submissive position. | Low whine or pleading bark. |
| Exerting dominance. | Erect or forward. | Staring at subject. | Closed. | Tall posture. Hackles up. | Stiffened. | Assertive growl. |
| Beginning of chase. | Upright. | Wide open and alert. | Open, possibly panting. | Tense. Crouched, legs bent ready to run. | Extended straight out from body. | None. |
| Excited. | Erect, pointing forwards | Wide open. | Open, possibly panting. | Well-balanced pose, possibly pacing or wriggling | Wagging. | Short yelps of excitement. |
| Playful. | Erect or relaxed. | Wide open. | Relaxed, slight panting. | 'Play bow' – forelegs bent, rear raised. Possibly circling round, running to and fro. | Vigorous wagging. | Excited barking, play-growling. |
| Submissive. | Down, laid against head. | Whites showing or narrowed. | Lips pulled back in 'submissive grin'. | Lying on back, belly exposed, one paw raised. | Between legs. | Whimper or low whine. |

# MAIN DOG TYPES

Breed-specific traits have been developed over many generations of selective breeding, and dogs are now grouped according to the work for which they were bred. There are six groups of dogs in Britain: hound, gundog (sporting), terrier, utility (non-sporting), working and toy. Dogs are divided into seven groups in the United States by the American Kennel Club (AKC): sporting, non-sporting, hounds, terriers, toy, working and herding. It is not always easy to classify a particular breed, and kennel clubs in different countries vary in their classifications. Most of the breeds that are popular today in the USA and Britain emerged only within the last two-hundred to two-hundred-and-fifty years, with a great many being bred during the nineteenth century.

Dogs were once bred for guarding, herding and hunting, utilising characteristics that had evolved through natural selection. The Victorians were the first seriously to breed dogs for their looks alone, and it was during the nineteenth century that kennel clubs began to lay down stringent rules governing the appearance of each breed. The genetic make-up of some breeds became governed by the whims of fashion, and some developed distorted features, such as massive heads, folded skin or short, squashed muzzles.

**BOSTON TERRIER**

Traits that had been maintained in some breeds through natural selection over generations were subordinated to the demands of dog-show judges, and some breeds continue to suffer from damaging recessive genes that are detrimental to their health. Bulldogs, for example, are prized for their large heads and narrow hips, but their physique means that many litters must be delivered by Caesarean section. Dalmatians suffer from deafness, King Charles spaniels are prone to heart trouble, while German shepherds are susceptible to hip problems. Veterinary science and breeders are making good progress in their efforts to minimise these problems, however.

**PYRENEAN MOUNTAIN DOG**

**AUSTRALIAN CATTLEDOG**

**BASSETT HOUND**

**LLASO APSO**

**BICHON FRISE**

**MALTESE TOY**

**CHOW-CHOW**

**MINI PINSCHER**

# DOG GROUPS

Hounds are hunting dogs and can be divided into two categories: sight-hounds (also known as gaze-hounds) and scent-hounds. Greyhounds, Salukis, whippets and borzois primarily use their sight to hunt, whereas beagles or bloodhounds hunt by following the scent of their prey. Aloof and independent, hounds generally concentrate on the world around them – the hunt – and can be deaf to the commands of their owners, so they may be tricky dogs to train well. However, they adapt easily to family life and make excellent companions.

Sporting gundogs excel at catching game, either birds or small, furry creatures. This group encompasses the setters and pointers that show huntsmen where the game is; the retrievers, which, as their name suggests, collect the dead game from either water or land; and the versatile spaniels that can do either job. Gundogs are adventurous, kindly animals and generally make good family pets.

Terriers were bred to trap rodents, and this group encompasses a wide variety of dogs that are generally extremely active and lively from puppyhood. Long-legged terriers include breeds over 35 cm (14 in) high at the withers, while short-legged terriers measure less than 35 cm (14 inches). Bull terriers are fearless, muscular dogs, and special terriers include such breeds as the Dandy Dinmont and the attractive and friendly West Highland terrier.

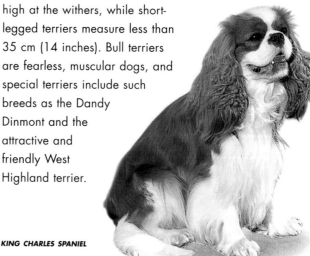

**KING CHARLES SPANIEL**

BEAGLE

BORZOI

AMERICAN COCKER SPANIEL

FRENCH BULLDOG

PEMBROKE CORGI

DANDY DINMONT

complete DOG

The working group includes the much-maligned Rottweiler, the massive Newfoundland and the Pembroke corgi, a favourite at Buckingham Palace. Another diverse group, working breeds are further subdivided into guard and working dogs, herding and shepherding dogs. Many breeds require particularly rigorous training to ensure their good behaviour, but they are level-headed dogs, with business-like dispositions.

Utility breeds (known as the non-sporting group in the USA) are a diverse group, although they are all generally good companion dogs. Their sizes and body shape range from the small chow-chow through Dalmatians and poodles to Tibetan breeds and bulldogs, such as the French bulldog, which was once used for bull-baiting.

Dogs in the toy group are not among the largest breeds, but have big characters. Dogs such as the Chihuahua and Yorkshire terrier are undoubtedly brave; others, such as the King Charles spaniel, make excellent pets; and as a group they are generally intelligent dogs. They have been bred to be companion dogs and thrive on affection. Many, such as the 'min pin', or miniature pinscher, are miniature versions of working dogs.

Critics of pedigree dogs believe that mongrels are healthier, more intelligent and easier to train than their purebred cousins, but pedigree animals are infinitely more predictable in their behaviour. Although breeding to accentuate useful natural characteristics is no bad thing in a domestic animal, it is surely cruel to breed simply to accentuate physical characteristics that are momentarily deemed attractive, but that may actually make the animal's life miserable.

**THE WEIMARANER IS A HANDSOME GUNDOG.**

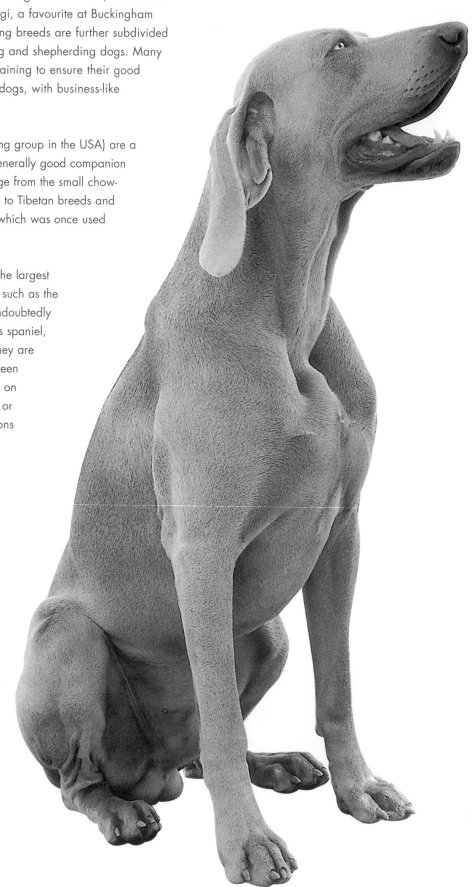

## CHAPTER 3

# OWNING A DOG

Choosing to become a dog-owner is not a decision to be made lightly, on impulse or under pressure from persistent small children. A dog will be an addition to your family, a creature that will require care and attention for many years (the average life span for a dog is thirteen years). A potential dog-owner must consider whether he or she has the time and patience necessary to invest in a dog that will require feeding, grooming, walking and stimulation. However, if you think that you can undertake this role, your time and effort will be repaid handsomely by the affection of a faithful friend, who will give you years of pleasure, fun and companionship. Above all, dogs are rewarding pets.

*RIGHT: FIERCELY PROTECTIVE, KERRY BLUE TERRIERS ARE GOOD WITH CHILDREN.*

*DOGS QUICKLY BECOME MUCH-LOVED MEMBERS OF THE FAMILY.*

*FRIENDLY ANIMALS WILL WELCOME THEIR OWNERS.*

Dogs have individual temperaments, but each breed exhibits certain general characteristics. By examining your lifestyle, you may be able to narrow down the sort of dog that will be right for you.

If you are usually inactive, and lack the time, ability or inclination to exercise, consider a relatively sedentary breed that will be content with a short walk around the streets or to lie in its basket. A dog from the toy group, such as a Yorkshire terrier or a King Charles spaniel, would be ideal.

*SMALL AND COMPACT, YORKSHIRE TERRIERS REQUIRE CONSIDERABLE GROOMING.*

Before acquiring a dog, consider carefully what you want. Do you want to train a puppy? Or would you rather acquire a mature dog from a rescue home? Can you provide a regular routine for your pet? Do you have time to exercise it and play with it? If you are away at work all day, or would regularly leave your dog for longer than four hours, a dog is probably not the ideal pet for you because dogs are social creatures that dislike solitude. Do not forget the cost of owning a dog – in addition to food, it will require a collar, tag, vaccinations, veterinary treatment and kennelling. Generally, large dogs cost more to maintain than small dogs.

*LEFT: VETERINARY CARE IS A VITAL PART OF A DOG'S LIFE.*

*RIGHT: ALL DOGS NEED TO LEARN OBEDIENCE.*

*INTELLIGENT BEARDED COLLIES ENJOY TRAINING.*

boxer, for example. It is worth mentioning that these dogs also require mental stimulation because they are highly intelligent animals; obedience classes or agility training will be useful and can help to prevent behavioural problems.

If you have an outdoor lifestyle and would like a dog to be with you all day, choose a dog who thrives on this way of life, such as a Siberian husky, a Dalmatian, a pointer or a retriever.

Families with children need a dog who will accept the rough and tumble of family life. Children must be taught how to treat a dog with respect, and a good family dog must be easy-going, love exercise and revel in attention.

If you fancy a daily walk of about an hour, but preferably only in fine weather, you'll need an adaptable, easy-going breed, such as a terrier or a Shetland sheepdog. A large number of breeds would be suitable.

A dedicated walker, who delights in exercise whatever the weather, would appreciate an active dog – a gundog or working dog, such as a golden retriever, a bearded collie or a

Gundogs, particularly Labradors, are popular family pets for precisely these reasons. A successful family dog must have been around children from puppyhood, so check the background of any animal that you may acquire from a rescue centre carefully. However gentle the dog, young children should never be left alone with it – small children are unpredictable creatures, as are even the most well-balanced dogs. (See also Chapter 5, page 70.)

*CHILDREN SHOULD BE TAUGHT TO RESPECT AND ENJOY DOGS AND NOT TO MISTREAT OR BULLY THEM.*

Many academic studies have shown that pet-ownership is beneficial for both children and their families. Dogs act as a source of play and learning, and children will also learn the importance of responsibilities to animals, as well as the facts of life and, because dogs have comparatively short lives, how to cope with death, too. One study at Vienna University found that dog-owning children were likely to be more popular at school, possibly because they were learning about non-verbal communication through playing with their dogs.

*LEFT: ENERGETIC DALMATIANS NEED A LOT OF EXERCISE.*

# LARGE OR SMALL?

*LONG-HAIRED SPANIELS NEED DAILY GROOMING.*

The decision as to the best size of dog for you depends largely on your domestic circumstances. Put simply, do you have the room to accommodate a large animal, or is your home better suited to a small pet, such as a spaniel? Large dogs are probably more costly to keep because they require more food, although small dogs are often picky eaters that demand specialised food.

Small dogs need almost as much exercise as their larger cousins, but do not require quite so much space in which to run around. Terriers, for example, must have regular exercise, whereas larger breeds, such as Irish wolfhounds, are more relaxed about the frequency of their exercise.

Large breeds with long-haired coats will drop hair around the house and will need frequent grooming, whereas dogs with

non-shedding coats, such as poodles, would suit people with allergies. Long-haired breeds require the investment of a certain amount of time, dedication and money to ensure that they look good.

Crossbreeds often make the best family pets. They can be friendly, healthier and longer-living than purebreeds and do not usually suffer from the painful congenital diseases that afflict many purebreeds. Mongrels are also more often in need of a good home than purebred dogs. On the other hand, pedigree dogs are known quantities: their behaviour is likely to conform to the expectations of the breed and their life expectancy is reasonably certain, as are any health problems.

Dogs vary widely in size and temperament, and it is important to match your individual needs to a suitable dog. Ask friends for recommendations, research the qualities of different breeds through books, magazines or the Internet, and do not hurry your decision. Once you have chosen a breed, try to meet dogs of that breed of both sexes and all ages to gain an idea of what to expect at different stages in the dog's life.

*THE SHIH TZU IS AN IDEAL PET FOR A SMALL HOME.*

*complete DOG*

# ADULT OR PUPPY?

It is vital to ascertain why an adult dog is being advertised. (Rescue centres, see page 49, will usually be able to furnish you with details of the dog's life and behaviour.) Be wary of a dog that has been rehomed several times: it may simply have been unlucky in its owners or it could have severe behavioural problems. Some – but not all – problems can be solved with a little patience. A dog with a destructive reputation may simply have been suffering from boredom, loneliness and lack of exercise, for example.

Adult dogs typically arrive fully house-trained, which is a big advantage, but may suffer from a number of hidden problems, such as separation anxiety or a dislike of children. Carry out a few simple tests on the dog that you are considering. Watch its reaction when you put a lead on it and take it for a walk. How does it react to strangers, other dogs and children? Is it easily frightened? Will it obey simple commands, such as 'Sit'? Leave it alone to play with a toy for a few minutes. A dog that is prone to separation anxiety will bark or whine. Approach the dog from the front and maintain eye contact with it. A relaxed dog will watch you expectantly, but a nervous dog may bark or cower.

**BAD BEHAVIOUR OFTEN RESULTS FROM POOR CARE.**

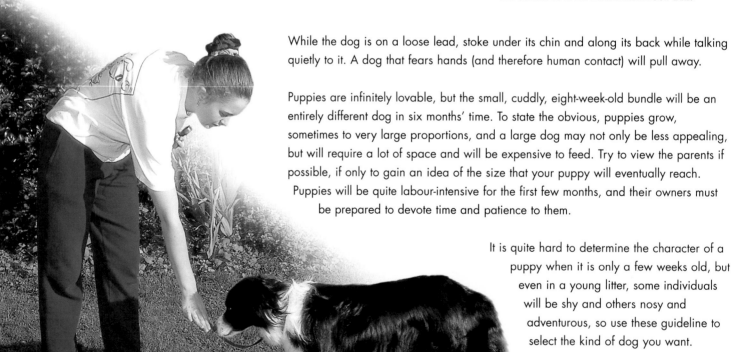

While the dog is on a loose lead, stoke under its chin and along its back while talking quietly to it. A dog that fears hands (and therefore human contact) will pull away.

Puppies are infinitely lovable, but the small, cuddly, eight-week-old bundle will be an entirely different dog in six months' time. To state the obvious, puppies grow, sometimes to very large proportions, and a large dog may not only be less appealing, but will require a lot of space and will be expensive to feed. Try to view the parents if possible, if only to gain an idea of the size that your puppy will eventually reach. Puppies will be quite labour-intensive for the first few months, and their owners must be prepared to devote time and patience to them.

It is quite hard to determine the character of a puppy when it is only a few weeks old, but even in a young litter, some individuals will be shy and others nosy and adventurous, so use these guideline to select the kind of dog you want.

**SPEND TIME ASSESSING HOW AN ADULT DOG INTERACTS WITH PEOPLE AND RESPONDS TO SIMPLE COMMANDS.**

# MALE OR FEMALE?

In general terms, male dogs from dominant breeds are more likely to roam and to be more aggressive than females. They will probably be more active, playful and little more difficult to train, too. Females are generally more placid, gentle and easier to train, but may demand more affection. (Note that females have two menstrual cycles per year, when they emit blood-tinged discharges.) Among small and more submissive breeds, temperamental differences between the sexes are less marked.

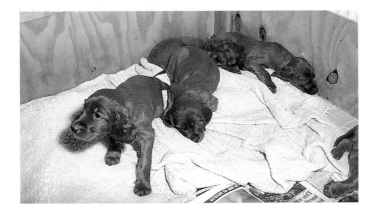

*PUPPIES NEED PLENTY OF CARE.*

## POINTS TO CONSIDER WHEN CHOOSING A DOG
- Large or small?
- Puppy or adult?
- Pedigree or crossbreed?
- The size of your house.
- Your lifestyle – are you out at work all day?
- How much exercise are you prepared to provide?
- The background of an adult dog.

# ADOPTING A DOG

## BREEDERS

Once you have decided on the breed of dog that is best suited to your situation, you'll have to decide where to get it from. Reputable breeders are probably the best source for pedigree animals, although these dogs will be more expensive than crossbreeds or rescue dogs. In Britain, breed-club details can be found by contacting the Kennel Club.

Dog-breeding is a specialised discipline, and good breeders choose their blood stock carefully and ensure that their animals have an excellent quality of life. They will never breed from an animal that is likely to pass on inherited medical problems, nor will they breed from a bitch under two years of age or over eight. Breeding bitches usually produce no more than three or four litters during their lifetime and are never mated in two consecutive seasons. (It is now illegal in Britain for breeders to mate a bitch before she is a year old, to allow a bitch to have more than six litters in a lifetime or to allow her to produce more than one litter a year.)

*REPUTABLE BREEDERS CAN PROVIDE HEALTHY DOGS.*

*complete DOG*

Breeders do not sell their dogs to pet shops, dealers or other commercial outlets. They should be knowledgeable about their breed and frank about the disadvantages of their dogs. They should be equally keen to learn about your circumstances. Good breeders will also offer to take a puppy back should your domestic circumstances change.

CAREFULLY CHECK A POTENTIAL PET.

Be prepared to put your name on a waiting list for a puppy – a well-bred puppy from a good breeder is worth waiting for. Once the litter has been born, visit it to watch the puppies interacting with the mother and ask to see the father if possible. Check that the puppies have regular human contact, preferably with more than one person, that the facilities are clean and that the puppies appear alert and healthy. Choose a puppy that is interested in its surroundings rather than one that hides in the background (but be aware that such a puppy may develop into a dominant dog). The puppy should be confident, mischievous, appealing and curious.

Once you have chosen a puppy, you will probably be asked to pay a deposit. Ensure that the breeder has prepared the relevant paperwork, which should include pedigree and registration

papers, as well as the parents' hereditary screening certificates. Ask for a written agreement that the purchase is dependent on a satisfactory examination by a vet within forty-eight hours of the purchase. Find out whether the puppy has been wormed and vaccinated (some breeders do this at eight weeks before releasing puppies to new homes).

On the day of collection, check that the puppy is healthy, with no sores, scabs, discharges from the nose or eyes, any kind of cough or other signs of illness. If the puppy appears poorly, do not take it, but arrange to pick it up on another day. Arrange to have your puppy examined by a vet on the day of collection, too. You and your family will bond strongly with the animal within twenty-four hours, and if the vet decides that it should be returned to the breeder for any reason, parting with it will be much harder once you have become attached to it.

COLLECT VITAL PAPERWORK FROM THE BREEDER.

# RESCUE CENTRES AND OTHER SOURCES

Rescue or rehoming centres house animals that have been surrendered by their owners for a variety of reasons. Many people, for example, have simply acquired the wrong dog for their circumstances and are unable to look after it adequately, while other animals arrive as a result of domestic upheaval and still more are the product of an unexpected litter of puppies.

**MANY UNWANTED PUPS END UP IN RESCUE CENTRES.**

Rehoming centres are committed to the welfare of dogs and are keen to prevent any further distress to their animals. They often make behavioural assessments of their dogs and carry out medical tests and neutering programmes. Such centres question prospective owners closely about their lifestyle, accommodation, family circumstances and their expectations of dog-ownership. Some especially rigorous organisations even arrange for a pre-adoption talk or ask for a reference from a vet.

The dogs available from rescue centres are mainly crossbreeds, but there are a number of specialist-breed rescue societies, too. If you are considering taking a puppy from a rescue centre, it is vital to visit it and see it with its mother first. A well-adjusted puppy will play and socialise with its littermates and will benefit from its mother's care. (If you are tempted to buy a puppy advertised in the small ads, you may not have the opportunity to assess its background, and if the puppy has been badly cared for, it could grow into an aggressive, troublesome dog with behavioural problems.)

Dog-owning friends are another good source, and you will usually be able to visit the mother, and possibly also the father, of your prospective dog. Local vets may be helpful, too, and if a dog is recommended, it is likely that the vet will know the animal's medical and behavioural background.

Dogs sold by pet shops are prone to diseases and behavioural problems created during the vital early months of a puppy's life because it may have suffered periods of isolation and inadequate contact with people.

# HEALTH CHECK

Before purchasing a dog, make a few basic checks to ascertain the state of its health. This is especially important with puppies.

Watch the whole litter of puppies running about in a small space; they are likely to empty their bladders and bowels, giving you the chance to check that their motions are reasonably formed, with no sign of diarrhoea. A puppy that does not join in the romping may be tired, lame or simply unsociable.

You should be able to pick up a puppy without it whimpering or showing signs of distress as you examine its body. Puppies must be held carefully in the crook of the arm (rather as you would hold a baby), with one hand supporting the hindquarters and the base of the spine and the other the forelimbs and head.

Anyone selling an adult dog should be able to supply details of its medical history and vaccinations.

### LOOK OVER THE PUPPY'S BODY, CHECKING THE FOLLOWING POINTS.

- Skin: depending on the breed, the skin should have loose folds.
- Coat: should be clean and shiny.
- Tail root: check for fleas.
- Anal area: should be clean.
- Belly: should be supple and reasonably flat.
- Ears: check the edges for lice.
- Nose: should be cool and moist, with no discharge.
- Eyes: should be open and bright.

# PREPARING YOUR HOME FOR THE ARRIVAL OF YOUR DOG

## OUTDOOR AND INDOOR SECURITY

Before bringing your new dog home, make sure that your house and garden are secure and that the dog will not be able to escape into the road either by digging or leaping. Garden fences and gates must be secured, pools and ponds covered and poisonous pesticides stored out of reach (and in some cases not used at all).

THIS CAGE OR CRATE PROVIDES A SECURE HOME.

Try to look at your garden through a dog's eyes and to see any potential hazards from a dog's eye level. It may be necessary to insert paving stones around your garden fence to prevent it from digging and burrowing. Check the whole garden for holes and gaps, which are especially attractive to puppies, which have tendency to explore every nook and cranny without giving any thought to how they might get out of small cracks and crevices. High-sided ponds are another potential hazard for puppies, which, if they fell in, would find it difficult to climb out of again. If your dog turns out to be a persistent digger, consider converting a corner of the garden into a sandpit where it can bury its toys. Instead of punishing it for digging elsewhere, reward it with a treat every time that it digs in the sandpit.

THIS DOG PATROLS HIS TERRITORY.

ENSURE THAT GARDEN HAZARDS LIKE THIS POND ARE ADEQUATELY FENCED TO AVOID ACCIDENTS.

Inside, carry out the same checks that you would make before the arrival of a toddler. Tidy away all trailing electrical wires, stabilise fragile furniture and, if necessary, remove treasured ornaments until the new dog or puppy has settled in. Place any toxic houseplants well out of the dog's reach, too. In the case of a puppy, remove anything that looks remotely chewable, such as shoes, gloves, children's toys and even the post on the doormat. Give the dog three chewable toys of different textures and never leave a dog that likes chewing alone in a room that contains live electric wires.

CHECK THAT YOUR DOG CANNOT DIG UNDER FENCES.

A HIGH, STURDY FENCE KEEPS DOGS SAFE.

# INTRODUCING A DOG TO OTHER PETS

Contrary to the image projected in cartoons, dogs and cats are not natural enemies and will happily co-exist if properly introduced. Try to ensure that the cat does not run away from the dog while they are being introduced – and restrain the dog – because this will simply induce the dog to chase the cat. It will then try to frighten the cat into running away each time that they subsequently meet simply for the fun of it, which will not make for a peaceful household. It may be worth putting the cat into a basket or cage for the first meeting, which will allow the dog to sniff it and satisfy its curiosity without making mischief.

*YOUNG DOGS CAN LEARN FROM OLDER ANIMALS.*

*MANY DOGS AND CATS CO-EXIST HAPPILY.*

Many owners fail to realise how much a single dog (rather like an only child) can miss the fun and companionship provided by another dog. Once a dog slows down in middle age, the introduction of another dog to the household may perk it up. Introduce them on neutral ground, away from sleeping or feeding areas. Never give either dog preferential treatment and do not leave the two dogs alone together until they have established a good relationship.

# POINTS FOR CONSIDERATE DOG-OWNERSHIP

- Remember that not everyone shares your love of your dog. Some people are genuinely scared of dogs, for a variety of reasons, and although their behaviour may appear irrational, the considerate dog-owner will respect their feelings.

- Never take your dog for a walk without a lead. If traffic is visible, even at a distance, it is simply too dangerous to allow a dog to run free: if something catches its eye, it may run off into the path of on-coming vehicles. Even in woodland areas, where dogs can run freely, it may either encounter horse-riders or small children or may disappear to chase rabbits, making a lead useful, if only for momentary control.

- Carry some doggy treats with which to bribe your dog. Give it one before letting it off the lead and another as a reward when it returns when called.

- Never leave your dog in an unventilated car.

- Although parks and beaches are excellent open spaces for exercising dogs, try to retain a degree of control over your dog. Some parents are nervous of dogs near children's play areas and few people appreciate being showered with water as a wet dog races past them on a beach.

- Never let your dog foul the pavement – make it defaecate in the gutter, 'scoop the poop' and dispose of it either in a toilet or a specially provided bin. At home, encourage your dog to use one corner of the garden so that you do not always have to watch where you're walking.

*THE POOP-SCOOP – A VITAL PIECE OF EQUIPMENT.*

# EQUIPMENT

Although there is a huge variety of equipment available with which to pamper dogs of all shapes, sizes and ages, the basic equipment needed to make your dog comfortable and safe is quite limited. At the very least, a dog needs a collar and lead, a comfortable sleeping area, a few items of grooming equipment and food and water bowls.

## COLLARS, TAGS, LEADS AND HARNESSES

Collars are available in leather, nylon or cotton in a range of styles and prices. Simple buckle collars suit many dogs, but a half-check collar with a 'choke chain' may be more suitable for restraining energetic animals. Rolled-leather collars make a smaller indentation in a dog's coat than flat collars.

A puppy's first collar should be lightweight and inexpensive (it will soon outgrow it). When fitting a collar, ensure that it is loose enough to allow you to slip at least two fingers underneath it and that it will not slip over the puppy's head when it pulls back against it. Allow a puppy gradually to grow accustomed to wearing its collar by fitting it for an hour or two at a time.

PRACTISE BASIC OBEDIENCE LESSONS AT HOME.

A BASIC ENGRAVED IDENTITY TAG.

AN ELECTRONIC TAG.

the back of a dog's neck. The chip carries a number unique to the dog, which is stored on a national database and refers to information about the dog and its vaccinations, its owner and address. The microchip is read by a scanner that uses low-frequency waves to activate it.

MICRO-CHIPPING IS A PAINLESS PROCEDURE.

In Britain, dog-owners are legally obliged to attach some form of identification to their dogs, so either fit an identity tag engraved with your address or telephone number to its collar or have your dog microchipped, a relatively new method of labelling dogs that must be carried out by a vet. Microchipping is an easy process, no more painful than a vaccination, in which a microchip, the size of a grain of rice (encased in biocompatible glass to prevent rejection by the dog's body), is implanted in the loose fold of skin on

It is imperative that you maintain control over your dog, particularly in public places, so once your dog is used to wearing a collar, attach a lightweight lead to it before taking it for walks. You will probably need a short lead, about 2 m (6 ft) in length; a long training lead, about 6 m (20 ft) in length, made of cotton or meshed nylon; and a long houseline for use at home.

*LEATHER LEADS ARE HARD-WEARING.*

*LONGER LEADS ARE USEFUL DURING TRAINING.*

Some boisterous dogs, or breeds with especially fragile windpipes, such as Yorkshire terriers, may need a body harness or halter instead of a lead. Head halters are similar to those used on horses and enable you to exert a little more control over energetic large dogs (when the dog runs off, pressure is applied to the halter, which pulls the head down). Ask your vet for advice if you are unsure about the best lead for your dog.

*BELOW: BODY HARNESSES PROVIDE EXTRA CONTROL.*

# BEDDING

All dogs appreciate a place of their own, where they feel secure. It must be away from draughts and provide sufficient warmth for the dog (obviously, long-haired breeds are better insulated than short-coated ones). A moulded-plastic dog bed lined with a small doggy mattress will provide both the security of 'walls' to lie against and the comfort of a soft surface.

**BEDS MUST BE PLACED AWAY FROM DRAUGHTS.**

**DOGS APPRECIATE THEIR OWN SPACE.**

Your dog's bedding needs to be washable and comfortable. As well as being washable, synthetic, fake-fur material is warm, and dogs appear to love snuggling into it. Bean-bag beds, another popular style, are well insulated, mould themselves to the dog's body and are exceptionally snug. Wicker baskets, which were once popular, are, however, both difficult to clean and, particularly in the case of puppies, eminently chewable.

Puppies' beds can be temporary affairs, but must be either disposable or easy to clean. A cardboard box with a piece cut out of the front and lined with newspaper and an old blanket are adequate to start with. As the puppy grows, it can graduate to a proper bed.

**BEDS CAN BE MADE FROM SIMPLE CARDBOARD BOXES.**

If you intend to keep your dog outside, you will need to provide it with a secure, weatherproof outbuilding furnished with a comfortable bed. (If it has a concrete floor, make sure that the bed is raised.) The kennel (or shed) must have ventilation and

**OUTDOOR DOG KENNELS MUST BE SNUG AND DRY.**

light provided by a window so that it will not become too hot in warm weather. Purpose-built kennels with runs attached are another option; usually constructed of wood, these are easy to scrub down and keep clean.

# GROOMING EQUIPMENT

All dogs need regular grooming, but it clearly takes longer to maintain the coats of long-haired breeds. Although it is important to train your dog to sit still during grooming sessions, most dogs accept – and even enjoy – basic grooming, which consists of brushing the coat, cleaning the face and checking the nails (which should be trimmed with special nailclippers for dogs).

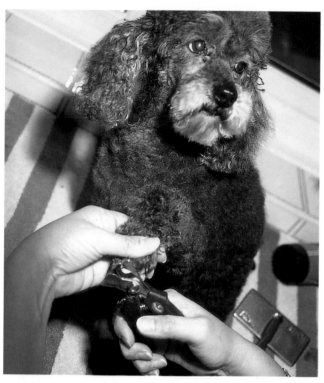

NAIL-CLIPPING IS PART OF REGULAR GROOMING.

There is a wide variety of grooming equipment on sale to suit every type of coat, and your choice should depend on your dog's coat, although every dog-owner will need a brush and comb. Short-haired dogs, such as boxers, require a hard brush that massages the skin while removing loose hair, but this would be entirely unsuitable on the long coat of a rough collie, for example. A rubber brush and a chamois cloth are also useful, the latter for 'polishing' the coat to produce a healthy shine. Fine-haired dogs, such as Yorkshire terriers, must be brushed with a soft pin brush and a wide-toothed comb, while breeds with thick coats, such as sheepdogs, require brisk brushing with a soft pin brush, a comb and a firm bristle brush. Long-haired dogs can be groomed with a 'slicker' brush to tease out tangles; a bristle brush to enhance the coat's shine; a comb to part the coat neatly and to comb the legs; and scissors to trim the hair around the paws. Trimmed breeds, such as poodles, will need trimming every two months or so with electric clippers, which must be sharpened regularly by a professional service. A breeder or vet will be able to advise on the most suitable grooming equipment for your pet.

# FOOD BOWLS

Dogs should have their own food and water bowls, which must be kept apart from human utensils. Although dogs are perfectly clean, a number of zoonotic diseases can be passed from animals to humans through poor hygiene. For the same reason, it is sensible to dedicate a special can-opener, spoon and fork to dog-food preparation.

Dogs' appetites vary according to the size of the animal: big breeds have hearty appetites, for instance, in which case buy large food and water bowls. Available in metal, plastic or ceramic designs, bowls must be robust, easy to clean, hard to tip over, unattractive to dogs that like chewing and reasonably heavy so that the dog cannot pick them up. If you have more than one dog, each must have its own food bowl. Place the bowls on a mat to absorb any spills.

Clean the food bowl after each meal and replenish the water bowl at least once a day.

A RAISED FEEDING BOWL FOR OLDER DOGS.

# TOYS

Dogs are naturally inclined to pull, chase and tug things, and puppies are especially keen on chewing, so if you want to avoid your home and possessions being damaged, invest in a few toys.

A CHEWY TOY SLIPPER.

CHEWY TOYS ARE POPULAR WITH DOGS OF ALL AGES.

Make sure that toys are well made and too large to be swallowed. Rubber and rope tug toys are ideal for indoors, while Frisbees, soft rubber balls and throw toys on a rope make good outdoor toys. Dogs also enjoy bone-shaped chewies or squeaky toys (although the sound of these may either irritate you or over-excite your dog).

# TRAVEL

Dogs often have to travel with their owners in cars, whether it be to a park for exercise, to the vet or on longer trips. Some dogs become very excited by car travel and will bark, leap around or pace, behaviour that is neither safe nor peaceful in the confined space of a family car. Although most dogs experience no ill effects during car journeys, there are a number of ways of both improving your dog's in-car safety and making the trip more comfortable for it.

A PET CARRIER IS USEFUL TO TRANSPORT PUPPIES.

MAKE SURE YOUR DOG IS SECURE IN THE CAR.

Try to accustom your dog to travelling by car from an early age. Young puppies are often car sick, but this is usually a problem that they grow out of. Do not feed a dog immediately before car travel. Before beginning a long journey, exercise your dog; it is also advisable to stop every two hours to allow the dog to have a run, relieve itself and have a drink.

Either put an old sheet or rug over the back seat or, if you have an estate vehicle or hatchback, settle your dog at the rear of the car (fit a metal grille to prevent the dog from leaping in to the seating area). A crate-trained dog will happily lie securely in its crate for journeys of any length; not only is this probably the most secure method of transporting a dog, but, in the event of an accident, it will ensure that the dog will not be flung around the car. Another alternative is to train your dog to sit in a purpose-built, moulded travel container secured within the car.

In hot weather, make sure that your car is well ventilated and carry a flask of water and a bowl so that your dog can have a drink. Try not to leave your dog alone in your car, but if you really must, ensure that it is well ventilated and park in the shade if possible. Never leave your dog in a car without opening the windows slightly: dogs have poor control of their body temperature and can easily become overheated, often fatally so. If the weather is really hot, leave the dog at home, where it will be more comfortable.

*A GRILLE PREVENTS DOGS LEAPING AROUND THE CAR.*

# HOLIDAYS

Before acquiring a dog, think about what you will do when you go away on holiday. Do you have a friend living nearby who could accommodate your pet? If not, consider kennels as an alternative. Ask dog-owning friends for their recommendations or get a list of local kennels from your vet.

*KENNELS ARE USEFUL WHILE DOG OWNERS ARE AWAY.*

All good kennels should be open for inspection. Check that the dogs are exercised and appear well groomed and try to chat to the staff – enthusiastic employees are a sign of a good kennels. The kennels staff should ask to see vaccination certificates to guard against the introduction of disease, and will also need information about your dog's diet, medication and infirmities. Prices vary according to the facilities; at the very least, kennels

should provide secure, weatherproof accommodation and adequate food. It is advisable to book well in advance of popular holiday periods.

Boarding can be upsetting for a dog, especially one with a strong attachment to its owner, so the younger a dog starts boarding, the better, because it will learn that the stay in kennels is only temporary. If you do your research properly, you will be able to leave your dog secure in the knowledge that it will be well cared for in your absence.

However, you may prefer to hire a dog-sitter to care for it in your home. Vets can usually provide a list of reputable house- and dog-sitting services.

*MOST DOGS IN KENNELS ARE VERY WELL-CARED FOR.*

## CHAPTER 4

# PUPPIES

Irresistibly cute, furry bundles of fun and mischief – and lots of hard work – puppies are especially appealing. Hard-boiled individuals who would never consider pet-ownership often find themselves bowled over by a desire to look after these little creatures, and children persistently pester their parents for a furry playmate. The desire to protect small creatures is inherent in us all, but what happens when the cuddly ball of fur grows into a large, demanding dog? And how can you get it to obey your commands? Most importantly, just how long does it take to house-train your pooch?

# THE FIRST WEEKS

For the first two weeks of life, puppies are completely dependent on their mother for warmth, food and protection as their senses develop, their eyes open and they gradually begin to respond to the world around them. During the next two weeks, puppies become a little more independent, wagging their tails, growling, barking and starting to move away from their mother as their bodies become able to control their temperature more efficiently. They then begin a period of intense socialisation, when they absorb smells, sights, sounds, touches and experiences, all of which will help them in adult life. It is vital that puppies have human contact during these early weeks so that they grow accustomed to people. The wider a dog's experience as a puppy, the more adaptable it will be in later life.

**PUPPIES SPEND THEIR FIRST FEW WEEKS SIMPLY EATING AND SLEEPING.**

**PUPPIES ARE FUN, UNDENIABLY CUTE. . . AND A LOT OF HARD WORK!**

# COLLECTING A PUPPY

Puppies are usually taken away from their mother between six and twelve weeks of age. This is inevitably a stressful time for a young dog, and it is important for new owners to establish a feeling of security and trust. Try to collect your new puppy in the morning so that it will have a day to explore its new home and get used to new faces, smells and sounds before going to sleep. Arrange for two people to collect the puppy so that one can sit with it in the back of the car (and remember to protect the seat with an old towel or blanket in case it is car sick).

**RIGHT: PUPPIES MUST GET USED TO BEING HANDLED.**

# BEDDING AND BEDTIME

Having carried out the safety checks recommended on pages 50 to 51, introduce the puppy to its sleeping area. Until it is house-trained, it probably makes sense to house him in the kitchen, where spills and accidents are more easily cleared up. Because the kitchen is also likely to be warm, and full of welcoming smells, it provides a good introduction to a new home.

Housing the puppy's bed within a playpen will enable it to have a secure place of its own, as well as preventing it from getting up to mischief. Puppies need a large amount of sleep, so it is important to provide a quiet site, away from the excitement of the household, where it can snooze after meals. Line its bed with newspaper to absorb the inevitable accidents.

THIS BEAN-BAG STYLE BED IS IDEAL FOR YOUNG DOGS AS IT IS WARM AND COSY – RATHER LIKE THEIR MOTHERS.

THE WALLS OF THIS BED PROVIDE A FEELING OF SECURITY FOR YOUR DOG.

There are several theories about how to deal with new puppies at night. Like human babies, puppies are likely to wake up, when they'll find a human presence very comforting. However, they must become used to falling asleep alone, and it is never too early to start training. Your approach will probably depend on how strong-willed you are in the face of a small, upset dog.

One recommendation is to tuck it up snugly next to a ticking alarm clock, which simulates the beating of its mother's heart, before leaving it to sleep. A few whines are inevitable, but it should settle eventually. (Remember to cover the floor with newspaper and not to leave it for longer than six hours without taking it outside to relieve itself.)

Another school of thought, however, advocates putting the puppy's bed in the owner's bedroom for the first few nights in a new home. This will provide the security of knowing that a human presence is close, and also means that you will not have to trek down to the kitchen if you need to re-settle the dog. If you opt for this approach, make sure that your puppy naps alone during the day and gradually extend this habit until it is spending the night alone in its designated sleeping area.

A MAT WILL PROVIDE A SOFT DRAUGHT-FREE SURFACE.

If your dog has been crate-trained, travel is made easier because you can use the crate in the car, thus providing your dog with a safe and secure travelling environment.

## CRATE-TRAINING

Crates may appear to be little more than cages, but if a dog has been accustomed to one since it was a puppy, it will regard it as a secure place. Crates, which differ from playpens in that they cover a smaller area, should only be used for resting or sleeping. Do not leave a puppy in a crate for more than two hours during the day.

**1** Place soft bedding, a bowl of water and a toy inside the crate. Leave the door open, and your puppy will probably wander inside out of curiosity.

**2** Show your puppy a treat, put the treat into the crate and say 'Go to your crate' to lure the puppy inside. Keep the door open.

**3** Do not close the door until your puppy is used to being in the crate – this may take a couple of sessions.

**4** Once your puppy appears happy inside its crate, take it outside for some exercise, then encourage it to return to its crate, where it will probably play quietly before falling asleep.

# HOUSE-TRAINING

Dogs are clean animals who will try to avoid soiling their sleeping areas, and house-training is simply about encouraging them to relieve themselves in a place that is convenient to the owner. It is a process that requires perseverance and patience, but daytime habits can probably be established within a week.

Dogs often sniff the ground before urinating, or else circle rapidly, so watch out for these signs and then act quickly because there will only be seconds between warning and performance. Puppies usually want to urinate as soon as they wake up and after a meal, so prepare for this either by taking your puppy outside or putting it on some newspaper on awakening, after each meal and last thing at night. Make sure that you provide regular opportunities for it to relieve itself throughout the day.

KEEP TEMPTING SHOES AWAY FROM YOUNG DOGS.

TREATS ARE USEFUL TO HELP TRAIN PUPPIES.

Dog faeces is both unpleasant and a health risk, so always clean up after your dog. Use a plastic bag or 'pooper scooper' to clear up the mess and either dispose of it in a dog bin or flush it down the toilet. Clean up any accidents inside the house with disinfectant, but try to avoid products which smell of ammonia because this may remind the puppy of the smell of its own urine.

TEACH PUPS TO ASK TO GO OUTSIDE – QUICKLY!

To encourage your puppy to use the same area again, keep a piece of soiled newspaper and put it underneath the top sheet of fresh newspaper. The puppy will recognise its own odour and quickly learn to use the same spot. If you take your puppy outside, take it to the same spot each time and encourage it with a command, such as 'Be quick' or 'Hurry up'. Praise your puppy extravagantly when it has urinated in the correct place.

Never discipline a puppy when it has had an accident on the floor, nor rub its nose in the mess, because these actions will simply make it scared of you. If you see it urinating (or worse) indoors, say 'No' very sternly, and then move it to your designated spot. Never play with your puppy outside until it has performed.

RIGHT: PUPPIES MUST BE TAUGHT TO GO TO SLEEP ALONE.

complete DOG

# FEEDING

Breeders often supply the owners of new puppies with a diet sheet, and it is sensible to follow it closely. If you suddenly change a puppy's diet, it may result in an upset stomach, so if you want to make any changes, do so gradually and allow the puppy to adjust itself to the new food.

Puppies are usually weaned off their mother's milk by the age of five or six weeks. Once they can eat and drink on their own, they like to eat little and often; an eight-week-old dog should probably have four small meals each day. Adjust this amount over time, so that by six months your dog is on two meals a day, and on just one by the time it is a year old. (Naturally, the amount of food must be increased!) As they become bigger, puppies' lack of enthusiasm for first one, then another, feed becomes obvious, so the reduction in the number of meals is a natural progression. Some small dogs, or breeds with sensitive stomachs, such as borzois, thrive better on two or three small meals even as adults.

The nutritional requirements of growing puppies are considerable, and it is essential for the dog's general health that it receives a balanced diet. A good diet helps to realise the puppy's potential for growth and development; a diet that

*ABOVE: ADJUST YOUR DOG'S DIET TO ACCOMMODATE HIS CHANGING NEEDS AS HE GROWS.*

*REAL BONES MAY SPLINTER INSIDE A DOG'S MOUTH, SO USE MANUFACTURED ONES LIKE THIS, INSTEAD.*

is in some way deficient may mean that a dog fails to reach the full physical potential of its breed.

Dogs need protein, essential fatty acids, mineral elements, vitamins and carbohydrates. Calcium is critical, but they do not need fruit or green vegetables because their bodies make plenty of vitamin C. Water is also, of course, essential, and every dog should have constant access to a clean bowl of water.

PROTECT YOUR HOME FROM A CHEWING PUPPY.

DRIED FOOD IS CONVENIENT AND DELICIOUS.

Dog-food manufacturers produce special foods for puppies, whose calorie requirement is quiet high in comparison to their size. Consult your vet if you are unsure about any aspect of your pet's diet. (See pages 98 for more information about diets.)

Puppies are relentless chewers. Teething occurs around the ages of four to six months and again at six to eight months, when the adult teeth erupt; chewing helps this process, as well as providing a bit of relief from teething pain. Protect vulnerable items in your home either by removing them from sight or sprinkling pepper on items like electric flexes to discourage damage. Alternatively, buy a non-toxic, bitter-tasting spray from your vet or pet shop to spray on objects that you do not want to be chewed. Give your puppy a chewable toy to play with, such as a large rubber bone, but not an old slipper because it will not understand that other shoes and slippers are out of bounds. Make sure that your puppy understands what it can chew and what it must not touch, otherwise poor behavioural patterns will become established, which will be hard to break.

# BEHAVIOUR AT FEEDING TIME

Dogs have a primitive instinct to guard their feeding bowls tenaciously, and are very competitive at meal times. Although such behaviour may seem sweet in a puppy, it is less amusing in an adult dog, so discourage it by deliberately approaching your puppy while it is feeding and then patting or moving its bowl slightly. Reward the puppy if it allows you to do this without complaint. As the puppy becomes used to this, it will understand that its food is safe and should become less defensive.

Dogs must also learn that they should eat after their owners and then only from their own bowls. This r einforces the fact that the owner is dominant and the 'pack leader' in the household.

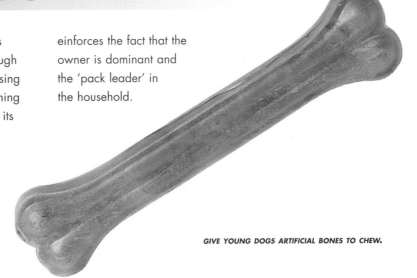

GIVE YOUNG DOGS ARTIFICIAL BONES TO CHEW.

# VACCINATIONS

Until a puppy has completed its course of vaccinations, it is at risk of infection, both from other dogs and from infections that may be carried into the house on visitors' clothes. Restrict its outings until it is protected.

The vaccination regime varies from puppy to puppy, and is dependent on the level of immunity passed to the young dog through its mother's milk, as well as disease problems in a particular area. Your vet will advise you on the best course of action, but puppies are generally inoculated at eight weeks, twelve weeks and eighteen weeks of age against distemper, hepatitis, parvovirus and leptospirosis. The first combined vaccination is given at eight weeks and repeated at twelve weeks, when the first dose of parvovirus vaccine is administered, which is boosted at eighteen weeks.

Leptospirosis is a bacterial disease that affects the liver and kidneys, while parvovirus is a highly infectious, and often fatal, viral disease that affects the heart and bowel. Kennel-cough vaccine may also be administered at the first-stage vaccination. Booster injections are given at regular intervals throughout the dog's life, although the hepatitis vaccination confers life-long protection.

*BELOW: ALL DOGS MUST BE VACCINATED AGAINST COMMON CANINE ILLNESSES.*

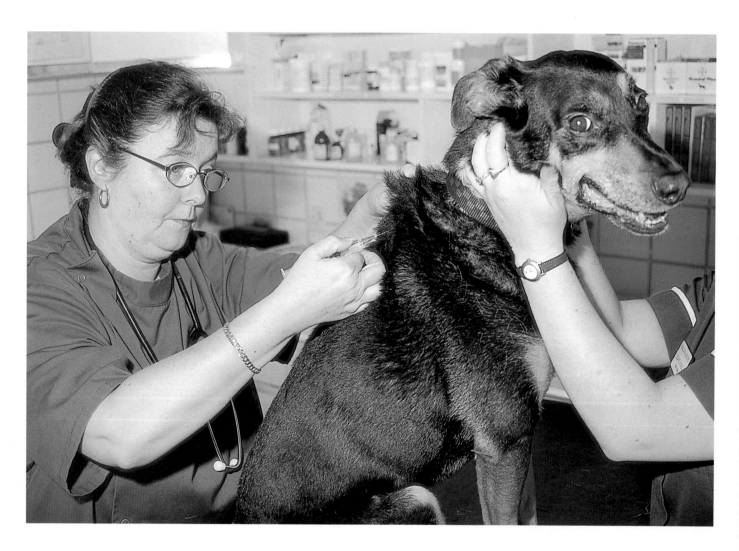

# BASIC TRAINING AND EXERCISE

YOU SHOULD IMPOSE YOUR RULES UPON A PUPPY AS SOON AS IT ENTERS YOUR HOUSEHOLD. IT MUST LEARN THE BASICS:
- to wear a collar and lead and obey the family
- to eat only from its own food bowl
- to sleep in its own bed
- to come when called
- to wait on command.

Choosing, and then using, a suitable name for your dog is an important part of a puppy's training. Pick a short, simple name and use it frequently when addressing your puppy.

A puppy understands only a few words and will respond more to tone of voice than to what is actually being said, so choose one word for a command and stick to it; do not, for example, alternate between 'come' and 'here' in recall training because this will confuse your dog. Speak softly to your dog – this forces it to listen hard to what you're saying. Use hand signals to reinforce your commands, especially outdoors.

Puppies are energetic creatures, but tire quickly. They obviously need less exercise than adult dogs; treat even large breeds with caution because they take longer to mature than smaller breeds and their legs and joints can be permanently damaged by too much exercise.

**COMMAND**

Because a puppy's attention span is limited, keep lessons short. Fifteen-minute sessions four times a day are probably enough for a young dog. Always praise your dog when it has obeyed a command. Edible treats are also an excellent way of showing your puppy that you are pleased with it, but as you repeat the exercises, decrease the treats until it responds to your

**ENCOURAGE**

commands without being bribed. Most importantly, keep training sessions fun and be aware that because your puppy regards your training sessions as just another play activity, you'll need to be patient and keep your sense of humour. Always end a training session with a short period of play time.

**REWARD**

complete DOG

# TRAINING A YOUNG DOG TO WEAR A COLLAR AND LEAD

**1** Let your puppy see and sniff the collar and lead while you are both indoors.

Put the collar and lead on your puppy for short periods so that it becomes used to them. Never use a choke or check chain on a puppy: a sharp tug may frighten it and a loose chain may snag on an obstacle, strangling the dog. (See also page 53.)

**2** Attach a lightweight lead to the collar, keep it slack and begin walking while calling the puppy by name. If the dog sets off in another direction, go with it, keeping the lead slack and talking to it. The aim is accustom the puppy to the feel of the lead.

After five or six lessons, when the puppy is used to wearing the collar and lead at home, take it for a short, fifteen-minute walk around the streets. Try to understand how overwhelming traffic, rushing people and the attendant noise may be for your dog.

# NEW EXPERIENCES

To a young dog, the world outside the house is strange, frightening and full of excitement, so you'll need to train it to deal with new experiences. To do this, train your puppy to understand simple commands in the house and introduce it to a variety of new experiences, such as meeting strangers and children, getting used to car journeys, playing with other animals and developing road sense.

*ALLOW PUPPIES TO SNIFF OTHER PETS.*

*RIGHT: SPEND AS MUCH TIME AS POSSIBLE WITH YOUR NEW DOG.*

become accustomed to the noises and smells, command it to sit every time that you come to a kerb. Your dog will soon learn to sit and wait for your command before crossing a road. Never let your dog off a lead in a busy urban area, however well-trained it may be.

To accustom your puppy to meeting strangers, try to introduce it to someone who looks completely dissimilar to you – perhaps someone with a beard, someone wearing a hat or someone carrying an unusual object. Let the puppy sniff this person until it realises that although he or she may look different, the stranger is just another friendly human being. Arrange for such meetings to take place both indoors and outdoors so that the dog becomes used to the approach of strangers.

Make sure that whoever is meeting the dog bends down to the dog's level and perhaps offers a small treat as an incentive.

When you think that your dog is ready, start to teach it road sense. This is nothing less than a survival technique for dogs, who must learn to stop at kerbs. To a small dog, cars and lorries may appear very intimidating at first, but once it has

**ROAD SAFETY: TEACH YOUR DOG TO STOP AT KERBS.**

## CHAPTER 5

# EXERCISES AND TRAINING

Dogs must be trained to teach them their place in life and their status within the family. Intelligent, untrained dogs will get into trouble, perhaps causing road accidents, worrying sheep, frightening strangers and generally making themselves unpopular within the neighbourhood. Owners who do not train their dogs in the basics of good behaviour are irresponsible: badly behaved dogs should not be blamed for any mayhem that they may cause – it is the fault of their owners. British legislation reflects this, and dog-owners are obliged to control their pets wherever they are. The 1991 Dangerous Dogs Act states that it is a criminal offence to allow your dog to be out of control in a public place, including your car, and if anyone feels threatened by your dog (let alone actually attacked by it), they are within their rights to report you, as its owner, to the police. If you are found guilty under this act, your dog could be destroyed, and you could receive a prison sentence of six months and/or a £5,000 fine.

# EXERCISE

Although exercise is vital for every dog, whatever its age, size or breed, each dog has, of course, different requirements. It is not enough just to let your dog run around the garden because dogs that are not adequately exercised may revert to destructive or unacceptable behaviour. Dogs benefit from organised exercise: not only does it provide a physical outlet for their energy, but they love games and find them mentally stimulating. You do not have to stick to a rigorous daily regime that never varies – change the route of your walk, alter the length or finish off with games in a park on some days, but if you don't want to do this every day, don't. Never forget who is supposed to be in charge!

Generally, bigger breeds need more exercise than smaller ones, but there are exceptions: Saint Bernards, for example, do not enjoy the same sort of terrain and distance that Border collies thrive on. Be aware that once it has been let off the lead, an active young dog will probably run two or three times the distance that you will walk. As a rough guide, a medium-sized dog, such as a golden retriever, will enjoy a walk of about five to six kilometres (around three to four miles) every day, and this distance is the minimum for larger dogs like mature Afghan hounds. Older dogs may prefer two short walks a day rather than one long one.

*ENTHUSIASTIC DOGS SHOULD BE TAUGHT NOT TO JUMP UP AT STRANGERS.*

*EXERCISING SHOULD BE AN ENJOYABLE TIME FOR YOU AND YOUR DOG.*

# GAMES

Playing games with your dog emphasises your control and dominance, but games are also fun and provide mental and physical stimulation. They are a great way of channelling your dog's energies, sustaining its attention and thus alleviating any risk of destructive behaviour. Make sure that you tailor the games to suit your pet. Don't overstretch old or frail dogs because they will simply become frustrated, while strenuous activity may endanger their health.

You can generally rely on the tried-and-tested game of fetch, in which you throw a stick for your dog to chase and retrieve, but there are a variety of doggy toys available, too. Use Frisbees, balls and tug toys to amuse your dog. It will enjoy trying to catch a Frisbee and then returning it to you. Dogs love ball games and will relish simply chasing a ball because this reflects natural canine behaviour in chasing prey. Try playing catch

DOGS LOVE PLAYING TOGETHER; AN OBSTACLE COURSE PROVIDES MENTAL AS WELL AS PHYSICAL STIMULATION.

*AGILITY TRAINING: CERTAIN BREEDS LOVE JUMPING THROUGH HOOPS AND OVER HURDLES.*

and drop by throwing a ball for your dog to catch and then encouraging it to surrender the ball to you. (Never throw a ball directly at a dog in case it injures it – throw it away from the dog so that it can jump for the ball.) If your dog enjoys playing tug-of-war, make sure that the tug toy is robust enough to stand the strain. Indoor games, like hunt the treat or hide and seek, are also stimulating and fun.

It is important to finish a session of games with a human 'victory', otherwise the dog will think that it is the dominant partner. When you have finished playing, put the toys away in a bag or box that is inaccessible to the dog. This will teach it that they are your toys and that it can only play with them when you allow it. These toys should be distinct from the one or two items that are your dog's toys, however, which should be available to it all of the time.

*TWO DOGS ENJOY A GAME OF 'TUG'.*

# PLAYING WITH OTHER DOGS

Dogs enjoy playing with each other, although females are usually more willing to play than males, who may appear territorial at first. Dogs are likely to meet others when out for a walk in an area that they regard as neutral territory. Let the dogs sniff each other, but watch their body language for any signs of aggression, such as staring eye contact. If this happens, divert their attention with a toy. Fighting is less likely between dogs of different sexes, but it is sensible to keep the dogs on their leads during their first meeting. If appropriate, praise your dog for its calm and alert behaviour.

*INTRODUCE OLDER DOGS TO PUPPIES. DO NOT LEAVE THEM ALONE UNTIL THEY ARE USED TO EACH OTHER.*

*IF TWO DOGS MEET, THEY WILL INVARIABLY SNIFF EACH OTHER TO LEARN ABOUT SEX, LOCALITY AND DOMINANCE.*

# TRAINING

Training falls into several different categories. Firstly, behavioural training teaches a dog basic 'good manners', including how to behave around people, how to walk on a lead and house-training. Secondly, obedience training teaches a dog to perform specific activities like walking to heel or sitting and staying. Thirdly, activity training trains a dog in actions, such as retrieving, herding or agility performances.

Training helps to establish the human position as pack leader. If a dog respects its owner, it will want to obey him or her, so when training your dog, do not shout or become angry if it does not obey you, but instead persevere and take the time to teach your dog commands. Remember that its 'disobedience' may simply be caused by puzzlement and a break-down in communication: if it doesn't understand what you want, it can't carry out your commands. Being shouted at or physically punished will both scare a dog, causing it to become apprehensive around an owner who displays this kind of behaviour (and which may actually teach the dog itself to become aggressive). The most effective punishment for a disobedient dog is to ignore it. Because most dogs want attention and to feel that they are part of the pack, withdrawing your attention (including not looking at it) for ten minutes will probably have a greater effect than administering any physical or verbal punishment.

A daily routine of twenty minutes or more will help to reinforce obedience training. Overnight success is unlikely, however, so be patient and consistent. Praise your dog frequently and extravagantly to encourage it. It helps to make the command word part of a praise phrase, for example, by saying 'Lovely sit' in an pleased tone of voice. Including the command word within a praise phrase thus serves to reinforce the action without actually repeating the command itself.

It is relatively straightforward to teach young dogs most commands, and training itself is much easier if you begin with a young puppy. We have all heard the phrase 'You can't teach an old dog new tricks', so bear this in mind and work patiently with your pet.

*HAND SIGNALS (LIKE THIS FOR 'STOP') ARE USED TO REINFORCE VERBAL COMMANDS WHILE TRAINING.*

# INTRODUCING CHILDREN AND DOGS

Children must be taught how to treat a dog properly, but, equally, dogs must learn how to behave around children. Dogs recognise that children, who are smaller than adults (and often smaller than a dog), are not 'pack leaders', so may try to dominate them by nipping or growling.

Make sure that your children do not tease dogs by pulling their tails, invading their personal space, trying to use them for rides or squeezing them as though they were teddies. Children should also learn that not every dog is friendly and that they should approach all dogs with caution. Explain to them why some dogs may jump up at them and how to react – it is important that small children realise that if they throw up their hands in horror and squeal, the dog may think they are playing and continue jumping up. Never leave a child and a dog alone together until a child is both old enough to understand these rules and physically large enough to dominate the dog.

**RIGHT: CHILDREN MUST LEARN TO TREAT DOGS PROPERLY.**

## HOW TO INTRODUCE A CHILD TO YOUR DOG

**1** Put a lead on your dog. Let the child approach it, but make sure that he or she maintains eye contact with you rather than the dog. A dog will feel threatened by a staring child because it interprets staring as aggressive behaviour.

**2** Let the child stroke the dog along its side, but tell the child not to pat its head.

**3** Praise the dog for its good behaviour if appropriate, but reprimand it if it snaps or growls.

Dogs should be taught to lie down and relax while children are playing around them,

**WITH CARE, DOGS AND CHILDREN MAKE GREAT FRIENDS.**

even if they are doing something exciting like playing with a ball. Once you are confident that your dog can cope with older children, it will probably be able to deal with toddlers. If your dog is particularly prone to guarding or chasing, however, or if it has ever threatened anyone, it is sensible to muzzle it in the presence of toddlers.

Dogs are generally curious about babies, so if one has recently joined your household, ask a friend or your partner to help you to introduce the dog to your new offspring. Babies' flailing limbs and cries may startle even the most placid of animals, so it's important that your dog becomes used to the new arrival. One of you should hold the baby and the other the dog's lead. Let the dog see and sniff the baby, but not touch it. If the dog behaves well, praise it and play with it while the baby is in the room. It is also sensible to feed the dog in the baby's presence to show it that it has not been supplanted in your affections.

But remember: however gentle your pet, never, ever leave it alone with a baby or small child.

# ENCOURAGING GOOD BEHAVIOUR

The best way of encouraging a dog to do what you want is to use positive reinforcement, that is, to reward good behaviour and ignore, or gently correct, bad behaviour. Physical or verbal punishment is not only unacceptable, but self-defeating. A reward should increase the occurrence of the desired behaviour; a correction should decrease it.

It is important to be consistent in your behaviour and to remain patient – it is all too easy for a dog to confuse rewards and corrections. For example, if your dog is on the other side of a field and persistently ignores your calls, you may become cross. If you shout at it or otherwise show your anger when it finally returns, you will actually be punishing the dog for obeying your command (however slowly!) when you should have rewarded it. A dog associates corrections or rewards with its most recent action, so in this case it will associate returning to its owner with being punished.

**ADMINISTER REWARDS FOR GOOD BEHAVIOUR.**

## USE OF FOOD?

The use of food as a motivation for learning is the subject of controversy. Most trainers seem to agree that it certainly helps in the initial stages of teaching a dog a new command, but others believe that dogs should obey their owners simply because they have been told to do so. Some people simply dislike using food as a reward.

Dogs undeniably perform better when there is the prospect of a reward in sight, whether it is a snack, a squeaky toy or just verbal praise. The trick is discovering what makes your dog work most productively.

When teaching a new command, reward the dog with a treat the first few times that it performs well, then reward it randomly. This way, the dog will try even harder to earn the reward.

*RIGHT: DOGS USUALLY PERFORM BETTER IF FOOD IS OFFERED.*

# SPECIAL EQUIPMENT

It is unlikely that you will need to acquire extra equipment for any of the training exercises included in this book. However, some excitable dogs or particularly large breeds may be easier to control if they are fitted with a head halter or body harness. Dogs with delicate windpipes or those with strong necks and small heads may also be more comfortable wearing a body harness than a lead. Head halters are similar to horse halters in that they pull the dog's head downwards if it tries to run off. They are especially useful for controlling large dogs. (See Chapter 3, page 53, for more information about harnesses, halters and leads.)

**USE A MUZZLE TO CURB AGGRESSIVE DOGS.**

Consider fitting a muzzle to your dog if it is a persistent scavenger and eater of unsuitable items or if it is destructive or seems aggressive. It may be prudent to muzzle your dog when it meets babies or small children for the first time, too. Dogs adjust very quickly to basket muzzles, which are spacious enough to enable barking and panting. Never leave a muzzle on an unsupervised dog.

## TRAINING TIPS

- Train your dog in a quiet area where there are no distractions.
- Never become angry with your dog or administer physical punishment.
- Reward your dog (with food, a toy or encouraging words) as soon as it has performed a task successfully.
- Keep training sessions short (ten to fifteen minutes to begin with) so that the dog does not become bored.
- Concentrate on encouraging your dog to master one task at a time.
- Try to make training fun!

**PERSISTENTLY AGGRESSIVE DOGS SHOULD BE MUZZLED WHEN THEY ARE IN PUBLIC TO AVOID DANGEROUS FIGHTS.**

# BASIC COMMANDS
## RECALL TRAINING: 'COME!'

'Come!' is a vital command, without which no progress can be made with further training. Begin recall training inside before moving on to an enclosed area outside. Don't let your dog off the lead if there is any danger of it running off and not returning. Never call your dog over to reprimand it because it will associate the action with punishment and will therefore be reluctant to repeat the experience.

## INSIDE

**1** Stand a short distance away from your dog, holding a food treat in your hand. Let the dog see the treat and then say its name, followed by the command 'Come!'

**2** As the dog comes to you, praise it in a warm voice by saying 'Good dog'. Bend your knees to bring the treat closer to the dog and open your arms in a welcoming manner.

**3** Once the dog has reached you, kneel down so that you are level with it, praise it, give it the treat and stroke it.

# OUTSIDE (IN AN ENCLOSED SPACE)

**1** Many dogs, and particularly puppies, dislike being kept in control and will run off once they've been let off the lead. If this happens, it won't want to surrender its freedom either, so let it run around for a few minutes. When it slows down, call it by name and then say 'Come!'

**2** Your dog will probably respond by taking a step or two towards you. Praise it for this, saying 'Good dog'.

**3** Take one step backwards and encourage your dog to come closer by patting your leg to show where you want it to go. If it comes, do not instantly put its lead on, but pat it on the head, give it a treat, tell it how good it is . . . and then attach the lead.

**4** It will probably take time and patience to train your dog to come on command, and it is unlikely to perform first time. If it comes halfway towards you and then wanders off, move out of its line of sight and it should follow you out of curiosity. Never punish your dog for failing to respond. Instead continue practising until it responds immediately. When you are sure that it has mastered the routine, try it out in an open space.

**Troubleshooting**
If your dog does not respond to edible treats, use a toy to encourage it. If it is easily distracted, use a squeaky toy to get its attention.

# 'SIT!'

When your dog has learnt to obey the command 'Come!', it's time to teach it to sit on command. It is possible to teach some dogs to do this simply by saying 'Sit!' and gently pushing down their rump. Others may require more formal training, however.

**1** Put a lead on the dog and talk quietly to it, keeping the atmosphere calm. Face the dog and then move away, holding the lead in your left hand and a snack treat in your right.

**2** Tell the dog to come to you and, when it arrives, gradually move your right hand up and over its head. The dog will watch the treat and, as you see it bend its legs to sit down, give the command 'Sit!' If it does, praise the dog and give it the snack.

**3** Practise this command on your dog and gradually reduce the food rewards until a verbal command alone does the trick.

**Troubleshooting**

If the dog refuses to sit, hold its collar in one hand and press its hindquarters down with the other while saying 'Sit!' Once it has accomplished this, show it that you are pleased with it by praising it.

# 'STAY!'

**1** Attach a lead to the dog's collar. Command the dog to sit, and then, holding the lead loosely, step away from it. Now give the command 'Stay!' You can reinforce the command with a hand signal, by holding the palm of your hand in front of its face. (Remember that you must be consistent, so if you decide to use the hand signal, you must do so every time.)

**2** Walk slowly around the dog in a circle, maintaining eye contact with it. If it tries to get up, make it sit down again. If it stays still for the count of five, go back to it, praise it and give it a treat. Repeat the exercise, gradually moving further away for longer periods.

**3** Once your dog has mastered it, repeat the whole exercise, but this time drop the lead. While your dog is sitting obediently, give it a treat and praise it. Make sure that you do this before allowing it to move.

PUPPIES MUST LEARN TO SIT STILL WHILE A LEAD IS PUT ON.

**Troubleshooting**
This exercise may be quite difficult for your dog because its natural instinct is to go to you. If it tries to get up and does not stay, hold its collar with one hand while pressing down its hindquarters with the other.

DO NOT LET YOUR DOG OFF THE LEASH IN A PUBLIC PLACE UNTIL YOU ARE SURE IT WILL RESPOND TO YOUR COMMANDS.

# 'DOWN!'

As your dog gets older, train it to lie down while distracting activity is going on around it. If you can teach your dog to obey this command in such circumstances, you will be able to exert control over it if it tries to jump up at people. Initial training should take place in a quiet place, however.

**1** Conceal a treat in one hand. Tell your dog to sit and then let it see the treat in your hand.

**2** Move the treat-holding hand to the floor while saying 'Down!' The dog will probably move into the 'down' position in order to reach the treat.

## Troubleshooting

If a puppy is reluctant to lie down, raise it into the begging position and then, with one palm under each of its forelegs, lie it down and praise it. If it tries to jump up, hold it down by gently pushing on its withers for a few seconds.

*REWARD AND PRAISE YOUR DOG – AND KEEP PRACTISING.*

# 'DOWN AND STAY!'

**1** With your dog on a lead in the 'down' position, give the command 'Stay!' and walk away, still holding the lead. Maintain eye contact with your dog as you are walking away. Repeat the command 'Stay!' and praise your dog. When practising this exercise, gradually make it stay down for longer periods.

**2** Train your dog to stay down when you are out of sight by repeating steps 1 to 3 and then leaving the room. Peer through a crack or use a mirror to make sure that it does not move. After a few minutes, return and praise your dog while it is still lying down. Do this calmly so that you don't excite it.

**Troubleshooting**

If the dog gets up while you are out of the room, return, make it lie down again, repeat the 'Stay!' command and then remain in the room, moving around as it watches you.

# WALKING AT HEEL WITHOUT A LEAD 'HEEL!'

Because they enjoy human company, puppies especially naturally follow their owners. This makes it reasonably simple to train a dog to walk by your side without a lead from a very young age.

**1** Position the dog on your left. Hold a treat in your right hand and gently grasp its collar with your left. Call the dog by name and let it see the treat.

**2** Walk in a straight line and let the dog follow the treat as you give the command 'Heel!'

**3** Say 'Wait!' and then bend down next to the dog's right side to show it the treat.

**4** Holding the snack near the dog's nose, make a right turn and repeat the command 'Heel!' The dog will speed up to follow you and the treat.

**5** Holding its collar with your left hand, gently steer the dog to the left. Position your right, snack-holding, hand at a low level so that the dog follows you round to the left.

**6** Give the dog its reward and lots of praise.

# WALKING AT HEEL ON A LEAD: 'HEEL!'

Most dogs learn to walk at heel on a lead as puppies. Dogs should never be allowed to pull on their leads, which results in cross owners with sore shoulder muscles and dogs that are gasping for breath – no way to take an invigorating walk.

It is best to begin training your dog to walk at heel somewhere quiet, such as your garden. The aim of the exercise is for your dog to follow you closely, walking at your pace, with its head close to your left leg. Hold the lead in your right hand, taking up the slack with your left hand. (This is the most natural stance for right-handed individuals, but can, of course, be reversed if you are left-handed.)

**1** Begin by attaching a lead to the dog's collar. Call the dog by name and then say 'Heel!' in a commanding voice. If it follows you, walk forward with the lead held slackly.

**2** If it fails to respond, jerk the lead firmly and repeat the command. If it tries to walk ahead of you, slide your left hand down the lead to its collar and gently pull it back.

**3** After a couple of minutes of walking at heel, praise your dog fulsomely.

**4** If it slows down or tries to wander off, pull sharply on the lead and say 'Heel!' It will quickly learn that it is more comfortable to follow you as required.

**5** To turn right, gently push your dog with your left hand and repeat the command 'Heel!' To make a left turn, use a food treat to entice your dog to move forward and follow you, again saying 'Heel!'

**Troubleshooting**
Climbing up the lead: respond by saying 'No!' or 'Off!' very sternly. Tell the dog to sit and then start the exercise again. Try training the dog in a quiet spot inside, where it will not become excited or distracted.
Immobile dog: if the dog refuses to shift and collapses onto the floor, try encouraging it with a favourite toy. Do not shout or become angry. Cajole it into obeying by using lots of praise so that its confidence increases.
Pulling forwards: tell the dog to sit every time that it pulls forwards. If your dog is very lively, try using a head halter.

# RETRIEVING

**1** Retrieving is quite an advanced skill, but most breeds respond excellently to training. Use something like an old dog toy rather than a stick or a ball, as the dog will find it easier to identify. First, show the dog the object you wish him to retrieve. Let him sniff it and perhaps clutch it in his mouth. Do not let him play with it, however.

**2** Throw the object across the garden or field and give the command, 'Fetch!'. Your dog will probably not need any more encouragement to chase across the field and collect the object.

**3** Once the dog has the object, say 'Come' to make him approach you, then tell him to 'Give' to surrender the object. Reward him with lots of praise and patting. As a final reward, you can return the object to the dog.

# CORRECTING INAPPROPRIATE BEHAVIOUR

Dogs that have been well trained from an early age are unlikely to provide major problems as they get older. However, poorly trained animals may exhibit some bad habits that are both annoying and dangerous. If you adopted your dog from a rescue home, you may have to work quite hard to correct a few anti-social facets of its behaviour. Although some problems are the result of poor training, others are simply uncontrolled natural canine behaviour, while still others result from boredom, anxiety or frustration. This section, as well as pages 8 to 10 in Chapter 1, may help to explain why your dog behaves as it does.

## BARKING PROBLEMS

It is natural for dogs to bark when they are excited, frustrated, bored or want to convey a warning when they are in 'guard' mode, so the arrival of visitors will often precipitate a lot of noise. A barking dog is a useful deterrent against intruders, and short bursts of barking are a natural outlet for canine excitement, but sometimes dogs bark simply to gain attention, sometimes out of fear and sometimes as a sign of anxiety when they have been left alone.

BARKING CAN IRRITATE, SO SHOULD BE ADDRESSED.

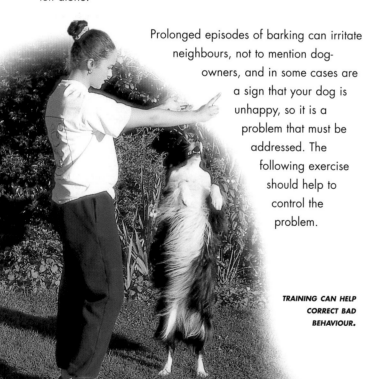

Prolonged episodes of barking can irritate neighbours, not to mention dog-owners, and in some cases are a sign that your dog is unhappy, so it is a problem that must be addressed. The following exercise should help to control the problem.

TRAINING CAN HELP CORRECT BAD BEHAVIOUR.

## AN EXERCISE TO CONTROL BARKING: 'QUIET!'

1 Show your dog a toy, but don't let it play with it. Reward it when it barks.

2 Put the toy in your pocket and verbally praise your dog when it barks, occasionally handing out a more tempting treat.

3 Watch the dog closely, give the command 'Speak!' and reward the dog when it barks.

4 When the dog understands the 'Speak!' command, say 'Quiet!' and reward the dog with the toy when it is silent. Put the toy away if it begins to bark again.

5 Repeat the exercise, but this time move further away from your dog.

Do not shout at your dog because it will think that you are simply sharing its excitement. It is best to ignore its barking for as long as you can and instead to accustom the dog to the events that wind it up. Initiate some obedience training to impose limits on the dog's behaviour on the occasions when it would normally bark. So if, for example, your dog scares the postman by barking ferociously every time that he approaches the house, train your dog to sit quietly during his daily visit. You could also incorporate a command that allows it to bark when you want it to, such as when visitors arrive. Use the training techniques illustrated earlier in this chapter, and remember that because altering this type of behaviour is unlikely to succeed overnight, you'll need to persevere. With time and patience, however, it is possible to train a dog to bark on command or under specific conditions.

Dogs that bark as a result of guarding behaviour usually stop as soon as the 'threat' to their territory has disappeared (unlike excited dogs, which continue to bark). Some dogs 'guard' the house because they are unsure about who controls the arrival of visitors. In such cases, it is important to teach your dog that you are in charge (although its guarding behaviour will probably continue when you are away and it has been left at home).

**DOGS NEED TRAINING TO AVOID BECOMING ANXIOUS OR STRESSED.**

Owners of dominant dogs like this must exert their control as 'pack leader' by imposing firm obedience training on their pets. Teach your dog to earn your attention by obeying a command, for example, but ignore it if it tries to demand it.

Attention-seeking dogs bark to attract notice and then stop as soon as someone approaches them (this behaviour is often learnt as a puppy). It can be exceptionally annoying if your dog barks while you are on the phone or talking to someone, behaviour that is simply the result of your dog feeling left out. Cure this problem by ignoring your dog's methods of attention-seeking, such as barking, nudging your hand or dropping toys expectantly at your feet. Tell it to sit and ask before you stroke it and give it all of your attention – it will need periods when it has your undivided attention, so play games and carry out training exercises for at least an hour a day.

Dogs that bark due to separation anxiety are often very attached to their owners and find being alone highly stressful. If this is the case, make sure that your dog has been well exercised before leaving it and train it to become used to spending time alone. Teach it to obey the 'Quiet!' command and then leave it in a room for a couple of minutes. If the dog begins barking, make a loud noise to startle it and then return to the room and praise it when it is quiet before leaving again. You will probably have to repeat this exercise several times, but once your dog has become accustomed to the idea of being quiet, build up the length of time that it is left alone. It also helps to give it a toy with your scent on it.

**DOGS CAN BE TRAINED BY A HUMAN 'PACK LEADER'.**

# AGGRESSION

Aggression is one of the most common problems that dog behaviourists are asked to deal with. Dogs behave aggressively for a variety of reasons, and while some will direct their aggression only towards other animals, others will behave aggressively towards humans.

If a dog considers itself to be the dominant animal in the 'pack', it may try to exert its power by threatening family members, especially vulnerable ones, such as children. Even small dogs like West Highland terriers will aim a nip at an adult owner if they have not been trained to accept their status. Animals who regard themselves as top dog may also damage their owner's possessions. A dominant dog will often stare directly at strangers, try to go through doors first and expect an immediate response to their demands for attention. Do not confuse the behaviour of a dominant dog with that of a frightened one – although both animals will snarl, and possibly bite, the frightened dog will probably cower behind its owner and will be apprehensive when encountering new faces and situations.

Dominant aggression is treated by training the dog to accept its position as a subordinate member of the 'pack'. It is important

*TWO DOGS TRY TO WARN OFF A HORSE AND RIDER.*

to minimise the risk that your dog poses to others, so fit a muzzle or adjustable head halter before taking it for walks; this will also encourage obedience. Groom your dog at least once a day because this reinforces human dominance. Fit a houseline so that you can control its movements more easily. Do not allow it to jump on to furniture and ignore all of its requests for attention. Do not respond until it stops making demands, and then command it to sit before stroking it. Ensure that you eat before the dog does because in wild wolf packs the leader always eats first: prepare the dog's food, but eat your meal first, only feeding the dog when you have finished. When exercising your dog, also initiate some retrieving exercises, which will further emphasise who is in control. Do not give it any treats while you are carrying out this training.

Dogs behave aggressively towards other dogs either to defend their own territory or because they have been poorly socialised

*MUZZLE AN AGGRESSIVE OR DANGEROUS DOG.*

and are unused to the company of other animals. Male dogs are more likely to exhibit this type of behaviour than females, and neutering reduces the problem in young dogs (around two years of age). Actual fighting is preceded by the display of aggressive body language (see page 33): the dog will stare intently at its adversary and will assume a forward stance, with its ears and tail raised. It may also snarl and bare its teeth (and if your dog becomes involved in a fight with another dog, be wary of intervening in case you are bitten).

Prevention is possible, although you must first learn to recognise the signs of brewing aggression. If you notice your dog making threatening eye contact with another animal, for example, divert its attention, if necessary physically turning its head away. Think ahead and take a toy with you, and if its aggression seems to be escalating, command it to sit and use the toy to reward good behaviour, thus diverting its attention. When a dog pulls on a lead, its feelings of aggression increase, so do not exacerbate the situation by forcibly pulling it back. Anticipate the problem by muzzling your dog if necessary.

In order to decrease the likelihood of a dog fight, reinforce your dog's recall training (see pages 79 to 80), first at home and then in an open area within sight of another dog. Reward your dog when it ignores the other animal, or at least when it does not demonstrate hostile behaviour.

ABOVE: DOMINANT DOGS MAY TRY TO IMPOSE THEIR WILL.

BELOW: STARING AND LEANING FORWARD ARE DANGER SIGNS.

# ANXIETY

After aggression, separation anxiety is probably the second most common behavioural problem in dogs and is characterised by a dog that whines when left alone and is extremely excited and clingy when its owner returns. The dog may follow its owner from room to room, demonstrating great affection, trying to maintain eye contact and demanding as much physical contact as possible. When left alone, it may howl, bark or wreck the room that it is in as it tries to find a way out. Such dogs must be trained to lessen their over-attachment to their owners and to feel more secure when left alone.

Try to discourage your dog from following you around by shutting doors and asking other family members and friends to entertain it. In this way, it will gradually become less dependent on you.

# JUMPING UP

Excited dogs often jump up to greet their owners, when they know that it is time for a walk or if they hear a visitor arriving. Some breeds are more likely to jump up to solicit attention than others: big, assertive breeds may try to enforce their dominant position in such a way, while others, such as standard poodles, do it to beg for affection. All puppies greet their mother by licking her face, and young dogs aged between six and eighteen months are likely to reproduce this behaviour with their owners. Some owners encourage their dogs to jump up by slapping their thighs, but many people, especially children, find this type of excited behaviour unsettling. It is generally better to teach your dog to greet you with all four paws on the ground.

**EXCITABLE DOGS JUMP UP TO GREET PEOPLE.**

Gradually increase the length of time that the dog is left alone. It may help to leave a radio on and to place one item of your clothing on its bed and another on the other side of the closed door.

Ignore your dog for about twenty minutes before your departure and for twenty minutes after your return. Do not greet it until it has calmed down.

**TEACH A JUMPING DOG TO CALM DOWN.**

If your dog jumps up at you, turn away, withdraw eye contact and say 'No!' or 'Down!' sternly. Tell the dog to sit and then say hello to it in your own way, praising it for obeying you.

# CHASING

Dogs that persistently chase vehicles are both annoying and dangerous in that they are endangering both themselves and others, especially car drivers, who may be distracted by them. It is very difficult to overcome this problem because all dogs are natural chasers: they chase in order to scare off predators, and because cars and cyclists (the usual targets) rarely stop, the dog will be satisfied that it has succeeded. One instantaneous preventative measure is to ask a friend, armed with a water pistol, to cycle past the offending dog. As the dog chases the bike, the cyclist should stop and squirt the dog, at the same time saying 'No!' firmly.

Generations of selective breeding have failed to eliminate the dog's basic instinct to chase prey, and this problem is most likely to surface on, or near, farms. Dogs must be kept on a lead if they are anywhere near farm animals; farmers are within their rights to shoot dogs that are known to worry sheep and cattle. If your dog seems tempted to give chase, divert its attention by throwing a toy in the opposite direction to the other animal and encourage it to chase and retrieve the toy. With luck, the dog will become so absorbed by the game that it will forget its desire to chase the other animal.

**DOGS WHICH CHASE CARS ARE ANNOYING AND A DANGER TO THEMSELVES RATHER THAN OTHERS.**

# DESTRUCTIVE BEHAVIOUR

Destructive behaviour is often an outlet for boredom or frustration. Chewing, scratching, destroying soft furnishings or personal possessions – all of these behavioural problems are undesirable, but it is vital to understand what has prompted them in the first place.

Puppies chew as part of the teething process, but can be easily trained to turn their attention from shoes and slippers to toys. Older dogs must also be taught what is unacceptable behaviour, although you should also make sure that you remove all tempting articles from sight.

*TEACH YOUR DOG TO STAY WHEN YOU LEAVE HOME.*

*USE A STAIR GATE TO RESTRICT YOUR DOG'S ACCESS.*

Frustrated dogs may also create damage around the house, often focused in one area. If a dog wants to get outside to chase a cat, for example, it may scratch or chew around a door or window. Owners either need to discover what is upsetting their pet and remedy it if possible or else keep it in a different room, away from the source of frustration. Once again, make sure the dog is well exercised before leaving it alone and ensure that it has some stimulating toys to play with while you're away, too.

Destructive behaviour, such as wrecking soft furnishings, or even destroying its owner's personal possessions, can become an outlet for an intelligent dog that is lacking in stimulation. Boredom is a major cause of destructive behaviour, and the only solution is to ensure that your dog is mentally stimulated and well exercised. Part of the cure obviously lies in denying the dog access to tempting articles. More importantly, however, if your dog is left alone for long periods, make sure that it has a couple of toys to play with and that it has also enjoyed a long walk, preferably with some obedience training beforehand.

*DO NOT LET DOGS HOG YOUR FAVOURITE CHAIR.*

# MOUNTING EMBARRASSMENT

Dogs that try to mount table legs or the legs of visitors may initially appear funny, but some people find this type of behaviour embarrassing, and it certainly becomes annoying. Because most male dogs rarely meet females in heat, they often attempt to mount their owners' legs. The simple answer is to neuter a male dog, which will certainly reduce the problem (females also mount things, but spaying has little effect). Like many potential problems, this one is best caught early, so do not allow your puppy or adolescent dog to mount legs – either yours or those of furniture – in order to prevent it becoming a habit that is hard to break in adulthood.

Cold showers and plenty of fresh air sound like old-fashioned remedies, but canine variations on this theme may reduce the problem. Use a water pistol to spray water at a dog that is thrusting into a rug or cushion – the dog will certainly be diverted and probably put off. A dog that mounts anything clearly needs some sort of stimulation, so make sure that it is well exercised. Control the behaviour of an over-sexed dog by making it wear a lead or houseline. If it tries to mount anything, say 'No!' firmly and remove it to another room for a minute. Once it has returned from isolation, ignore it for a few minutes, then tell it to sit, reward it and play with it.

# OBEDIENCE CLASSES

Dogs that try to mount table legs or the legs of visitors may initially appear funny, but some people find this type of behaviour embarrassing, and it certainly becomes annoying. Because most male dogs rarely meet females in heat, they often attempt to mount their owners' legs. The simple answer is to neuter a male dog, which will certainly reduce the problem

(females also mount things, but spaying has little effect). Like many potential problems, this one is best caught early, so do not allow your puppy or adolescent dog to mount legs – either yours or those of furniture – in order to prevent it becoming a habit that is hard to break in adulthood.

**FIND A CLASS WITH A LOW TEACHER-PUPIL RATIO.**

Cold showers and plenty of fresh air sound like old-fashioned remedies, but canine variations on this theme may reduce the problem. Use a water pistol to spray water at a dog that is thrusting into a rug or cushion – the dog will certainly be diverted and probably put off. A dog that mounts anything clearly needs some sort of stimulation, so make sure that it is well exercised. Control the behaviour of an over-sexed dog by making it wear a lead or houseline. If it tries to mount anything, say 'No!' firmly and remove it to another room for a minute. Once it has returned from isolation, ignore it for a few minutes, then tell it to sit, reward it and play with it.

**CLASSES HELP NEW OWNERS TRAIN THEIR DOGS.**

**DOGS BENEFIT FROM EXPERT TUITION, AS DO OWNERS.**

**INDOOR CLASSES ARE CALMER THAN OUTDOORS.**

**LEARNING TO STAY.**

## CHAPTER 6

# A DOG'S LIFE

# DIET

Dogs are carnivores. Their digestive system is designed to absorb protein from meat and their teeth are configured for ripping flesh. Having said that, however, dogs, like humans, are not equipped to survive on an all-meat diet. Like us, dogs need a judicious mix of nutrients that contains the right balance of carbohydrates, fats, proteins, minerals and vitamins. Dogs are descended from scavenging ancestors and can survive on an intermittent diet of virtually anything, but this would undoubtedly result in nutritional deficiencies.

Most adult dogs should have one or two meals a day and continuous access to a bowl of water. Many dogs have a main meal in the morning and a few biscuits in the evening. Dogs' energy levels vary throughout their life, and their calorie requirements reflect this. Puppies have a higher calorie requirement than adult dogs, working dogs need more food than sedentary animals and older dogs will probably eat less than when they were younger. Always seek professional advice if you are unsure about how much to feed your pet.

The essential nutrients for a dog are broadly similar to those required by humans. Protein is necessary for growth and plays a vital role in building cell membranes and regenerating healing tissues within the body. It is derived from either plant or animal sources, but plant proteins lack some of the amino acids necessary for mammalian health. Carbohydrates provide much of the body's energy and, for dogs, are derived from biscuit meal, rice bread or commercially manufactured biscuits and snacks. Finally, fats are essential as a concentrated energy source and to provide fatty acids or polyunsaturates. Minerals, such as calcium, phosphorus and salt, and vitamins are usually present in a well-balanced diet, but can be provided as supplements if a vet deems it necessary.

**DOGS NEED REGULAR AND HEALTHY MEALS.**

# WEIGHT-WATCHING

It is important not to overfeed your dog, because obesity will make it unhealthy, placing extra strain on its joints, digestive system and internal organs.

Ultimately, a fat dog will have a shorter life expectancy than a thinner one, and most obese dogs are overweight because they are being overfed and underexercised. A healthy dog should exhibit some sort of waist when viewed from above, and you should be able to feel, but not see, its ribs. Do not become obsessed by your dog's weight, however, and never impose a crash diet on your pampered pooch. Ask your vet for advice if you think that your dog is overweight and needs to lose a few pounds.

Regularly weighing your dog will enable you to spot any tendency towards obesity, as well as weight loss, which may be a sign of illness. The easiest method of weighing your dog is to hold it while standing on the bathroom scales and then to subtract your weight from the figure shown. If you have a large dog, try to coax it to stand on the scales alone. Pedigree breeders and vets will be able to give you an idea of the average weight for your dog's breed or size.

**RIGHT: CALCULATE YOUR DOG'S WEIGHT.**

# WHICH FOOD?

Modern dogs – or rather their owners – are faced with an almost bewildering choice of food, ranging from the traditional table scraps to scientifically adjusted diets that target animals with special requirements, such as puppies or nursing bitches.

Deciding which food is right for your dog is not easy. It is important to bear in mind the breed and size of the animal, and how much time you can devote to preparing your dog's meals. Some owners prefer to prepare fresh food for their pets, but not only is this time-consuming, surveys have shown that over 90 per cent of home-made dog foods are nutritionally unbalanced. Pet-food manufacturers have spent vast sums of money researching the field of dog food in order to create products that combine convenience, the best nutritional mix and palatability. It is not only easier to use manufactured pet food than to prepare fresh food yourself, but ensures that your dog receives the correct mix of vitamins and nutrients. Make sure that you follow the manufacturer's recommendations for portion size (see also the table on page 102).

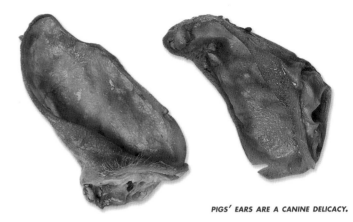

*PIGS' EARS ARE A CANINE DELICACY.*

There are three main types of commercially available dog food – moist or wet foods, complete dry meals and semi-moist food – along with special foods and treats.

## MOIST OR WET FOODS

Most of the tinned dog foods that are sold in supermarkets are carefully calibrated to provide dogs with a healthy diet. Some provide a complete diet, while others have a lower carbohydrate level and must be supplemented with dog meal. They are composed of meat, offal, poultry or fish and incorporate vitamin and mineral supplements. As a caveat, they often have a high protein content, which can make some dogs very energetic and over-excited, which may be a problem in a big, dominant dog.

## COMPLETE DRY MEALS

These products are extremely convenient. A mixture of cereals and protein, they are available in the form of pellets or other shapes and are coated with fat to improve their palatability. Some types must be rehydrated with water before consumption. They have as much as four times the calorie content of tinned food and must therefore be fed in smaller portions.

*DRIED FOOD ALLOWS OWNERS TO FEED THEIR DOGS A PRECISE CALORIFIC AMOUNT.*

## SEMI-MOIST FOOD

Semi-moist food is not intended as the only source of nourishment and must be supplemented with biscuits or meal to provide adequate carbohydrates.

*DOG BISCUITS MAKE A USEFUL NIGHT TIME SNACK.*

## SPECIAL FOODS AND TREATS

Manufacturers also produce special foods, such as high-energy food for puppies and vitamin- and mineral-enriched varieties for elderly dogs or nursing bitches. Some manufacturers provide prescription diets for dogs with specific health problems, such as diabetes, heart trouble or kidney disorders. These should only be given to a dog on the advice of a vet.

There is also an infinite variety of snacks and treats, from meaty treats and bone-shaped biscuits to doggie chocs. Never give your dog human sweets, however, especially chocolate, which can poison dogs if eaten in large enough quantities. So if you offer your dog treats, make sure that they are special doggy snacks and, because they are high in calories, remember to include them in the daily calorie count.

*DOGGY TREATS ARE USEFUL AS REWARDS.*

## EATING PROBLEMS

There is no convincing evidence that dogs become bored by being offered the same type of food every day, although some dogs, particularly small breeds, do become fussy about food. In some cases, battles over food are part of the dog's struggle to establish its dominance within its 'pack' – in the wild, the pack leader has first choice of food – and it may be trying to assert itself by refusing one food in favour of another.

Do not give in to this behaviour. First check with your vet that your dog is not unhealthy in any way and then impose a new mealtime regime. Leave the food in its bowl for an hour or so and then, if it remains uneaten, remove it. Your dog can survive without food for a couple of days and will give in when it becomes really hungry.

Some dogs appear to like eating grass, and although this is not inherently dangerous, it can lead to infections and disease. It is thought that dogs eat grass to ease stomach discomfort because it often induces vomiting. It may also be a sign that the dog needs more fibre in its diet.

Other dogs seem to delight in eating their own faeces, a condition known as coprophagia. There are various explanations for this habit. It may be that the dog is suffering from a deficiency of certain B vitamins or vitamin K, which is produced by bacteria in the gut. However, the behaviour seems to become habit-forming and is often prevalent among dogs who have been kennelled in unsanitary conditions. Clean up after your dog as quickly as possible to limit the possibility of faeces consumption. In severe cases, your vet can supply a drug called Cythiomate to taint the faeces, which will make the dog feel very ill after it has eaten it.

Scavenging is a natural canine habit to which most dogs will succumb if food is left temptingly within reach. Do not let your dog sniff around discarded food when you are out for a walk and keep all foodstuffs out of its reach at home. Persistent scavenging may be a sign of illness: pancreatic insufficiency, for example, increases a dog's appetite, causing it to try to obtain food at every opportunity.

# FEEDING GUIDE FOR ADULT DOGS

This chart is simply a rough guide. Individual dog's food requirements vary according to their activity levels and mood. Remember that this is the daily requirement, not per meal.

| DOG SIZE | APPROX. DAILY CALORIE NEEDS | CANNED FOOD/MEAL (420 G/14 OZ TIN) | SEMI-MOIST FOOD | DRY FOOD |
|---|---|---|---|---|
| Toy breeds less than 4.5 kg (10 lb), e.g., Yorkshire terrier, Chihuahua, Pomeranian | 210 | 105 g (4 oz) meat + 35 g (1 oz) meal | 70 g (2.4 oz) | 60 g (2 oz) |
| Small breeds 4.5–9 kg (10–20 lb), e.g., West Highland terrier, beagle. | 590 | 300 g (11 oz) meat + 100 g (4 oz) meal | 200 g (8 oz) | 170 g (6 oz) |
| Medium breeds 9–22 kg (20–50 lb), e.g., springer spaniel, basset hound. | 900 | 450 g (16 oz) meat + 150 g (5 oz) meal | 300 g (11 oz) | 260 g (9 oz) |
| Large breeds 22–34 kg (50–75 lb), e.g., German shepherd, Labrador, Irish setter. | 1,680 | 850 g (30 oz) meat + 280 g (10 oz) meal | 550 g (19 oz) | 480 g (17 oz) |
| Giant breeds 34–63 kg (74–140 lb), e.g., Great Dane, Newfoundland, Irish wolfhound | 2,800 | 1,400 g (49 oz) meat + 460 g (16 oz) meal | 900 g (32 oz) | 800 g (28 oz) |

# ALTERING A DIET

If you decide to change your dog's food, do so gradually. If you are switching from a wet food to a dry diet, for instance, begin by placing a half-and-half mix in your dog's feeding bowl and gradually reduce the amount of wet food over time – say a week or two.

# DENTAL HYGIENE

As a follow-up to feeding your dog well, make sure that you clean its teeth every day. Severe gum and plaque disease can lead to heart problems in older dogs and, at the very least, keeping its teeth and gums clean will prevent unpleasant 'dog's breath'. Your vet will be able to recommend a canine toothpaste (dogs dislike the minty human varieties) to use to keep your pet's teeth and gums healthy, or else use dilute salt water. Use an adult-sized toothbrush for a large dog and a small one for a medium-sized or small dog. Special canine toothbrushes are also available.

In some cases, chewing a large, raw (not cooked) bone will help to clean a dog's teeth and massage its gums, but it must be a large bone, such as an ox shank. Never give your dog chicken, fish or lamb bones or ones that are likely to splinter or become stuck in its throat. Small dogs that are unable to cope with big bones can chew on raw carrots, and an even better option is a chew toy or a rawhide stick, available from pet shops.

**CHEWING A HARD ITEM HELPS CLEAN DOGS' TEETH.**

*AVOID BONES AND GIVE YOUR DOG A RAWHIDE TOY TO CHEW.*

# HOW TO CLEAN A DOGS TEETH

**1** Settle your dog quietly on the floor or on your lap.

**2** Place your left hand across its muzzle, with a finger or thumb under the chin to keep its mouth closed. Using your right hand, gently insert the toothbrush inside its lips.

**3** Starting at the back and working forwards, brush the outer surface of the teeth (the tongue does a reasonable job of keeping the inside clean). Move the brush gently in a circular motion – do not scrub the teeth. Make sure that you clean the gum line, too.

*DOGGIE TOOTHBRUSHES HAVE ANGLED HEADS.*

HOLD THE DOG'S JAW WHILE CLEANING ITS TEETH.

IT IS EXTREMELY IMPORTANT TO KEEP A DOG'S TEETH AND GUMS CLEAN AND HEALTHY. CHECK TEETH REGULARLY FOR ANY PROBLEMS. IF IN DOUBT, CONSULT A VET.

# GROOMING

Regular grooming is important for most dogs, particularly the longer-haired breeds, because it removes dead hair. But grooming is not merely for cosmetic purposes: it is also a valuable means of detecting fleas and other skin parasites, or thorns or burrs that have adhered to the dog's coat during a walk.

Grooming is part of the bonding process between owner and dog, too, and can be very pleasurable and relaxing for the dog. Dogs who are accustomed to being groomed from a young age will settle quickly and enjoy their grooming sessions – as will the owner because it is obviously far easier to groom a compliant dog than a wriggling animal! In addition, it is an important part of your dog's training: by insisting that your pet stands still while you groom it, you are emphasising your control and dominance.

Begin by simply grooming a small puppy with a brush and comb – more serious grooming can wait until it is older. Long-coated breeds should be groomed daily in order to prevent their fur from matting; dealing with matted fur is a tricky task which the dog may find painful, so it is worth spending a short time each day grooming your dog to avoid this.

# ROUTINE GROOMING

The grooming needs of dogs vary tremendously from breed to breed, but the basics are the same.

Welsh corgis and other short-coated dogs have dense layers of hair close to the skin which both insulates them and is water-resistant. They have another layer of thick, straight hair on top, which needs less attention than that of many other breeds, but their coats do tend to moult, covering their owners and homes in dog hairs. Daily grooming will help to prevent this. Use a stiff brush all over the body (but be sensitive when brushing the head and face) and follow up with a wire-bristled glove. The whole routine will probably take no more than ten minutes. Smooth-coated dogs require little maintenance, but their coats may provide inadequate protection against the cold and require weekly brushing. Some smooth-coated dogs, such as Great Danes and Dobermans, suffer when the coarse hairs on their body's pressure points (the elbows and hocks) penetrate the skin. Treat these areas with conditioner to soften the hair.

Rough-coated dogs do not moult in the same way as their short-coated cousins, but they do 'cast' every six months or so, when their hair comes out in great chunks, particularly if the dog has not been groomed regularly. Terriers and other rough-coated breeds therefore benefit from a daily brushing-out to prevent the coat from matting. Use a stiff brush and a comb with which to penetrate every knot and make sure that the coat is trimmed regularly, preferably by a professional groomer (see below).

*ASK A VET OR PROFESSIONAL GROOMER TO CUT CLAWS IF YOU FIND IT TRICKY.*

Silky-coated breeds, such as King Charles spaniels and Irish setters, need the same attention as rough-coated breeds, but do not use too stiff a brush. Their coats may become rather heavy and will require trimming once or twice a year.

Long-haired dogs are the most time-consuming to groom, making grooming them a labour of love. A dog with fine, silky hair, such as an Afghan hound or Yorkshire terrier, will need a thorough daily grooming with a slicker brush, pin brush and wide-toothed comb for the feathering on the back of the legs. Be careful not to brush too hard or pull on any tangles in case you hurt your dog.

Place your dog on a table. (Although grooming can be carried out on the floor, dogs associate this area with play, so it may be difficult to keep it still. Dogs must be trained to sit still for grooming or veterinary treatment at an early age.) Put one hand around the dog's chest and shoulders to steady it and then, using a hound glove or rubber brush, brush down its body (starting at the back of the neck and moving to the sides, then between the hind legs and under the body) to remove dead or loose hairs. Note that dogs are sensitive about their paws, and especially their tails and anal regions, being touched. Talk to your dog, especially when you are grooming its head and face, and reward it at the end of the session.

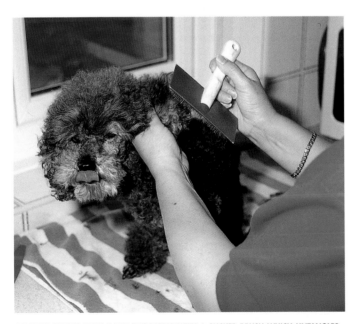

*POODLES BENEFIT FROM DAILY GROOMING WITH A SLICKER BRUSH WHICH UNTANGLES FUR.*

# PROFESSIONAL GROOMING

Some dogs – poodles, Afghan hounds and Old English sheepdogs, for example – will benefit from the attentions of a professional dog-groomer, in other words, a trip to the proverbial poodle parlour every month or so. This is worthwhile, not only because it will ensure that your dog looks its very best, but you will probably pick up some professional tips and hints to help you to keep your dog in top condition. If you intend to show your dog, professional grooming is a necessity.

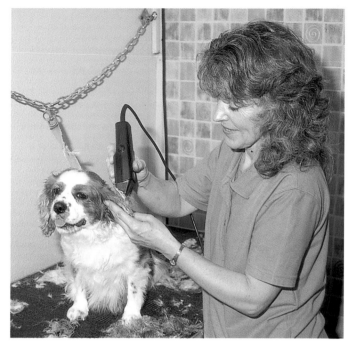

A dog grooming salon is equipped with a variety of equipment to make washing a dog easier than it may be at home. The dog is restrained with a loose lead clipped to a wall chain.

Once washed, the fluffy ears of this spaniel are gently dried with a hair dryer.

Dog groomers can offer an expert service with a high level of attention to detail. Their experience means that they are able to wash even the most fractious dog quickly and with the minimum of fuss.

Very wiry-coated dogs like schnauzers, border terriers and Airedales may need professional attention, too. Their coats must be stripped every three to four months, with the dead hair being pulled out by hand or with a stripping knife. This is completely painless and helps to maintain their naturally wiry coats. It can be rather a long job, and may best be tackled in short sessions over two or three days. Alternatively, clip the coat regularly and ask a professional groomer to trim around the face.

Many dogs enjoy the attention lavished on them while being groomed. A professional dog groomer has the skills to tidy up any breed of dog, but long-haired dogs in particular will benefit from his or her skills.

# A REGULAR HEALTH CHECK

Grooming also provides an opportunity for you to check your dog's general health. Every few days, clean away the mucus around its eyes, using a different piece of dampened cotton wool for each eye. If your dog has a wrinkled face or many folds of skin, clean around these, too, checking for odour or inflammation.

Lift the flaps of the ears to check for inflammation or redness (if the dog is scratching around an ear, take it to the vet for examination). Dogs with long ears, such as spaniels, must be carefully checked.

Next, check your dog's teeth and gums for inflammation. If it is reluctant to open its mouth, hold its lower jaw firmly with one hand while blocking its nostrils. Use a soft toothbrush to remove any debris and massage the gums every day (see also dental hygiene, pages 103 to 105).

Inspect your dog's anal region and clean away accumulated debris. If your dog is dragging its bottom along the ground, its anal sacs may need emptying (ask your vet for advice about this).

Examine its paws, too, especially between the toes, and remove any matted fur, grit, small stones or seeds that may have become trapped. Grass seeds are prone to stick and can be removed with tweezers, although it may be sensible to consult a vet. Check the pads and clean off any mud with a moistened piece of cotton wool. Trim away any long fur to prevent foreign bodies becoming lodged in it.

Regular walks along hard pavements will help to keep your dog's claws short, but, if necessary, cut them using specially angled, doggy nailclippers. Cut above the quick, the pink area on the claw – this is usually obvious in clear nails, but may be more difficult to see in dark ones. If you are unsure, a vet will show you the best way to trim your dog's claws.

*THE CLAWS OF SOME DOGS REQUIRE THE ATTENTIONS OF A VET.*

# WASHING A DOG

Left to their own devices, dogs keep themselves reasonably clean by rolling on the ground, scratching and chewing at matted fur and licking themselves. Because they also love to roll in mud – and worse – there will undoubtedly be a time when a sign of your dog's presence wafts into the room before it does. Time for a bath!

Unless your dog has become extremely muddy or smelly, it will probably only need a bath once every couple of months (although some breeds, according to their breeders, should never be washed). In tropical or subtropical countries, dog are often bathed weekly to minimise the risk of tick-borne diseases. Dried mud falls off short-coated breeds easily, but a bath will get rid of lingering odours.

Larger dogs can be washed in the bath (put down a rubber mat to stop the dog from slipping), but it is probably better to use an old baby bath and also less messy if you bathe your dog outside. Use warm (not hot) water and either baby shampoo or a medicated shampoo rather than any type of detergent. Special dog shampoos are also available: medicated shampoo, anti-parasitic shampoo and varieties prescribed by vets to treat specific skin conditions. Try to make the experience fun – and wear something waterproof.

Beginning with the hindquarters, lather the coat well and gently massage the dog, working forwards along the body and trying to make sure that the bubbles do not enter any orifices, especially the eyes. Rinse the dog thoroughly, working from the head backwards, and paying particular attention to the area between the forelegs and hind legs where shampoo may remain and cause irritation.

After you've bathed it, your dog will probably want to have a vigorous shake, but try to dry it first. Use a chamois leather and a towel to dry short-coated breeds. Long-haired dogs must be dried with a towel using a squeezing motion because rubbing tends to mat the coat. Terriers usually enjoy a rub with a rough towel, and dachshunds and other short-legged dogs are liable to develop colds if their stomachs become cold, making drying them especially important. Follow this rough-drying with a blast of air from a hairdryer on a low setting, but remember that your dog may be startled by the hairdryer if it is not used to it, so introduce its use gradually. Once dry, your dog will look great, but don't be surprised if it immediately rolls around on the ground to cover itself in some familiar smells!

**1** This dog is small enough to be washed in the sink. Use either baby shampoo or a special dog shampoo.

**2** After shampooing, gently rinse off the suds with warm water, avoiding the eye area.

**3** Wrap your dog in an old towel and rub him dry before he has a chance to shower you with water.

**4** Finally, dry your dog with a hair dryer on a low setting. Keep it moving so that you do not scorch the animal.

# HEALTH

## THE SIGNS OF A HEALTHY DOG

Most dogs are hardy and healthy, keen-eyed and bushy of tail. Check the following vital areas, and if your dog does not exhibit the points noted, consult your vet.

- Abdomen: tapering towards the back legs; neither sensitive to touch nor distended.
- Anus: clean.
- Appetite: hearty, fast eater.
- Breathing: quiet and even when at rest; panting when cooling down; no coughing.
- Claws: no splits or interdigital cysts; well trimmed.
- Coat: clean and glossy; no loose hair, dirt or parasites.
- Ears: clean, no dark wax, no redness; held at correct angle for breed; alert.
- Eyes: clear, no discharge.
- Faeces: varies according to diet, but bowel motions should be regular and reasonably solid.
- Manner: alert; quick response to sounds and instructions.
- Movement: even gait; even weight distribution over all four legs.
- Nose: cold and damp on a walk, dry and warm inside; no discharge.
- Skin: supple, clean and free from inflammation or sores.
- Teeth: clean and strong; pink gums.
- Urine: passed easily.

# NEUTERING

The advantages of neutering far outweigh the disadvantages, and it is notable that all dogs bred as guide dogs in Britain are neutered at the age of six months to ensure that they are stable, peaceable animals. The coats of some breeds become fluffy rather than silky after neutering, which is an aesthetic shame for Irish setters or cocker spaniels. More seriously, a bitch may develop urinary incontinence in later life, but hormone-replacement therapy usually solves this problem. Owners are often worried that neutering their dogs will cause them to put on weight, but if a dog is fed properly, this will not happen. Owners may give their neutered pets more food out of guilt, but studies have shown that neutered dogs have lower calorie requirements (up to 15 per cent less) than unneutered animals, so if they are given smaller amounts of food they will not put on weight.

Dogs become sexually mature between six and twelve months of age, although in many cases they are not mentally mature until eighteen months. This means that a young bitch who has a litter when she is still under a year old may find it hard to cope with the demands of motherhood. (In Britain, it is illegal for breeders to breed from such a young animal.) Most owners do not want to breed from their bitches and so have three choices: spaying, controlling the dog's activities during her 'seasons' or using hormonal birth-control drugs.

Most bitches come into season every six to nine months throughout their lives. An average season lasts between fifteen and twenty-one days, and most bitches suffer from abdominal pain and moodiness. Unless she actually does become pregnant, a season is followed by a false pregnancy, when the bitch will display signs of pregnancy and maternal behaviour, as well as restlessness. Spaying, which is carried out under general anaesthetic, eliminates these problems and will make your dog more stable.

Most male pet dogs are castrated, an operation that is carried out by a vet using a general anaesthetic. Unneutered males may exhibit behavioural problems, such as mounting people or furniture, aggression and straying in search of an oestrous female, caused by an increase in testosterone. Castration can be carried out at any age, but it is probably best for the dog to be aged between nine and eighteen months.

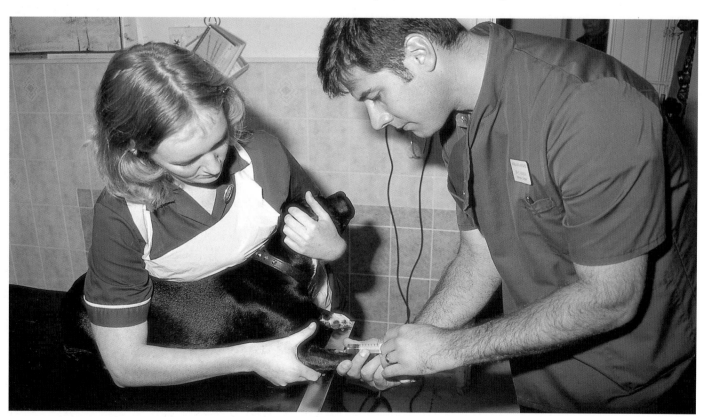

**A DOG IS INJECTED WITH ANAESTHETIC PRIOR TO SURGERY.**

# BREEDING

*A CHOCOLATE-BROWN BUNDLE OF FUN AND MISCHIEF.*

Deciding whether or not to breed from your female dog is an important decision. Consider what you would do with the puppies – and remember the scenes from A Hundred and One Dalmatians! It is unlikely that you will want to keep them all, so think about what will happen to them. Will you be able to sell them or give them away? Or will you be left with four or five rapidly growing puppies which will exhaust both your energy and your cash? It is irresponsible to allow your dog to breed if the future of the puppies is uncertain. It is cruel to send them to unsuitable homes, and although rescue centres will look after them more than adequately, their resources are not infinite.

Remember that if you own a crossbreed, the chances of the puppies looking like their mother are reasonably small, and that if both parents have mixed ancestry, it is almost impossible to predict what the puppies will look like. If you are the owner of a purebred dog, however, mating it with another dog of the same breed will at least produce puppies whose looks and behaviour will be predictable. Purchasers of purebred puppies want the best, so try to ensure that the chosen mate has shown its quality, is of sound temperament and has the relevant Kennel Club and breed certificates.

If you feel that you have the necessary resources to breed from your female dog, contact your vet, who will be able to suggest a reputable breeder (to help you to find a prospective mate) and will advise you on how to care for her during pregnancy.

## MATING

A bitch's season usually lasts about three weeks. Her vulva swells and there will be a blood-stained discharge; male dogs (although not humans) will be able to detect a powerful odour signifying that she is in season. She is fertile about twelve days from the first signs of coming into season and remains so for about five to seven days. This is the time to mate her with a suitable sire – and male dogs are always ready to mate! Do not breed from a bitch until she is at least two years old because she will not be physically or mentally mature enough to cope with motherhood properly until then.

Pregnancy lasts for sixty-three days, but is hard to spot. After every season, hormonal changes occur (known as a 'false pregnancy') whether the bitch is pregnant or not, so no blood or urine tests can confirm the presence of puppies. About six weeks into the pregnancy, the bitch's abdomen will become noticeably fuller and her mammary glands will be enlarged – these are obvious signs of impending motherhood.

The mother-to-be will need extra food and rest from now on. Increase her food gradually until, by the end of her pregnancy, she is eating about two-thirds more than normal, and give her two meals a day. Smaller dogs will probably double their normal diets. A few days before the arrival of the litter, she may lose interest in food and vomit up her last meal.

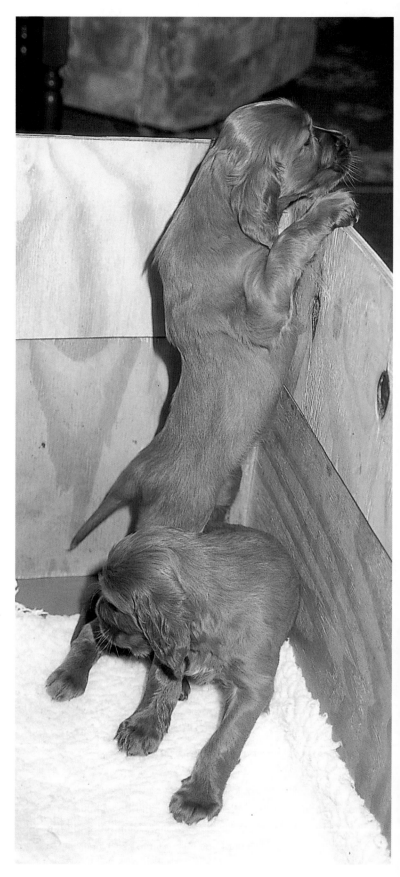

*MAKE SURE YOU HAVE THE TIME TO DEAL WITH A LITTER.*

# WELPING

About two weeks before the puppies are due, prepare a whelping box and introduce your dog to it. It should be sited in a warm, quiet spot, but make sure that it is accessible in case you or the vet need to help with whelping. Whelping boxes are sold through pet-supply shops; alternatively, you can make one. Line it with a warm, washable, synthetic fleece and newspaper – whelping is a messy business. Prepare a box of old towels, disinfectant and scissors and keep it nearby.

Most bitches whelp without difficulty, but it is sensible to talk through the process with your vet in advance. A day or so before the birth, the dog will probably become uninterested in food and very restless, perhaps trying to make a nest somewhere. Shortly before labour starts, the dog will pant and

her temperature will drop by two or three degrees (a dog's normal temperature is 38°C or 100.4°F). It may take several hours from the beginning of the contractions until the arrival of the first pup, but once the first has appeared, the remainder should follow at intervals of ten to eighty minutes.

Owners will probably be little more than observers at the birth, but make sure that one placenta is delivered for each pup. If your dog appears to be having an unproductive labour, with lots of straining but no sign of a puppy emerging, contact your vet. She may need a Caesarean, which is relatively common for breeds with large heads, such as bulldogs.
Do not let your dog become exhausted by labour because, at the very least, this will impede her recovery.

*MOST BITCHES REQUIRE LITTLE HELP WHEN WHELPING.*

Puppies are born either head or tail first – either way is normal. The mother will lick the newborn pups vigorously to remove the membranes and will chew through the umbilical cord to separate it from the placenta, which she will later eat. She will continue to lick each puppy to stimulate it, clear away mucus and warm it.

Once all of the puppies have been delivered, their mother will feed them and lick their bottoms to stimulate the elimination of faeces and urine. She will consume all of the puppies' waste for three weeks (this is a throwback to the behaviour of dogs' wild ancestors, which needed to hide the presence of vulnerable young from predators). For the first three weeks, the puppies are entirely dependent on their mother and will do little more than feed and sleep, huddling together for warmth and security. Their eyes open at about ten days.

Some breeds are prone to cannibalism and will lick their puppies obsessively before taking this process to a natural conclusion and consuming them. Bull terriers are most likely to do this, and a nursing mother must therefore be watched closely until the puppies' umbilical cords have dropped off.

Owners should ensure that the mother is comfortable, warm, healthy and well fed, which will help her milk production. Handle the puppies, but do not upset their mother, who will be very protective of them. Check that they are all gaining weight by weighing them daily. By four weeks of age they will be more active and learning how to interact with their peers.

Weaning can begin at three weeks, when you will need to supplement the puppies' diet (this will also lessen the strain on their mother). They should be completely weaned at six weeks, when they can be fed on puppy food. Consult your vet about worming and vaccinations. And by the age of eight weeks, the puppies will be ready to leave home.

**BELOW: PUPPIES ARE SWEET, BUT DO YOU WANT A HOUSE FULL OF THEM?**

# OLDER DOGS

Given the wide variety of types of dog, it is not surprising that life expectancy varies from breed to breed. Generally, smaller dogs live longer than larger dogs; terriers, for example, may live for as long as twenty years, although miniature dogs are less fortunate. Giant dogs, such as Great Danes, rarely survive beyond the age of ten, while bulldogs average about seven years. The average life expectancy for a crossbreed dog is thirteen years, and most dogs are considered old at the age of seven or eight.

One of the most important factors contributing to its longevity is the quality of the care that the dog has received throughout its life. If untreated, illnesses or infections contracted early in life, for instance, may weaken an organ and result in health problems a few years later.

Certain breeds are prone to particular diseases in old age (see Chapter 7), to which a breeder or vet will certainly alert you when you acquire a dog. Arthritis and incontinence, which afflict many old dogs, can be alleviated by medical treatment. There are many pet-insurance schemes which will help to keep the expense of vets' bills to a minimum, and it is prudent to take out a policy before your dog reaches five years of age.

Older dogs are generally less energetic than younger ones, but the ageing process is gradual, and it is often hard to recognise the signs of ageing until problems occur. Ideally, dogs over seven years of age should have a check-up at the vet's every six months.

The behaviour of older dogs alters subtly over time. They generally sleep more and may become more irritable,

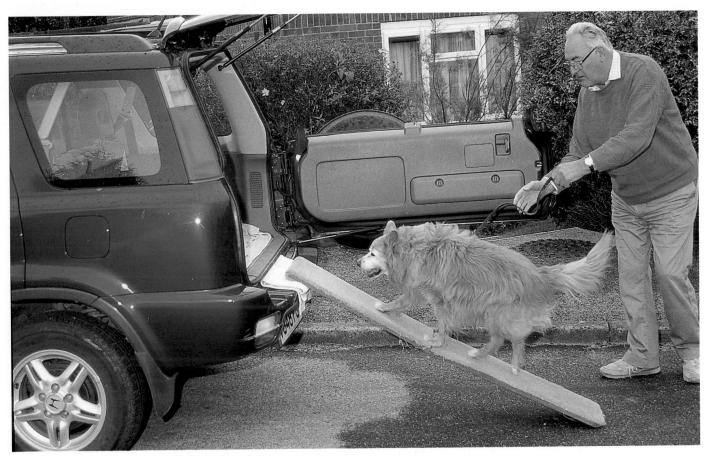

**PROVIDE PRACTICAL HELP FOR AGEING DOGS, SUCH AS THIS RAMP UP TO THE CAR.**

especially around exuberant youngsters – human or canine. They sometimes bark more often, which may be a sign of deafness or that something else is troubling the animal. You may need to be flexible in your routines to accommodate the changing needs of your dog. It will probably eat less, for example, and may prefer a couple of smaller meals each day instead of one large one. If your dog has a stiff neck, raise its feeding and drinking bowls to head height. Mobility may become a problem, and joint stiffness may occur in the morning or after exercise. However reluctant your old dog seems, try to make sure that it is well exercised to keep its joints mobile, stimulate its mind and improve its bowel function. Frequent short walks are probably easier for an old dog to manage than long ones, particularly if it is suffering from heart, respiratory or arthritic problems.

Your dog may become upset and confused by its ageing body, as well as frustrated that it can no longer do the things it used to. Try to avoid inflicting stressful situations on an older dog. Routine and familiarity are more important than ever, so try not to make any sudden changes to the dog's circumstances.

OLDER DOGS WILL LIVE LIFE AT A SLOWER PACE, BUT ARE STILL LIVELY ENOUGH TO ENJOY A CAR RIDE.

BELOW: THE ARRIVAL OF A NEW DOG MAY PERK UP AN OLDER ANIMAL.

**OLDER DOGS NEED LESS EXERCISE.**

# AGE-RELATED HEALTH PROBLEMS

- **Tumours and benign growths:** if you spot one, consult the vet immediately.

- **Heart:** your dog may be reluctant to exercise and may be prone to coughing after lying down for long periods.

- **Teeth:** dental disease is common in dogs aged over three years old. Brush your dog's teeth daily (see page 103) and consult your vet at the first sign of trouble. If left untreated, dental disease can affect a dog's overall health.

- **Anal sacs:** if your dog has a habit of dragging its bottom along the floor, its anal sacs probably need emptying. Consult the vet.

- **Nails:** nails will require clipping more frequently if they are not being kept short by exercise.

- **Incontinence:** poor bladder control is relatively common in older dogs. Make sure that the dog has waterproof bedding in a bed that is easy to clean. Don't punish your dog for any accidents – it really can't help it.

- **Obesity:** old dogs may put on weight if they take less exercise. Regulate your dog's diet to avoid obesity, which can lead to more serious health problems.

- **Hearing:** if your dog's hearing begins to decline, it will not be able to hear certain frequencies. Because it may not hear your voice clearly, non-compliance with commands may not be disobedience, merely the result of deafness. Because it may not be able to hear traffic noise, ensure that it is kept on a lead near roads. Check its ears for infection or a build-up of wax.

- **Eyes:** eyes may appear cloudy, which could be a sign of cataracts. If your dog shows signs of deteriorating vision, try to avoid repositioning any furniture within the house and do not let it off the lead when out walking.

- **Coat:** the coat will probably become flecked with grey and feel coarser.

*OLD HABITS DIE HARD – THIS AGEING DOG IS STILL AN ALERT GUARD DOG.*

# THE LAST KINDNESS

If your dog has a physical problem or disease that considerably reduces its quality of life, or if it is in constant pain, your vet will advise you on the most humane course of action. Consider what your dog can still do and whether it seems happy. Is it able to walk and feed itself, for example, and is it continent? Confronting death is hard, but if your pet is suffering, ending its pain is the greatest kindness that you can bestow on it.

## CHAPTER 7

# DISORDERS AND ILLNESSES

It is unlikely that your dog will cruise through life without incurring any health problems. This section offers guidance on how to spot signs of trouble, how to prevent some common illnesses or infections and how to look after a sick dog. If your dog's behaviour alters dramatically, for example, if it rejects its food or the frequency with which it empties its bowels or bladder changes, consult your vet.

Your dog is far more likely to remain healthy if it is given basic inoculations as a puppy (see page 66). These will protect it against common, but unpleasant, and potentially fatal, diseases. Boosters are usually given annually, and it is vital that your dog receives them to maintain its immunity. Preventative medicine is a crucial part of canine healthcare. Distemper vaccinations must be boosted every other year to maintain immunity, while leptospirosis jabs, which only give short-lived protection, must be administered more regularly. Kennel cough, which is caused by several infectious agents and is transmitted through fairly close contact between dogs, can be prevented by a nasal-spray vaccine, which wards off most, if not all, components of the infection. Most kennels advise owners to treat their dogs before installing them in kennels for any length of time.

Your vet will become an important partner in maintaining your dog's health, so it is important that you find one with whom you feel comfortable. Ask friends for their recommendations or, if it seems adequate, simply register with the practice nearest to your home. Check the facilities, opening times and appointment system, and make sure that you keep the phone number in a prominent place in case you need it urgently. Veterinary advice and treatment does not come cheap, and new dog-owners will be well advised to take out a suitable insurance policy. These vary tremendously in terms of their cost and coverage: the most expensive policies will pay out in the event of your dog's death, but others are far more limited with regard to which illnesses or treatments they will pay for. Do a little research to find the best policy for your circumstances – your vet may be able to advise you.

**AN ALERT PAIR LISTEN TO THEIR OWNER.**

# INHERITED DISEASES

In the wild, only the fittest survive, which means that inherited diseases are a relatively minor problem. However, the dog, which has been domesticated and selectively bred for so long, is prone to more inherited disorders than any other species of animal apart from humans.

Inherited diseases are passed from one generation to the next through the affected genes of the sire or dam – and sometimes from both. Even healthy dogs can pass on a problem if they carry a recessive gene.

Large breeds, such as German shepherds, retrievers and Great Danes, are prone to degenerative hip dysplasia, which causes pain and lameness in the hind legs. It can be treated with medication, but surgery is necessary in severe cases. Progressive retinal atrophy, an eye disease which leads to blindness, can be a problem for Irish setters, cocker spaniels, collies and retrievers, while Dalmatians may suffer from hereditary deafness.

*ROUGH COLLIES ARE PRONE TO PROGRESSIVE RETINAL ATROPHY, A SERIOUS VISUAL DISORDER.*

*LARGE DOGS, GREAT DANES COMMONLY SUFFER FROM ARTHRITIS OR HIP DYSPLASIA.*

*AMERICAN COCKER SPANIELS OFTEN SUFFER FROM EPILEPSY.*

Breeders have begun to co-operate to eliminate genetic diseases from some breeds. Progressive retinal atrophy, for example, has a straightforward inheritance pattern, and Irish setter breeders have worked to reduce the occurrence of the condition in the breed. Progress is slow, however, because eliminating affected dogs from breeding programmes is only part of the solution. Other diseases, such as hip dysplasia, are hard to eliminate because they sometimes do not manifest themselves until relatively late in a dog's life, and certainly beyond the prime breeding age. As scientists learn more about genetics and the canine genome, it is likely that DNA tests will become available to pinpoint genetic diseases and, in time, eliminate them.

*IF YOUR DOG SEEMS OFF-COLOUR, TAKE IT TO THE VET.*

*ABOVE: IRISH SETTERS MAY SUFFER FROM VISUAL DEFECTS.*

*RIGHT: SMOOTH COLLIES ARE RARE IN BRITAIN.*

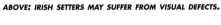

# DISEASES SHARED WITH HUMANS: ZOONOSES

There are a number of diseases (known as zoonoses) and parasites that spread from dogs to humans, but most can be combated with a stringent routine of basic hygiene.

Regular de-worming and the removal of dog faeces from the environment are especially important to prevent the transmission of the Toxocara canis roundworm eggs that can survive in soil for up to two years. Children are most susceptible to worms, so make sure that they do not come into contact with dog faeces when playing in parks, and do not allow dogs to lick their faces. Encourage children to wash their hands after they have played with a dog before a meal, too. If infectious Toxocara roundworm larva are swallowed by humans, they can produce allergic reactions and, in extreme cases, blindness. (See page 135 below for details of worming treatments.)

Ringworm infections cause circular skin lesions in humans and should be treated by a doctor, while flea and tick bites irritate human skin and transfer diseases like Lyme disease.

Rabies, a potentially fatal disease, is transmitted in saliva, usually via bite wounds. It exists almost everywhere in the world apart from a few islands and peninsulas, among them Britain, Australia, Scandinavia and the islands of the Caribbean. All mammals are susceptible to rabies, but it is commonly carried by foxes, raccoons, mongooses, bats, skunks, cats and dogs. In Africa and Asia, dogs are the usual source of infection, and it is

**CHILDREN AND DOGS MUST RESPECT EACH OTHER.**

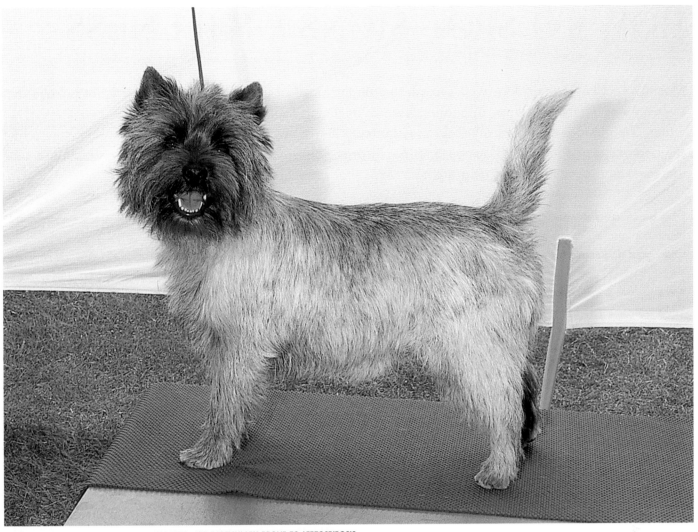

*TERRIERS LIKE THE CAIRNS VARIETY SHOWN HERE, ARE PARTICULARY PRONE TO LEPTOSPIROSIS*

foolhardy to handle a stray dog in these regions, but if you are bitten, immediately seek medical advice about being given the rabies antiserum. An infected dog is usually aggressive and salivates a great deal (although foaming at the mouth is an exaggeration).

Leptospirosis exists in two forms, one of which is linked to rats, which means that terriers are particularly prone to it, especially on farms, where they may encounter the bacterium via rats' urine. (It can be transferred to humans as Weil's disease.) A farm dog could also infect another animal. The second form, Leptospira icterohaemorrhagiae, leads to jaundice, and early symptoms include diarrhoea, vomiting and fever. Antibiotics usually clear it up and it can also be prevented via vaccination. In the later stages of the illness, an infected dog may appear permanently thirsty and experience breathing difficulties.

*A RELAXED DOG WITH ITS NEW OWNER.*

# HOW TO SPOT SIGNS OF ILLNESS

Most owners know their dogs well enough to spot the signs of illness. Poorly dogs may not behave in their normal manner, perhaps appearing listless, declining food or drinking prodigious quantities of water. Weight loss over several weeks may indicate illness, while slowly developing swellings may be the beginning of some sort of tumour (not necessarily cancerous). Hair loss, skin problems, slight lameness and occasional vomiting are also signs that something is not quite right.

Daily grooming is a chance for you to check your dog's health and also accustoms your pet to being handled. Check your dog carefully using this checklist.

- Are its eyes bright and clean? Sores, discharge or ulcers should not be present.

- Is its nose clean, slightly moist and free from crusty discharge?

- Check your dog's mouth to ensure that it looks pink. The gums should be pink (but are sometimes naturally mottled with black), the teeth should not be discoloured and there should be no foreign bodies or traces of food in the mouth.

- Are its ears clean and free from waxy discharge or odour?

- Check its paws for cuts, abrasions and foreign bodies trapped between the toes.

- Is your dog scratching or worrying at part of its body?

- Does your dog appear lame? Sometimes lameness is obvious, but in other cases it is manifested by changes in the dog's posture or a subtle alteration in its gait.

- Does it have a raised temperature? A normal canine temperature ranges between 38 and 39°C (100.4 and 102.2°F).

If you are concerned about your dog's health, write down the symptoms and note how long they have lasted – these details will help the vet to diagnose the dog's problem.

*GROOMING ENABLES YOU TO CHECK A DOG'S HEALTH.*

*CHECKING EARS FOR INFECTION.*

*GROOMING IS AN IDEAL TIME TO CHECK FOR ANY SIGNS OF ILL HEALTH*

# CALL THE VET...

. . . if you are in any doubt about your dog's health. Medical intervention is vital if your dog collapses, appears unable to breathe, loses consciousness or has convulsions. If your dog has been injured, is bleeding profusely, has been scalded, poisoned or in danger of drowning or is having difficulties whelping, get veterinary attention as quickly as possible.

Other potentially serious problems include the following.

- A swollen stomach that is obviously tender, accompanied by panting and salivation. This may be bloat or gastric torsion and is an emergency situation.
- Vomiting: if this persists for more than twelve hours, consult a vet.
- Diarrhoea lasting for more than twenty-four hours or blood-stained faeces require veterinary treatment.
- Breathing difficulties, gasping or choking require medical help.
- Collapse or unconsciousness require immediate veterinary attention.

*SERIOUS PROBLEMS MAY NEED SURGICAL INTERVENTION.*

*complete DOG*

# ADMINISTERING MEDICINE

**1** Tablets can be crushed and disguised within food, but if you need to be absolutely certain that your dog has swallowed its medication, you must place the tablet at the back of the dog's mouth.

**2** Do this by holding the muzzle with one hand while tilting the head slightly upwards. Grasp the lower jaw with your other hand and use your index finger and thumb to place the pill on the dog's tongue as far back as possible.

**3** Hold the mouth shut and gently massage the throat to encourage the dog to swallow the tablet.

**4** Liquid medicine is most easily given by using a plastic syringe to shoot the medicine to the back of the dog's mouth. A syringe enables you to measure the quantity precisely, and if you pipe the medicine in steadily, the dog will swallow it reasonably easily. Wash the syringe afterwards and reward your dog for its good behaviour. Eye drops can be administered by holding the dog's head steady (you may need an assistant) and tipping it slightly backwards. Apply the drops to the corner of the eye.

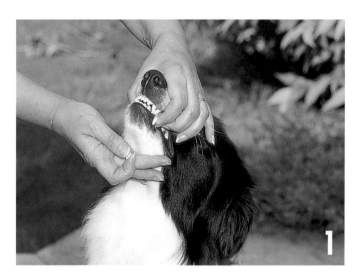

# DISORDERS

## EYES

Dogs' eyes are very expressive, and because eye contact is an important dog–human form of communication, owners are usually quick to notice any ocular problems. A dog may try to scratch its eye with its paw if there is an irritant in it, which may actually damage the eye. Discharges are the most common form of eye complaint, but more serious problems are harder to spot. If you are in the least worried by your dog's vision or eyes, consult a vet.

### CLEAR DISCHARGE

Tears, or clear discharge, are usually produced to wash away irritants. If the tear duct is blocked by mucus or an infection, tears can overflow and run down the face, which, if prolonged, can stain the fur. Light-coloured dogs, such as poodles, often display brown fur around their eyes, the result of 'poodle eye', or blocked tear ducts. If left untreated, surgical intervention may be necessary to clear the blocked duct. Excessive tears may also be a symptom of another problem, so always consult your vet.

### DRY EYE

Insufficient tear production may lead to dry eye, or Keratoconjunctivitis sicca, in which the eyeball's normal, healthy moistness is replaced by a sticky discharge and inflammation. This is most common in older dogs and can lead to blindness, but your vet can treat it with antibiotics and eye drops.

### CLOUDY OR INFLAMED EYES

Keratitis, a severe inflammation of the cornea or outer-eye surface caused by injury or infectious disease, must be treated by a vet. The cloudy, blue-grey cornea caused by Keratitis should not be confused with blue eye, a condition usually associated with a specific viral infection like hepatitis (in most cases, the eye recovers within a few days). Cataracts also cause cloudiness within the eye, and although they are associated with other eye diseases, they are more usually a problem of old age. Cataracts cause a deterioration in vision and can be removed if a vet thinks that the operation will result in an improvement in the dog's sight.

**RIGHT: A VET CHECKS A DOG'S EYES FOR DISCHARGE, REDNESS OR INFLAMMATION.**

### VISUAL PROBLEMS

Visual problems are hard to spot and diagnose until a dog begins to bump into furniture, at which point you should seek professional help. Some breeds are more likely to suffer from inherited eye disorders. Collie eye anomaly, for example, is the faulty development of the retina that occurs in rough and smooth collies and produces visual defects ranging from mild short-sightedness to total blindness.

### PROGRESSIVE RETINAL ATROPHY

Progressive retinal atrophy (RPA) first manifests itself as night-blindness, but may not be apparent until the dog begins to bump into things. Although it is an inherited and incurable condition, many blind dogs live contented and fulfilled lives.

# EARS

Most dogs shake their heads on waking, but persistent head-shaking, ear-scratching or signs of discharge indicate an ear problem. Dogs with long, floppy, hairy ears, such as spaniels, are more prone to ear diseases than those with erect ears, and their ears should be cleaned regularly. The insides of healthy ears look shiny and pale pink and are free from wax and odour. Do not insert anything into your dog's ears with which to clean out wax unless you are certain that there is no underlying problem.

## EAR-MITE INFESTATIONS

Ear-mite infestations are common in puppies and spread quickly from dog to dog, irritating the lining of the ear and increasing the production of wax. A vet will prescribe insecticidal ear drops to treat the problem.

## INFLAMMATION

Grass seeds often cause inflammation in spaniels' ears, and the first sign of such a problem is often excessive shaking of the head as the dog tries to dislodge the foreign body. A vet will probably remove the source of irritation with forceps and administer anti-inflammatory drops to restore the ear to health.

## INNER-EAR INFECTION

If your dog exhibits problems in balancing, such as appearing unsteady on its paws and tilting its head in the direction of one ear, it may have an inner-ear infection. Antibiotics usually solve the problem, although the infected ear may need to be drained by a vet. It is also sensible to restrict your dog's movements while it appears wobbly.

**EARS MUST BE KEPT CLEAN. CHECK FOR EAR MITE INFESTATION, EXCESSIVE WAX OR INFLAMMATION.**

# ORAL DISORDERS

## GUM DISEASE

Gum disease, or gingivitis, affects over 70 per cent of adult dogs and is caused by bacteria breeding in the remnants of food trapped between the teeth. Gum disease can be prevented by rigorous dental hygiene, that is, cleaning your dog's teeth every day (see page 103). The first sign of this condition is often bad breath followed by sore, inflamed gums, and if it is untreated, it will lead to tooth decay.

## EXCESSIVE DROOLING

Excessive drooling may be caused by a cyst on a salivary gland. Such cysts look like blisters and usually appear under the tongue, but also develop under the skin in the neck by the jaw. Consult your vet, who will probably drain the cyst and remove the salivary gland.

*RIGHT: A DOG HAS ITS TEETH CLEANED BY THE VET.*

*BELOW: TEETH AND GUMS MUST BE REGULARLY CHECKED FOR GINGIVITIS AND TOOTH DECAY.*

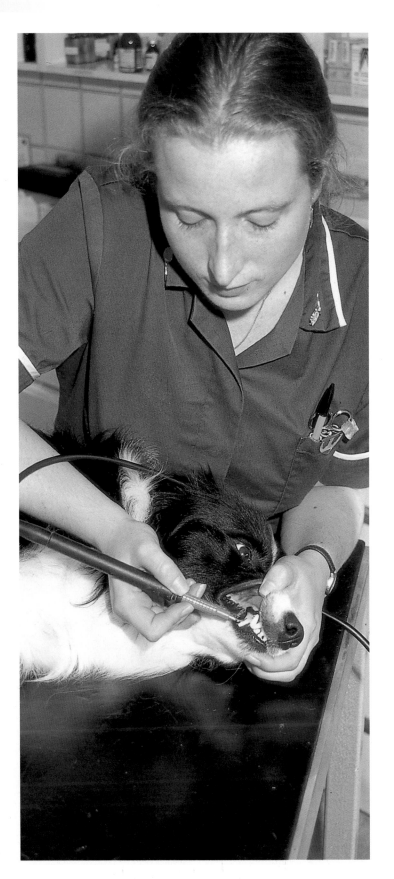

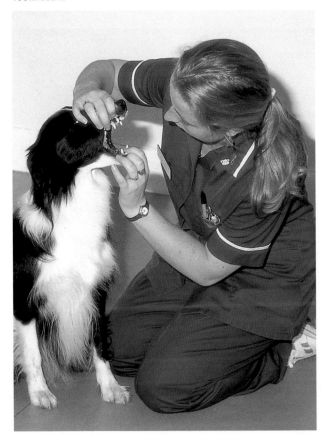

# EXTERNAL PARASITES

Fleas afflict nearly every dog at some point in their lives and flourish in warm environments. They are not immediately visible unless they are present in large numbers, but you may see flecks of reddish-brown dirt, the traces of blood that are left behind after fleas have bitten their host. Fleas move swiftly through a dog's coat and are extremely difficult to catch, although special combs help to sweep them out. If you place the specks of dirt on a piece of white tissue paper and find that the traces of blood stain the paper red, this confirms the presence of fleas.

A female flea lays her eggs on the floor or in bedding. After a week, the eggs hatch into larvae, which mature within two or three weeks. Because fleas can live in carpets and bedding, once you have treated the dog, vacuum its bedding and the surrounding area and apply a biological spray to kill any surviving fleas. If any remain, they will breed and re-infect the dog. Fleas also act as hosts for the larvae of the common tapeworm (see below), making it doubly important to treat an infestation. Ask your vet for an insecticide which will kill the fleas and prevent the eggs from hatching.

Mange mites and lice are usually caught from other dogs. Demodex mange mites live deep within the hair follicles, particularly of short-coated breeds. Invisible to the naked eye, they mainly afflict young puppies and elderly, infirm dogs. They can be treated by bathing your dog once a week in a special insecticide. Demodetic mange is more unsightly than irritating, but the affected areas often become infected, the skin may thicken and become wrinkly, like elephant hide, and pustules may form. If left untreated, hair follicles may be destroyed and, in severe cases, any skin changes may become permanent. Sarcoptes mites can invade a dog's ear tips and elbows by burrowing into the skin, causing these sites to become itchy and scabby. (They can inflict itchy, mosquito-like bites on humans, too). Infested dogs must be bathed weekly for at least four weeks to kill the parasites.

Harvest mites, or chiggers, only infest dogs during their larval stage during the autumn, when they usually attach themselves to dogs' paws, causing severe irritation. Insecticidal shampoo usually kills them, although anti-inflammatory medicine may also be necessary.

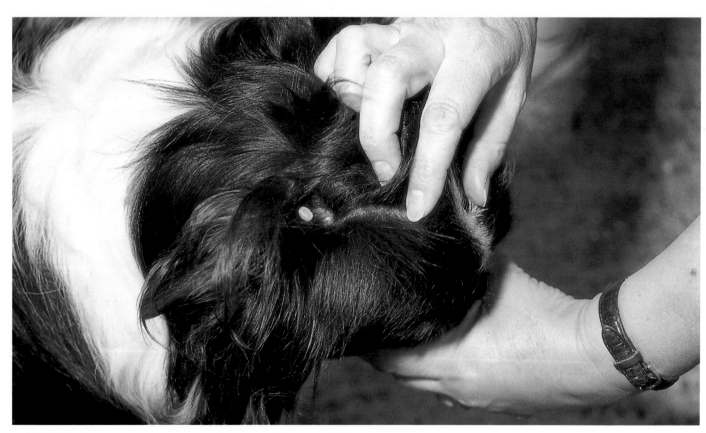

**PARASITES INFEST MOST DOGS AT SOME POINT. A TICK HAS SET UP HOME ON THIS ANIMAL.**

**FLEA AND TICK INFESTATIONS CAN BE TREATED WITH SPRAYS, POWDERS AND TABLETS.**

# INTERNAL PARASITES

All dogs lick their bottoms, but constant licking of the anal region or dragging the bottom along the ground can be signs that your dog is infected with worms. The two most common worms in dogs are roundworms and tapeworms.

Roundworms (Toxocara canis or Toxocaris leonina) infect most puppies, partly because they are transmitted from dog to dog via faecal contamination. The larvae can also be transmitted from a mother to her unborn puppies, which means that puppies may have mature worms within them at the age of only two weeks. Infected puppies may appear pot-bellied and will gain weight only slowly. Most breeders will treat the entire litter with worming medicine at the age of three or four weeks, and the treatment should be repeated every month or so until the dogs are six months old. Your vet will advise you on the best course of treatment, but it is sensible to worm adult dogs every three months because roundworms also pose a hazard to human health.

Tapeworms are more common in older dogs than in puppies and have a life cycle based upon two hosts: the dog and its fleas. It is hard to know when tapeworms are present, the only sign being small 'rice grains' (the tapeworms' dried egg sacs) around the dog's anus and in its faeces. Treatment is usually a medicine prescribed by the vet, but prevention, as they say, is better than cure, and this depends on controlling the flea problem. Never allow your dog to eat animal carcasses or offal from animals such as sheep because both are sources of tapeworm infection.

Dogs living in unhygienic conditions are susceptible to other species of worm, too, such as whipworms and hookworms, both of which live within the intestine and can cause diarrhoea, while hookworms can result in serious bleeding and anaemia in the host dog. Veterinary treatment is vital in both cases.

# COMMON AILMENTS OF THE NERVOUS SYSTEM

Diseases of the nervous system are often caused by viruses, such as rabies or distemper, and viral damage can lead to paralysis, behavioural changes, loss of balance or seizures. Viruses or bacterial infections may inflame the lining of the brain, while head injuries resulting in damaged brain tissue may cause epilepsy.

## CHOREA

Chorea, or involuntary muscle-twitching, is usually a symptom of another disease, such as distemper. It often begins a couple of weeks after apparent recovery from the disease and is most noticeable when the dog is asleep. Because it can progress to cause major muscle spasms and then convulsions, veterinary advice is vital.

## DISTEMPER AND HARD PAD

Although the majority of puppies are inoculated against distemper, some still catch this miserable illness. Highly infectious, and sometimes fatal, it usually afflicts young dogs.

The classic signs are thick discharge from the nose and eyes, forming a crusty residue, persistent coughing, fever, vomiting and diarrhoea. It can lead to encephalitis (inflammation of the brain) and fits, but, with good care, most dogs recover. Hard pad occurs when the virus affects the horny layer of the dog's paws, making them feel leathery. Veterinary intervention is vital.

## LOSS OF BALANCE

Loss of balance may be a sign of an inner-ear infection (see page 132), when the dog may cock its head quite obviously towards the affected side. An inner-ear infection can be treated with antibiotics.

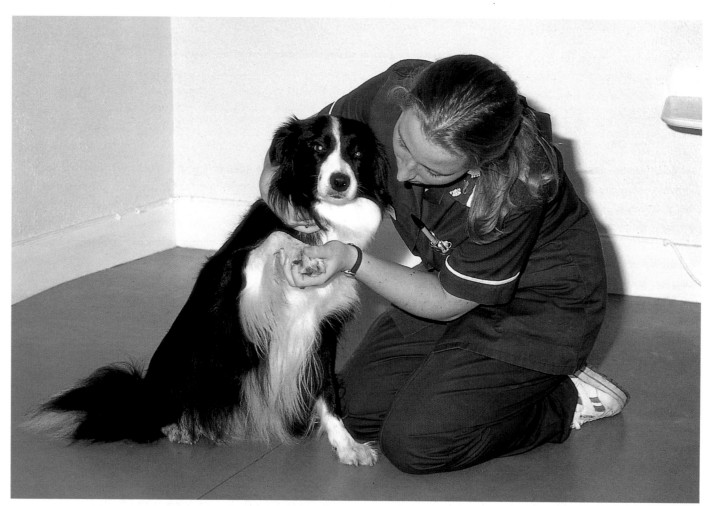

*GRASS SEEDS OFTEN CAUSE INFECTION IF THEY BECOME TRAPPED IN A DOG'S SOFT PAW PAD.*

## RABIES

Although behavioural changes are sometimes prompted by neurological problems, rabies is the most serious cause (but this disease has currently been eradicated from Britain). The first sign is often a change of temperament: gentle dogs become more aggressive and active dogs quieter. As the disease progresses over the course of about ten days, gradual paralysis sets in and the dog eventually dies from respiratory failure.

## SEIZURES

Seizures can be controlled by drugs, but may be a sign of another problem, such as encephalitis, epilepsy or a brain tumour. Encephalitis can be treated with antibiotics, and tumours can sometimes be removed from the brain. Whatever the cause, consult a vet if your dog has a convulsion.

# DIGESTIVE AILMENTS

Dogs are natural scavengers, and if they are allowed to grab food at any opportunity, they will inevitably become ill. Some dogs eat grass regularly and others do it sporadically to ease abdominal discomfort because it usually provokes vomiting. Persistent vomiting, or vomiting blood or bile, are signs of a serious problem, however, as is persistent diarrhoea.

If your dog has vomited, do not give it any solid food for a day, but allow it unlimited access to water. If, after twenty-four hours, it is still vomiting, take it to the vet's. Severe vomiting may be caused by gastric torsion, a life-threatening condition, or an infection, such as canine parvovirus. (Puppies are inoculated against canine parvovirus, but this infectious, potentially fatal, virus may still take hold, manifesting itself as chronic vomiting and blood-stained diarrhoea). In both instances, seek veterinary help. Loss of appetite may also indicate that your dog is not well.

## CONSTIPATION

The consistency of dogs' motions, and the frequency with which they are passed, vary, but constipation is obvious when a dog has difficulty passing stools, straining or showing other signs of discomfort.

Constipation is more usually a problem in ageing dogs than in young ones, when it is often a symptom of poor gut motility. It may also be a sign of blocked anal sacs, which, although they can be squeezed to empty them, may require antibiotic treatment. Ingested bones also cause digestive troubles.

Dogs sometimes produce greasy motions when they have difficulty digesting fat (which may be a sign of pancreatic failure), and if this is the case, avoid giving your dog an oily

*CHOREA IS MOST NOTICEABLE WHEN THE DOG IS ASLEEP*

laxative. Otherwise, ask your vet's advice for a suitable laxative, such as liquid paraffin.

## GASTRIC DISTENSION, BLOAT OR GASTRIC TORSION

Gastric distension (also known as bloat or gastric torsion) usually affects large dogs, such as Great Danes, although it can also occur in Pekinese and dachshunds. The dog may show obvious signs of pain two to four hours after feeding, the abdomen may appear distended and hard and the dog may also try to vomit. This is a surgical emergency, so get veterinary help immediately.

## WEIGHT PROBLEMS

If your dog suddenly develops a voracious appetite and great thirst and also steadily loses weight, ask your vet to test it for diabetes. In most cases, diabetes can be treated with daily injections of insulin to control the dog's blood-sugar level.

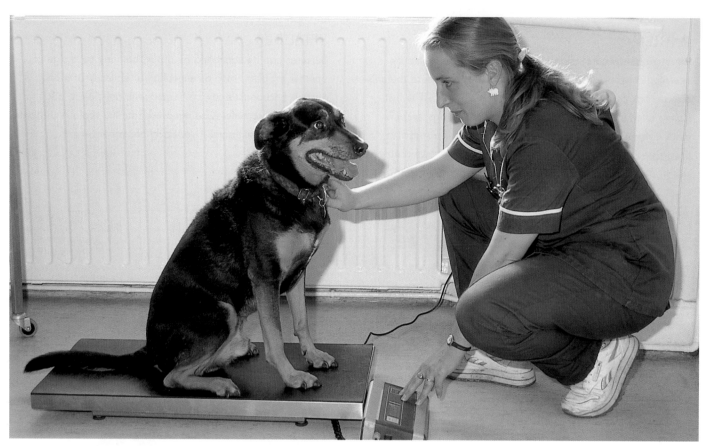

*EXCESSIVE WEIGHT GAIN OR WEIGHT LOSS MAY BE A SIGN OF ILLNESS.*

Equally, if your dog becomes lethargic and starts to put on weight when you have made no changes to its diet, consult your vet because an underactive thyroid gland may be slowing down its metabolism. This problem is easily treatable with drugs.

In most cases, however, weight gain is the result of lack of exercise and over-feeding. Try not to let your dog become overweight – obese dogs have a shorter life expectancy and, in some cases, a poorer quality of life than slim ones.

## URINARY PROBLEMS

Any change in your dog's ability to urinate, or frequency of urination, should be investigated by a vet.

If your dog appears to strain to urinate, it may be a sign of a bladder infection or of stones, which can lodge in the urinary system anywhere from the kidneys through the urethra to the bladder. Dogs with bladder stones usually urinate frequently in small amounts because they are unable to empty their bladder properly. If the problem is caused by an infection, antibiotics will usually relieve it. If there is a serious blockage, however, the vet

may use a catheter to empty the bladder. Bladder stones are visible on X-rays and, in many cases, can be treated using dietary changes.

Incontinence is reasonably common in older dogs, who are usually unaware of leaking urine. It also occurs in younger dogs, usually in spayed females, when it is caused by a hormonal imbalance that can be treated with a hormone spray. Male dogs may experience similar problems when they have an enlarged prostate gland.

An increase in the frequency of urination may be caused by a bladder or kidney infection, or possibly by diabetes or a liver problem. Consult a vet, who will probably want to take a urine sample for analysis.

Kidney disease (rather than merely an infection) is often a cause of serious illness in adult dogs. Acute kidney failure usually manifests itself as fever, increased thirst and decreased urination, the urine itself being dark in colour and almost sticky. Immediate veterinary attention is necessary to administer fluids intravenously.

# CIRCULATORY AND RESPIRATORY PROBLEMS

Although blood disorders are rare in dogs, heart disease is almost as common in dogs as in humans. Sudden heart failure is unusual, but is more common in large breeds, such as the Doberman. Some breeds are prone to progressive valvular heart disease, particularly King Charles spaniels. Heart conditions can be treated with drugs and careful monitoring of the dog's lifestyle – exercise is vital.

Coughing is usually an attempt to dislodge mucus or foreign bodies from the respiratory system, but it may be a symptom of a more serious disease, such as distemper or kennel cough.

Kennel cough is a rasping, unproductive cough that often occurs in dogs that have recently returned from a stay in kennels. The dog may not appear particularly ill, but the cough is caused by the Bordetella bacterium, and secondary infection can lead to pneumonia. It is sensible to vaccinate your dog against kennel cough prior to a stay in kennels.

A moist cough, sometimes known as 'heart cough', may be a sign of circulatory problems and occurs after exercise, usually in older dogs. Any persistent cough requires veterinary treatment, particularly if it is accompanied by a refusal to eat or any sign of distress.

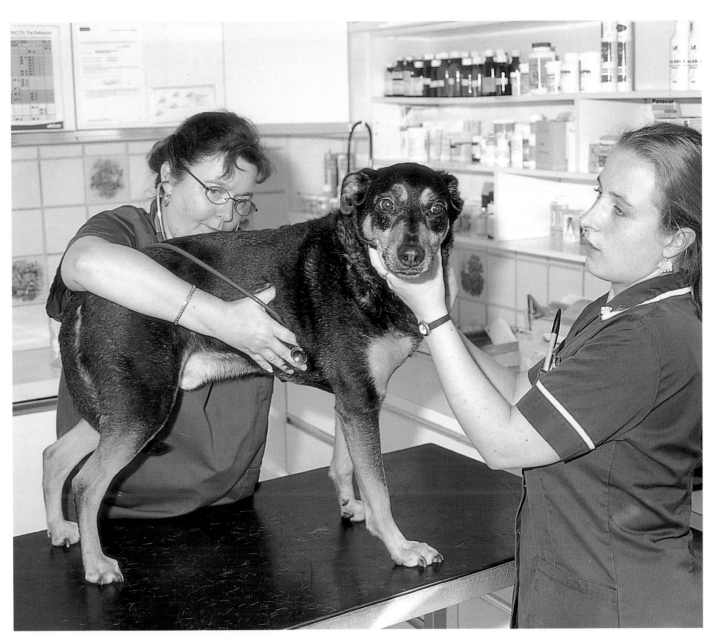

**A VET USES A STETHOSCOPE TO CHECK THIS ELDERLY DOG'S HEART RATE.**

# EXTERNAL DISORDERS

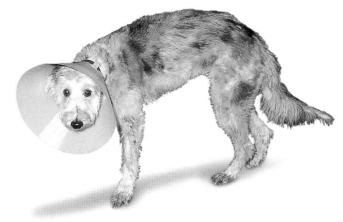

*AN 'ELIZABETHAN COLLAR' TO PREVENT SCRATCHING.*

## LICK GRANULOMA

Lick granuloma usually occurs on the fore leg (often in Labradors and short-hared dogs), when a small cut or abrasion is opened up by the constant licking of a bored dog and does not heal properly. The skin becomes itchy and eventually ulcerates. Bandaging the leg sometimes prevents licking, but the best cure is to fit a funnel-shaped 'Elizabethan collar' around your dog's neck to prevent it licking itself.

## ANAL SACS

Anal sacs are two pockets, one on each side of the anus, containing glands that produce the pungent secretions used by dogs to communicate scent-marking and whether a bitch is in oestrus. Dogs occasionally empty their anal sacs involuntarily in stressful situations.

If the anal sacs become blocked, they will first cause irritation and then pain, and an affected dog may drag its behind along the ground. (It is easy to confuse this behaviour with the symptoms of fleas or worms.) Although evacuation of the anal sacs is relatively simple, it is best to ask a vet to do it because the cause of the problem needs to be diagnosed.

# SKIN AND COAT DISORDERS

## SEBORRHOEA

Seborrhoea, or an overproduction of the sebum, produced by the sebaceous glands, that lubricates the skin, produces a dull, greasy coat with a mouse-like smell. It is most common in cocker spaniels, although terriers are also affected. Dry seborrhoea looks like dandruff, and both types are easily treated with an anti-sebum shampoo. Seborrhoea is caused by parasites, a yeast infection, a hormonal imbalance or poor diet.

*SOME SMOOTH COLLIES SUFFER FROM DEAFNESS.*

*EXCESSIVE SCRATCHING MAY BE A SIGN OF FLEAS.*

## HAIR LOSS

Hair-loss patterns vary from breed to breed and, indeed, from dog to dog. Some breeds shed their hair almost perpetually, especially in spring and autumn, when a new coat grows. However, some dogs shed excessive amounts of hair without it thinning the coat, which is probably the result of a hormonal imbalance or possibly environmental factors, such as central heating. Frequent grooming is vital, both to maintain a healthy coat and to prevent itchiness.

Localised hair loss may be caused by ringworm (see page 126 or parasites, such as mange mites (see page 134), both of which are easily treated. In some breeds – particularly collies – sunburn can lead to hair loss on the muzzle, and vulnerable dogs must be protected by a high-factor sun cream. Other dogs suffer hair loss on the elbows, which is simply caused by too much pressure being applied to hard surfaces. Calluses may also develop, but a moisturising cream will help to combat this problem, while soft bedding will minimise any discomfort.

## WARTS, CYSTS AND TUMOURS

Warts are common in older dogs of most breeds, especially spaniels and poodles. They can become infected, at which point your vet may advise their surgical removal. Cysts feel like hard lumps under the skin, whereas tumours, which are usually benign and affect older dogs, can be felt as soft, fluctuating masses beneath the skin.

MINIATURE POODLES MAY ENDURE BONE DISORDERS.

# REPRODUCTIVE DISORDERS

Many reproductive disorders, such as womb infections in females, can be avoided by having your dog neutered (see pages 112). All sexually active dogs should be checked for sexually transmitted diseases, such as brucellosis, which can cause infertility.

Prostate disease, in which the prostate gland becomes enlarged, is a problem of older male dogs. The prostate gland is sited by the exit to the bladder and underneath the rectum, so the first sign of trouble may be urinary incontinence and/or constipation (because the swollen gland obstructs the rectum). Some cases may be treated either by hormonal drugs or castration.

Pregnancy can be hard to detect in dogs, but after pregnancy has been diagnosed look out for the danger signal of vaginal discharge. Bloody discharge may warn of miscarriage, while a discharge of pus may be a sign of a womb infection. In both cases, contact the vet immediately.

Most bitches give birth without difficulty, but labour is nevertheless hazardous for a dog. If your dog is due to whelp, alert your vet, just in case he or she is needed. (See Chapter 6 for more information about whelping.)

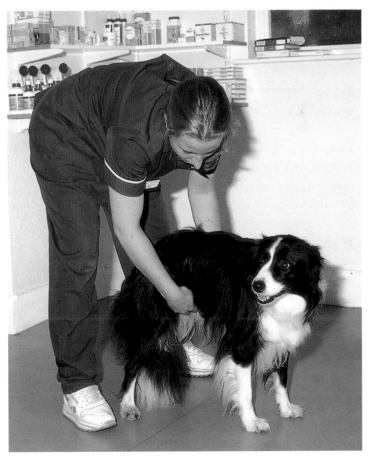

IF YOU SUSPECT YOUR DOG IS PREGNANT, ASK A VET TO CONFIRM IT.

complete DOG

# EMERGENCIES AND FIRST AID

If you are in any doubt about your dog's health, contact your vet immediately. In the case of emergency situations, there are a number of ways of relieving your dog's pain and distress or administering first aid. You can treat less serious injuries yourself with first-aid measures before taking your dog to the vet.

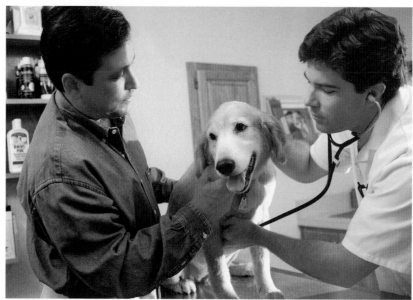

IF IN DOUBT, ALWAYS CONSULT A VET.

## FIRST-AID KIT

Never mix up items in human and canine first-aid kits. Keep a separate kit for your dog and make sure that the vet's telephone number is included in it. You will need the following items:

- cotton wool
- cotton buds
- adhesive and gauze bandage in two widths, 5 and 10 cm (2 and 4 in)
- adhesive tape
- sharp-pointed scissors
- blunt-ended forceps
- a thermometer
- antiseptic cream and/or spray.

# UNCONSCIOUSNESS

If your dog collapses or becomes unconscious after an accident, you will need to check its airways, perhaps removing any foreign bodies and gently pulling its tongue forwards to stop the dog's breathing from being obstructed.

Watch your dog's chest to observe its breathing – there should be between twenty and thirty breaths a minute. If exhaling seems forced, it may have an injured diaphragm.

Check its pulse on the inside of the hind leg, or press a hand on its chest, behind the elbow. Large dogs should have a pulse rate of between fifty and ninety beats per minute, and small dogs one of about a hundred and fifty beats per minute.

Do not spend too much time doing these things: an unconscious dog needs urgent veterinary treatment, so wrap it in a blanket and take it to the vet's.

KEEP AN UNCONSCIOUS DOG WARM AND CALL A VET IMMEDIATELY.

# BLEEDING

If your dog is bleeding severely, it is an emergency. Try to control the bleeding while you are on the way to the veterinary surgery by applying a pressure bandage to the wound. (A tourniquet should not be used.) Place a large wad of cotton wool on the wound and bandage it firmly into place. If your dog is injured when you are not at home and have no access to a bandage, use whatever comes to hand, such as a scarf, sock or T-shirt. The important thing is to slow the bleeding down.

Lighter wounds, which will probably stop bleeding within a short time, will probably only need to be cleaned with antiseptic. Trim the hair from around the wound to prevent it from becoming infected and watch out for any swelling, which would indicate an infection.

A dog's skin does not readily bleed, and it is therefore easy to miss even deep cuts and scratches. A wound that is longer than about a centimetre (half an inch), or that appears to be quite deep, may need stitching. Unless it is bleeding profusely, do not attempt to administer any first aid and take your dog directly to the vet's.

If your dog has been injured in a traffic accident, or has suffered a serious fall, it may be bleeding internally. If it suddenly becomes pale and lethargic, alert the vet immediately.

*SERIOUS INJURIES REQUIRE VETERINARY HELP.*

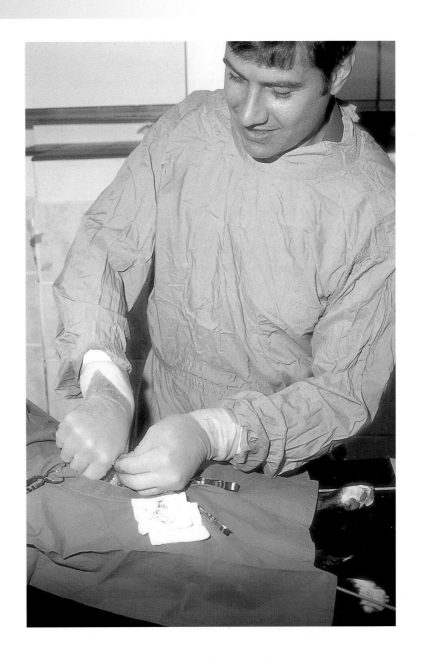

# ROAD ACCIDENTS

Many road accidents involving dogs can be prevented by ensuring that dogs are kept under control in urban areas.

A badly injured dog may be in shock and may bite you, so fit a muzzle using a lead, scarf or rope before trying to examine it. If the dog is unconscious, try to put it on to a coat or blanket to make it easier to move it and avoid touching any visible injuries. Ask someone to help you to carry it to a car, using the coat or blanket as a stretcher, and take it to a vet's as quickly as possible.

If the dog appears to have a fractured leg, pick it up by supporting its chest under one arm and its hindquarters under the other, thereby allowing the affected limb to hang free.

## BITES

Unless the dog is bleeding profusely from a bite or has been really savaged, a bite is not an emergency situation. When dog bites take the form of puncture wounds they often become infected, so clean the wound with antiseptic and wait for twenty-four hours before deciding if you need to take your dog to see the vet, who will determine whether antibiotics are necessary.

## STINGS

Dogs are unlikely to die from insect stings unless the resultant swelling blocks the dog's airways or it has been subjected to multiple stings. Veterinary treatment is usually unnecessary unless the mouth or throat begin to swell. If it is visible, remove the sting with tweezers and apply a soothing cream or icepack to relieve the swelling.

## HEAT EXHAUSTION

Heat exhaustion is usually inflicted on dogs by careless owners, but some breeds, such as chows and bulldogs, are more susceptible to it than others. Never leave a dog in a car without adequate ventilation and water: even on a cloudy day, the temperature can build up and heat exhaustion can kill a dog.

The signs of heat exhaustion are heavy panting, obvious distress and an inability to breath deeply. In severe cases, the tongue may appear swollen and blue. In such instances you must try to revive the dog immediately by bathing it in cold water, especially its head. Put it in a cold bath if possible, or a cattle trough if you happen to be near one, or drape a towel soaked in cold water over it. This really is life-saving treatment. Once it appears to be breathing more easily, take it to the vet's.

**LARGE HEADS AND NARROW HIPS OFTEN CAUSE WHELPING PROBLEMS FOR BULLDOGS.**

# POISONING

Dogs may either ingest poisons or suffer external contamination or burns from chemicals. If your dog has been in contact with caustic chemicals, sponge its coat with warm, soapy water. Do not use anything on your dog that you would not apply to your own skin, so do not, for example, use paint-stripper to clean paint from its coat, which is in any case highly toxic to dogs. Ask your vet for advice.

Internal poisoning can be fatal, so keep all toxic substances well out of your dog's reach. However, if it is clear that it has swallowed something untoward, take it to the vet's immediately, preferably with a sample of whatever it has consumed, along with its packaging. Vomiting, diarrhoea, fits, collapse and coma are all signs of poisoning. If you know that the poison has been ingested within the past hour, try to induce vomiting by making your dog swallow a salt-water solution. Mix one teaspoon of salt with a cup of tepid water, administer the solution with a syringe and stand by with newspaper or a bucket because vomiting will occur quite swiftly. Take your dog to the vet's as soon as possible, along with a sample of the vomit.

| COMMON POISONS | SYMPTOMS |
| --- | --- |
| Rat poisons are dangerous when consumed in in great quantities. They are coloured to show their active ingredient, so take a sample or the packaging to the vet's to assist diagnosis. | Bleeding gums and bruising to the skin. |
| Household drugs: aspirins, tranquillisers or barbiturates. | Appetite loss, depression, staggering and coma. |
| Slug and snail bait (metaldehyde). | Tremors, salivation, fits and coma. |
| Antifreeze. | Vomiting, staggering, convulsions and coma. |
| Lead paint. | Vomiting, diarrhoea, stomach pain and paralysis. |
| Household cleaners. | Inflamed skin, vomiting, diarrhoea, ulcerated tongue and fits. |
| Toads: dogs may lick toads, some of whose skins are toxic. | Redness, swelling of the mouth and tongue. |

## CHAPTER 8

# BREEDS

The classification of breeds and breed types is quite arbitrary. The ancient Romans classified dogs as 'house dogs', 'shepherd dogs' and 'sporting dogs', and even in the late Middle Ages when Dr. Caius made his classification he divided them into three groups: 'hunters', 'homely dogs' and 'curs'. The three groups were further subdivided: hunters were divided into terriers, harriers, bloodhounds, gazehounds, greyhounds, spaniels, setters and water spaniels. Homely dogs also found 'gentle' spaniels included, as well as dogs described as 'comforters', while curs were divided into shepherds, mastiffs and 'bandogges' – an ancient term for a dog that was tied up by day and released at night, the medieval equivalent of a modern, trained professional guard dog.

# CLASSIFICATION OF BREEDS

In the 1700s the Swedish scientist Dr. Carolus Linneaus (1702–1778) published his text The System of Nature in which he listed and named 35 breeds of dog, while the French naturalist, the Comte de Buffon (1707–1788) further classified dogs into five groups according to their shape and behaviour. In the following century, as the interest in science grew, new breed classifications were explored and, in 1878, the German scientist Professor Fitzinger classified 180 dog breeds and varieties according to their external features.

**TOY (KING CHARLES)**

**TERRIER**

Even with the founding of the world's first Kennel Club in 1873, all dogs were shown together. Soon however two categories of dogs were devised, called simply 'sporting' and 'non-sporting'. Sporting dogs were soon subdivided and had three groups: gundogs, hounds and terriers. Non-sporting dogs proved a little more difficult to classify but, eventually, toy dogs were separated out, followed by working dogs and the miscellaneous breeds, labelled as utility dogs. (In the US, gundogs are still known as 'sporting dogs' and utility dogs as 'non-sporting dogs').

Today the K.C. has breed standards for six main groups of dogs: hounds, terriers, gundogs, utility, toy, and working dogs. Each of the original breed clubs retains the rights to define the standards for their own breed of dog, but all the clubs that are affiliated to the F.C.I. submit their standards to them for international recognition. This does mean that the F.C.I. may recognise certain breeds of dogs, while the K.C. in the UK and the A.K.C. (American Kennel Club) may not! Furthermore, the breed

standards are often interpreted in different ways in different countries, so there may be distinctive differences in appearances between dogs from different countries.

The F.C.I. classification of breeds is a complicated, one based on the origins and physical characteristics of the breeds as well as on their behaviour. In its most basic form, the F.C.I. classification contains eight categories, which, once again, are arbitrary since some breeds could very accurately be included in another category! The eight F.C.I. categories are:

Primitive dogs (once again an arbitrary classification applied to a small group of dogs descended from Canus lupus pallipes, or the Indian Plains wolf. The group includes 'genuine primitives' such as the dingo and the New Guinea singing dog as well as the basenji and Mexican hairless dogs, both of which are the result of human intervention in breeding); sight hounds; scent hounds; spitz-type dogs; terriers; gundogs; livestock dogs; and, companion dogs.

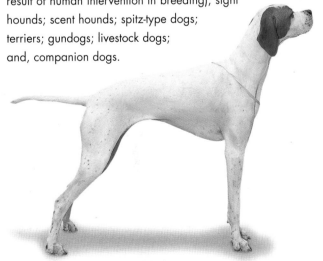

**GUN DOG**

# GUN DOGS

Throughout the great part of man's history of hunting for food – and for sport – it was sight and scent hounds that accompanied them. Such hounds were the preserve of the nobility and rich land–owning classes, and were used for hunting 'large game' such as deer or wild boar, while the lower orders in society were largely prohibited from owning and using them. The peasant and farming classes developed their own 'hunting dogs' – terriers that would hunt 'vermin' by digging and tunnelling after smaller mammals such as rats, rabbits or foxes.

**CURLY–COATRED RETRIEVER**

**LABRADOR RETRIEVER**

The introduction of firearms encouraged breeders to take a further, deeper interest in the natural instincts of hounds and terriers to scent, track, 'go to earth' and even to swim. What was needed now were dogs that could find game, but would then stand or crouch stock still, or, on command, leap into icy water to 'retrieve' shot game – not eat the game but deliver the dead animal back to the hunter. This type of dog not only had the natural instincts that hounds and terriers already demonstrated, but also needed a willingness to be trained. In the 16th and 17th centuries, using a genetic base derived from hounds and dogs with a 'herding instinct', breeders developed some 50 breeds of gun dogs. These gun dogs are usually divided into five subgroups: water dogs, pointers, setters, flushing dogs and retrievers. Water dogs, which will

**SPRINGER SPANIEL**

retrieve shot game from rivers and lakes, require both an urge to swim and a tight, waterproof coat, like that of the curly–coated retriever. Pointers and setters were employed originally to accompany hunters armed with nets. The dogs followed the air scent of game, silently searched for the animal on the ground and then stopped in their tracks and remained completely still: the pointer freezes with one of its forelegs 'bent' and 'points' at the quarry; the setter works in the same manner except that it crouches down or 'sets'. In both cases, the dog's natural instinct to capture the prey has been 'stopped' by training.

Flushing dogs work their way through dense undergrowth and 'flush' the game birds towards the hunters. At one time all British spaniels were classified as land, field or water spaniels depending on the terrain in which they worked, but with developments in breeding for show standards, classifications became more 'distinct': English and Welsh 'springers' (so called because their flushing technique also involved 'springing' birds into nets) were separated from the 'cockers' (so called because their small size made them suitable for small game such as woodcock), while field, Sussex and clumber spaniels became distinct breeds.

Using the water–loving dogs of Newfoundland (see page 164), British breeders developed retrievers. These dogs had the natural ability to carry game 'softly' in their mouths – without marking them with their teeth – coupled with the dog's great intelligence, and a willingness to learn and obey. These outstanding qualities, seen in Labrador retrievers and golden retrievers not only makes them popular gun dogs, but firm favourites as family pets, and as 'service dogs' – in particular, as guide dogs for the blind.

# ENGLISH COCKER SPANIEL

**OTHER NAMES:** Cocker spaniel

**DATE OF ORIGIN:** 19th century

**PLACE OF ORIGIN:**
Great Britain

**ORIGINAL USE:** Small game
flushing and retrieving

**MODERN USE:** Companion

**SIZE:**

**HEIGHT:** 38–41 cm (15–16 in)

**WEIGHT:** 13–15 kg (28–32 lb)

**COLOURS:** Various including
black, red, blue roan, strawberry
roan, black–and–white and tricolour

**RECOGNIZED BY:** K.C.

The term 'spaniel' has been in use since the Renaissance and it refers to the original home of the breed, Spain, which in the 16th century was at the height of its cultural and political powers and where the 'new' methods of hunting and the dog breeds were first developed. Such dogs were well established on the Continent and were probably known in England during the reign of the Plantagenet kings (from 1154–1485). The term 'spaniel' was however generic: in the 17th century both 'large' and 'small' spaniels were evident, as well as those with either long or short bodies which were 'fast' or 'slow' dogs. From the melting pot of spaniels the distinct breeds such as the English and American cocker spaniels, the Sussex, the springer, and the field spaniels were developed.

The cocker is said by some to have earned its name because it was used for small game bird hunting, such as woodcock, while others maintain it was because the spaniel 'sprung', 'started' or 'cocked' the game – first for the net, and later for the gun. Whatever the origins, the name was so widely used that, in 1873, the English Kennel Club recognised the breed under that name. Game hunters claim that the cocker is the most efficiently designed of all the spaniels: robust and strong, but small enough to push through dense undergrowth, a neck that is strong enough to lift game that is large and heavy relative to the dog itself, and long enough to keep the game lifted clear of the floor in the retrieve. The forelegs are solid and short – perfect for concentrated power – while the elegantly shaped head has a well–defined, square muzzle and a well–developed nose.

# AMERICAN COCKER SPANIEL

**OTHER NAMES:** Cocker spaniel

**DATE OF ORIGIN:** 19th century

**PLACE OF ORIGIN:**
United States of America

**ORIGINAL USE:** Small game
retrieving

**MODERN USE:** Companion

**SIZE:**

**HEIGHT:** 36–38 cm (14–15 in)

**WEIGHT:** 11–13 kg (24–28 lb)

**COLOURS:** Variety

**RECOGNIZED BY:** K.C.

'Cocker spaniel' is in fact the proper name for two distinct breeds: the English cocker spaniel and the American cocker. The English cocker is the older of the two breeds, although legend tells of how the American cocker's ancestor arrived in the New World with the Pilgrim Fathers aboard the Mayflower in 1620. While the term spaniel had been in use in England in the Middle Ages, the real history of the cocker spaniel begins with the birth of a dog called 'Obo' in 1879 and all cockers, English or American, can trace their ancestry back to him.

The American cocker spaniel was developed in the USA from the working English cocker, but while the American cocker still retains its hunting instincts and attempts have been made to work dogs, its greatest appeal lies in the gentle, loyal and affectionate companionship the American cocker offers as a household pet. In the 1920s American breeders developed cockers with a more distinctly domed head to the English cocker, and one which displayed more height at the shoulder, a shorter back and a slightly longer neck. The American cocker is also distinguished by its' beautiful long, silky and wavy coat of dense, fine hair which needs careful grooming on a daily basis to prevent it from matting.

Regrettably, the American cocker spaniel, like its English cousin, does suffer from a range of health problems including skin and eye complaints and, sometimes, epilepsy. Despite these problems, the American cocker spaniel, with it's wonderful character, remains America's most popular 'home–grown' breeds.

*complete DOG*

# CLUMBER SPANIEL

**OTHER NAMES:** None

**DATE OF ORIGIN:** 19th century

**PLACE OF ORIGIN:**
Nottinghamshire, England

**ORIGINAL USE:** Tracking, game
retrieving

**MODERN USE:** Tracking,
companion

**SIZE:**

**HEIGHT:** 48–51 cm (19–20 in)

**WEIGHT:** 29–36 kg (65–80 lb)

**COLOURS:** Plain white (lemon
markings permitted)

**RECOGNIZED BY:** K.C.

The clumber is the heavyweight of the spaniel world. They are both large and deceptively slow moving – except when you want to catch up with one! The clumber is named after the Duke of Newcastle's Nottinghamshire estate, Cumber Park. According to legend, this spaniel's ancestors were retrievers owned by the French Duc de Noialles, who, at the outbreak of the French Revolution, sent his dogs to safety in England. The clumber's ancestors may, therefore, include the basset hound – which would account for its long back – and the St. Bernard, which would account for the very large, square–shaped head.

A more likely explanation however, is that the clumber was bred in Nottinghamshire using existing dogs in the region, which would rule out the St. Bernard as a possible influence. Whatever dogs were used, the aim was to produce a gun dog that would be less volatile during a shoot than other breeds, and whose speed was dictated by its size: in essence the clumber was 'designed' to flatten the dense undergrowth to a suitable width, allowing the armed huntsmen on foot (and who, in the 19th century, were also large in the girth) to follow at a decent 'leisurely' pace! Working clumber spaniels operate as a team, rather leisurely beating the game towards the hunters.

This gentlemanly pace of the shoot ensured that the clumber became a firm favourite with the Royals: King Edward VII, a dedicated huntsman and bon viveur, who earned himself the nickname of 'Tum–Tum' on account of his ever increasing waist, was particularly fond of the clumber spaniel and he kept a large number of them at Sandringham, in Norfolk. Later, King George V also used clumbers exclusively on the Royal Estates in Norfolk, and the bloodline of these dogs was a great influence on the breed. Today, the preference for working spaniels is for faster animals which can cover more ground, and the clumber spaniel is more likely to be found tracking and retrieving sticks and fallen leaves in back gardens!

# FIELD SPANIEL

**OTHER NAMES:** None

**DATE OF ORIGIN:** 19th century

**PLACE OF ORIGIN:** Great Britain

**ORIGINAL USE:** Game retrieving

**MODERN USE:** Companion

**SIZE:**

**HEIGHT:** 51–58 cm (20–23 in)

**WEIGHT:** 16–23 kg (35–50 lb)

**COLOURS:** Black, roan, liver

**RECOGNIZED BY:** K.C.

The field spaniel, although popular in the early part of the 20th century, is now quite a rare dog. The breed has an ancestry similar to that of the cocker spaniel and both, in their early days, were classed simply as either 'field spaniels under 25 lb (11.5 kg)' and 'field spaniels over 25 lb (11.5 kg)'. In 1892, however, the two breeds were separated as distinct as cocker spaniel and field spaniel. While the cocker became shorter and a more robust dog, breeders of field spaniels worked towards producing low, long dogs with heavy–boned legs. These dogs looked more like heavily built dachshunds than working dogs and, consequently, the field spaniel lost the greater part of its ability to work outside of the show ring.

By the end of World War II, the field spaniel was nearly extinct, but was saved by the efforts of breeders who rescued the breed from complete obscurity. In the 1960s numbers were increased after breeders introduced English cocker spaniels (see page 149) and springer spaniels (see page 153) in order to regenerate the breed and produce today's good looking and affectionate dog.

Field spaniels today have a moderate length body that is well ribbed and carried on strong, muscular hind quarters and straight front legs. The shoulders slope well back while the skull is well developed with a distinct occiput. Like all spaniels, the field's ears are long, wide and beautifully feathered. The glorious silky and glossy coat is flat, but can be slightly waved, and dense enough to resist wet weather. Field spaniels should always be 'self coloured' (solid, or 'whole' coloured): black, liver, roan or any of these colours with tan markings over their rather serious–looking eyes, on the cheeks, feet and pasterns.

# SUSSEX SPANIEL

**OTHER NAMES:** None

**DATE OF ORIGIN:** 18th century

**PLACE OF ORIGIN:** Hastings, Sussex, England

**ORIGINAL USE:** Game tracking

**MODERN USE:** Companion

**SIZE:**

**HEIGHT:** 38–41 cm (15–16 in)

**WEIGHT:** 18–23 kg (40–50 lb)

**COLOURS:** Golden–liver

**RECOGNIZED BY:** K.C.

In 1795, Mr. Fuller of Rosehill Park, Hastings in East Sussex, England began breeding dogs for a special purpose: gun dogs to work in districts where the terrain was rough and the undergrowth very dense. What was most needed in the dog was strength and the ability to 'give tongue'– a trait not desirable in other spaniels but one which in the county of Sussex at least, was highly desirable. This is because in such dense undergrowth of bracken and brambles where dogs couldn't be seen, they at least could be heard and the experienced hunter was able to distinguish the quarry of the dog – whether it is 'furred' or 'feathered' – from the variations in the tone of the Sussex's voice.

Mr. Fuller's breed was the result of crossing various existing spaniels, including the now–extinct liver–and–white Norfolk, the field spaniel (see page 151) and possibly, some early 'springing' spaniels. The result was a dog of the most gorgeous colour – and a colour unknown inn any other breed – a rich 'golden–liver' which shades to gold at the tips of the hairs. The Sussex first reached the show rings in 1862 in London but occupied such a modest place in the dog world that World War I threatened their existence. A brief recovery in the 1920s and 1930s was set back once again by the outbreak of World War II: in 1947 only 10 Sussex spaniels were registered in the English Kennel Club. Accidental inbreeding and selective breeding among such few specimens is a hazardous affair and, consequently, inherited defects such as drooping lower eyelids and flews are common, and such conditions can lead to infections.

Today, this rare breed is safeguarded by only a handful of dedicated breeders, largely in the USA, so the Sussex continues to be rare – and even rarer in its homeland of England.

# ENGLISH SPRINGER SPANIEL

**OTHER NAMES:** Spaniel

**DATE OF ORIGIN:** 17th century

**PLACE OF ORIGIN:**
Great Britain

**ORIGINAL USE:** Game flushing,
retrieving

**MODERN USE:** Gundog,
companion

**SIZE:**

**HEIGHT:** 48–51 cm (19–20 ins)

**WEIGHT:** 22–24 kg (49–53 lb)

**COLOURS:** Black–white,
liver–white

**RECOGNIZED BY:** K.C.

Many claim that the English springer spaniel is the oldest of all the sporting spaniels. Long before the invention of firearms, spaniels were used to spring or flush game, causing it to leave cover so that a hunter's waiting hawks and falcons could swoop in on the quarry. Spaniels were also used to 'spring' birds and small mammals into nets, hence 'springer spaniels'.
There is uncertainty as to what these early dogs actually looked like: it was not until the 19th century, and the formation of dog shows, that the spaniels began to be separated into 'land' and 'water' spaniels. Land spaniels were divided into categories according to their weight, and the English springer spaniel emerged in the heaviest classes, as distinct from the cockers. Today, the English springer spaniel is still Britain's most popular working spaniel: an all–rounder in the field with seemingly unlimited stamina and a great love of the water. It is the tallest in the leg – and the raciest – of all the British land spaniels and one of the most intelligent. Consequently, these dogs need constant mental and physical activity to keep them from being bored. The show and working strains in the breed have become quite distinct: the show dogs are bigger in general and have heavier bones: they are especially good at retrieving tennis balls in parks, and find it difficult to resist duck ponds!
The most commonly seen coat colours in English springer spaniels is liver and white, but black and white is also acceptable, as are these colours combined with tan markings. Their straight coats are firm and require regular grooming.

# BRITTANY SPANIEL

**OTHER NAMES:** Armoricon,
Armorique, Epagneul Breton, Brittany

**DATE OF ORIGIN:** 18th century

**PLACE OF ORIGIN:** Brittany, France

**ORIGINAL USE:** Retrieving

**MODERN USE:** Retrieving,
companion

**SIZE:**

**HEIGHT:** 46–52 cm (18–20 1/2 in)

**WEIGHT:** 13–15 kg (28–33 lb)

**COLOURS:** Black–white, liver–white,
tricolour

**RECOGNIZED
BY:** K.C.

Originating in the region in northern France from which it takes its name, the Brittany is the breed which 'bridges the gap' between the spaniels and the setters and pointers. Spaniels work within the range of the gun and flush birds inside that range, which works well when there is dense ground cover hiding lots of birds. On more open ground, such as moorlands, a faster and lighter dog is needed – one that is capable of covering a greater range. Pointers and setters are such dogs: quartering the ground in front of the guns, scenting the air with wide nostrils to find hidden birds. In this way, the dogs will find sitting birds often at some distance from the guns: when they do, they point or set the bird, standing or crouching in a rigid position that indicates the bird's location and with luck, keeps the bird there until the guns come into range. The most popular native breed in France, and still a working dog there, as well as in Canada and the United States, the Brittany is the only spaniel breed that points – and probably the world's only 'stumpy–tailed' pointer as well! The dog is born either tailless or, if naturally long, is docked to 10 cm (4 in) and the ears are also shorter than those of other spaniels and are set above eye level.
Like the English, the French developed sporting dogs to suit the regions in which they worked, but in the 19th century, British breeders crossed the Channel to France to shoot woodcocks and took with them their own dogs, especially setters. It seems that, from crossings between English dogs and local Breton spaniels, the breed known as the Armorique emerged, until 1905, when it was officially recognised as the Brittany Spaniel.

# WELSH SPRINGER SPANIEL

**OTHER NAMES:** Once known as the Welsh cocker

**DATE OF ORIGIN:** 17th century

**PLACE OF ORIGIN:** Wales, Great Britain

**ORIGINAL USE:** Game flushing, retrieving

**MODERN USE:** Gun dog, companion

**SIZE:**

**HEIGHT:** 46–48 cm (18–19 in)

**WEIGHT:** 16–20 kg (35–45 lb)

**COLOURS:** Red–white

**RECOGNIZED BY:** K.C.

The Principality of Wales has given the canine world three breeds: the Welsh terrier, the Welsh corgis (see page 249) and the Welsh springer spaniel. Three dogs – though not these three breeds – were mentioned in the Laws of Howel Dda, a 10th century ruler of Wales. The three dogs mentioned were a 'tracker', a 'greyhound' and a 'spaniel'. This last dog is described further as being of equal value to a stallion or the king's 'buck hound' (a buck is a male deer).

The mention of a spaniel is curious at this time because it predates the introduction of Spanish dogs to Britain. Even more curious, an old Welsh law dating from ad 300 also mentions 'our native spaniel'. Most people in Britain would not have known of the existence of Spain at this time so it seems that both the breed and the name here are unconnected with Iberia. One theory is that these spaniels came to Wales from Gaul ('ancient' France) in pre–Roman times and consequently the Welsh springer spaniel may well share a common ancestry with the equally ancient and similarly coloured, Brittany (see page 153).

While never a 'popular' dog, the Welsh springer spaniel has always been a highly respected working dog, capable of driving herds of cattle or sheep and excelling at flushing or 'springing' game birds. The colouring of the Welsh springer spaniel is very distinctive: it was commented upon by Dr. Caius, in his book English Dogges of c.1570, who wrote of Spaniels whose 'skins are white and if they are marked with any spottes, they are commonly red'. Dr. Caius did however mention how remarkably white – almost pearly white – the white part of the coat was. Such as distinctive appearance made the dog attractive also to artists: they make numerous appearances in the sporting prints of the 18th century and in a number of family portraits by such artists as John Copley and Joseph Wright.

The flat, silky coat is less profuse on the Welsh's legs and ears than on some other breeds, and it stays quite clean because of its natural oiliness – for this dog is also a fine retriever from water. The ears are also an unusual shape: smaller than an English springer's, they are best described as shaped like a 'vine–leaf'. When they were first introduced into the show ring, they were known as 'Welsh cockers'. In 1902, the Kennel Club recognised their existence as 'Welsh springers' and as a breed distinct from the cocker spaniel (see page 149).

# ENGLISH SETTER

**OTHER NAMES:** Setting spaniel

**DATE OF ORIGIN:** 19th century

**PLACE OF ORIGIN:** Great Britain

**ORIGINAL USE:** Game retrieving, bird setting

**MODERN USE:** Retrieving, companion

**SIZE:**

**HEIGHT:** 61–69 cm (24–27 in)

**WEIGHT:** 25–30 kg (55–66 lb)

**COLOURS:** Tricolour, lemon–white, black–white, liver–white

**RECOGNIZED BY:** K.C.

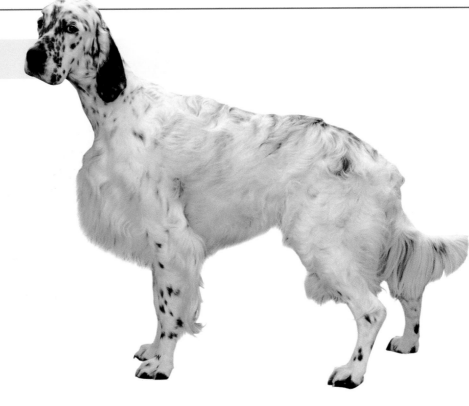

The English setter, with its delicate dappling or 'freckles' and shading of colours, has a very long history: a bond signed in 1485 by a Mr. John Harris states that, in exchange for a 10 shillings (50 pence) he could keep 'certain spaniels to set partridges, pheasants and other game' for six months. These dogs, called 'setting spaniels', had their names later shortened to 'setter', and finally to English setter, to distinguish them from the many other types that evolved during the same period. Such setting spaniels were longer in the leg than today's spaniel breeds, but they did work with the same lashing tails that setters do when quartering the ground. Until the 19th century however, these setters were not the beautiful, elegant or swift–footed dogs we know today. The modern English setter is the result largely of the efforts of two breeders: Sir Edward Laverack, who, in 1825, brought a brace of setters called Ponto and Moll. With these dogs from a pure, recognised line, Laverack began a sustained programme of inbreeding which resulted in a strain of beautiful and very able dogs. Inbreeding fixes the virtues or 'positive points' in a breed; but, while inbreeding does not introduce faults in dogs, it can, and does, intensify existing faults. Consequently, while the breeding programme succeeded in producing an elegant, easily trainable dog that was an excellent worker in the field, it also meant that the English setter can suffer inherited diseases: allergic skin reactions are common in predominantly white coloured dogs and, in all varieties, there is a tendency to blindness caused by the deterioration of the retinas. The development of the English setter was continued shortly afterwards by Sir Purcell Llewellin who successfully continued the long–term breeding programme.

The modern English setter is shorter in the leg than its ancestors – and the other setter breeds – since it was developed to work on grassland and stubble rather than rough moorlands and bog, where they pointed out game in the traditional manner, and then, on command, stealthily inched forward towards the game until the bird broke cover. In the 20th century, the use of the English setter as a gun dog in Britain declined and, today, it is no longer used. In the United States and Canada however, the breed split into two different types: smaller strains were developed for hunting and field trials, making the English setter one of the most popular breeds of hunting dogs among the bird dogs, while the larger dog is reserved for show.

# GORDON SETTER

**OTHER NAMES:** Black–and–tan setter

**DATE OF ORIGIN:** 18th century

**PLACE OF ORIGIN:** Banffshire, Scotland

**ORIGINAL USE:** Bird setting

**MODERN USE:** Gun dog, companion

**SIZE:**

**HEIGHT:** 62–66 cm (24–26 in)

**WEIGHT:** 25–30 kg (56–65 lb)

**COLOURS:** Black with tan markings

**RECOGNIZED BY:** K.C.

The Gordon setter is the largest, strongest, heaviest and slowest of the setters. It is also the only gun dog to be produced by Scotland – in spite of the country's strong sporting traditions. In fact, the Gordon setter is a very versatile gun dog: they are hardy enough to endure the harsh Scottish weather of early season shoots; they can withstand the heat of an summer shoot (the season starts on the 'Glorious 12th August); they can go without water for long periods and their legs and feet are strong enough to work over baked fields and the most brittle and prickly stubble. Scotland really had no need of other gun dogs when it had the magnificent Gordon setter already!

Black–and–tan setters existed in Britain in the 17th century, but the Gordon setter was developed and established by Alexander, 4th Duke of Richmond and Gordon, at his estate in Banffshire in Scotland, who continued to perfect the breed until his death in 1827. It is believed that the Gordon setter is the result of a cross between the Black–and–tan setter and bloodhounds (see page 180). This would account for the colour – and the Gordon's habit of hunting with its nose to the ground. There is also reputed to be collie (see page 241) blood: local history relates that one of the Duke's shepherds owned a black 'colley' who was a natural at finding game – even when the Duke's setters had failed! Moreover, this 'colley' froze and pointed, which earned her invitations to the ducal shoots and, it seems, to the kennels. This would also seem to account for the Gordon's earlier tendency: on finding game, the Gordon tended to circle it – like a sheepdog – holding the game in place rather than the more usual 'setting'. Moving around the game would be dangerous for the dog as it could end up on the 'wrong' side, in the line of fire. Through breeding, and through careful training, this tendency has now been eliminated.

The magnificent coat, jet black in colour with rich chestnut–tan markings, is fairly flat and a moderate length on the body. Elsewhere – on the head, front of the legs and tips of the ears – it is short and fine. The feathering on the belly, chest and throat makes a wonderful 'fringe'. The tail is fairly short and straight and is carried horizontal or just below the line of the back.

# IRISH SETTER

**OTHER NAMES:** Modder rhu
(Gaelic for 'red dog'), red setter

**DATE OF ORIGIN:** 18th century

**PLACE OF ORIGIN:** Ireland

**ORIGINAL USE:** Game
retrieving, setting

**MODERN USE:** Companion

**SIZE:**

**HEIGHT:** 64–69 cm (25–27 in)

**WEIGHT:** 27–32 kg (60–70 lb)

**COLOURS:** Chestnut red

**RECOGNIZED**

**BY:** K.C.

Often called a red setter, the Irish setter was also once called a 'red spaniel', and is one of the most popular breeds of setters – much more widely known than its cousins the Irish red–and–white setter (see below) and the English setter. The red setter is undoubtedly a good–looking and affectionate dog, but they can also be very exuberant and love nothing more than galloping through fields and parks – especially with other dogs!

In common with most other Irish breeds, the exact origins of the Irish setter are uncertain: it is possible that the Old Spanish pointer, a breed unknown outside of Spain, setting spaniels and early Scottish setters may have been contributed to the development of the breed which is known to have existed in the early 18th century and was used by the Irish landed gentry to find game on their estates. Today Irish setters still have a 'good nose' but few are used for working because the breed has unfortunately gained a – largely undeserved – reputation for being 'flighty' and 'excitable', which lead them to be unpredictable in the field. Like its red–and–white cousin, the Irish setter takes more time to obedience–train than other gun dogs. This is because as a breed, they are late to mature – they retain their youthful 'joie de vivre' for much longer! But, once trained, they do indeed make very reliable companions.

The breed standard for these gorgeous, gregarious dogs calls for a 'racy' dog, with a kind expression in the oval–shaped eyes, and the rich, glowing, chestnut–red coat, which is silky and flat to the body but abundantly feathered at the top of the ears, on the legs and the tail. The sensitive nose is usually black or a lovely chocolate colour.

# IRISH RED AND WHITE SETTER

**OTHER NAMES:** Parti–coloured
Setter

**DATE OF ORIGIN:** 18th century

**PLACE OF ORIGIN:** Ireland

**ORIGINAL USE:** Setting, game
retrieving

**MODERN USE:** Gun dog,
companion

**SIZE:**

**HEIGHT:** 58–69 cm (23–27 in)

**WEIGHT:** 27–32 kg (60–70 lb)

**COLOURS:** Red–white

**RECOGNIZED BY:** K.C.

As with most Irish breeds, very little is known of their exact origins. We know that setters existed in the 18th century in Ireland, where they were used by the landed gentry to find game on their large estates. It may be possible that they evolved through some crosses with the Irish water spaniels, English setters (see page 155), Gordon setters (see left), springer spaniels and pointers. Most people when they think of Irish setters think first of the 'modder rhu' or 'red dog' as it is called in Gaelic, the whole–coloured, red Irish setter. A century ago, working Irish setters were not always red though; in fact, they were more often chestnut and white or red and white. The breeders began to concentrate on the red–and–white variety. Before 1877, in Dublin, Irish Setter classes were divided by colour and the red–and–whites were in the majority. In the 20th century, the breed came close to extinction before being revived as a separate breed.

The Irish red–and–white setter is a little less tall than its red cousin and its deep chest, makes the breed prone to gastric torsion, commonly called 'bloat'. This is a sudden, painful and, sometimes, fatal disease where the stomach has become twisted, trapping gas, which then causes the abdomen to bloat. Surgical intervention is vital to save the dog. Like its redheaded cousin, the Irish red–and–white setter is exuberant, extrovert and enthusiastic with a highly refined sense of smell, but this character does mean that it takes more time to obedience–train than other gun dogs.

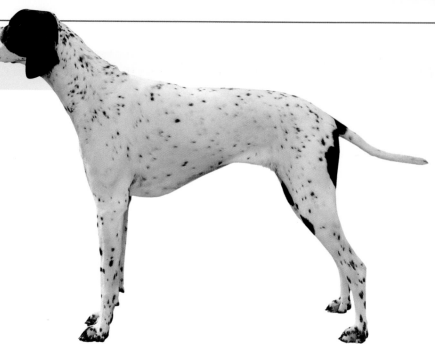

# POINTER

**OTHER NAMES:** English pointer

**DATE OF ORIGIN:** 17th century

**PLACE OF ORIGIN:** Great Britain

**ORIGINAL USE:** Tracking game

**MODERN USE:** Gun dog, companion

**SIZE:**

**HEIGHT:** 61–69 cm (24–27 in)

**WEIGHT:** 20–30 kg (44–66 lb)

**COLOURS:** Black–white, liver–white, lemon–white, orange–white

**RECOGNIZED BY:** K.C.

It is likely that the name of this breed started out as a general description: 'pointing dogs', which described the dog's work and gradually became shortened and then a proper name, 'pointer'. Its work was to find game in open country, which it did with its nose, and when it found it, the dog froze in the classic pose: nose held high, one foreleg lifted and bent, the tail held still, straight out, and level with the back. While it is believed the pointer came to England from Spain in the 18th century (where it had been developed in the 16th century), such dogs also existed in many European countries and in slightly differing forms: The Netherlands (once a Spanish dominion), France, Germany and Denmark all had their own variations to suit the regions in which the dogs worked. The pointer – in this instance the name refers to the breed developed wholly in Great Britain – is a dog with an excellent nose but a slow, ponderous nature. This speed was ideally suited to huntsmen armed with the early, muzzle–loading guns. Later technological developments improved the guns, which meant that instead of having to shoot at birds while they roosted, flying birds could now be accurately targeted. Consequently faster and more skilful gun dogs were required.

To make the pointer more robust, and to give it more speed, early breeders made crosses with foxhounds (see page182): this nearly proved disastrous since hounds work with their noses to the ground and their instinct is to chase and kill the quarry, while the pointer scents the air, stalks its prey but holds back from the kill. The offspring of these crosses tended to inherit the hounds 'skills'. Breeders tried again, this time it is suggested they used bulldogs, greyhounds and bloodhounds and, chances are, the offspring of these crosses were even more 'useless' as pointers! It was actually the dog show that rescued the breed from more 'tinkering': the first dog show in Newcastle, England, in 1859 was less a 'show' or exhibition, and more a competition, especially among the shooting men who argued incessantly over which dogs were not only the finest gun dogs, but which were also the most 'handsome'. The show excited such interest that 'pointer men' now strove to breed a dog with the purest of forms, the result of which can be seen today. Even though few pointers are worked today, their good looks, and calm characters, which have made them firm favourites in many homes as loving pets, will surely ensure the pointer will never disappear.

# GERMAN POINTER (SHORT HAIRED)

**OTHER NAMES:** Deutscher Vorstehhund

**DATE OF ORIGIN:** 19th century

**PLACE OF ORIGIN:** Germany

**ORIGINAL USE:** General hunting

**MODERN USE:** Gun dog, companion

**SIZE:**

**HEIGHT:** 60–65 cm (24–26 in)

**WEIGHT:** 27–32 kg (60–70 lb)

**COLOURS:** Liver, liver–white, black–white, black

**RECOGNIZED BY:** K.C.

German pointers are a diverse group of breeds, with a variety of origins, and the result of intense breeding activity which took place in Germany in the late 19th century. The most well–known German pointers are the German short–haired pointer and the German wire–haired pointer, and the Weimaraner (see page 161). These three breeds are recognised by the Kennel Club. There are however, other less well know German pointers such as the German long–haired pointer (see page 160) and the Pudelpointer, both of which are recognised by the F.C.I. but not by the K.C.

The 'native' German pointers were heavy, slow, dogs and as with so many breeds, the German short–haired pointer was developed in the period from 1860 to 1880 when the Germans were searching for an 'improved' all–purpose hunting dog. To achieve this, dogs of Spanish pointer origins were crossed with St. Hubert Hounds. This at least gave the dogs an excellent trailing nose.

One early breeder was Prince Albrecht zu Solms–Bauenfels of the House of Hanover, who, in 1870, laid down the dictum that the dog's form should follow its function and ability. Subsequently, Christian Bode of Altenau is said to have introduced English pointer blood to give the German dogs a greater wind–scenting nose and a more 'stylish', lean and athletic appearance. In 1883, the foundations of the breed were established by two dogs: Nero and Treff, who tied for the German Derby that year.

The German short–haired pointer made its first appearance in Britain in 1887, but it would not be until 1950 that a breed club was established in the U.K.

Nevertheless, the German short–haired pointer became a great favourite with weekend hunters in Germany and in America, where it was introduced in 1925 by Dr. Charles R. Thornton of Missoula, Montana. Soon afterwards a breed club was established in the USA and in 1930, the breed was admitted to the American Kennel Club.

The German wire–haired pointer, known in its homeland as the Deutscher Drahthaariger was developed by crossing the offspring of German short–haired pointers with a number of other breeds including the wire–haired pointing griffon, the Pudelpointer and the Stichelhaar (broken–coated pointer). This produced another all–purpose dog, which could work on land and in water, flushing, pointing and retrieving.

# GERMAN POINTER (LONG HAIRED)

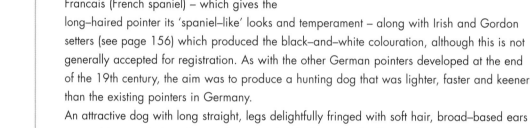

**OTHER NAMES:** Deutscher Vorstehhund

**DATE OF ORIGIN:** 19th century

**PLACE OF ORIGIN:** Germany

**ORIGINAL USE:** General hunting

**MODERN USE:** Gun dog, companion

**SIZE:**

**HEIGHT:** 60–65 cm (24–26 in)

**WEIGHT:** 27–32 kg (60–70 lb)

**COLOURS:** Red–and–black

**RECOGNIZED BY:** F.C.I.

One of the three distinct German pointer breeds developed in the late 19th century using 'native' stock and imported breeds, the German long–haired pointer is not well known outside of its homeland, where it is primarily still a working dog, and it is recognised only by the F.C.I. The breed made its first appearance in Hanover, Germany in 1879 and is the result of crossings of pointers with long–haired continental bird dogs such as the epagneul Francais (French spaniel) – which gives the long–haired pointer its 'spaniel–like' looks and temperament – along with Irish and Gordon setters (see page 156) which produced the black–and–white colouration, although this is not generally accepted for registration. As with the other German pointers developed at the end of the 19th century, the aim was to produce a hunting dog that was lighter, faster and keener than the existing pointers in Germany.

An attractive dog with long straight, legs delightfully fringed with soft hair, broad–based ears covered in wavy hair and a gentle expression in the eyes, the German long–haired pointer also makes an excellent companion dog and a very good watchdog. Such attributes will no doubt ensure its continued existence and perhaps, greater notice outside of Germany.

# MUNSTERLANDER (LARGE)

**OTHER NAMES:** Grosser Münsterlander Vorstehhund

**DATE OF ORIGIN:** 19th century

**PLACE OF ORIGIN:** Germany

**ORIGINAL USE:** Tracking, pointing, retrieving

**MODERN USE:** Gun dog, companion

**SIZE:**

**HEIGHT:** 59–61 cm (23–24 in)

**WEIGHT:** 25–29 kg (55–65 lb)

**COLOURS:** Black–white

**RECOGNIZED BY:** K.C.

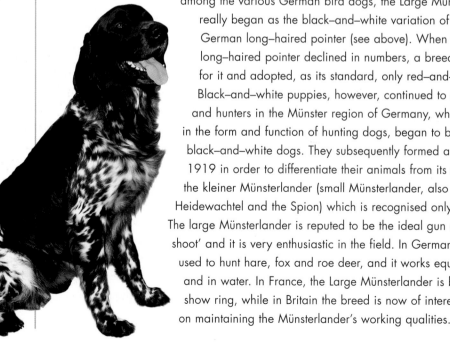

The black–and–white coloured Large Münsterlander is an all–purpose gun dog with a superb nose for scents, that was developed in Germany in the 19th century. While its ancestors were among the various German bird dogs, the Large Münsterlander breed really began as the black–and–white variation of the red–and–white German long–haired pointer (see above). When the German long–haired pointer declined in numbers, a breed was established for it and adopted, as its standard, only red–and–white specimens. Black–and–white puppies, however, continued to appear in litters and hunters in the Münster region of Germany, who were interested in the form and function of hunting dogs, began to breed from the black–and–white dogs. They subsequently formed a breed club in 1919 in order to differentiate their animals from its smaller relative, the kleiner Münsterlander (small Münsterlander, also known as the Heidewachtel and the Spion) which is recognised only by the F.C.I. The large Münsterlander is reputed to be the ideal gun dog for the 'rough shoot' and it is very enthusiastic in the field. In Germany, the dog is still used to hunt hare, fox and roe deer, and it works equally well on land and in water. In France, the Large Münsterlander is best known in the show ring, while in Britain the breed is now of interest to owners keen on maintaining the Münsterlander's working qualities.

# WEIMARANA

**OTHER NAMES:** Weimarana Vorstehhund (Weimar Pointer)

**DATE OF ORIGIN:** 17th century, but developed in early 19th century into modern form

**PLACE OF ORIGIN:** Germany

**ORIGINAL USE:** Large game tracking

**MODERN USE:** Gun dog, companion

**SIZE:**

**HEIGHT:** 56–69 cm (22–27 in)

**WEIGHT:** 32–39 kg (70–86 lb)

**COLOURS:** Grey

**RECOGNIZED BY:** K.C.

A painting by the artist Anthony van Dyke (1599–1641) provides one of the earliest records of this uniquely coloured breed. There is no other evidence to indicate the origins of the Weimarana but most assume that it is the result of crosses between the St. Hubert hound, bloodhounds (see page 180), and pointers. However, by the early 19th century, a distinctly grey-coloured hunting dog was evident in Germany, and credit for developing and popularising the breed is generally given to Grand Duke Karl August of Weimar, the capital of Thuringia. The Grand Duke's work was carried on by enthusiastic sportsmen keen on producing an 'all-purpose' hunting dog that would not only enter water to retrieve fowl, but to blend the abilities of the tracking dogs with those of the pointers. The result was the gorgeous Weimarana, rippling with muscles – but also available in the lesser known long-haired variety. The Weimarana was recognised in Germany as a distinct breed in 1896 and the following years, owners met at Erfort to form a breed club – not to popularise the breed though, but to save it from extinction by enforcing strict breeding rules with which owners had to abide. In 1943, the breed was recognised in the USA where it has grown steadily in popularity. While the Weimarana has proven itself more than proficient in field trials and obedience work, as a hunting dog and as a watchdog, it is undoubtedly its appearance that has captured most peoples' hearts: the shimmering grey coat – which earned it its nickname of 'Grey Ghost' – coupled with distinctive and arresting eyes ranging from amber, through grey to blue and physical grace, make the Weimarana a universally admired breed.

# GOLDEN RETRIEVER

**OTHER NAMES:** None

**DATE OF ORIGIN:** 19th century

**PLACE OF ORIGIN:**
Great Britain

**ORIGINAL USE:** Retrieving game

**MODERN USE:** Gun dog,
companion, guide dog for the blind

**SIZE:**

**HEIGHT:** 51–61 cm (20–24 in)

**WEIGHT:** 27–36 kg (60–80 lb)

**COLOURS:** Cream, gold

**RECOGNIZED BY:** K.C.

Quite possibly, the golden retriever is the most benign, good–natured, easiest to train – and the most willing to learn – breed of all dogs. A brilliant gun dog, wonderful family pet and excellent guide dog for the blind, it is also one of the most popular breeds today. In the late 19th and early 20th centuries, the popular account of the breed's origins was based on a rather 'tall story', according to which, in 1858, Sir Dudley Majorbanks, while visiting the circus in Brighton, saw a troop of trained Russian sheepdogs perform. Sir Dudley was so impressed by their tricks and beauty that he wanted to have a pair immediately himself. The trainer of the dog troupe refused to sell two dogs claiming it would ruin his act, so Sir Dudley promptly bought all eight dogs in the act and took them home to his estate to breed.

The public 'lapped up' the story, but if these dogs were in fact herding dogs or 'sheepdogs', they would not make good retrievers: sheepdogs round up and hustle their charges along – and are not adverse to nipping the heels of slow movers to hurry them – while gun dogs must work in exactly the opposite manner: finding the object of interest with as little fuss as possible and taking it in their mouths without marking or damaging it any further. In the end, the mystery was solved when Sir Dudley's kennel records from 1835 to 1890 were published: Majorbanks had been breeding from 'sports' – animals which deviate slightly from the expected norm – and the original animal of the golden retriever breed was called Nous, a yellow dog bred from black, flat–coated retriever (see right) parents. Nous was mated with a small liver–coated tweed water spaniel (itself a small retriever), and the result was four golden retriever puppies, called delightfully, Crocus, Ada, Primrose and Cowslip. Not a hint of Russian sheepdog in them! Instead the golden retriever was a 100% gun dog.

Since its introduction, four breed lines have been established: one continues to produce working gun dogs, the second line was developed for field trials, the third line (the largest) is for show dogs and family pets, while the fourth line produces dogs bred exclusively for training as assistants to blind and disabled people.

# FLAT-COATED RETRIEVER

**OTHER NAMES:** Originally called 'wavy–coated retriever'

**DATE OF ORIGIN:** 19th century

**PLACE OF ORIGIN:** Great Britain

**ORIGINAL USE:** Retrieving game

**MODERN USE:** Gun dog, companion

**SIZE:**

**HEIGHT:** 56–61 cm (22–24 in)

**WEIGHT:** 25–35 kg (60–89 lb)

**COLOURS:** Liver, black

**RECOGNIZED BY:** K.C.

Once game birds have been shot, they must be found. 'Springing' dogs, whose job it was to 'spring' the birds into the air, as well as most setters and pointers, were to the greater extent, uninterested in retrieving game for their masters. What was needed was a dog who would concentrate just on this task, and the early candidate was the flat–coated retriever, known originally as the wavy–coated retriever.

The first 'representative' of the breed to be seen in England was a dog called Wyndham, which was shown in Birmingham in 1860, and who aroused a great deal of interest among huntsmen, but from whose owner very little information about the breed could be gleaned. In the end it was concluded that the foundation stock for the breed came from smaller working dogs from the St. Johns region of Newfoundland. These dogs had come to Britain on fishing boats and were possibly used as guard dogs, but game keepers in the late 19th century were soon to discover its special talents and, following further crossings with setters (which 'flattened' out the wavy coat), the sleek, flat–coated retriever was soon a favourite gun dog. The arrival on the scene of the Labrador retriever and the golden retriever however, meant that by the end of World War II, the flat–coated variety was almost extinct. In the 1960s this handsome breed was rescued once more to become a much sought–after gun dog, whose numbers are sure to increase in line with its growing popularity as a companion dog.

# LABRADOR RETRIEVER

**OTHER NAMES:** Labrador, small water dog

**DATE OF ORIGIN:** 19th century

**PLACE OF ORIGIN:** Great Britain

**ORIGINAL USE:** Gun dog

**MODERN USE:** Gun dog, field trails, companion, guiding/assistance dog

**SIZE:**

**HEIGHT:** 54–57 cm ( 21½ –22½ in)

**WEIGHT:** 25–34 kg (55–75 lb)

**COLOURS:** Yellow, black, mid–brown

**RECOGNIZED BY:** K.C.

One of the world's most popular breeds, the waterproof, and water–loving Labrador was first used in its native Newfoundland, Canada, a natural–born retriever – though not of birds! Their task was to go over the side of the fishing boats and drag the ends of the nets full of fish to the shore where they could be hauled up: the rocky inlets of the Labrador coast made it dangerous for fishing boats to approach the shores too closely. Once this task was done, the Labrador swam back to the boat, retrieving any objects lost overboard in the process. When the St. John's fishermen sailed to British ports to sell the catch, their dogs came with them and some remained in this country. In their native land, these Labradors were called 'small water dogs' in order to distinguish them from the giant Newfoundland (see page 241) also found in the region. An early owner was the Earl of Malmesbury who wrote in a letter of 1879 that he had acquired such dogs from a Newfoundland fisherman, in Poole, Dorset. The earl began breeding the dogs for use as gun dogs and wrote that he always called them 'Labradors' and the name has stuck firm ever since. While still widely used as gun dogs, retrieving game on shoots, the Labrador, being among the most affable breeds, has found many a home as a loving and well loved pet. Regrettably, some dogs suffer from hereditary cataracts and hip and elbow arthritis. As they get older, they are also prone to weight gain, which can exacerbate any underlying joint problems.

# CURLY-COATED RETRIEVER

**OTHER NAMES:** None

**DATE OF ORIGIN:** 19th century

**PLACE OF ORIGIN:** Great Britain

**ORIGINAL USE:** Retrieving waterfowl

**MODERN USE:** Gun dog, companion

**SIZE:**

**HEIGHT:** 64–69 cm (25–27 in)

**WEIGHT:** 32–36 kg (70–80 lb)

**COLOURS:** Black, liver

**RECOGNIZED BY:** K.C.

The origins of this breed lie in the lesser Newfoundland dog – the 'small water dog' (see Labrador retriever, above) brought to England by the cod fishermen of St. John's, Newfoundland in the late 18th and 19th centuries, and the now extinct old water dog or English water spaniel. It also seems likely that further crosses with poodles (see page 223) were made, which would have improved the retrieving skills, though not the coat!

The curly–coated retriever is the largest, oldest (early evidence suggests that it existed as early as 1803) and the least well known of the British retrievers. It is distinguished by it's marvellous coat of crisp, tight and extremely waterproof curls. The result looks more like the finest astrakhan rather than dog, and can be either jet black or liver in colour. One good shake is all it takes to get the coat almost completely dry. This is useful for the curly–coated retriever delights in swimming and earned its place in the hearts of many 19th–century game keepers for its robust character and willingness to cross marshes, rivers and streams. The curly's kind and playful nature also made it a firm favourite among families with children. In 1896 a club was formed to promote the breed and, for a while, the curly prospered – in the field, in the show ring and in the home. Its heyday was undoubtedly during the interwar period (1918–1939) but the breed was soon eclipsed in popularity by its 'cousins' the Labrador retriever (see above) and the golden retriever (see page 162). In recent years interest in the breed has been revived and soon, no doubt, this calm, even–tempered and delightful–looking breed will become firmly established in the hearts of many admirers once more.

# HUNGARIAN VIZSLA

**OTHER NAMES:** Magyar vizsla, drotszoru Magyar vizsla, Hungarian yellow pointer

**DATE OF ORIGIN:** Middle Ages (wire–haired version developed in 1930s)

**PLACE OF ORIGIN:** Hungary

**ORIGINAL USE:** Hunting, falconry

**MODERN USE:** Gun dog, companion

**SIZE:**

**HEIGHT:** 57–64 cm (22½ –25 in)

**WEIGHT:** 22–30 kg (48½–66 lb)

**COLOURS:** Solid colours ranging from rusty–gold to dark, sandy yellow (darker shades are preferred)

**RECOGNIZED BY:** K.C.

Elegant and energetic, the vizsla is Hungary's most famous native hunting dog. The name was first used in 1510 to describe the result of a crossing between the now extinct native pannonian hound with a yellow Turkish dog. It is more likely though that the breed is much more modern and its background may include Transylvanian pointing dogs and the Weimarana (see page 161) of Germany.

Whatever its origins, by the 1850s the 'Hungarian yellow pointing dog' was well established and was widely employed as a dual–purpose, pointing and retrieving dog. In Hungary the dogs were trained to work close to the hunter on foot. While this meant that it was not as fast or wide ranging as a pointer, it was a very careful and diligent searcher with fine scenting abilities for both tracking and airborne scents.

The beautiful vizsla owes its survival today to the concerted efforts of Hungarian expatriates who fled their homeland during World War II, taking their beloved dogs with them to new lives in other parts of Europe and in North America. Since then the dual working purposes of the vizsla have been extended to include a third role, to which it is also ideally suited: as a steady, reliable, obedient, and well–loved family pet. Back home in Hungary, the breed has been revived once again as a working gun dog, while in Canada, the wire–haired variety, developed in the 1930s, with its distinguishing 'old gentleman's whiskers', is a favourite among weekend hunters.

# BRACCO ITALIANO

**OTHER NAMES:** Italian pointer, Italian setter

**DATE OF ORIGIN:** 18th century

**PLACE OF ORIGIN:** Italy

**ORIGINAL USE:** Tracking, pointing, retrieving

**MODERN USE:** Gun dog, companion

**SIZE:**

**HEIGHT:** 56–67 cm (22–26½ in)

**WEIGHT:** 25–40 kg (55–88 lb)

**COLOURS:** White, white–orange, white–chestnut

**RECOGNIZED BY:** K.C.

Until very recently the powerfully built and unique–looking breed with its long bloodhound–like ears was extremely rare. It was rediscovered by Italian dog breeders and then by breeders elsewhere in Europe. Similar looking dogs had been extremely fashionable hunting dogs with the nobles at the Renaissance courts of Italy. The breed evolved in the northern regions of Italy, in Piedmont and Lombardy, where it proved to be a versatile hunter, capable of scenting, pointing and retrieving on both land and in water.

It's ancestry is largely unknown: some breeders claim that it was a result of crosses between the segugio (see page 186) and an ancient Asiatic mastiff. Others maintain that the bracco is descended from the St. Hubert hound – which would account for the ears!

# ITALIAN SPINONE

**OTHER NAMES:** Spinone Italiano, spinone

**DATE OF ORIGIN:** Middle Ages

**PLACE OF ORIGIN:** Italy

**ORIGINAL USE:** Game retrieving

**MODERN USE:** Gun dog, field trials, companion

**SIZE:**

**HEIGHT:** 61–66 cm (24–26 in)

**WEIGHT:** 32–37 kg (71–82 lb)

**COLOURS:** White, white–orange, white–chestnut

**RECOGNIZED BY:** K.C.

Like the bracco Italiano (see above) the spinone developed in Piedmont and Lombardy in northern Italy. Although developed into its present form through selective breeding, the spinone is an ancient breed and is known to have existed – or at least varieties of the breed existed – in the 13th century. It is possible that it descended from the segugio (see page 186), while some claim descent from the ancient korthals griffon. In Italy the spinone is worked as a pointer, searching out and indicating the presence of game by the sudden freezing, the rigid posture, that makes the dog look as if it has turned to stone. The spinone is a solid–looking dog, strongly boned and well muscled, with a rather reserved look – largely due to its long whiskers. In character, the spinone thrives on work and is generally calm and easy going. But it can also be far from reserved and very playful – though its rather large size makes it a little clumsy! The spinone also has a tendency to dribble and drool somewhat and can have a rather pungent 'doggy' aroma! Fortunately these 'faults' are totally insufficient to detract from the positive attributes of this very obedient and happy breed: it has recently found great popularity beyond its native Italy in the USA and Canada, Scandinavia and Great Britain as well as throughout the European Union countries.

# KOOIKERHONDJE

**OTHER NAMES:** Kooiker dog, Dutch decoy spaniel

**DATE OF ORIGIN:** 18th century

**PLACE OF ORIGIN:** The Netherlands

**ORIGINAL USE:** Bird flushing and retrieving

**MODERN USE:** Gun dog, companion

**SIZE:**

**HEIGHT:** 35–41 cm (14–16 in)

**WEIGHT:** 9–11 kg (20–24 lb)

**COLOURS:** Red–white

**RECOGNIZED BY:** K.C.

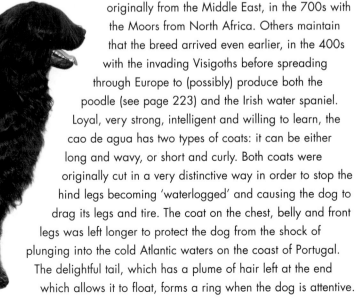

This breed is known to date back to the time of Dutch ruler, William of Orange (1650–1702) who, in 1688, became William III of England. Like the now–extinct English red decoy dog, the kooikerhondje assisted Dutch hunters by waving its bushy white tail around, luring curious ducks and geese forwards into nets or traps made of rush matting. At one time, the waterfowl were netted for food, but today, the dogs assist in conservation programmes where the ducks are leg–banded for identification.

During World War II, like many European breeds, the lovely kooikerhondje, seriously declined in numbers and virtually disappeared: only 25 of the dogs survived the war. This small number formed the stock from which Baroness van Hardenbroek van Amerstool worked to recreate the breed. While, today, numbers are increasing, such a small gene pool does mean that inherited diseases do occur.

The kooiker's body is covered with a heavy, luxurious top coat of waterproof hair which conceals layers of insulating down. Most distinctive, however, are the ears with their dark, black 'ear–drops' of long hair.

# PORTUGUESE WATER DOG

**OTHER NAMES:** Cao de Agua

**DATE OF ORIGIN:** Middle Ages

**PLACE OF ORIGIN:** Portugal

**ORIGINAL USE:** Fisherman's dogs

**MODERN USE:** Retrieving, guarding, companion

**SIZE:**

**HEIGHT:** 43–57 cm (17–22½ in)

**WEIGHT:** 16–25 kg (35–55 lb)

**COLOURS:** Black, brown, white, black–white, brown–white

**RECOGNIZED BY:** K.C.

Found principally today in the Algarve region of Portugal, this ancient breed was used by Portuguese fishermen to help pull nets in the water, and, as 'couriers' or message bearers, between boats. Meanwhile, on land, they also proved to be adept rabbiters. The cao de agua ('water dog') is said by many to have come originally from the Middle East, in the 700s with the Moors from North Africa. Others maintain that the breed arrived even earlier, in the 400s with the invading Visigoths before spreading through Europe to (possibly) produce both the poodle (see page 223) and the Irish water spaniel. Loyal, very strong, intelligent and willing to learn, the cao de agua has two types of coats: it can be either long and wavy, or short and curly. Both coats were originally cut in a very distinctive way in order to stop the hind legs becoming 'waterlogged' and causing the dog to drag its legs and tire. The coat on the chest, belly and front legs was left longer to protect the dog from the shock of plunging into the cold Atlantic waters on the coast of Portugal. The delightful tail, which has a plume of hair left at the end which allows it to float, forms a ring when the dog is attentive.

*complete DOG*

# HOUNDS

The hound group of dogs includes various breeds which, for centuries, all over the world, helped man to hunt – for food and for sport. The hounds divide roughly into two groups: those like the greyhound and Afghan which hunt by sight, and pursue their quarry with great speed and agility, and, those like the basset hound and beagle which use their noses and great stamina to wear down their prey. Both types of hound do use all their senses when hunting but, while the scent hound will bark and howl when it encounters the scent of its quarry, the sight hound will chase silently.

**SLOUGHI**

**BLOODHOUND**

There is a third group of dogs known as 'primitive dogs': these are descended from the Indian Plains wolf, Canis lupus pallipes and genuinely 'primitive' dogs such as the Australian dingo, the New Guinea singing dog, and dogs such as the basenji, Canaan, Ibizan and pharaoh hounds, which share the same ancestry but have been 'developed' through breeding programmes.

The sight, or, gaze hound, is the product of selective breeding which began thousands of years ago. Arabia is the original homeland of the Saluki and sloughi where, 5,000 years ago, they were bred to outrun the swift desert gazelles. Around 3,000 years ago, the ancient

**BEAGLE**

Egyptian were depicting greyhound–type dogs in their art. Sight hounds were most likely introduced into southern Europe, around the shores of the Mediterranean, and into North Africa by Phoenician traders, and it is thought that, around 2,500 years ago, these traders also introduced sight hounds to Great Britain, where they were further selectively bred and then crossed with mastiff breeds to produce the muscular and powerful sight hounds like the Irish wolfhound and the Scottish deerhound. Like their Middle–eastern relatives, these hounds have the same elegant carriage and noble bearing that made them the sight hounds of the 'aristocracy', the clan chiefs of Scotland and Ireland. A certain coolness and aloofness are the hallmarks of sight hounds: they are neither 'bouncy' nor exuberantly affectionate. But, while most sight hounds are now kept as companions, they still have their instinct to chase other 'fur'! One of the problems of having a sight hound in the home is the need for free exercise in a safe place: as they are not readily obedient, they must be exercised in a well–fenced area. Because they are agile dogs who can – and do – both jump and dig, garden fences need to be at least 2m (6 ft) high, with an additional 30 cm (1 ft) buried in concrete at the base! The scent hounds are heavier dogs with a 'lower build' and are not as speedy as sight

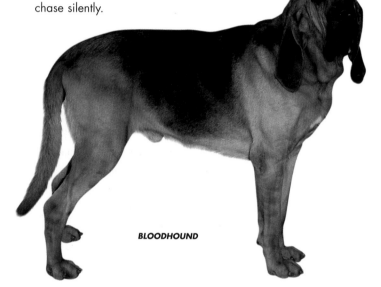

hounds. They do, however, have wide nostrils for picking up scents, pendulous ears which circulate air currents that carry scents, and deep flews, pendulous upper lips, which also act as scent 'traps'.

Medieval France was the undoubted leader in developing scent hounds and, often, 1,000 dogs at a time worked the parks and forests of France in the service of the king. The oldest breed of French scent hound is thought to be the Porcelaine, a descendent of the now extinct

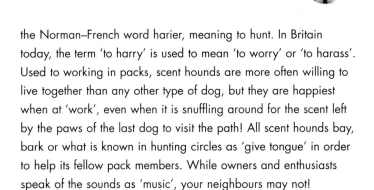

**CANAAN**

**GRIFFON**

Montaimbeouf. For over 1,000 years, until the French Revolution in 1789, the abbots of the Benedictine monastery of St. Hubert (now in modern Belgium) annually gave the king of France six St. Hubert hounds: today the descendants of these dogs is the famous bloodhound, the world's largest scent hound. Some scent hounds were smooth haired, others were wire haired – the griffons. Some were bred with short legs – the bassets (from 'bas' meaning 'low') – so that hunters could accompany these less speedy dogs on foot rather than horseback. Other small scent hounds developed in France, called harriers, which is derived from

the Norman–French word harier, meaning to hunt. In Britain today, the term 'to harry' is used to mean 'to worry' or 'to harass'. Used to working in packs, scent hounds are more often willing to live together than any other type of dog, but they are happiest when at 'work', even when it is snuffling around for the scent left by the paws of the last dog to visit the path! All scent hounds bay, bark or what is known in hunting circles as 'give tongue' in order to help its fellow pack members. While owners and enthusiasts speak of the sounds as 'music', your neighbours may not!

**AFGHAN HOUND**

**IRISH WOLFHOUND**

# BASENJI

**OTHER NAMES:** Congo dog

**DATE OF ORIGIN:** Antiquity

**PLACE OF ORIGIN:** Central Africa

**ORIGINAL USE:** Hunting

**MODERN USE:** Hunting, companion

**SIZE:**

**HEIGHT:** 41–43 cm (16–17 in)

**WEIGHT:** 9.5–11 kg (21–24 lb)

**COLOURS:** Black–white, tan–white, black

**RECOGNIZED BY:** K.C.

One of the more unusual hunting dogs, the basenji has a very long history. Similar dogs with erect ears and very tightly curled, ring tail were depicted in ancient Egyptian art. In the 19th century, British explorers 'discovered' similar dogs in the Congo basin where they were used by their owners to point, retrieve, drive game and track wounded prey. The basenji has a number of 'unique' features: they cannot bark, but like wolves, howl or 'yodel'. When tracking game they are completely silent. Because of their silence, owners attached little wooden bells to their necks to help find their dogs when they were busy in dense undergrowth. Unlike other dogs, which have two breeding cycles a year, the basenji (again like the wolf) has only one, and, they clean themselves all over with their paw rather like a cat!

The first basenjis arrived in Britain in 1895, where they were entered at Crufts as 'Congo dogs' and aroused great interest. It was not until 1937 however, that a successful breeding programme was established in Britain, because many of the 'imports' died of distemper: coming from a country where the disease was unknown made them particularly vulnerable. Soon after, in the early 1940s, the basenji became successfully established in the USA.

The lightly built basenji is perfectly designed for it's warm native climate: the loose skin covered by a short, silky textured coat help with heat tolerance, while the coat colours provide camouflage in the bush. The basenji also has a rather wrinkled forehead which gives the dog a very 'quizzical' expression. The ears are set high and forward, and are very mobile, alert to every sound, and the jaws are long, typical of the most ancient breeds of dogs. The muzzle tapers from the dark, almond–shaped eyes to the tip of the black nose, while the long legs allow the basenji to move freely, in a graceful movement, rather like a trotting horse.

# IBIZAN HOUND

**OTHER NAMES:** Ca Eivissenc, Podenco Ibiceno, Balearic dog, Charnique (in France)

**DATE OF ORIGIN:** Antiquity

**PLACE OF ORIGIN:** Balearic Islands, Spain

**ORIGINAL USE:** Sight/scent/sound hound

**MODERN USE:** Hunting/retrieving, companion

**SIZE:**

**HEIGHT:** 56–74 cm (22–29 in)

**WEIGHT:** 19–25 kg (42–55 lb)

**COLOURS:** White, fawn, fawn–white, red, red–white

**RECOGNIZED BY:** K.C.

Hailing originally from Ibiza, in Spain's Balearic Islands – although now found also on the mainland and in France where it is known as the Charnique – three types of the strongly built Ibizan hound exist: smooth–haired, wire–haired and long–haired. Highly agile, the Ibizan hound can jump great heights without a 'take off' run! Incredibly versatile, these hounds hunt largely by scent and by sound, but do use sight as well, and will only bark when they sense their quarry. Furthermore, the Ibizan hound will hunt alone or work in a pack, and will both point and retrieve game. The Ibizan hound has a long, narrow 'cone–shaped' head with a prominent occipital bone and a lightly defined 'stop'. The length from the eyes to the point of the muzzle is always the same as from between the eyes to the occiput. The ears are pricked and can be turned forwards, horizontally sideways and backwards, and when the dog is alert, they are carried very high. The eyes are slanting and quite small, and a lovely amber colour which matches the flesh–coloured nose (which becomes lighter in colour if the dog is unwell). The hind legs are strong and lean, well suited to bursts of speed and the feet are rather like a hare's, with a light feathering between the toes and light coloured claws. The tail is long and low set: in action it sometimes looks like a sickle!

# PHARAOH HOUND

**OTHER NAMES:** Kelb–tal kenek

**DATE OF ORIGIN:** Antiquity

**PLACE OF ORIGIN:** Malta

**ORIGINAL USE:**
Sight/scent/sound hound

**MODERN USE:** Hunting, companion

**SIZE:**

**HEIGHT:** 53–64 cm (12–25 in)

**WEIGHT:** 20–25 kg (45–55 lb)

**COLOURS:** Tan with white markings on extremities

**RECOGNIZED BY:** K.C.

Called Kelb–tal Fenek (rabbit dog) on the island of Malta, from where it originates, the pharaoh dog only received this newer name when it reached the British show scenes in the 1960s because they bear a very strong resemblance to the hounds with large, erect ears seen in ancient Egyptian tomb paintings from around 4,000 bc. Furthermore, in the ancient Egyptian religion, the god Anubis was depicted with the head of an 'Egyptian hound', and so the name 'pharaoh hound' seemed highly appropriate. This elegant, lithe hound, noted for its speed and agility, is probably descended from a small wolf, native to the Arabian Peninsula. The breed is thought to have been taken to the Mediterranean islands of Malta and neighbouring Gozo by Phoenician traders around 2,000 years ago. Because of the isolated nature of the islands, the breed remained unadulterated and 'pure', and retains its ability to hunt by sight, sound and scent. A rich red colour with white tips at the feet and tail, the coat is fine, glossy and short. Where white on the chest appears, a star–shape marking is preferred. The long, lean, chiselled head has powerful jaws, a nose that is flesh coloured (to blend with the coat and which becomes flushed when the hound is excited!), oval, close–set amber eyes for excellent binocular vision to assist sight hunting, and high–set ears, broad at the base and fairly large, which are carried erect when the hound is alert. The tail is fairly thick at the base, but tapers to a point: when excited the tail may be carried high and circular, but it should never touch the back.

# GREYHOUND

**OTHER NAMES:**
English greyhound

**DATE OF ORIGIN:** Antiquity

**PLACE OF ORIGIN:** Egypt/ Middle East, but developed to present form in Great Britain

**ORIGINAL USE:** Game coursing

**MODERN USE:** Coursing, racing, companion

**SIZE:**

**HEIGHT:** 69–76 cm (27–30 in)

**WEIGHT:** 27–32 kg (60–70 lb)

**COLOURS:** White, fawn, red, red–brindle, black–brindle, black as well as of the colours with white

**RECOGNIZED BY:** K.C.

The earliest images of greyhounds appear in ancient Egyptian mural paintings. When the Romans invaded Egypt 2,000 years ago, similar dogs were spread around the Mediterranean, and around 400 bc the dogs arrived in Britain where they were developed to their present form. The origins of the name 'greyhound' is a matter of debate: some hold it is from 'grais' meaning 'Grecian; 'grei' the Anglo Saxon word for 'beautiful', 'grech' an old English word for 'dog', or even that is was a mispronunciation of the word 'gaze', descriptive of hounds which hunt by sight.

Whatever the origins of the name, for hundreds of years ownership of greyhounds in Britain was restricted to the nobility: in 1016 King Canute decreed that 'No mean (ordinary) person may keep any greyhounds'. Under King John, the penalty for killing a greyhound was the same as for murdering a man, and the exalted status of the hound is further evidenced by the King's willingness to accept greyhounds from nobles in lieu of taxes! While the landowners of Britain made full use of the greyhound's hunting abilities, by the 18th century, the hound's sporting potential was also recognised and coursing grew in popularity. With a top speed of up to 60 km/h (37 mph) greyhounds entered a new arena: racing. The first record of a race was in 1876 of a meeting held in Hendon, north London, but it did not seem to 'catch on'. It was in the United States that the sport developed: greyhound races appeared in 1890 in Miami as an added attraction at horse racing events. In 1909, in Tucson, Arizona the greyhound track in its modern form was born.

complete DOG

# AFGHAN HOUND

**OTHER NAMES:** Tazi, Baluchi hound

**DATE OF ORIGIN:** Antiquity

**PLACE OF ORIGIN:** Afghanistan

**ORIGINAL USE:** Large game hunting

**MODERN USE:** Companion, guarding, hunting

**SIZE:**

**HEIGHT:** 64–74 cm (25–29 in)

**WEIGHT:** 23–27 kg (50–60 lb)

**COLOURS:** Any colour

**RECOGNIZED BY:** K.C.

The Afghan is a member of the greyhound family which first appeared in the eastern Mediterranean region several thousands of years ago, although it is not clear how it made its way from the Middle East to Afghanistan. Local legend says the hound was brought to Afghanistan in the Ark by Noah, but the most likely explanation is that it travelled with humans along the ancient trade routes, to eventually become the hunting dog of the Afghanistan royal family. Today, in Afghanistan, the hound exists in three varieties: short–haired (like the kyrghyz taigan, from Kyrgyzstan, the central Asian republic to the north of Afghanistan), fringe–haired (like the Saluki, see page 176), and the more familiar, long–haired dog, that we see in the West.

The British Museum in London has in its collection a pictorial fabric from ancient Athens called The Departure of Warriors which is dated to around the 6th century bc. This picture shows a variety of greyhound with a 'feathered' tail and bears an uncanny resemblance to the Afghan hound. Another ancient source is a papyrus scroll from Sinai dating from around 3,000 bc which refers to a cynocephalus, which translates roughly as, 'a monkey– or, baboon–faced hound'. Wherever it actually originated, and however this magnificent animal came to be found in Afghanistan, when the first European explorers arrived in the country in the late 15th century, the Afghan hound was already there.

The remote nature of the country and the use of selective breeding modified the 'original' greyhound into a hound more suited to the climate and terrain of Afghanistan. In addition to the long, thick, warm and protective coat, a distinctive feature is the feathered tail, carried high and ending in a circle or ring so the hunters could locate their dogs as they worked in the thick undergrowth. The Afghan's high and wide–set hipbones enables the dog to twist and turn on rocky hillsides and to leap like a monkey.

Highly prized by the Afghan nobility and aristocratic families, the hounds were difficult for 'mere foreigners' to obtain, and it was not until 1894 that the first Afghan hound reach Britain where its stunning appearance caused great interest. The hounds that followed over the next ten years or so however, did not prove to be as 'interesting', and it may be that they were not pure–bred animals. Then, Captain Banff imported his Afghan hound called Zardin, which was shown at the K.C. show at the Crystal Palace in 1907: Zardin won in sensational style and was such a topic in the press that Queen Alexandra, wife of King Edward VII, requested that Zardin attend a 'royal audience' at Buckingham Palace!

In conformation, their heads are long but not too narrow, with a slight stop (the indentation between the eyes where the nasal bone meets the skull) and long, strong jaws. The eyes are preferably dark although sometimes they are a glorious golden colour, and nearly 'triangular' in shape. The ears are set low and well back, close against the head. The back is level, but falls away slightly at the 'rump end' where the hips are wide and prominent and the hind legs powerful and with a good length between the hip and the hock. Thick hairs cover the large strong feet, ideally designed for rough terrain. The tail, which is lightly feathered and ends in the distinctive ring or circle, is set low when the hound is not in action, but raised high when the dog is running. The beautiful coat, which is acceptable in any colour, is long and fine – and requires daily grooming to avoid thick mats – except on the 'saddle' from the shoulders backwards and on the fore face.

# BORZOI

**OTHER NAMES:** Russian wolfhound

**DATE OF ORIGIN:** 17th century

**PLACE OF ORIGIN:** Russia

**ORIGINAL USE:** Wolf coursing

**MODERN USE:** Companion

**SIZE:**

**HEIGHT:** 69–79 cm (27–31 in)

**WEIGHT:** 35–48 kg (75–105 lb)

**COLOURS:** Any colour

**RECOGNIZED BY:** K.C.

The Russian word borzoi is a general term for sight hounds: the taigan, tasy, south Russian Steppe hound and chortaj are all classed as borzoi. Until fairly recently, the borzoi was known as the Russian wolfhound which, although a descriptive name, can be a little misleading. Pairs of borzoi were used in Imperial Russia for coursing wolves – a ceremonial kind of hunting and fashionable country pursuit among nobles. These dogs were never required to attack and fight wolves unaided, but 'to harry' wolves into open areas where human hunters could effect a kill more easily. The whole event was something of a spectacle, since symmetry and elegance in the paired dogs was highly valued, and both dogs were required to be matched in colour and markings, as well as in size and speed, since one dog alone reaching and harrying a wolf would not stand a chance! The two borzois' task was to seize the wolf by the neck and throw it to the ground, holding it there until the mounted hunter sprang from his horse and dispatched the unfortunate wolf in a suitably 'heroic' manner, with a dagger at close quarters.

The origins of the borzoi date back to the 17th century when a number of Arabian greyhounds similar to the Saluki (see page 176) were brought to Russia as hunting dogs. While they were fast, unfortunately their coats were not suited to withstand the severe cold of harsh Russian winters and they perished. When further greyhounds arrived, these were crossed with a native, long–legged collie–type dog which had a more suitable thick, heavy and wavy coat. The borzoi had arrived – in Russia at least. For the next 200 years the only borzois to leave Imperial Russia were those given as gifts to other royal households. In 1842, Queen Victoria was presented with the first of many borzois as gifts from the Russian Tsar. Victoria was immensely fond of the breed and as a 'fashion leader', she soon made the borzoi the 'most wanted' among the aristocracy of Britain. Early exhibitors of the breed at shows in the 19th century included the Duchess of Manchester, the Duke of Hamilton, the Duchess of Newcastle, and King Edward VII and his wife Queen Alexandra. Around 1889, the Borzoi arrived in America: the first dogs came from England but, in 1903, Russian dogs, supplied by Grand Duke Nicholas Romanoff, arrived in the USA.

The borzoi has an exceptionally long and lean head, measuring the same from the inner corner of the eye to both the nose and the occiput, with dark, almost almond–shaped eyes set obliquely and strong jaws. The body is best described as a series of graceful curves and, helping to give the borzoi its impression of streamlined strength, is a well–muscled body, an arched back nearer the shoulders, powerful quarters that are set wider than the shoulders and strong, well–muscled hind legs. The long, graceful almost hare–like feet – which some liken to the graceful arches of a Kirov ballerina – are covered in short, flat hairs. The coat is long and silky, with a lovely frill on the neck, but short on the head, ears and front legs. The hind quarters and tail on the other hand are wonderfully 'feathered' so that, even when still, the borzoi looks as if it is speeding through the wind!

# DEERHOUND

**OTHER NAMES:** Scottish deerhound, Highland greyhound

**DATE OF ORIGIN:** Middle Ages

**PLACE OF ORIGIN:** Great Britain

**ORIGINAL USE:** Deer hunting

**MODERN USE:** Companion

**SIZE:**

**HEIGHT:** 71–76 cm (28–30 in)

**WEIGHT:** 36–45 kg (80–100 lb)

**COLOURS:** Fawn, red, red–brindle, blue–grey, grey, black–brindle

**RECOGNIZED BY:** K.C.

Once the exclusive companion to the kings and noblemen of Scotland in the Middle Ages – many were owned by the chiefs of Highland clans and for a time, men of rank lower than an Earl were forbidden to own them – the deerhound is another descendent of the greyhound (see page 171). The exact date when these dogs reached the British Isles is unknown, but many believe it was first introduced by Phoenician traders around 3,000 years ago and then 'went north' to Scotland, where they proved to be of the greatest value, and where, possibly, they developed their heavy coats to withstand the tough Scottish climate.

The breed was developed to course deer through the densely wooded forests of the Scottish Highlands. During the 16th century, this was a favourite sport and pastime of the rich and powerful lairds, but when firearms became widespread in the 18th century, along with the clearing of much of the forests and the near collapse of the clan system following the Battle of Culloden in 1745, the favoured position of the deerhound was ended. Thanks to the efforts of Duncan McNeil, later Lord Colonsay, who took a particular interest in the deerhound, the near–extinct breed was successfully brought back to enjoy true glory by a careful and systematic breeding programme.

19th–century lovers of the breed included such notable figures as Queen Victoria and the great Scottish novelist, Sir Walter Scott, who had a monument erected to his deerhound, Maida, with the inscription: 'Beneath this sculptured form which late your wore, Sleep soundly Maida, at your Master's door'. So beloved was his dog that he described him as 'the most perfect creature of heaven', and wrote of how, because Maida had so often had his portrait painted, he would get up and walk away whenever he saw anyone with a palette and brushes!

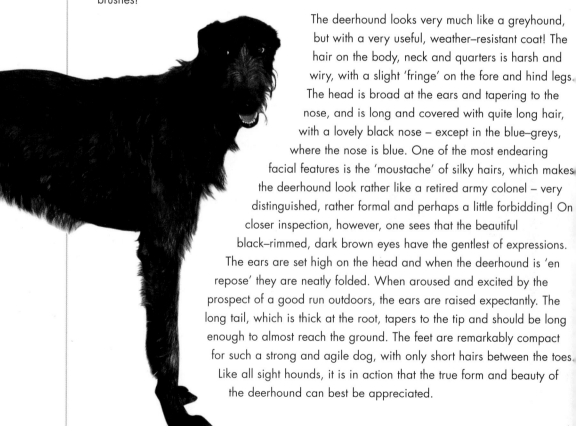

The deerhound looks very much like a greyhound, but with a very useful, weather–resistant coat! The hair on the body, neck and quarters is harsh and wiry, with a slight 'fringe' on the fore and hind legs. The head is broad at the ears and tapering to the nose, and is long and covered with quite long hair, with a lovely black nose – except in the blue–greys, where the nose is blue. One of the most endearing facial features is the 'moustache' of silky hairs, which makes the deerhound look rather like a retired army colonel – very distinguished, rather formal and perhaps a little forbidding! On closer inspection, however, one sees that the beautiful black–rimmed, dark brown eyes have the gentlest of expressions. The ears are set high on the head and when the deerhound is 'en repose' they are neatly folded. When aroused and excited by the prospect of a good run outdoors, the ears are raised expectantly. The long tail, which is thick at the root, tapers to the tip and should be long enough to almost reach the ground. The feet are remarkably compact for such a strong and agile dog, with only short hairs between the toes. Like all sight hounds, it is in action that the true form and beauty of the deerhound can best be appreciated.

# IRISH WOLFHOUND

**OTHER NAMES:** None

**DATE OF ORIGIN:** Antiquity, but breed 'recreated' in 19th century

**PLACE OF ORIGIN:** Ireland

**ORIGINAL USE:** Wolf hunting

**MODERN USE:** Companion, guarding

**SIZE:**

**HEIGHT:** 71–90 cm (28–35 in)

**WEIGHT:** 40–55 kg (90–120 lb)

**COLOURS:** Variety

**RECOGNIZED BY:** K.C.

The Irish wolfhound is not only among the tallest breeds in the world, it is also one of the oldest. In ad 392, Symmachus wrote from Rome to his brother Flavinius, then in Britain, thanking him for the gift of seven Irish hounds and added that 'all Rome viewed them with wonder'. Not surprising given their great size! Throughout Irish history the wolfhound appears: King Cormac, who reigned in the 4th century, owned numerous wolfhounds; the 12th–century King of Ulster was so desperate to own a wolfhound called 'Aibe' that he offered six thousand cows for him and went into battle when the offer was declined! In the 16th century, a pair were sent to the King of Spain as a gift, but later, in 1652, Oliver Cromwell forbade their export because the hounds were too rare and wolves were too plentiful! The last wolf to be killed in Ireland by the hounds was in 1780: their work was over and just fifty years later, it seemed the Irish wolfhound was extinct until English Army officer Captain G. A. Graham set about reviving the breed – although questions abound as to whether he found true Irish wolfhounds to breed from, or whether he 'manufactured' the breed from foreign breeds such as Great Danes (see page 234), deerhounds (see left) and mastiffs (see page 232).

In spite of their enormous size and strength, the Irish wolfhound is one of the gentlest breeds and is affectionate and loyal. It is only its size which makes it unsuitable for many homes, which generally lack the space needed to exercise such a magnificent animal. The head is long and not too broad, the muzzle long and moderately pointed. Underneath the shaggy brows are dark, soft, and good–natured eyes, shaded by black eyelids. The muscular thighs are long and strong, and the feet are large and round. The rough, topcoat is wiry on the body, legs and head, but longer over the eyes and under the jaws.

# SALUKI

**OTHER NAMES:** Gazelle hound,
Arabian hound, Persian greyhound

**DATE OF ORIGIN:** Antiquity

**PLACE OF ORIGIN:** Middle east

**ORIGINAL USE:** Gazelle hunting

**MODERN USE:** Companion, hare
coursing (in countries where legally
permitted)

**SIZE:**

**HEIGHT:** 58–71 cm (22–28 in)

**WEIGHT:** 14–25 kg (31–55 lb)

**COLOURS:** White, cream, red,
golden, black–tan, fawn, tricolour

**RECOGNIZED BY:** K.C.

The Saluki is a member of the greyhound family –
one of the oldest families of dogs – and the Saluki may
be the oldest member of this family! In the tomb of
Rekma–re in Egypt, dating from around 1400 bc there is
a painting of dogs that are remarkably 'Saluki–like',
showing the same ear and leg feathering, similar hind
quarters and tails. But even earlier paintings, such as
those at Heirakonapolis dating from around 3600 bc,
show similar dogs. According to legends, the Saluki takes its name either from the
disappeared southern Arabian town of Saluk, once famous for its armour as well as its fine
sight hounds, or from the town of Seleukia, in Syria. Its nickname of 'gazelle hound', however
indicates its original use and it was highly prized by the Arabs and Persians – as prized as
their horses! It is said that, to protect their feet from the hot sands, Salukis were carried to the
hunt on horse– or camel back. According to the tenets of Islam, dogs are considered as
'unclean' animals, but a special dispensation was accorded to the Saluki, which allowed them
to share the living quarters of their owners. The nomadic Bedouin tribesmen of North Africa
continue to hand down the genealogy of their prized Salukis as part of their oral tradition and
continue to course game – although their dogs are more likely to be carried in
four–wheel–drive vehicles! The Saluki carries its head like a true aristocrat. The small, deep–set
eyes have an expression described as 'far seeing' – indeed they will watch birds far in the
distance, a legacy of their desert past when they worked hunted alongside hawks.

# SLOUGHI

**OTHER NAMES:** Slughi, sleughi,
Arabian greyhound, eastern greyhound

**DATE OF ORIGIN:** Antiquity

**PLACE OF ORIGIN:** North Africa,
possibly Morocco

**ORIGINAL USE:** Hunting, guarding

**MODERN USE:** Companion

**SIZE:**

**HEIGHT:** 61–72 cm (24–28 in)

**WEIGHT:** 20–27 kg (45–60 lb)

**COLOURS:** 'Sand' and fawn colours

**RECOGNIZED BY:** K.C.

Like the Saluki (see above) the sloughi, or Slughi, as it is called in colloquial Arabic, is a
member of the greyhound family. At one time, the term greyhound was used as a 'catch all'
name to describe a whole group of loosely related dogs, but when it became necessary to
give individual names to the breeds, Britain, who was responsible for the naming process,
decided that the term 'greyhound' be applied to the short–coated 'English breed', and all
others types – such as the Saluki, Afghan, and sloughi be known as Eastern greyhounds.
Today, since many of the 'Eastern greyhounds' now have their 'own' precise breed name, the
term has largely fallen into disuse. While the Saluki's origins are firmly rooted in the Middle
East, the sloughi may have originated in the Yemeni town of Saloug and travelled into North
Africa with the invading Arab tribes over 1,000 years ago, where it became established as a
breed in Morocco. Like the Saluki, the sloughi was highly prized in a culture whose
religion decreed dogs to be unclean: unlike 'ordinary' dogs, the sloughi shared
their owners' homes and, it is said, were mourned as family when they died.
The sloughi, is less well known than the Saluki, and is often confused with it. It is
similar in size and shape to the Saluki, with a smooth, close coat designed to rid the
body of excess desert heat. What the sloughi doesn't have are the Saluki's ear, leg and
tail 'feathers'. The sloughi coat is also 'sand', 'biscuit' or fawn coloured – ideal
camouflage for hunting desert prey such as gazelles, foxes and hares. The sloughi's large
ribcage gives the dog its vast lung capacity; the leg muscles however, and the long, lean
paws, are less developed and lighter than a greyhound's.

# WHIPPET

**OTHER NAMES:** Snap dog, 'Poor man's greyhound'

**DATE OF ORIGIN:** 19th century

**PLACE OF ORIGIN:** Great Britain

**ORIGINAL USE:** Coursing, racing

**MODERN USE:** Companion, racing

**SIZE:**

**HEIGHT:** 43–51 cm (17–20 in)

**WEIGHT:** 12.5–13.5 kg (27–30 lb)

**COLOURS:** Any

**RECOGNIZED BY:** K.C.

While the names 'whappet' and 'wappet' are recorded in early English writings about dogs, these names in fact referred to any small – and noisy – dog of uncertain breeding. A 'miniature' greyhound, the perfect aerodynamic form of the whippet makes it a very fast mover, capable over short distances of reaching speeds of up to 65 km/h (40 mph). Often called 'the poor man's greyhound' – perhaps because of the early edicts outlawing commoners from owning 'true' greyhounds in Britain – but more likely because these dogs were popular with working men in the north of England, who spent their weekend leisure time coursing rabbits. Terriers, the original breeds used for this 'sport' were not really fast enough to excel at the 'snap' (on the spot or hastily arranged) dog trials favoured by the working classes, so careful crossing with small greyhounds began.

When anti–cruelty laws were introduced, owners turned to straight racing, training their dogs to run, grip and 'worry' a rag shaken by the owners. Rag racing required dogs with improved bodies and speed as well as a handicapping system: little dogs, the whippets, started at the front, bigger ones – greyhounds – at the rear! With purpose–built race tracks and commercial backing for greyhound racing in the 20th century, rag racing for whippets all but ended. Racing was revived as an amateur sport in the 1950s, using miniature starting traps – but no betting is allowed! Furthermore, unlike the divisions of greyhound 'type', a whippet can win in the show ring on one day, and the next day, be a winner at the races!

The immense power and speed of the whippet is more remarkable given the dog's outward appearance of great fragility, which is further enhanced by their habit of 'quivering' or 'shivering' when standing still and regarding you with quiet eyes! The truth is that the whippet is incredibly robust and has a supreme disregard for bad weather, and is so fearless that many suspect it to have the heart of a lion!

# BASSET HOUND

**OTHER NAMES:** None

**DATE OF ORIGIN:** 16th century

**PLACE OF ORIGIN:** France

**ORIGINAL USE:** Rabbit/hare hunting

**MODERN USE:** Companion

**SIZE:**

**HEIGHT:** 33–38 cm (13–15 in)

**WEIGHT:** 18–27 kg (40–60 lb)

**COLOURS:** Tricolour, lemon–white

**RECOGNIZED BY:** K.C.

The basset takes its name from the French word basset which means 'dwarf', and this breed of dog originated in France in the 16th century. The short legged hunting hounds are distinguished not only by their lowness to the ground, but also by the remarkable scenting skill. The pendulous ears – which should reach at least to the end of the muzzle – may well have been useful for directing scents: as they flapped and brushed against the undergrowth, they circulated currents of air carrying the scent of quarry to their noses.

Today the breed is considered a gentle and benign creature – if often a little obstinate – and worldwide they are famous as the symbol of the comfortable, well–fitting shoes! However, some lighter boned, slightly longer–legged bassets do take part in field trials, displaying the skills that made them prized as hunting dogs for centuries.

The typical pet basset however, is more likely to be the heavily boned dog on short, rather crooked legs. Weighing an average of about 25 kg (55 lb) and coming in at under 38 cm (15 in), basset hounds may be low slung, but they are certainly not small dogs! The wrinkled skin, heavy flews, floppy ears and soft, slightly sunken eyes (which give the Basset a rather doleful expression) are also misleading, for they are playful dogs, with hearty appetites for food and exercise!

# GRAND BASSET GRIFFON VANDÉEN

**OTHER NAMES:** Large Vendéen griffon basset

**DATE OF ORIGIN:** 19th century

**PLACE OF ORIGIN:** France

**ORIGINAL USE:** Gun dog, hare coursing

**MODERN USE:** Companion, gun dog (in France)

**SIZE:**

**HEIGHT:** 38–42 cm (15–16 in)

**WEIGHT:** 18–20 kg (40–44 lb)

**COLOURS:** White, grey, black/white, tan/white, tricolour

**RECOGNIZED BY:** K.C.

The basset griffon Vendéen (from the Vendée region of France) comes in two sizes: grand (large) and petit (small) (see page 179). A scenting dog from the region, with the short (bas) legs that give the breed its name was known in the 19th century, but the modern grand basset griffon was established in the mid 1940s by selective breeding by Paul Desamy who fixed the characteristics of the breed. The grand basset griffon is a little taller and a little 'longer in the legs' than most bassets, and unlike the basset hound (see above) its conformation is less exaggerated, the skin is not so wrinkled and it does not have the same 'serious expression'. The basset griffons coat is also much harsher and shaggier! Like all bassets their pendulous ears – which should touch the end of their noses when scenting – help to circulate air currents carrying the scent of their quarry. They are also well–muscled dogs, with a heavy bone structure, which allows them the strength to be persistent – some would say obstinate – hunters.

# PETIT BASSET GRIFFON VENDÉEN

**OTHER NAMES:** Little griffon Vendéen basset

**DATE OF ORIGIN:** 18th century

**PLACE OF ORIGIN:** France

**ORIGINAL USE:** Hare coursing

**MODERN USE:** Companion, gun dog (in France)

**SIZE:**

**HEIGHT:** 34–38 cm (13–15 in)

**WEIGHT:** 14–18 kg (31–40 lb)

**COLOURS:** White, orange–white, tricolour

**RECOGNIZED BY:** K.C.

Like its 'big brother' the petit basset griffon has its origins in the Vendée region of France in the 18th century, where it was used for hunting rabbits and hares. In the 1940s, selective breeding by Abel Desamy fixed the breed's modern characteristics and helped to establish it as one of the most popular basset breeds – both inside France and abroad. The petit basset griffon is a more 'true' basset in shape: with the typical firm, short legs of the breed – although the front legs do not turn inwards at the knees like the basset hound (see page 178). The petit shares the same deep chest as the grand basset: placed side by side the only discernible difference is in leg length: both have the shaggy coat, robust neck and domed, elongated head. The shortened legs combined with the length of the back and the deep chest do mean that the petit does have a tendency to suffer from back pain.

# BEAGLE

**OTHER NAMES:** English beagle

**DATE OF ORIGIN:** 11th century

**PLACE OF ORIGIN:** France, then developed in Great Britain

**ORIGINAL USE:** Rabbit/hare hunting

**MODERN USE:** Companion, gun dog, filed trials

**SIZE:**

**HEIGHT:** 33–41 cm (13–16 in)

**WEIGHT:** 8–14 kg (18–30 lb)

**COLOURS:** Any hound colour

**RECOGNIZED BY:** K.C.

The beagle is the smallest of the British scent hounds, whose ancestors are believed to date back to the arrival of the Norman–French forces in Britain, led by William the Conqueror in the 11th century. As well as invading Britain, the Normans also introduced hares to the country to widen both the culinary (a pleasant change to the native rabbits!) and sporting opportunities of the English!

The name 'beagle' may have originated in one of three sources: from the Celtic word 'beag', from the Norman–French word 'beigh' or from the Old English word 'begle', but all three mean the same thing: 'small'. In the late 18th century, beagles were often so small – under 25 cm (10 in) they were called 'pocket beagles' because the hunters could carry them in their saddle bags. The slightly larger sized 'modern' beagle was used almost exclusively as a working dog until the late 1940s in Britain, while in tropical countries, oversize beagles are still used in packs for hunting jaguars and leopards! While the beagle may vary in size and looks from country to country – some have smooth coats, others can be wiry – one characteristic they all share is its 'voice' – described as 'harmonious music' by enthusiasts – who listen for changes in 'song' if a rabbit – or dinner bowl – comes into view! One of the saddest – and most controversial – roles of the beagle in recent years has been as a research dog in laboratories, both for medical research and commercial research. Because of their small size and uniformity in weight, large numbers of genetically bred beagles are produced specifically for this 'market'.

# BLOOD HOUND

**OTHER NAMES:** Chien St. Hubert, St. Hubert hound

**DATE OF ORIGIN:** Middle Ages

**PLACE OF ORIGIN:** Abbey of St. Hubert, Ardennes, Belgium

**ORIGINAL USE:** Tracking ground scent of deer

**MODERN USE:** Tracking, companion

**SIZE:**

**HEIGHT:** 58–69 cm (23–27 in)

**WEIGHT:** 36–50 kg (80–110 lb)

**COLOURS:** Red, liver–tan, black–tan

**RECOGNIZED BY:** K.C.

The largest of the scent hounds, the bloodhound also has the keenest nose, able to detect the coldest of scents, and the unique ability to track people. While the movies depict a fearsome, drooling animal, baying after the scent of escaped criminals and ready to kill, in truth, the bloodhound lives only for tracking, with little or no interest in the 'end product'. Rather than bite their 'prey', bloodhounds are more likely to slobber all over them! The use of the word 'blood' in their name refers not to their killing instinct, but to the fact that the hound was a member of an 'aristocracy' – rather like the way pedigree or thoroughbred horses are described.

The bloodhound traces its origins back to the Abbey of St. Hubert, which had been founded in ad 687 in the Ardennes, in Belgium, and where the monks bred these superb hounds for tracking deer. At the same time in Britain, identical hounds were being bred, most likely derived from the St. Hubert stock, but brought to England by nobles returning from the Crusades. At this time, these hounds occurred in a wide variety of solid colours, including white, which was called the talbot hound. Today all bloodhounds are red, black and tan, or liver and tan. By the 17th century, the white strain had died out as a breed, but the gene continued and can be seen in white boxers and in tricolour basset hounds (see page 178). Size and 'song' apart, a bloodhound's head is its most distinctive feature, with its abundance of loose skin which, when the dog lowers its head to scent, hangs in folds over its forehead and the sides of its face. The lower lips hang 5 cm (2 in) below the jaw bone. The powerful neck and shoulders and the exceptionally strong back, allow the bloodhound to work for extended periods without rest.

# DACHSHUND

**OTHER NAMES:** Kaninchenteckel (rabbit–hunting) Normalschlag (standard), Zwergteckel (miniature), 'sausage dog'

**DATE OF ORIGIN:** 19th century

**PLACE OF ORIGIN:** Germany

**ORIGINAL USE:** Badger flushing

**MODERN USE:** Companion

**SIZE:**

**HEIGHT:** Standard and miniature: 13–25 cm (5–10 in)

**WEIGHT:**
Miniature: 4–5 kg (9–10 lb)
Standard: 6.5–11 kg (15–25 lb)

**COLOURS:** Variety of colours, but white markings undesirable in show dogs

**RECOGNIZED BY:** K.C.

The German name 'dachshund' translates as 'badger dog', which describes the dog's original role, in scenting and flushing out badgers which had 'gone to earth'. Its long, sausage–like body, short legs and rather big feet, allowed it to travel down narrow holes and tunnels and to dig out the quarry. Alternatively, the dachshund could hold a badger at bay in its earth, by barking continuously – its big ribcage gives this little dog a bark with tremendous resonance – until the badger was dug out with shovels. Technically then, the dachshund, is actually an 'earth dog', a terrier, but when the breed was first introduced to Britain by Prince Albert, the German husband of Queen Victoria, 'hund' was translated as 'hound' and the dachshund was placed in this group.

The dachshund today exists in six breeds: smooth–haired, long–haired and wire–haired, with miniature and standard varieties in each. The standard dachshunds – of all coats – vary in size. In Germany, where the dogs are still worked, they are categorised by their chest measurements: Kaninchenteckel (rabbit–hunting dachshund) has a maximum of 30 cm (12 in) chest circumference; Zwergteckel (miniature) measures 31–35 cm (12–14 in); Normalschlag (standard) measures over 35 cm (14 in).

While the smooth–haired standard dachshund, with its lustrous coat, is perhaps the oldest of the breed, the long–haired standard, with its silky–smooth, rather glamourous coat, seems to have been developed by crossing smooth–haired standards with short–legged spaniels such as the Sussex spaniel (see page 152) or field spaniel (see page 151). Miniature versions of each were then created. The wire–haired dachshund, with its thick and wiry, but flat, topcoat coupled with a fine undercoat, was the result of crossing the smooth–haired dachshund with wire–haired pinschers, with further crosses of the offspring with Dandie Dinmont terriers ( see page 191). Evidence of this ancestry can be seen in the way wire–haired dachshunds do not share the same 'tapering' nose of the other 'dachs' and it is further distinguished by the wiry 'beard' and bushy 'eyebrows'.

*complete DOG*

# FOXHOUND

**OTHER NAMES:** Known in USA as 'English' foxhound to distinguish it from the 'American' foxhound

**DATE OF ORIGIN:** 13th century

**PLACE OF ORIGIN:** Great Britain

**ORIGINAL USE:** Fox hunting

**MODERN USE:** Fox hunting (in areas where still legal) or hunting alternatives

**SIZE:**

**HEIGHT:** 58–69 cm (23–27 in)

**WEIGHT:** 25–34 kg (55–75 lb)

**COLOURS:** Bicolour, tricolour

**RECOGNIZED BY:** K.C.

While never a pet – although they do make excellent companions – nor really a show dog, the foxhound is nevertheless, probably one of the most instantly recognised breeds, and one which is currently subject to a great deal of public debate with regard to the legislation of fox hunting. Organised fox hunting became established in Britain in the 13th century: prior to that it had simply been a method of culling vermin, with stag hunting the more fashionable sporting pursuit. The first objective in the new sport of fox hunting, was to produce a lighter and faster dog than the St. Hubert–type hounds (see bloodhound, page 180) then available for hunting.

Imported French hounds, crossed with native animals, produced faster, leaner dogs, but each of the regions developed hounds that varied in shape and size: Yorkshire hounds were considered the fastest, while Staffordshire hounds were larger, a little slower but with a deeper voice. The differences were largely due to the types of terrain in which the hounds worked. In the 18th century, stag hunting declined and, by 1800, large, standardised packs of hounds were being bred and careful records were being kept that were incorporated into stud books kept by the Master of Foxhounds Association. These stud books provide valuable data and allow many packs to trace their hounds back over 200 years, making the English foxhound the oldest recorded pedigree. Years of selective breeding have produced an efficient hound, with a keen nose for scenting, a good voice, stamina – hunt distances of 50 miles (30 km) are not unusual, with many hounds racing to the start under their own steam on their powerful legs – and enthusiasm.

# ELKHOUND

**OTHER NAMES:** Norwegian Elkhound, Norsk Elghund (Gra) (Grey), grahund, Swedish Grey Dog

**DATE OF ORIGIN:** Antiquity, show standards developed in 1879

**PLACE OF ORIGIN:** Norway

**ORIGINAL USE:** Elk hunting

**MODERN USE:** Companion, gun dog, search and rescue

**SIZE:**

**HEIGHT:** 49–52 cm (19–21 in)

**WEIGHT:** 20–23 kg (44–50 lb)

**COLOURS:** Varied shades of grey with black tips to long outer coat, lighter on chest, neck buttocks and underside of tail

**RECOGNIZED BY:** K.C.

The elkhound – or more correctly, the Norwegian elkhound, the national dog of Norway – is a member of the spitz group of dogs that evolved in the Arctic regions of the world: Scandinavia, Canada, Russia, and Alaska. In conformation, spitz–type dogs are close to the northern wolf. The sharp, erect ears, the rather straight hocks, the lovely ruff around the neck and the tightly curled tail over their backs are the telltale signs of the elkhound's origins, and they are indeed well suited to harsh northern climates. Spitz dogs have an insulating, water–resistant undercoat that is as dense as the top coat; the small ears reduce any heat loss and minimise the risk of frost bite, while thick fur grows between the toes to protect them on snow and ice.

From Stone Age fossils found in Norway, it is evident that the breed has existed in Scandinavia for some 5,000 years and was originally bred for hunting elk (moose in US). In Britain, the elkhound is classified in the hound group because it hunts by scent to locate the quarry before alerting the huntsman by barking. The hound holds the elk at bay by 'dancing' around and in front of it – for up to an hour – always dodging the elk's formidable hooves and antlers.

Today, the versatile elkhound can be found herding farmyard livestock, working as a gun dog and, increasingly – owing to their scenting skills – as mountain search–and–rescue dogs.

# FINNISH SPITZ

**OTHER NAMES:** Suomenpystykorva, Finsk spets, barking bird dog

**DATE OF ORIGIN:** Antiquity

**PLACE OF ORIGIN:** Finland

**ORIGINAL USE:** Tracking animals – from bears to squirrels

**MODERN USE:** Gun dog, guarding, companion

**SIZE:**

**HEIGHT:** 38–51 cm (15–20 in)

**WEIGHT:** 14–16 kg (31–35 lb)

**COLOURS:** Bright reddish –brown or yellowish–red, but lighter on cheeks, under muzzle, on breast, inside legs, at back of thighs and under tail

**RECOGNIZED BY:** K.C.

The national breed of Finland, this is another spitz–type dog that has been around for thousands of years and, for centuries, inhabited the eastern part of Finland and the Karelian region of Russia (following the Russian Revolution in 1917, the hounds living in this region became known as Karelo–Finnish laikas). Legend says the ancestors of the Finnish spitz lived in the primeval forests where they helped the tribes or clans of Finns to track bears and elks. They have a particularly good nose for scent – which is why they are included in the hound group – but are also adept at listening to the forest floors for the sounds of animals and bird wings, they would force the animal out of cover to seek sanctuary in a tree. Then, using its bark to alert the hunter, the Finnish spitz would stand in rigid point marking the bird's or squirrel's position. This ability to track earned the spitz its nickname of the 'barking bird dog'.

By the 20th century, however, the breed had become repeatedly crossed with other Scandinavian spitz breeds and few pure specimens remained until expeditions to the far north of the country returned with magnificent animals with which the Finnish Kennel Club was able to begin a breed register and maintain detailed pedigrees. These handsome hounds, popular in their native land and growing in popularity abroad, are distinguished by their bushy, bright red–gold coats (double for weatherproofing), which shade off into rich creamy fawn on the under parts and their curled tail held against the thigh.

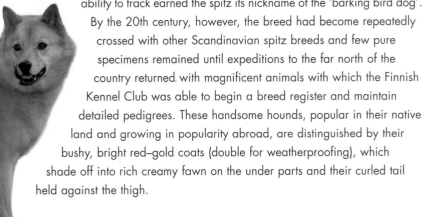

# GRAND BLEU DE GASCOGNE

**OTHER NAMES:** Large blue gascony hound

**DATE OF ORIGIN:** Middle Ages

**PLACE OF ORIGIN:** France

**ORIGINAL USE:** Deer/boar/wolf hunting.

**MODERN USE:** Gun dog

**SIZE:**

**HEIGHT:** 62–72 cm (24–28 in)

**WEIGHT:** 32–35 kg (71–77 lb)

**COLOURS:** Blue

**RECOGNIZED BY:** K.C.

The grand bleu de Gascogne is thought by many to be descended from racing breeds brought to France by Phoenician traders. While this cannot be proven, the grand bleu is certainly one of the world's oldest hounds. Developed in the middle ages in the arid Gascony region of southwest France to hunt large game, the breed is now popular outside of France, especially in the United States where it has been bred since the 18th century. In most cases, the grand blue continues to be a scent–trailing working dog, even though wolves and wild boars may have declined in numbers!

The coat is fairly thick and quite long– designed to give protection from angry teeth, tusks and horns. The forelegs are incredibly well–muscled and support exceptionally strong shoulders. The pendulous ears are quite distinctive being very low set and slightly curled!

Through selective breeding of the grand bleu de Gascogne for reduction in size to hunt smaller quarry, the petit bleu de Gascogne (small blue gascony hound) was also developed in the Middle Ages. This smaller hound has the same remarkable nose for scents as its 'big brother', but lacks the curled ears and usually has tan–coloured feet.

# HAMILTONSTOVARE

**OTHER NAMES:** Hamilton hound

**DATE OF ORIGIN:** Middle Ages, developed further in 19th century

**PLACE OF ORIGIN:** Sweden

**ORIGINAL USE:** Hare and fox hunting

**MODERN USE:** Hunting, companion

**SIZE:**

**HEIGHT:** 49–61 cm (19–24 in)

**WEIGHT:** 23–27 kg (50–60 lb)

**COLOURS:** Tricolour

**RECOGNIZED BY:** K.C.

The Hamiltonstovare is a Swedish hound named after the breed's creator, Adolf Patrick Hamilton, who was also the founder of the Swedish Kennel Club in 1889. The Hamiltonstovare was developed by crossing varieties of German beagle with the English foxhound (see page 182) and local Swedish hounds in the 1860s. The resulting Hamiltonstovare is a single, rather than pack hunter, capable of both scent tracking and flushing game, while baying in a typically hound like manner when it finds its quarry.

The harsh climate and difficult terrain in which the hound has to work calls for a very hardy animal, with a strong dense topcoat covering a short, thick, yet soft undercoat to protect it from the cold, and, in winter, the Hamiltonstovare's coat also thickens very considerably While the breed remains little known outside of its native Sweden, the Hamiltonstovare is among the country's ten most populous breeds, where its attractive appearance – due to its calm brown eyes, long muzzle, tipped with a lovely large black nose, its striking tricolouration – and, most of all, its affectionate nature, have made the Hamiltonstovare both a magnificent show dog and a loyal companion dog. Without doubt, the Hamiltonstovare will become a firm favourite with dog lovers in many other countries too.

# OTTERHOUND

**OTHER NAMES:** None

**DATE OF ORIGIN:** Antiquity

**PLACE OF ORIGIN:**
Great Britain

**ORIGINAL USE:** Otter hunting

**MODERN USE:** Companion

**SIZE:**

**HEIGHT:** 58–69 cm (23–27 in)

**WEIGHT:** 30–55 kg (65–120 lb)

**COLOURS:** Any hound colours

**RECOGNIZED BY:** K.C.

In Britain, different hounds were bred for different game, such as foxhounds for foxes, and harriers for hares. It is possible that the otterhound is descended from the bloodhound (see page 180) – its 'nose' for scents is equal to that of a bloodhound – with some foxhound, spaniel and large, rough coated terrier (like the Airedale, see page 188) blood.

The otterhound was bred to swim in the coldest of rivers: it has a double coat with a thick, oily woolly undercoat under coarse, outer hair that is also oily, insulating it from the iciest of water; its toes are webbed, and its legs are well muscled for swimming – for hours at a time!

Otters live in holes dug underneath the banks of rivers with the entrance hole (the holt) under water. On land, the scent or trail left by an otter is called a 'drag', while scent left on water is called a 'wash'. The sensitive nose of the otterhound can follow a drag that is ten hours old. But otters, who swim for long distances under water, surface occasionally to take a breath. When they submerge again, the otter leaves behind a small trail of bubbles, marking its course. It is this trail (the wash) that the otterhound follows, swimming sometimes for up to five hours after its quarry.

Now that otters are no longer hunted, the otterhound's original function no longer applies. Fortunately their lovely looks and even temperament have made them an attractive companion. They do have some drawbacks though as pets: Firstly, their absolute dedication to following and unravelling elusive scents on land makes them deaf to all commands! Secondly, they are irresistibly drawn by the sight or smell of water – no matter how deep or dirty – and they will paddle and swim around happily for hours, ignoring the requests of their owners to 'come out'. Thirdly, the oily nature of their coat, without frequent bathing or swims, makes the otterhound a rather pungent hound!

# RHODESIAN RIDGEBACK

**OTHER NAMES:** African Lion Hound

**DATE OF ORIGIN:** 19th century

**PLACE OF ORIGIN:** South Africa

**ORIGINAL USE:** Hunting

**MODERN USE:** Companion, guard dog

**SIZE:**

**HEIGHT:** 61–69 cm (24–27 in)

**WEIGHT:** 30–39 kg (65–85 lb)

**COLOURS:**
Light–wheaten to red wheaten

**RECOGNIZED BY:** K.C.

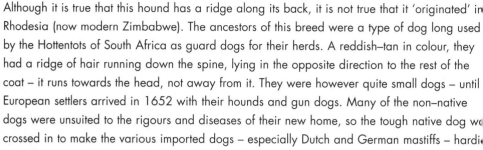

Although it is true that this hound has a ridge along its back, it is not true that it 'originated' in Rhodesia (now modern Zimbabwe). The ancestors of this breed were a type of dog long used by the Hottentots of South Africa as guard dogs for their herds. A reddish–tan in colour, they had a ridge of hair running down the spine, lying in the opposite direction to the rest of the coat – it runs towards the head, not away from it. They were however quite small dogs – until European settlers arrived in 1652 with their hounds and gun dogs. Many of the non–native dogs were unsuited to the rigours and diseases of their new home, so the tough native dog was crossed in to make the various imported dogs – especially Dutch and German mastiffs – hardier. In the process, the small ridge–backed dog grew in size and developed a keen nose for scenting.

This was very fortuitous, since at the time, the Cape region of South Africa teemed with big game. Later, South African big–game hunters took the breed north to 'lion country' – to what was then Rhodesia. The ridgeback was never used to attack lions, but instead was expected to act like a true hound: scenting and trailing the game, barking to hold both the lion at bay and to attract the hunter's attention. For its defence, the ridgeback relied on its sheer size and strength as it snapped, dodged, feinted and backed off to hold the lion's attention. The breed was still somewhat 'rough and ready' until 1922 when an official standard was drawn up in Bulawayo, Zimbabwe, taking and combining the best attributes of five existing dogs. Few Rhodesian ridgebacks are worked today in big game tracking, instead serving as guard dogs on remote farmsteads.

# SEGUGIO ITALIANO

**OTHER NAMES:** Segugio, Italian hound

**DATE OF ORIGIN:** Antiquity

**PLACE OF ORIGIN:** Italy

**ORIGINAL USE:** Game hunting

**MODERN USE:** Gun dog, companion

**SIZE:**

**HEIGHT:** 52–58 cm (20–23 in)

**WEIGHT:** 18–28 kg (40–62 lb)

**COLOURS:**
Fawn, black–tan

**RECOGNIZED BY:** K.C.

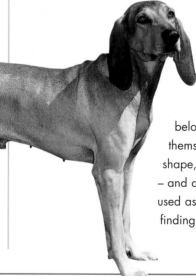

The segugio Italiano is Italy's only native scent hound and it is very similar to the coursing hounds seen in ancient Egyptian art although its stamina was later greatly increased with the introduction of mastiff (see page 232) blood. Consequently the segugio has the long legs of a sight hound with the face of a scent hound! During the Renaissance in Italy, the segugio was highly prized – and is often to be seen in many paintings depicting hunting scenes at this time. Once it has a scent, the segugio is as single minded in its determination to track as a bloodhound, but unlike that breed, the segugio is also very interested in the capture and kill of its quarry.

When not working, the segugio is a quiet and gentle dog, with an elegant outline, and a wonderful fawn, or black–and–tan coat which is dense and glossy. The tail is that of a sight hound – delicate and thin, even at the root – while the scent hound's pendulous triangular ears are set just below eye level and reach to the tip of the nose. The eyes themselves are large, dark and bright, while the feet are oval in shape, rather like a hare's – which it still hunts today in its native Italy – and are covered in short, dense hair. The segugio is not normally used as a pack hound: more often it is worked singly or as a pair, finding, tracking and driving quarry towards waiting guns.

# TERRIERS

The majority of the world's terriers evolved in Britain from various hounds. The name 'terrier' is derived from the Latin 'terra', meaning 'earth', and the Roman invaders of Britain called these dogs 'terrarii' on account that they were expert tunnellers, willing to 'go to ground' after badgers, rats, rabbits or foxes. In later centuries, terriers were associated, first, with the 'peasant classes' and then with the working classes of industrialised Britain. This is probably due to the fact that hounds and spaniels were the hunting dogs of the nobility – ancient laws in Britain and Ireland prohibited peasants from owning hunting dogs – and consequently, little reference is made of terriers until 1560 when Dr. John Caius remarked that

**CAIRN**

**STAFFORDSHIRE BULL**

terriers were quarrelsome, 'snappy' and fit only to live in stables! Terriers were, nevertheless, valuable dogs in both countryside and towns for their efficiency as vermin 'killing machines' and also for sport. The Patterdale and Yorkshire Terriers were renowned for their ratting skills, and sport ratting – where the dogs were placed in pits and killed 'against the clock' – was popular across England and Ireland. In other regions, other terriers were developed to fight against each other, or other animals, in pits or in open fields.

Dogs used for bull baiting were large mastiff-type animals with added terrier blood to give them the edge when it came to fearlessness and aggression: the American pit bull terrier, Staffordshire bull terrier, and English bull terrier were all produced as a result of this 'sport'. The 'lamb-like' Bedlington terrier is the only racing terrier – said to be descended from whippets – and was bred by gypsies in the Rothbury Forest on the Scottish border! In the 19th century, breeders seriously began breeding to type and produced the numerous regional variations: in Scotland, the generic, short-legged dogs became the Skye and Scottish terriers, Sealyham, cairn Terriers – the white-coloured dogs becoming the West Highland whites – and the delightfully named, though utterly fearless, Dandie Dinmont. Similar developments occurred across England, Wales and Ireland so that, today, there are 29 British breeds of terrier, as well as European, Japanese, Russian and Australian terriers. While they continue to retain their independent, tenacious characters and, if truth be told, remain completely convinced of their own 'self importance', terriers do make wonderful companions and pets.

**DANDIE DINMONT**

**HIGHLAND WESTIE**

# AIREDALE

**OTHER NAMES:** Waterside terrier, Warfedale terrier, Bingley terrier

**DATE OF ORIGIN:** 19th century

**PLACE OF ORIGIN:** Yorkshire, England

**ORIGINAL USE:** Badger/otter hunting

**MODERN USE:** Companion, guard dog, police dog (especially in Germany)

**SIZE:**

**HEIGHT:** 56-61 cm (22-24 in)

**WEIGHT:** 20-23 kg (44-50 lb)

**COLOURS:** All colours

**RECOGNIZED BY:** K.C.

The 'king of terriers', the Airedale, is the largest of the terriers, and is, in fact, too large to 'go to earth'! The Airedale, from the district in Yorkshire of the same name is thought to be a 'mixture' of otterhound (see page 185), and the now extinct 'black-and-tan' or old English broken-haired terrier. While other terriers were bred to deliberately reduce them in size, the Airedale was encouraged to grow in order to produce a dog that would take on an adult badger or otter. Its ancestry in the otterhound gave it both size, and its notably water skills, which earned it the nick name 'waterside terrier'. The Airedale, in true terrier style, also excelled at rabbit and rat hunting.

In 1879 the breed was officially classified at a dog show – in Bingley, Yorkshire – under the auspices of the Airedale Agricultural Society and, from then on, in spite of its large size, the Airedale grew in popularity. Some dogs went to the USA where they excelled in the show ring while others went to Germany, where they went to work pulling carts! Realising their working abilities, the Germans began using them as guard dogs – they are born watchdogs and owners tell of how their behaviour changes when dusk falls! – as border/frontier control dogs and as police dogs.

Undoubtedly their most attractive feature is their coat: a harsh, dense, wiry coat usually rich tan and black, which requires regular trimming.

# AUSTRALIAN TERRIER

**OTHER NAMES:** None

**DATE OF ORIGIN:** 19th century

**PLACE OF ORIGIN:** Australia

**ORIGINAL USE:** Rat hunting, snake hunting

**MODERN USE:** Farm 'pest controller', companion

**SIZE:**

**HEIGHT:** 24–25 cm (10 in)

**WEIGHT:** 5–6 kg (12–14 lb)

**COLOURS:** Blue–tan, sandy

**RECOGNIZED BY:** K.C.

Australia might be said to be the country that has specialised in producing unique animals: kangaroos, wallabies, koala bears, as well as the world favourite pet bird, the budgerigar. The Australian terrier may be more orthodox, but it is no less significant – it is the only true terrier accepted by the world which did not originate in Britain.

Described as a 'canine cocktail' the Australian terriers were bred for work and, by the time they were shown in Australia in 1899, these tough and tenacious little dogs had been around for some twenty years. Most breeders today believe the terrier to be descended from numerous British terriers – especially the Yorkshire terrier on account of its size – as well as cairns, Irish, and Scottish terriers and possibly, Dandie Dinmonts, Skye and Norwich terriers!

All these breeds travelled 'down under' with their owners and the welcome result was this low–set, compact, active and agile dog that was able to kill a rat or rabbit in seconds. The Australian terrier, with its rugged appearance, made itself even more indispensable on remote farms where, as well as acting as an ever alert guard or watchdog, unlikely to back down from any confrontations with other dogs – or dingoes – or man, its keen eyesight and quick reflexes made them excellent snake hunters, killing by leaping off the ground, turning in mid–air to land behind the snake, which was then seized behind the neck. While they are reasonably easy to train and make good companions, Australian terriers, like all terriers, have a strong independent streak.

# BEDLINGTON TERRIER

**OTHER NAMES:** Rothbury terrier
**DATE OF ORIGIN:** 18th century
**PLACE OF ORIGIN:** Rothbury, on
England/Scotland Borders, later
Bedlington, Northumberland,
England
**ORIGINAL USE:** Rat/badger
Hunting
**MODERN USE:** Companion
**SIZE:**
**HEIGHT:** 38–43 cm (15–17 in)
**WEIGHT:** 8–10 kg
(17–23 lb)
**COLOURS:**
Liver, sandy, blue
**RECOGNIZED BY:**
K.C.

This graceful, muscular British terrier, with its distinctive 'pear–shaped' head has existed for some 200 years and has a very different appearance from most other terriers: it's best described as a terrier in sheep's clothing. Not only does this rather accurately describe the Bedlington's outward appearance, but also its instincts as an effective hunter and killer. Legend has it that the breed originated in the Rothbury Forest, on the Northumbrian borders of England and Scotland, where they were bred by gypsies for poaching, hunting badgers, and for racing. The Bedlington's distinctive hind legs and its speed do suggest that the whippet (see page 177) featured somewhere in its ancestry! The earliest recorded Bedlington – although not known by that breed name – is said to be a dog called Old Flint, owned by Squire Trevelyan in 1872, and whose descendants were said to be directly traceable until 1873. When the English Kennel Club was formed, more accurate records were kept, but the breed was then known as the Rothbury terrier, largely because one famous terrier called Piper Allan lived in that town. In 1825, Joseph Ainsley gave his dog Young Allan the breed name of Bedlington Terrier – once again a Northumbrian name – and this became universally accepted. At the beginning of the 20th century, this one time 'gypsy' poaching dog became a firm favourite in smart drawing rooms – where it cleverly displayed both good manners and a liking for the 'good life'!

# BORDER TERRIER

**OTHER NAMES:** None
**DATE OF ORIGIN:** 18th century
**PLACE OF ORIGIN:**
Great Britain
**ORIGINAL USE:** Ratting,
harassing foxes from lairs
**MODERN USE:** Hunt follower,
companion
**SIZE:**
**HEIGHT:** 25–28 cm (10–11 in)
**WEIGHT:** 5–7 kg (11–15 lb)
**COLOURS:** Wheaten, tan–red,
grizzle, blue–tan
**RECOGNIZED BY:** K.C.

In 1800, a Mr. James Davidson of Hyndlee wrote to a friend that he had bought 'twa (two) red devils o' terriers that has hard wiry coats and would worry any damned thing that crepit (moved)'. The 'red devils' he was describing were Border terriers. Although the exact origins of the Border terrier are uncertain, it seems to have originated in the Cheviot Hills, the border between England and Scotland, where the breed has been known in its present form since the early 18th century. Small enough to follow a fox down a hole, but strong enough to enable it to keep up with horses at a hunt meet, the Border is quite possibly the terrier which has remained truest to its form and function – even though it may not now be used for its original uses of ratting and harassing foxes as most Borders are destined to be companions and pets, for they are immensely loyal and particularly good with children.

Its durable coat – which does not need to be stripped – protects it from the harshest northern weather, while its tail is a natural length – never docked – and is thick at the base, then tapering, set high and carried 'gaily'. Equally distinctive is the Border's head, which is required to resemble and otter and be moderately broad in the skull with a short, strong muzzle. The small, 'V'–shaped ears drop forwards to lie close to the dog's cheeks.

*complete DOG*

# CAIRN TERRIER

**OTHER NAMES:** None

**DATE OF ORIGIN:** Middle Ages

**PLACE OF ORIGIN:**
Great Britain

**ORIGINAL USE:** Ratting, fox
hunting

**MODERN USE:** Companion

**SIZE:**

**HEIGHT:** 25–30 cm (10–12 in)

**WEIGHT:** 6–7 kg (13–16 lb)

**COLOURS:** Cream, wheaten, red,
grey, nearly black

**RECOGNIZED BY:** K.C.

One of Britain's most popular terriers, the cairn may have originated on the Scottish Isle of Skye. Scotland is the home of no fewer than five of the short–legged terrier breeds. The cairn terriers were a working breed which earned their living hunting vermin in the cairns – heaps of stones set up as landmarks and border markings – and searching for foxes.

It was not until the early years of the 20th century, at dog shows, that the cairns became well known outside of the districts in which they lived and worked – the Western Highlands and Islands off the west coast of Scotland. Nevertheless, a cairn–type terrier can be seen in one of the most beautiful paintings, Jan Van Eyck's Arnolfini Marriage painted in 1434, and now in th National Gallery in London. In some ways this anonymity meant that the cairn would not be 'prettied up' for the show ring, but would largely retain its sturdy body, natural shaggy coat an its terrier instincts. The breed standard sums them up quite nicely: they are required to be fearless, gay, hardy, shaggy and strong.

Standing under 30 cm (12 in) high and weighing an average of 14 lb (6.5 kg), the cairn is happy to be picked up and carried under one arm – but much happier when running across a moor. They have a modest appetite for food – but a great lust for life, they like children and wi even tolerate the family cat! All this and a terrier too! No wonder they are such a popular dog

# CESKY TERRIER

**OTHER NAMES:** Czech terrier,
Bohemian terrier

**DATE OF ORIGIN:** 1940s

**PLACE OF ORIGIN:**
Czech Republic

**ORIGINAL USE:** Burrowing and
hunting

**MODERN USE:** Hunting, companion

**SIZE:**

**HEIGHT:** 28–36 cm (10–14 in)

**WEIGHT:** 5.5–8 kg (12–18 lb)

**COLOURS:** Blue–grey,
tawny

**RECOGNIZED
BY:** K.C.

This fearless and somewhat stubborn little dog was developed by a geneticist Dr. Frantisek Horak, from Klanovice, in former Czechoslovakia (now the Czech and the Slovak Republics) in the 1940s. Dr. Horak was interested in breeding a dog that worked like German hunting terrie – both above and below ground, in land or water, tracking and retrieving – but with shorter le for more efficient tunnelling and working under ground. Tough British terriers like the Sealyham the Scottish and the Dandie Dinmont were used in the breeding process which resulted in the delightful cesky. It has all the 'ground' attributes of the typical terrier combined with persistence and strength which enable it to subdue animals – and people – much larger than its average 3 cm (12 in) in height.

The cesky, like all terriers, is also a very fine looking anima with a lovely blue–grey or fawn coat. The darker, wavy hair on the legs is not usually clipped, making for a lovely 'rippling' when the dog moves. The hair is not clipped on the head either, leaving prominent – and very distinguished looking – eyebrows and a beard over and around a well–developed nos set off by triangular–shaped ears which fold forwards and lie close to the head. The tail is strong and tapers to a point and, when the dog is at rest, i carried down. Inquisitive and friendly – though like all terriers, apt to snap fi and ask questions later – it's not surprising that the cesky is such a popular terrier, especially in its home countries of the Czech and the Slovak Republic

# DANDIE DINMONT TERRIER

**OTHER NAMES:** None

**DATE OF ORIGIN:** 17th century

**PLACE OF ORIGIN:**
Great Britain

**ORIGINAL USE:** Badger/rat
hunting

**MODERN USE:** Companion

**SIZE:**

**HEIGHT:** 20–28 cm (8–11 in)

**WEIGHT:** 8–11 kg (18–24 lb)

**COLOURS:** Pepper, mustard

**RECOGNIZED BY:** K.C.

It is not certain whether the Dandie Dinmont is descended from the Skye, otterhound, Flanders basset hound, or even 'old–type' Scottish terriers, but we do know that the breed dates back to the 17th century. Paintings in many of the grand houses and castles of Scotland and the north of England show that it was owned by the aristocracy for centuries, although it was named after a character in Sir Walter Scot's 19th–century novel Guy Mannering. 'Dandie Dinmont' was a borders farmer who kept a pack of six terriers called Auld Pepper, Auld Mustard, Young Pepper, Young Mustard, Little Pepper and Little Mustard. Scot wrote that these dogs 'fear naething that ever cam wi' a hairy skin on't.'

One of the early owners of the 'type', if not the breed itself, was 'Piper' Allan of Northumberland – the same man credited with the development of the Bedlington terrier (see page 189). Allan's short–legged terriers caught the eye of the Duke of Northumberland, who evidently coveted a particular dog called Hitchem. When money was refused, the Duke offered Allan a farm in exchange for the dog – which was also refused. The Piper's son is said to have carried on the strain and one of the descendants of Hitchem was said to have been Auld Pepper.

Scot's novel did much to popularise 'all things Scottish', including the Dandie Dinmont terrier. Unlike other terriers, which are more 'square' in outline, Dandies are all flowing curves: a large round skull with a domed forehead, a gently arched back due to its long back legs and short front legs (which do make them prone to back pain and 'slipped discs') and a 'scimitar' like tail, about 20–25 cm (8–10 in) long. Even the hair colour is different: officially, Dandies are 'pepper' or 'mustard': more prosaically, the former is light grey to dark grey, and the latter, reddish brown to pale fawn. The Dandie's coat and beard texture are also unique, made up of a combination of hard and soft hairs.

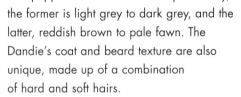

# IRISH TERRIER

**OTHER NAMES:** Irish red terrier, 'The dare devil'

**DATE OF ORIGIN:** 18th century

**PLACE OF ORIGIN:** Ireland

**ORIGINAL USE:** Vermin hunting, watchdog

**MODERN USE:** Companion

**SIZE:**

**HEIGHT:** 46–48 cms (18–19 in)

**WEIGHT:** 11–12 kg (25–27 lb)

**COLOURS:** Always 'whole coloured', either red, wheaten–red, yellow–red

**RECOGNIZED BY:** K.C.

Many enthusiasts of this handsome breed claim a long history and that it originated in the districts around Cork, Ireland and is descended from old black–and–tan and wheaten terriers. The first official mention of the Irish terrier, however, was not made until 1875 when a show in Dublin was organised for their debut. To most peoples' surprise, some fifty specimens of this formerly 'unknown' terrier were turned out for the event! The 'rules' – if that's what they could be called – were pretty 'loose', which no doubt was why, among the fifty entrants, dogs of various shapes, sizes and colours appeared: there was a class for dogs under 9 lb (4 kg) – no Irish terrier today weighs that little, so this was most likely cairn Terrier in a bad disguise! Meanwhile, the winner of the Open Class weighed in at a hefty 30 lb (12.5 kg), while one specimen was also said to be pure white in colour! Although every dog was required to have a pedigree, the first–prize winner called Boxer, had a hand–written note attached to him stating 'bred by owner but pedigree unknown'!

Inevitably, arguments followed – no doubt along with plenty of good stout! But, in 1879, a breed club was formed and the breed standard was issued – which is little changed today. Irish terriers soon grew in popularity, not only because they excelled as gun dogs, were brilliant at ratting, rabbiting, fox hunting, and badger–facing (while their superb aquatic skills made them ideal otter hunters) but, because they were hardy, courageous, even–tempered, and trainable. Add to this their good looks and a delightful strutting walk – charming with a touch of Irish 'blarney' – the Irish terrier is, perhaps, one of the most elegant of all terriers. Yet a terrier it is: inquisitive, feisty and, as its nickname suggests, a bit of a dare devil, willing to take on any other dog it meets!

# JACK RUSSELL TERRIER

**OTHER NAMES:** None

**DATE OF ORIGIN:** 19th century

**PLACE OF ORIGIN:**
Great Britain

**ORIGINAL USE:** Ratting

**MODERN USE:** Companion

**SIZE:**

**HEIGHT:** 25–26 cm (10–12 in)

**WEIGHT:** 4–7 kg (9–15 lb)

**COLOURS:** White–brown,
white–black, tricolour

**RECOGNIZED BY:** Not
recognised as a breed! Only
recognised as a 'type'.

When is a breed not a breed? When it's a Jack Russell! In fact the Kennel Club insists that this immensely popular terrier is not a breed but a 'type', because, to be recognised as a breed, there must be a breed standard which lays down the physical requirements. While every recognised breed has one – and there are around 400 recognised breeds – the Jack Russell doesn't. This is mostly because, while everyone can instantly identify them, they can't come to an agreement about exactly what they should look like! Arguments rage over leg length; whether ears should drop or be pricked up; coat colours and whether the coats should be smooth and soft, or wiry and shaggy. One thing is certain though, the Jack Russell terrier is not to be confused with the longer legged, officially recognised breed, the Parson Jack Russell terrier! This breed was developed for fox hunting: its longer legs enabled it to keep up with the horses. The Jack Russell terrier, which may be the result of accidental cross breeding with Wire–haired fox terriers is also a hunter, but its speciality was rats – where there are horses there is corn and where there is corn, there are rats! The Jack Russell's continued existence is due to the fact that these crossbred terriers were extremely valuable in controlling rodent populations – in the countryside and in towns: In the late 1970s, the Portuguese government employed a number of particularly enthusiastic Jack Russells from Yorkshire to help rid the capital city, Lisbon, of rats.

Like all terriers, Jack Russells can be snappy: when one goes for a wander, most people sensibly give them a wide berth – just in case! Nevertheless, they also have a great sense of humour, are devoted to their owners and are known to be among the best soccer players in the canine kingdom – although they're not too keen on passing the ball, generally defending it until it bursts, and tend to argue with the referee!

# KERRY BLUE TERRIER

**OTHER NAMES:** Irish blue terrier

**DATE OF ORIGIN:** 18th century

**PLACE OF ORIGIN:** Co. Kerry, southwest Ireland

**ORIGINAL USE:** Badger/fox/rat hunting

**MODERN USE:** Field trials, rat/rabbit hunting, companion

**SIZE:**

**HEIGHT:** 46–48 cm (18–19 in)

**WEIGHT:** 15–17 kg (33–37 lb)

**COLOURS:** Any shade of blue

**RECOGNIZED BY:** K.C.

This handsome terrier from County Kerry, in the southwest of Ireland, is by government decree, the national dog of Ireland. Some legends maintain that the Kerry blue arrived in Ireland aboard Noah's Ark, while others tell of a dog shipwrecked off the coast, which swam a shore and proved to be such a fighter that he killed every dog he encountered and thus established the breed. The county never claimed the Kerry blue as its own however: the link with the specific county in fact comes from Mrs. Casey Hewitt, from Tralee in County Kerry who first exhibited her dog at Cruft's in 1922. The same year, the Kennel Club officially recognised the breed.

Dogs of the Kerry blue 'type' are in fact indigenous to Ireland – there are also the Soft–coated wheaten (see page 199) and Irish terriers (see page 192). The Irish peasant classes were forbidden to own hunting dogs like the Irish wolfhound (see page 175), but were permitted terriers because they hunted vermin. It seems likely that, either by chance or design, matings between the squires' Irish wolfhounds and the farmers' terriers did occur. Kerries were – and still are – excellent terriers, guard dogs, hard working farm dogs who will herd sheep and cattle, and who because they like water, will also retrieve water fowl, as well as excellent household companions. The blue colour of their coats, possibly originally a cloudy black, has been intensified by years of selective breeding.

# LAKELAND TERRIER

**OTHER NAMES:** Variety of names depending on exact region, including Cumberland, Patterdale (see note below), fell terrier

**DATE OF ORIGIN:** 18th century

**PLACE OF ORIGIN:** Cumberland (Lake District), England

**ORIGINAL USE:** Small mammal hunting (inc. foxes)

**MODERN USE:**

Companion

**SIZE:**

**HEIGHT:**

33–38 cm (13–15 in)

**WEIGHT:** 7–8 kg (15–17 lb)

**COLOURS:**

Black, blue, black–tan, blue–tan, red, wheaten

**RECOGNIZED BY:** K.C.

The Lakeland Terrier was bred in the Lake District, in the English county of Cumberland which borders onto Scotland. With lakes, mountains and dales the region also had numerous foxes, which this agile terrier proved adept at pursuing and killing. Fox hunting in the region was not the 'well–dressed sport' of the more southern counties, and nor was it necessarily conducted on horseback, since most of the terrain was unsuitable for this type of pursuit. Instead, terriers were the order of the day because they would follow their quarry relentlessly over and under ground. The breed is likely to have descended from the now extinct black–and–tan terrier, which also gave rise to the Welsh terrier. Lakeland terrier is the name given in 1921 to describe dogs previously known by a variety of names. Each local area of this vast and beautiful county bred 'killer terriers' with powerful jaws to see off the foxes that preyed on the sheep. Some of these terriers were called Cumberland terriers, some were called fell terriers, and some were called Patterdale terriers. This last terrier, which is also known as the black fell terrier continues to flourish, although it is not officially recognised as a breed by the Kennel Club.

In 1928 Lakeland terriers made their first appearance at a Kennel Club show: some doubted whether the terrier would ever be a success in the show ring, but they were very wrong. In 1967 Champion Stingray of Derryabah was judged Supreme Champion at Cruft's and the following year, was crowned Best In Show at Westminster.

# MANCHESTER TERRIER

**OTHER NAMES:** English gentleman's terrier, black–and–tan

**DATE OF ORIGIN:** 16th century

**PLACE OF ORIGIN:** Manchester, Great Britain

**ORIGINAL USE:** Ratting, rabbit hunting

**MODERN USE:** Companion

**SIZE:**

**HEIGHT:** 38–41 cm (15–16 in)

**WEIGHT:** 5–10 kg (11–22 lb)

**COLOURS:** Black with tan markings

**RECOGNIZED BY:** K.C.

At the end of the 18th century, terriers were divided roughly by size (long or short legged), coat (smooth or wiry) and colour (white, or black and tan). The Manchester was the long–legged, smooth–coated, black–and–tan terrier and then called simply the black–and–tan (although there was a wire–haired version which later became extinct, but left its tell–tale marks in other breeds such as the Airedale, (see page 188).

The Manchester terrier is one of the few smooth–coated terrier breeds. Said to have originated in the city of Manchester in England – although it was only named as such in the 1920s – it is thought to be the result of a mating between a much earlier breed known as the 'English terrier' and a whippet (see page 177). In general though, credit is given to Mr. John Hulme of Crumpsall, of Manchester, for developing the breed in the 19th century, which was as adept at catching rabbits in the field as it was at killing rats in a pit.

When the 'sport' of ratting in pits was outlawed, the Manchester declined in numbers. This decline was further enhanced when the cropping of the dog's ears was outlawed: to protect the terriers ears from attack by vermin, the ears had always been cut short. Breeders received a shock when they saw the rather oversized ears of the Manchester for the first time in centuries! Breeders were soon able to produce ears that are as neat and attractive as any other terrier's, however.

# NORFOLK TERRIER

**OTHER NAMES:** Known in Britain until 1964, and still known in the USA as Norwich terriers

**DATE OF ORIGIN:** 19th century

**PLACE OF ORIGIN:** East Anglia, Great Britain

**ORIGINAL USE:** Ratting

**MODERN USE:** Companion

**SIZE:**

**HEIGHT:** 24.5–25.5 cm (9½– 10 in)

**WEIGHT:** 5–5.5 kg (11–12 lb)

**COLOURS:** Grizzle, black–tan, red, wheaten

**RECOGNIZED BY:** K.C.

From around 1880 until 1965, the Norfolk terrier was known as the Norwich Terrier (see page 196). This is because the Norwich terrier produced puppies with both erect ears and with dropped ears. The two varieties existed side by side, were mated together, and competed against each other in the same class at shows. However, neither variety dominated and, far from merging together into one breed, the two varieties diverged in certain important characteristics, which inevitably led to arguments among breeders. In January 1965, the Kennel Club ruling was that the terriers with the pricked up ears would continue with their original name of Norwich terriers, after the city, while the drop eared terriers would be known as Norfolk terriers, after the county. (In the United States however, both varieties continue to be known as Norwich Terriers.)

So, while a new breed was officially 'born' in 1965, the fact was that the Norfolk terrier had already been around for nearly 100 years. The small, low dog makes a good companion today, yet it was bred for work – and is still very capable at doing it – displaying the true terrier–like desire to attack any rodent (and other small animal) that dares to show itself.

The coat is hard, straight and wiry, rarely are they 'barbered' or 'trimmed' in an overly elegant fashion, and most owners are happy for them to be 'natural' in appearance. This attitude has proved fortunate since it has preserved the weather proof qualities of the Norfolk terrier's coat .

# NORWICH TERRIER

**OTHER NAMES:** Trumpington terrier, Jones terrier, Cantab terrier

**DATE OF ORIGIN:** 19th century

**PLACE OF ORIGIN:** East Anglia, England

**ORIGINAL USE:** Ratting

**MODERN USE:** Companion

**SIZE:**

**HEIGHT:** 25–26 cm (10–10½ in)

**WEIGHT:** 5– 5.5 kg (11–12 lb)

**COLOURS:** Grizzle, black–tan, red, wheaten

**RECOGNIZED BY:** K.C.

The Norwich terrier is among the smallest of the terriers and, with the Norfolk, is England's only short–legged terrier. The Norwich terrier has existed in the eastern counties of England for well over 100 years. Packs of small terriers, which had evolved from Irish terriers (see page 192) were in existence in the 19th century: in 1870 a gentleman known locally as 'Doggy Lawrence' made a good living for himself selling 'small red terriers' to the undergraduate students at Cambridge University, who kept the dogs as their mascots.

Others who acquired dogs from Doggy Lawrence included a Mr. Fred Law of Norfolk, who sent some to Mr. Jack Cooke, a well–known master of stag hounds, who in turn, employed one 'Rough–rider Jones'. When Jones left the master's employ, he took a few of the 'red terriers' with him – but rumour says he had already crossed these with Bedlington terriers and Staffordshire bull terriers. The red dogs at this time had no official name but were known locally as Trumpington terriers – although in parts of England and America, Rough–rider's legacy lived on in the name of Jones terrier, while their association with Cambridge University suggested to many the name of Cantab terriers.

Principally, these 'red terriers' were working dogs, ideally suited to ratting in the agricultural region of East Anglia, but their compact form also made them ideal pets. In 1932, they were granted official recognition as Norwich terriers, but were allowed to have either pricked up or dropped ears. Then, in 1965, came the split: the pricked–up–eared variety kept their name of Norwich terriers, while the drop eared variety were now Norfolk terriers. In fact, the ear difference is often overplayed as the reason for the split: in truth, the two varieties of dog had developed along significantly different lines so that really, the ears had dogs of different shapes. The Norwich is a somewhat more 'low–slung' dog than the Norfolk!

# SCOTTISH TERRIER

**OTHER NAMES:** Aberdeen terrier, 'Scottie dog'

**DATE OF ORIGIN:** 19th century

**PLACE OF ORIGIN:** Scotland, Great Britain

**ORIGINAL USE:** Badger, fox and vermin hunting

**MODERN USE:** Companion

**SIZE:**

**HEIGHT:** 25–28 cm (10–11 in)

**WEIGHT:** 8.5–10.5 cm (19–23 kg)

**COLOURS:** Black, black–brindle, red brindle, wheaten

**RECOGNIZED BY:** K.C.

One of the favourites among the terriers – and one of the 'heavyweights' among the small terriers – the 'Scottie' was previously known as the Aberdeen terrier. In the 18th century, the Highlands of Scotland were remote and quite inaccessible places, and the terriers varied from one district to the next, largely because most dogs resembled their parents who were local dogs and because breeders were keen on producing animals that were ideally suited to the land in which they worked. The Scottie's job was to destroy vermin: foxes, badgers, and other small mammals found in the rough countryside. Consequently a brave, tough dog, with an instinct for digging – preferably 'weatherproof' – was the order of the day. When the Scottie was first shown at dog shows in the 19th century, it competed alongside the Dandie Dinmont and Skye terriers in 'Scotch terrier' classes, but in 1882, a breed club was formed and it was given a separate register, with the name Scottish Terrier. Although we tend to think that all Scotties are black in colour – perhaps largely because of its starring role alongside the white West Highland terrier in advertising a famous whisky – the first standard of breed points said that the most desirable colour was red–brindle with black muzzle and ear tips. Black Scotties were not even mentioned and don't seem to have 'been around' until 1890, and it would be another 40 years or so before they became the most popular colour.

Although the Scottie is no longer used for its original purpose, this fine terrier still retains all the attractive features of the breed: a little reserved and aloof – it leaves the 'excited nature' to the Westie! – as well as independent and fiercely loyal to its owners.

# SKYE TERRIER

**OTHER NAMES:** None

**DATE OF ORIGIN:** 17th century

**PLACE OF ORIGIN:** Isle of Skye (in the Western Islands of Scotland)

**ORIGINAL USE:** Small game hunting

**MODERN USE:** Companion

**SIZE:**

**HEIGHT:** 23–25 cm (9–10 in)

**WEIGHT:** 8.5–10.5 kg (19–23 lb)

**COLOURS:** Black, grey, fawn, cream

**RECOGNIZED BY:** K.C.

This terrier, with its exceptionally long hair, hails from the Hebridean Island of Skye in Scotland where local legend claims that long–haired dogs swam ashore when ships of the Spanish Armada were wrecked by storms off the islands. (The same legend – but of surviving Spanish sailors – is also said to account for the magnificent patterns of Fair Isle jumpers!) The only flaw in the story is the fact that the long coat of the Skye terrier is, in fact, a recent 'invention'. The long coat was not apparent on one of the most famous terriers, Rona, owned by Queen Victoria. In Scotland, the dog's role was to catch and destroy vermin: foxes, badgers, even wild cats! This meant burrowing and digging and fighting in confined spaces – activities not to be hampered by an elaborate 'coiffure'.

Their powerful jaws are today hidden under magnificent whiskers: but it's still a brave – or foolhardy – person who tries to look! While Skyes are gentle and good natured with their owners, they are very intolerant of strangers and will do more than snap! Skye owners are happy with the appearance and the character of these delightful terriers, and stand by the motto of the Skye Terrier Club of Scotland: "Wha dour meddle wi' me?" (Would you want to meddle with me?).

No reference to the Skye terrier could ever be complete without mentioning the world famous Greyfriar's Bobby, one of the few dogs in Britain to have a memorial in Edinburgh, Scotland – and one that is a major tourist attraction as well.

# SMOOTH FOX TERRIER

**OTHER NAMES:** Fox terrier

**DATE OF ORIGIN:** 18th century

**PLACE OF ORIGIN:**
Great Britain

**ORIGINAL USE:** Fox flushing,
vermin hunting

**MODERN USE:** Companion

**SIZE:**

**HEIGHT:** 38.5–39.5 cm
(15–15½ in)

**WEIGHT:** 7–8 kg (16–18 lb)

**COLOURS:** Black–tan, white–tan,
white

**RECOGNIZED BY:** K.C.

At one time, all dogs that 'went to earth' in the pursuit of foxes were called fox terriers, and every English county had its own version. It was not until 1850 that breeding was regularised, resulting in the breed today. The 'smooth' while never the most 'fashionable' of terriers, has always been popular because of its hard–working 'no–nonsense' character, always ready to get on with the job. This breed began life in the stables, where it proved itself extremely adept at killing vermin, especially rats. And, if they had to dig them out first with their strong legs, then so much the better! Soon huntsmen began to exploit this tenacity to dig out foxes that had escaped down holes. This is probably how the terrier got its name – it's certainly more appealing than 'rat terrier', and the adjective 'smooth' exists to distinguish from its 'relative', the wire fox terrier.

In the early days of the breed, both varieties – smooth and wire – were bred together: a smooth called Jack is in fact the 'big daddy' of all the great wires as he was mated with a bitch of unknown ancestry – but obviously rough coated – called Trap.

The abundant coat of the smooth fox terrier is straight, flat and hard in texture.

Three years after the English Kennel Club was established, in 1876, the smooths were given their separate register. While they have left their working past behind, fox terriers are still predominantly white in colour, with black or tan patches, although smooths come also in black and tan colours: many of the huntsmen preferred largely white dogs since this readily distinguished the dogs from the quarry in the turmoil of the hunt.

# WIRE FOX TERRIER

**OTHER NAMES:** Fox terrier

**DATE OF ORIGIN:** 19th century

**PLACE OF ORIGIN:** Great Britain

**ORIGINAL USE:** Fox flushing, vermin hunting

**MODERN USE:** Companion

**SIZE:**

**HEIGHT:** 38.5–39.5 cm (15–15½ in)

**WEIGHT:** 7–8 kg (16–18 lb)

**COLOURS:** White–black, white–tan, white

**RECOGNIZED BY:** K.C.

Like many other terriers, The wire fox terrier was 'Made in Britain' and designed to 'go to earth' after foxes. Shape was not so important as long as the dog was sturdy enough to gallop alongside horses. Ancestry was even less important since huntsmen who used terriers generally developed local varieties to suit the terrain in which they hunted, adding touches of 'outside' blood whenever they thought it advantageous. In the 18th century – and earlier – no one bothered to record the details, except to mention a particularly outstanding dog.

It seems likely that Old English rough terriers were used: in their own rights, these already were early types of dachshunds and beagles. Staffordshire bull terrier types were also likely to have been used which in time, would bring about the division in the two coats. From 1876, different registers were established for the different coated varieties, but crossbreeding between them was still allowed. Around this time, the Fox Terrier Club was set up in England and it drew up the breed standard: straight legs, strong jaw, compact feet, a short back, well–curved stifles and sloping shoulders. It is said that the fox terrier was to be as close to being a horse as a dog could ever be! And, like a horse, fox terriers don't merely walk, they prance and dance – right on their tip toes! But some characteristics of the fox terrier are still truly terrier–like: these dogs just adore digging – almost as much as they like challenging other dogs to a fight! Where the smooth fox terrier's coat is hard and flat, the wire fox terrier has a dense wiry coat with a lovely dense set of facial whiskers. The wire fox terrier is permitted in white, white and tan, and white and black.

# SOFT-COATED WHEATEN TERRIER

**OTHER NAMES:** None

**DATE OF ORIGIN:** 18th century

**PLACE OF ORIGIN:** Munster, southwest Ireland

**ORIGINAL USE:** Herding, vermin hunting

**MODERN USE:** Companion

**SIZE:**

**HEIGHT:** 46–48 cm (18–19 in)

**WEIGHT:** 16–20 kg (35–45 lb)

**COLOURS:** Wheaten

**RECOGNIZED BY:** K.C.

Although this terrier has a long history, it was not officially recognised until 1937 by the Irish Kennel Club and by the Kennel Club in England in 1943. A native of the Munster region in southwest Ireland, for centuries the soft–coated wheaten – whose name perfectly describes both its colour and coat – was an 'all–purpose' working dog, used for driving cattle home, guarding and as an efficient 'pest controller'. Versatile dogs like these were developed to overcome the ancient laws in Ireland which prohibited peasants from owning hunting hounds. Terriers fitted the bill perfectly!

The soft–coated wheaten may have descended from the now extinct black–and–tan terrier and, although a slightly smaller and stockier dog, it is a relative of – and some hold, the ancestor of– the Kerry blue terrier (see page 194) and the Irish Terrier (see page 192). The breed is distinguished by its gorgeous, abundant , moderately long, soft and silky, and, slightly wavy coat that is the colour – as the lyrical Irish say – 'of a field of ripening wheat in the morning sun'. Since its official recognition this attractive and remarkably easy–going, even–tempered terrier has justifiably, become a firm favourite with owners on both sides of the Atlantic.

# STAFFORDSHIRE BULL TERRIER

**OTHER NAMES:** None

**DATE OF ORIGIN:** 19th century

**PLACE OF ORIGIN:** Great Britain

**ORIGINAL USE:** Dog fighting, ratting

**MODERN USE:** Companion

**SIZE:**

**HEIGHT:** 36–41 cm (14–16 in)

**WEIGHT:** 11–17 kg (24–38 lb)

**COLOURS:** Brindle, red, fawn, black, blue, white, or white with any of these colours

**RECOGNIZED BY:** K.C.

The well–muscled 'Staffie' did indeed originate in the Midlands county of Staffordshire, England. In the early 19th century, the two most popular 'sports' were bull baiting – in which dogs fought with bulls – and dog fighting, where a pair of dogs, matched in size and weight fought in a wooden sided pit. The dogs used to bait bulls were the earlier version of the modern bulldog (see page 216) with short legs, deep chests and short, massive jaws. The fighting dogs on the other hand, could be of any shape whatsoever. What was needed was the strength and tenacity of the bulldog combined with the speed and agility of the terrier. It seems likely then that the Staffie is the result of crossing between bulldogs and Old English terriers.

In the 19th century, there was still a wide range of types in these fighting dogs – with each region claiming their dogs to be the 'perfect' combination. In 1835 bull baiting was outlawed in England; this led to an increased interest in dog fighting, using dogs variously described as 'pit dogs', 'pit bull terriers', and 'half and halfs'. When dog fighting was outlawed, many fights went 'underground' and continued well into the 20th century: some say it is because of these illegal fights that the breed survived. In 1935, however, the Staffie, shook off its fighting background and entered the show ring. A club was formed, a breed standard set and respectability earned in the form of official recognition in 1939 by the Kennel Club and a separate register for the breed. Staffies are the terrier that many 'love to hate' for it has suffered from its former role as a fighter. Like all dogs of any breed, it thrives on affection, returning it tenfold, and is docile, unless encouraged to fight or attack.

# WEST HIGHLAND WHITE TERRIER

**OTHER NAMES:** 'The Westie'

**DATE OF ORIGIN:** 19th century

**PLACE OF ORIGIN:** Scotland

**ORIGINAL USE:** Ratting

**MODERN USE:** Companion

**SIZE:**

**HEIGHT:** 25–28 cm (10–11 in)

**WEIGHT:** 7–10 kg (15–22 lb)

**COLOURS:** White

**RECOGNIZED BY:** K.C.

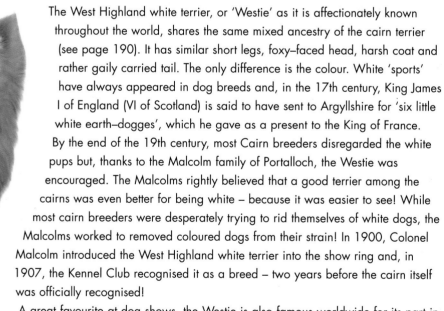

The West Highland white terrier, or 'Westie' as it is affectionately known throughout the world, shares the same mixed ancestry of the cairn terrier (see page 190). It has similar short legs, foxy–faced head, harsh coat and rather gaily carried tail. The only difference is the colour. White 'sports' have always appeared in dog breeds and, in the 17th century, King James I of England (VI of Scotland) is said to have sent to Argyllshire for 'six little white earth–dogges', which he gave as a present to the King of France. By the end of the 19th century, most Cairn breeders disregarded the white pups but, thanks to the Malcolm family of Portalloch, the Westie was encouraged. The Malcolms rightly believed that a good terrier among the cairns was even better for being white – because it was easier to see! While most cairn breeders were desperately trying to rid themselves of white dogs, the Malcolms worked to removed coloured dogs from their strain! In 1900, Colonel Malcolm introduced the West Highland white terrier into the show ring and, in 1907, the Kennel Club recognised it as a breed – two years before the cairn itself was officially recognised!

A great favourite at dog shows, the Westie is also famous worldwide for its part in advertising a particular Scotch Whisky. It is also a great favourite in the home: it has all the courage of a terrier, but will seldom pick a fight; it enjoys the outdoor life but is equally happy and content on the sofas of suburbia. It likes modest amounts of exercise followed by a snooze, and it's a very smart–looking dog that doesn't need a great deal of 'primping': although it is white, the harsh coat sheds dirt as easily as it sheds water – but mostly over those sofas!

# TOY DOGS

Toy dogs were generally bred as pets and companions, although many, like the affenpinscher (see page 202) also did very useful jobs as 'pest controllers' and acted as fearless guard dogs in spite of their size. Toy dogs are not a recent development: some toy breeds have been around for at least 2,000 years in both Europe, where they were also known as 'lap dogs', and in the Far East, where some were called 'sleeve dogs' because their size enabled them to be carried in the silk sleeves of kimonos and similarly styled robes.

AFFENPINSCHER

PEKINGESE

Most toy breeds are related to larger breeds in other groups and, in spite of their size, they maintain all of the characteristics of their larger relatives. 'Toys' only in name  they are most definitely dogs, and some toys can be as formidable as their 'big brothers'!
The most ancient of the toy breeds is thought to be the 'lion dog of Peking' better known toady as the Pekingese (see page 213) which was bred to reflect the leonine spirit of the Buddha. This little dog later became a favourite at the Imperial Chinese court and was often given as a diplomatic gift to visiting dignitaries from other countries. The cult of the lap dog in China reached its peak between 1820 and 1850 under the reign of the Dowager Empress Tzu Hsi,

whose 4,000 eunuchs housed in the 'forty–eight palaces' were employed solely to breed Pekingese.
In the West, the Romans are credited with developing the oldest European toy breed, the little white Maltese (see page 204). Throughout European history, toy dogs were a symbol of luxury and wealth to be enjoyed – and pampered – by the rich and leisured classes. Many toy dogs became firm favourites at the royal and noble courts and appear in some of the most famous paintings of Western art: Veronese, Rubens and Rembrandt painted papillons (see page 211), as did the American–born artist, Benjamin West. Many of Thomas Gainsborough's elegant subjects for his portraits chose to be accompanied by their Pomeranians (see page 212).

PAPILLON

MALTESE

# AFFENPINSCHER

**OTHER NAMES:** Monkey dog

**DATE OF ORIGIN:** 17th century

**PLACE OF ORIGIN:** Germany

**ORIGINAL USE:** Vermin hunting, companion

**MODERN USE:** Companion

**SIZE:**

**HEIGHT:** 25–30 cm (10–12 in)

**WEIGHT:** 3–3.5 kg (7–8 lb)

**COLOURS:** Black

**RECOGNIZED BY:** K.C.

In German, affen means 'to mock' or 'tease', and affenartig means 'monkey-like'. The delightful little affenpinscher, is sometimes called the 'monkey terrier' and people who see the dog for the first time invariably comment on its resemblance to this animal. Despite this comical appearance the affenpinscher's tightly compressed jaws still make it a formidable mouser and ratter given the chance. The origins of the breed are obscure but thought, perhaps, to be from crosses between pug-like dogs from Asia and small German pinschers. The affenpinscher is also thought to be the likely progenitor of the griffon Bruxellois (Brussels griffon) and a relative of the miniature schnauzer. Today, in Germany, the breed is quite rare, but is thriving in North America where despite the fact that it is an incredibly stubborn little dog – so is quite hard to obedience train – and, like all terriers, has a tendency to snap, it has found itself a happy niche as a lively companion dog.

# AUSTRALIAN SILKY TERRIER

**OTHER NAMES:** Silky, silky terrier, Sydney silky

**DATE OF ORIGIN:** 20th century

**PLACE OF ORIGIN:** Australia

**ORIGINAL USE:** Companion

**MODERN USE:** Companion

**SIZE:**

**HEIGHT:** 22.5–23.5 cm (9 in)

**WEIGHT:** 4–5 kg (8–11 lb)

**COLOURS:** Blue–tan

**RECOGNIZED BY:** K.C.

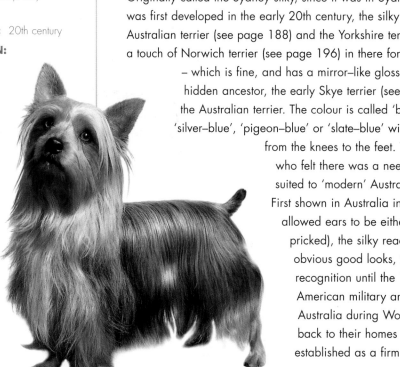

Originally called the Sydney silky, since it was in Sydney, New South Wales, that the breed was first developed in the early 20th century, the silky is basically a cross between the Australian terrier (see page 188) and the Yorkshire terrier (see page 214) – with perhaps just a touch of Norwich terrier (see page 196) in there for good measure. The gorgeous silky coat – which is fine, and has a mirror–like gloss to it – comes from the influence of a hidden ancestor, the early Skye terrier (see page 197) that was used to develop the Australian terrier. The colour is called 'blue' by breeders and may be 'silver–blue', 'pigeon–blue' or 'slate–blue' with rich tan coloured hairs growing down from the knees to the feet. The breed was developed by fanciers who felt there was a need for a small terrier which would be suited to 'modern' Australian life in city apartments.

First shown in Australia in 1907, when the breed standard allowed ears to be either pricked or folded (today they are pricked), the silky reached England in 1928. Despite its obvious good looks, the silky did not gain widespread recognition until the 1940s.

American military and civilian personnel, who arrived in Australia during World War II, took it to their hearts – and back to their homes overseas, where the little dog is now established as a firm favourite.

# BICHON FRISE

**OTHER NAMES:** Tenerife dog
**DATE OF ORIGIN:** Middle Ages
**PLACE OF ORIGIN:** Southern Mediterranean regions
**ORIGINAL USE:** Companion
**MODERN USE:** Companion
**SIZE:**
**HEIGHT:** 23–30 cm (9–11 in)
**WEIGHT:** 3–6 kg (7–12 lb)
**COLOURS:** White
**RECOGNIZED BY:** K.C.

The term 'bichon' is often used to refer to a family of small, usually white, dogs, to which the bichon frise, and the Maltese (see page 204) belong, and which originated in the Mediterranean region around 500 bc. 'Bichon' in French means 'lap dog', and these animals have always been bred as companions and pets.

'Frise' (or curled) refers to the coat of soft corkscrew curls which, with careful trimming, for the show ring, makes the delightful little dog look as fluffed up as a pyjama case! Attractive, happy, lively – in short, downright cute! – the bichon frise is also a real 'go–er': Norwegian farmers have found that this toy breed is very adept at rounding up sheep! Perhaps the sheep mistake them for very clever lambs!

By the 14th century, Spanish sailors introduced the bichon frise to Tenerife in the Canary Islands, where it was rediscovered by Italian sailors who took them home, where they became favourites in the palaces of nobles before spreading across Europe. Although it has an ancient lineage, the bichon frise is a relative newcomer to the official canine world: it was only officially recognised in both Britain and the United States in the 1970s. Nevertheless, the bichon frise has a firm, loyal and growing following of admirers.

# BOLOGNESE

**OTHER NAMES:** Bichon Bolognese
**DATE OF ORIGIN:** Middle Ages
**PLACE OF ORIGIN:** Italy
**ORIGINAL USE:** Companion
**MODERN USE:** Companion
**SIZE:**
**HEIGHT:** 25–31 cm (10–12 in)
**WEIGHT:** 3–4 kg (5–9 lb)
**COLOURS:** White
**RECOGNIZED BY:** K.C.

Although this white dog takes its name from the northern Italian city of Bologna, it seems likely that the Bolognese is descended from the bichons that originated in the more southern Mediterranean regions. The Bolognese, like all the bichons, has a very long history and numerous descriptions of the breed have been recorded since the 12th century. Like other toy dogs, the Bolognese was a companion dog and highly desired at the courts of Renaissance princes including the Medici in Florence, the d'Este family in Ferrara, and the Gonzagas in Mantua. A very similar looking dog to the Bolognese appears in a fresco painted between 1465–74, in the Palazzo Ducale in Mantua, by Andrea Mantegna. The Bolognese is, however, still quite rare in Italy: by nature it is more reserved and shy and is often overlooked in favour of its more 'cuddly' cousin, the bichon frise (see page above). Nevertheless in future, this button–nosed, cottony–coated breed – ideally suited for warmer climates – is sure to become a firm favourite.

# MALTESE

**OTHER NAMES:** Bichon Maltais

**DATE OF ORIGIN:** Antiquity

**PLACE OF ORIGIN:**
Mediterranean region

**ORIGINAL USE:** Companion

**MODERN USE:** Companion

**SIZE:**

**HEIGHT:** 20–25 cm (8–10 in)

**WEIGHT:** 2–3 kg (4–6 lb)

**COLOURS:** White

**RECOGNIZED
BY:** K.C.

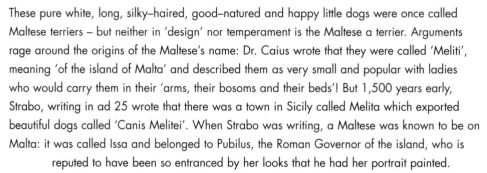

These pure white, long, silky–haired, good–natured and happy little dogs were once called Maltese terriers – but neither in 'design' nor temperament is the Maltese a terrier. Arguments rage around the origins of the Maltese's name: Dr. Caius wrote that they were called 'Meliti', meaning 'of the island of Malta' and described them as very small and popular with ladies who would carry them in their 'arms, their bosoms and their beds'! But 1,500 years early, Strabo, writing in ad 25 wrote that there was a town in Sicily called Melita which exported beautiful dogs called 'Canis Melitei'. When Strabo was writing, a Maltese was known to be on Malta: it was called Issa and belonged to Pubilus, the Roman Governor of the island, who is reputed to have been so entranced by her looks that he had her portrait painted.

I like to think though, that whichever Meliti or Melitei the Maltese came from, both names are derived from the Latin word melli which means 'honey' and perfectly describes the sweet nature of the breed! However, archaeological evidence suggests that in fact the Maltese has an even longer history than even Strabo suggested, for images of similar looking dogs are to be found in ancient Egyptian tombs. It seems the good fortune of the Maltese to have been captured on canvas: Sir Joshua Reynold's 1763 portrait of Nellie O'Brien includes an unmistakable Maltese, while later, Sir Edward Landseer, incorrectly prophesied the breed's demise in his 1840 painting The Last of the Race. With so many admirers across the world, the Maltese is certain to remain one of the most popular toy breeds.

# HAVANESE

**OTHER NAMES:** Bichon
Havanais, Havana silk dog

**DATE OF ORIGIN:**
18th-19th Centuries

**PLACE OF ORIGIN:**
Mediterranean regions/Cuba

**ORIGINAL USE:** Companion

**MODERN USE:** Companion

**SIZE:**

**HEIGHT:** 20–28 cm (8–11 in)

**WEIGHT:** 3–6 kg (7–13 lb)

**COLOURS:** Silver, cream, gold,
blue, black

**RECOGNIZED BY:** K.C.

The shy, gentle Havanese, which becomes a devoted companion to its human 'family' may be descended from Bolognese (see page 203) crosses with small poodles (see page 223): many Bolognese found their way to Argentina as the pets of wealthy Italians in the 18th and 19th centuries before arriving in Cuba, while Spanish–owned Maltese were already likely to be present on the island. In post–revolutionary Cuba the little Havanese did not fare very well: in the aftermath of most political revolutions, the political and cultural signs and symbols of the former system of rule are obliterated – either deliberately or through neglect. Consequently, the Havanese is rare in Cuba but is immensely popular in the United States – especially among Cuban expatriates. Although similar to the other 'bichon' breeds, unlike them, the Havanese appears in a range of gorgeous colours: cream, silver, gold, blue and black – but not white! With its large dark eyes, and lovely feathery–haired coat and tail of long, silky hair, coupled with a delightful character, the Havanese is set to win plenty of hearts!

# CHIHUAHUA

**OTHER NAMES:** None

**DATE OF ORIGIN:** disputed: 16th century or 19th century

**PLACE OF ORIGIN:** Mexico

**ORIGINAL USE:** Companion

**MODERN USE:** Companion

**SIZE:**

**HEIGHT:** 15–23 cm (6–9 in)

**WEIGHT:** 1–3 kg (2–6 lb)

**COLOURS:** Any

**RECOGNIZED BY:** K.C.

The origins of the Chihuahua, named after the Mexican state from which it was first exported, are shrouded in myth and legend. What is fact is that the little Chihuahua is the world's smallest breed of dog – a mere 2–4 lb (2–2.5 kg) is the average weight. It is also remarkable as the Chihuahua sometimes has a hole in its head: this is the mollera or fontanelle, an area of membranous space between the cranial bones that exists in foetal life and in infancy – even in human babies – but which, in some Chihuahuas, fails to close. Not all Chihuahuas have a mollera, but the condition is largely restricted to the breed.

Some claim the Chihuahua was a breed developed by the Aztecs from dogs brought to the New World by the Spanish Conquistadors. Others, that the ancestor of the Chihuahua was already in the region when the Spanish arrived: the Aztec name Xoloitzcuintli is often taken to refer to the Chihuahua but, in truth this was a much larger animal, possibly a coatimundi. There are also further unsubstantiated legends that Chihuahuas with red coats were ritually sacrificed on funeral pyres. However, since the Aztec civilisation was destroyed by the European invasion, it may be that the dog was in fact 'rescued' by the Spanish who then developed the breed. There is no mention of such a small dog between the time of Cortes conquest in 1519 and the late 19th century: the Pelon or Mexican hairless dog was known to be inhabiting the border towns of Mexico and America in the 1840s and, in the 1850s, the Chihuahua was being exported to the USA. The first Chihuahua to be registered in the USA was the appropriately named Midget in 1904. Many breeders believed that the long–coat Chihuahua was the 'original', but it was the short–coated variety that caught the attention of the public.

Whatever the origins of the Chihuahua, there is no doubting the immense popularity of the breed, which is happiest when it is in the lap of its owner! These may be tiny dogs, but they possess giant personalities: fearless and very agile, they could easily be called 'Mexican spitfires'.

# CHINESE CRESTED DOG

**OTHER NAMES:** Powderpuff,
Turkish hairless, Chinese hairless

**DATE OF ORIGIN:** Antiquity

**PLACE OF ORIGIN:** China/Africa

**ORIGINAL USE:** Companion

**MODERN USE:** Companion

**SIZE:**

**HEIGHT:** 23–33 cm (9–13 in)

**WEIGHT:** 2–5.5 kg (5–12 lb)

**COLOURS:** Variety

**RECOGNIZED BY:** K.C.

The Chinese crested is one of a small group of hairless breeds – although a luxuriously coated powderpuff variety does also exist. Hairless dogs have appeared in many parts of the world and, in general, they have been named after their place of origin, such as the African sand dog, the Mexican hairless, and the Abyssinian hairless dog. There is however, no documented proof that the Chinese crested originated in China, since evidence suggests that hairless dogs did indeed originate in Africa before they were transported to Asia and America. The reason for hairlessness has been attributed to an incompletely functioning gene, to a blood factor deficiency and to a skin ailment involving pigmentation. Whatever the cause, hairlessness is sex–linked to missing or abnormal teeth and toenails, so hairless dogs do not breed very successfully. However, matings between two hairless dogs can also result in 'coated' puppies, called powderpuffs. These powderpuffs are genetically more 'sound' and are the key to safeguarding the future of this interesting and delicate breed of dogs.

The skin of the Chinese crested is soft and smooth – and can be any colour, including spotted and dappled with bronze, blue or grey. The colours do vary in summer and winter: a careful watch needs to be kept that they don't get sunburn or chilled. Because of the lack of hair, the Chinese crested is odourless, and it won't leave hair all over your chairs! The only hair is the very fine, silky crest on the top of the skull, feathering on the feet and a plume on the end of the tail. The ears, which are large and erect may also be 'fringed' with hair. The powderpuffs have a coat of very fine hair which can be either long or short: among breeders the coat is called poetically, a 'veil coat'. At first sight, it is easy to be shocked or put off by a hairless dog but, after a few minutes, the expressive face, the liveliness and affectionate character of these little dogs invariably wins over many hearts.

# ENGLISH TOY TERRIER

**OTHER NAMES:** Black–and–tan toy terrier, toy Manchester terrier

**DATE OF ORIGIN:** 19th century

**PLACE OF ORIGIN:** Great Britain

**ORIGINAL USE:** Ratting, rabbit hunting

**MODERN USE:** Companion

**SIZE:**

**HEIGHT:** 25–30 cm (10–12 in)

**WEIGHT:** 3–4 kg (6–8 lb)

**COLOURS:** Black–tan

**RECOGNIZED BY:** K.C.

These terriers are relatively rare – even in Britain where they originated. They descended from runt Manchester terriers (see page 195) and were called toy Manchesters, before being called toy black–and–tan terriers and then miniature black–and–tan terriers before they adopted their present name in 1962 (although in the United States they are still called toy Manchesters!). Small, yet spirited, these are terriers through and through.

The first known mention of them occurs in Dr. Caius' Of Englishe Dogges from 1570, although he did not make any distinction between the 'normal–sized' Manchester terrier and the bantam version and it seems that small offspring were often the product of normal–sized parents. In the mid–19th century, the mini–dogs were quite common, and were especially favoured in the 'sporting' rat pits in the north of England. Around the same time there were rumours of crosses to other breeds, in particular the dachshund (see page 181) and the whippet (see page 177) as well as Italian greyhounds (see page 208) which would have stabilised the English toy terriers size and would account for the slightly arched or, 'roached' back. At various stages in its development, breeders have emphasised different characteristics: at one time, the small size was all important, at other times, it was the 'candle–flame' ears. One thing that was 'insisted' on at all times was the precise black–and–tan markings.

# GRIFFON BRUXELLOIS

**OTHER NAMES:** Brussels griffon, griffon Belge

**DATE OF ORIGIN:** 19th century

**PLACE OF ORIGIN:** Belgium

**ORIGINAL USE:** Vermin hunting

**MODERN USE:** Companion

**SIZE:**

**HEIGHT:** 18–20 cm (7–8 in)

**WEIGHT:** 2.5–5.5 kg (6–12 lb)

**COLOURS:** Black, black–tan

**RECOGNIZED BY:** K.C.

It would be nice to think of the delightful griffon bruxellois as the perfect symbol of European unity and accord: here is a breed that is the result of blending bloodlines from diverse regions to produce a friendly, alert, attractive companion. Their mixed ancestry is thought to include among others, the griffon d'ecurie (stable griffon) which was crossed with the English toy spaniel in the 19th century, plus additions from the German affenpinscher (see page 202), the miniature black–and–tan terriers, Yorkshire terriers (see page 214), the Dutch smoushond, the French barbet, and pugs (see page 214). But dissent remains – in the naming of the breed! In some countries (especially Belgium) three dogs are classified as Belgian griffons while, in other countries, each dog is recognised as a unique breed.

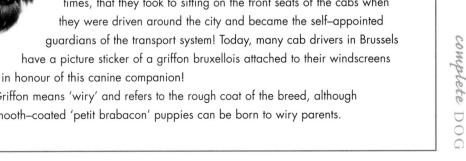

Originally, the griffon bruxellois was used as a pest controller in the stables of Brussels – especially those which housed the horses that pulled fiacres (hansom cabs). It seems that these dogs were so determined to be with their owners – or possibly the horses – at all times, that they took to sitting on the front seats of the cabs when they were driven around the city and became the self–appointed guardians of the transport system! Today, many cab drivers in Brussels have a picture sticker of a griffon bruxellois attached to their windscreens in honour of this canine companion!

Griffon means 'wiry' and refers to the rough coat of the breed, although smooth–coated 'petit brabacon' puppies can be born to wiry parents.

# ITALIAN GREYHOUND

**OTHER NAMES:** Piccolo Levrieri Italiani (little Italian 'hare–dog')

**DATE OF ORIGIN:** Antiquity

**PLACE OF ORIGIN:** Italy

**ORIGINAL USE:** Companion

**MODERN USE:** Companion

**SIZE:**

**HEIGHT:** 33–38 cm (13–15 in)

**WEIGHT:** 3– 3.5 kg (7–8 lb)

**COLOURS:** Black, blue, fawn, cream

**RECOGNIZED BY:** K.C.

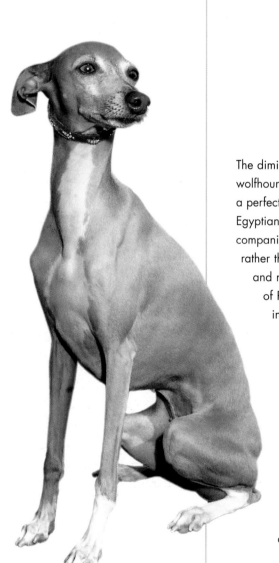

The diminutive Italian greyhound belongs to the same family of sight hounds as the Irish wolfhound – the largest breed in the world (see page 175). The high–stepping little Italian is a perfect miniature of 'big' greyhounds, and the breed dates back to ancient Greece and Egyptian times, since there are numerous representations of them in ancient artworks as companions to pharaohs and heroes. Elegant and graceful, and a dog purely for pleasure rather than utility, it is not surprising that the Italian greyhound found favour with the rich and noble families of Europe from the Renaissance onwards: Frederick II the Great, King of Prussia (1712–1786), owned more than fifty of the little dogs and took great interest in employing only 'suitable people' to care for them. Charles I of England (1600–1649), known for his love of dogs – and condemned by his critics for it – was familiar with the breed: his mother, Anne of Denmark was painted with five of the companion dogs. More surprising is the story that the 19th century Matabele chief, King Lobengula, was so fascinated with the high–stepping gait of the Italian greyhound that he 'paid' 200 head of cattle for one! Owners and admirers of the breed would argue that this was a very small price to pay for such an ideal companion.

With their slim, highly refined body and delicate pencil–slim legs, the Italian greyhound does need a little extra special care: they injure easily – largely because they 'forget' their size and enjoy bursts of activity – and they are more susceptible to cold and wet. But, perhaps because they are Italians, they are able to wear those special little 'doggy jackets' with such style!

# KING CHARLES SPANIEL

**OTHER NAMES:** English toy spaniel, 'Charlie'

**DATE OF ORIGIN:** 17th century

**PLACE OF ORIGIN:** Great Britain

**ORIGINAL USE:** Companion

**MODERN USE:** Companion

**SIZE:**

**HEIGHT:** .25–27 cm (10–11 in)

**WEIGHT:** 4–6 kg (8–14 lb)

**COLOURS:** Tricolour, black–tan, red–tan, Blenhiem (pearly white with chestnut–red patches)

**RECOGNIZED BY:** K.C.

The King Charles Spaniel is a compact little dog with a larger head and less tapered muzzle than its close relative the Cavalier King Charles. Small spaniels were well known in Britain (and Europe) from the Middle Ages onwards, as spaniels of various sizes often occurred in single litters. Selective breeding in the 16th century of the smallest individuals led to the 'toy spaniel': Mary, Queen of Scots had a pack and, at the time of her execution, one devoted dog is said to have crept under her skirts and fought with the executioner who tried to remove it.

It was King Charles II, who was to give his name to the breed, and who was one of its most devoted fans. The diarist of the Great Plague and the Fire of London, Samuel Pepys noted that the spaniels had access to all parts of the palace of Whitehall, even on state occasions. The king would also be condemned for spending more time with his dogs than with affairs of state. King Charles' dogs were slightly larger and had longer noses than today's breed: interbreeding with Pekingese (see page 213), pugs (see page 214) and in particular, Japanese Chin (see page 210) were responsible for achieving the modern form. A trace of the Japanese Chin ancestry can be seen in the white blaze on the King Charles' forehead: this mark is said to be the thumb mark of the Buddha, left behind on the Chin when he blessed the dog.

# JAPANESE CHIN

**OTHER NAMES:** Japanese spaniel, Chin

**DATE OF ORIGIN:** Middle Ages

**PLACE OF ORIGIN:** Japan

**ORIGINAL USE:** Companion

**MODERN USE:** Companion

**SIZE:**

**HEIGHT:** 23–25 cm (9–10 in)

**WEIGHT:** 2–5 kg (4–11 lb)

**COLOURS:** Black–white, red–white

**RECOGNIZED BY:** K.C.

Dainty is word often used to describe the Chin – also known as the Japanese spaniel. While it is similar to the Pekingese (see page 171) the Chin is more likely to have evolved from the Tibetan spaniel (see page 199), which may have been introduced to Japan by Buddhist monks as early as 520 ad. They then became favourites in the royal households as highly prized, and very valuable, companion pets: even when Portuguese traders arrived in the 16th century few Chin left Japan save for some presented to Princess Catherine of Braganza. The American naval commander, Commodore Perry took some Chins home on his return voyage in 1853. Only two survived the long sea journey to New York where they were presented to August Belmont. These two are reputed to have died without issue but it was the start of great interest in the breed in the west and led to a great number of importations – and a fair number of myths. One legend says that the Chin was dwarfed through sake, Japanese rice wine! The Chin arrived in Britain in 1880 where it was crossed with 'native' toy spaniels – which accounts today for the close similarity between the Chin and the King Charles Spaniel (see page 166). Like all breeds with flat faces, the Chin can suffer from respiratory and related cardiac problems. Still a popular in Japan, the Chin was largely eclipsed in the West with the arrival of the Pekingese but, since the 1960s, there has been a resurgence of interest in these stylish little dogs with their large dark eyes and long straight coats.

# LÖWCHEN

**OTHER NAMES:** Petit chien lion (little lion dog)

**DATE OF ORIGIN:** 17th century

**PLACE OF ORIGIN:** France

**ORIGINAL USE:** Companion

**MODERN USE:** Companion

**SIZE:**

**HEIGHT:** 25–33 cm (10–13 in)

**WEIGHT:** 4–8 kg (9–18 lb)

**COLOURS:** Any

**RECOGNIZED BY:** K.C.

Many dogs have been called 'lion dogs' because of their appearance, but few look more leonine than the little löwchen, particularly when its coat has been clipped in the rather fancy manner! An ancient breed, the löwchen is possibly related to the small 'barbets' or water spaniel and to the bichon dogs from the Mediterranean regions. It can also be seen in a number of paintings by the masters of European art including Lucas Cranach the Elder and Francisco Goya.

Although the modern löwchen can be up to 33 cm (13 in) high, it has been classed with the toy dogs since it was first registered in 1971.

It is a strongly built dog with well–muscled hind quarters. These are left 'nude' for the show ring: the coat on the hind quarters is clipped out like a poodle (see page 223) but left on the forequarters to form a mane. Tufts of hair are left on the end of the tail – which is carried over the back when the dog is on the move – and there are bracelets of hair around the 'wrists' and ankle joints. The clipped area is often a different shade and makes a tonal contrast with the longer coat.

# MINIATURE PINSCHER

**OTHER NAMES:** Zwergpinscher, reh pinscher 'min pin'

**DATE OF ORIGIN:** 18th century

**PLACE OF ORIGIN:** Germany

**ORIGINAL USE:** Ratting

**MODERN USE:** Companion

**SIZE:**

**HEIGHT:** 25–30 cm (10–12 in)

**WEIGHT:** 4–5 kg (8–10 lb)

**COLOURS:** Nearly black, chocolate, blue, red

**RECOGNIZED BY:** K.C.

The miniature pinscher belongs to the pinscher–schnauzer group of breeds which were developed in Germany. By no means a modern breed, small pinschers have been around since at least the 16th century, although unlikely to have been as small as today's 'min pin'. Nevertheless, the min pin shares its ancestor's love of hunting and chasing, and was kept in German farms and warehouses as an effective pest controller. Although today's min pin is strikingly similar to the English toy terrier, the two breeds evolved along different lines. The min pin also looks like a 'miniature Doberman': in fact the min pin predates the Doberman by some 200 years.

It has been suggested that, in the 19th century, to improve the quality and reduce the size of the miniature pinscher, dachshunds (see page 181) and Italian greyhounds (see page 208) were used in breeding programmes. The clear red colouring could well have come from the dachshund, and may have led the min pin to be called 'reh pinscher' after the roe deer which were abundant in Germany at this time. Black, blue and chocolate dogs with clearly defined rich tan markings are also recognised in the show rings. From the Italian greyhound the min pin could have obtained its distinctive high–stepping gait: each foot is lifted high like a little Hackney horse. A true terrier, the miniature pinscher's 'ratting abilities' remain undiminished and, like many terriers, it will challenge anyone – and any dog – snapping first and asking questions later.

# PAPILLON

**OTHER NAMES:** Continental toy spaniel

**DATE OF ORIGIN:** 17th century

**PLACE OF ORIGIN:** Continental Europe

**ORIGINAL USE:** Companion

**MODERN USE:** Companion

**SIZE:**

**HEIGHT:** 20–28 cm (8–11 in)

**WEIGHT:** 4–4.5 kg (9–10 lb)

**COLOURS:** White with patches of any colour except liver

**RECOGNIZED BY:** K.C.

'Papillon' is French for 'butterfly' and is the name given to this little spitz–type dog for an obvious reason: their heads have a thin white blaze running down the eyes and are framed on either side by pricked flared and fringed ears to make them resemble butterflies. Drop ears are also permissible, however, but these dogs are correctly called phalene – which means 'moth' (in North America they are known as Epagneul Nain). The delightful papillon is probably the most painted dog in the history of European art: they appear in paintings by Rubens, Van Dyck, Rembrandt and Fragonard, and famous owners in the past have included Madame de Pompadour and Queen Marie Antoinette.

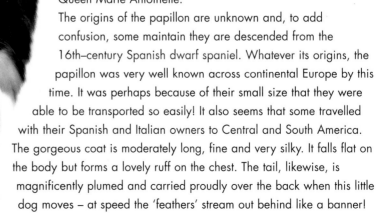

The origins of the papillon are unknown and, to add confusion, some maintain they are descended from the 16th–century Spanish dwarf spaniel. Whatever its origins, the papillon was very well known across continental Europe by this time. It was perhaps because of their small size that they were able to be transported so easily! It also seems that some travelled with their Spanish and Italian owners to Central and South America. The gorgeous coat is moderately long, fine and very silky. It falls flat on the body but forms a lovely ruff on the chest. The tail, likewise, is magnificently plumed and carried proudly over the back when this little dog moves – at speed the 'feathers' stream out behind like a banner!

# POMERANIAN

**OTHER NAMES:** Dwarf spitz, loulou

**DATE OF ORIGIN:** Middle Ages, developed in the 19th century

**PLACE OF ORIGIN:** Germany

**ORIGINAL USE:** Companion

**MODERN USE:** Companion

**SIZE:**

**HEIGHT:** 22–28 cm (8½–11 in)

**WEIGHT:** 2–3 kg (4–5½ lb)

**COLOURS:** Black, brown, grey, blue, red, orange, cream, white, sable

**RECOGNIZED BY:** K.C.

The classic spitz shape, 'fluffy' coat and curled tail, illustrate the early origins of the Pomeranian in the larger spitz dogs of the Arctic Circle. In the Middle Ages, when the breed was first noted, it was found only in northern Germany – in Pomerania – from where it took its name. These early dogs were larger – and whiter – than the modern version: some were used as herding dogs and some were so large they were used as draught animals. When they first arrived in England in the 19th century, the Pomeranian did not excite any particular interest – England had its own herding breeds and didn't use dogs as draught animals and, since it had no sporting use, it came to be ignored.

That was until Queen Victoria visited Florence, Italy, in 1888, saw some Pomeranians and accepted one as a gift. Soon after she founded a kennel of the breed and began to exhibit them regularly, favouring the smaller sized dogs between 12–16 lb (6–9 kg). Following her royal example, other breeders began bantamising and produced dogs of a mere 6 lb (3 kg) in weight – so even the Queen's smallest 'Poms' started to look enormous! Breeders were also able to extend the range of colours to develop a wide range of 'pastels' that are unknown in any other breed. Their attractive features have made them a success in the show ring, which in turn has made them one of the most 'expensive' breeds – especially if you 'weigh them up' dollar or pound sterling per ounce of Pom! Despite its miniaturisation, like all toy breeds, the Pom still thinks and acts like a big dog. A fine bark makes it a terrific watchdog and the heart of a lion makes it a fearless – and devoted – companion.

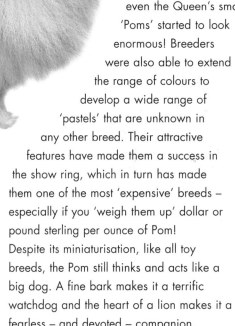

# PEKINGESE

**OTHER NAMES:** Peking palasthund, Peke

**DATE OF ORIGIN:** Antiquity

**PLACE OF ORIGIN:** China

**ORIGINAL USE:** Companion

**MODERN USE:** Companion

**SIZE:**

**HEIGHT:** 15–23 cm (6–9 in)

**WEIGHT:** 3–6 kg (7–12 lb)

**COLOURS:** Any colours

**RECOGNIZED BY:** K.C.

Now among the favourite toy dogs in the West, the Pekingese is almost extinct in its native China following the edicts of the Cultural Revolution, which banned all dogs from mainland China. The Chinese bred miniature dogs some 1,500 years ago: in ad 565 the emperor gave the name ch'ih hu or 'red tiger' to one such dog which rode with the emperor on his horse. Peke was, at one time, bred exclusively at the royal courts of the Chinese emperors and the cult of the lap dog really reached its peak in the 19th century under the Dowager Empress, Tzu Hsi.

The Empress encouraged the development of 'lion dogs' linking them – and herself – to the spirit lions of the Buddha, and maintained 4,000 eunuchs whose task it was to produce these dogs. One of her acts was to compose a set of rules regarding their appearance: they were to have a 'swelling cape of dignity' round their necks, bent legs so they couldn't wander far from the palace – and her presence – and the coat the colour of a lion. She also recommended a diet of sharks' fins, curlews' livers, and the breasts of quails. Such a pampered upbringing may account for the distinctly 'snobbish' character of the Peke and its stubborn streak – so superior is it that it will steadfastly refuse to do anything – even move – if it doesn't want to! More poetically, Chinese legend claims that the Peke is the result of a union between a lion and a monkey: it certainly has the nobleness of the former, while the monkey perhaps is responsible for its wilful streak!

Legend tells of how the Peke came to the West: on the sacking of Peking in 1860, four Pekes were 'captured' and one was presented to Queen Victoria.

# TOY POODLE

**OTHER NAMES:** Caniche, barbone

**DATE OF ORIGIN:** 16th century

**PLACE OF ORIGIN:** France

**ORIGINAL USE:** Companion

**MODERN USE:** Companion

**SIZE:**

**HEIGHT:** 25–28 cm (11–15 in)

**WEIGHT:** 6.5–7.5 kg (14–16 lb)

**COLOURS:** All solid colours

**RECOGNIZED BY:** K.C.

In Britain, the toy poodle is classified alongside its 'bigger brothers', the standard and miniature poodles, in the utility dog category, while in the USA, it appears in the toy dog category. The original standard–sized dog was bred in Germany in the Middle Ages, as a 'water retriever', and was most likely taken from Germany to France in the 16th century, where it appears to have been 'bantamised' to produce the miniature version. In turn, the miniature poodle was 'bred down' to produce the toy version. While the dog may have been in size, the toy poodle loses nothing in character, and retains the same lively personality and fiercely independent nature of its larger relatives. What it lacks in stature, the delightful toy poodle more than compensates for in affection, loyalty and its courageous spirit.

# PUG

**OTHER NAMES:** Carlin, mops
**DATE OF ORIGIN:** Antiquity
**PLACE OF ORIGIN:** China
**ORIGINAL USE:** Companion
**MODERN USE:** Companion
**SIZE:**
**HEIGHT:** 25–28 cm (10–11 in)
**WEIGHT:** 6–8 kg (14–18 lb)
**COLOURS:** Apricot, fawn, black, silver
**RECOGNIZED BY:** K.C.

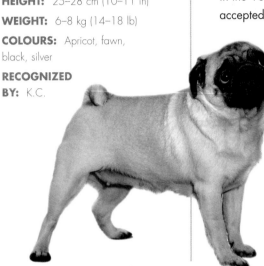

The pug is often said to take its name from the Latin pugnus which means 'fist' – suggesting that the dog's profile resembles a clenched fist. The name pug, however, was not used until the late 18th century: today Latin countries still prefer to call these little dogs 'carlin'. An alternative theory for the name 'pug' is that the word was used in England to refer to pets in general, but to pet monkeys in particular! Like the name itself, the origins of the pug are also disputed: at one time the breed was thought to have come from Holland, but was in fact introduced there in the 16th century by traders with the Dutch East India Company. Today it is generally accepted to have originated in China, where miniaturised mastiffs were produced some 2000 years ago. The pug arrived in Britain in 1688 when the court of William of Orange came to England. Originally, fawn was the most popular colour – a colour set off most attractively by the black mask and dark, shining eyes. By the 18th century the pug had truly become a popular fashion accessory among the royal and the aristocratic set – so popular that even German and French porcelain factories made pug 'ornaments' which are now highly collectible, and valuable! The curled tail was delighted in, but the ears were cut off close to the head in the belief that the pain suffered by the pug would make the wrinkles on their faces deeper! Fortunately this practice is long gone.

Despite the breathing problems suffered by all breeds with 'flattened' faces – especially in hot summer months – the pug remains a very happy, tolerant and good-natured breed. Sharing these fine qualities are pug owners – who have to endure their dog's quite tremendous snores!

# YORKSHIRE TERRIER

**OTHER NAMES:** 'Yorkies'
**DATE OF ORIGIN:** 19th century
**PLACE OF ORIGIN:** Great Britain
**ORIGINAL USE:** Ratting
**MODERN USE:** Companion
**SIZE:**
**HEIGHT:** 22.5–23.5 cm (9 in)
**WEIGHT:** 2.5–3.5 kg (5–7 lb)
**COLOURS:** Steel blue and rich tan in show dogs
**RECOGNIZED BY:** K.C.

One of the world's most instantly recognised breeds and one of the world's most popular too, the delightful Yorkie originated in the early 19th century in the West Riding of Yorkshire. They were bred by miners who wanted a terrier who was good at ratting but small enough to be carried in their pockets! The Yorkie is most likely the result of crosses between early black-and-tan terriers, Paisley and Clydesdale terriers. Originally Yorkies were somewhat larger dogs: but wise Yorkshire miners soon realised they could 'make a few bob' by selling the smaller, 'prettier' animals to their bosses! Soon size and quality were being refined further through selective breeding.

As a show dog, the Yorkie betrays nothing of this tough origin: its long silky coat sweeps the ground like a glossy curtain: they are brushed with the softest of brushes, bathed and oiled to keep them in the finest condition and rolled up neatly in little protective bandaged bundles so the Yorkie can play without spoiling its hairdo! Even pet Yorkies are inevitable pampered and spoiled – and wear at least one little ribbon! Nevertheless underneath it all, Yorkies are true terriers: tenacious and stubborn, they are veritable dynamos of energy, and possess some of the fastest little legs on any dog! And, if there were medals for 'yapping', some Yorkies would be world champions!

# UTILITY DOGS

**ST. BERNARD**

The group system used to 'organise' the various breeds is largely arbitrary, as some dogs can 'fit' easily into more than one category. It is, in fact, possible to divide the breeds into any kind of category, for example, according to type, which would allow spitz–type dogs to be grouped together or the 'giant' breeds like the Newfoundland and St. Bernard to be grouped together. But it would be equally as reasonable to group together curly–haired dogs, or long–haired dogs or wire–haired dogs, or to class short, long or tall dogs together! The British group system, which is pretty closely followed by Commonwealth countries, is also substantially similar to the system adopted by North, Central and South American countries. The only real differences are in the naming of groups and the British tendency to include toy or miniature varieties in the same group in which the standard–sized dogs appear. The toy, terrier, hound and working dog groups are named the same in the USA and Britain. The gun dog group in the USA is known as the sporting group, while the utility group is known in the USA as the nonsporting group.

**DALMATION**

Within these groups, the breeds are pretty much the same, but with the following notable exceptions: In Britain, all three varieties of the schnauzer are grouped in the utility group (in the USA, they are split between the terrier group and working group).
Toy poodles in Britain are also kept with the other varieties in the utility group (instead of being placed with the toys as they are in North America).
Shih–tzus and lhasa apsos are included in the utility group in Great Britain (instead of being placed with the toys as they are in the USA – although not in Canada!).
The utility group is a 'catchall' group for breeds which do not fit 'exactly' into the other groups. Some choose to call utility dogs 'special dogs' and certainly some of them are unusual and unfamiliar breeds. Many of these dogs, however, are ancient breeds that were developed for a particular purpose or occupation, but which since that time, they have left behind. Two fine examples are the Dalmatian and the poodle: the former was a 'carriage dog' bred to trot alongside coaches and carriages, simply to demonstrate the wealth and status of the carriage owner. The poodle is descended from German gun dogs and was once used as a water retriever and guard of herds. Today, although still feisty and still very brave, the poodle is almost exclusively a companion dog.

**NEWFOUNDLAND**

**GERMAN SPITZ**

# BOSTON TERRIER

**OTHER NAMES:** Boston bull

**DATE OF ORIGIN:** 19th century

**PLACE OF ORIGIN:**
United States of America

**ORIGINAL USE:** Fighting, ratting

**MODERN USE:** Companion

**SIZE:**

**HEIGHT:** 38–43 cm (15–17 in)

**WEIGHT:** 4.5–11.5 kg (10–25 lb)

**COLOURS:** Black–brindle,
red–brindle

**RECOGNIZED BY:** K.C.

The Boston terrier is one of many breeds and varieties developed in the United States, and is one of the most popular breeds in the country (for many, it is the 'national dog' of the USA. It often comes as a surprise that the well-mannered, considerate, spry and entertaining Boston terrier, which today is a delightful companion dog, was used in pit fighting in the Boston area. Bulldogs (see below) and bull terriers (see page 199) were crossed with boxers (see page 235) and the now extinct white terrier to produce dogs with 'improved' fighting qualities. Common practice was to name the dog after its owner and the name would then change as the dog was passed to a new owner: for example, the dog would be known as O'Toole's Bob but when passed to a new owner would become Smith's Bob. The known history of the Boston terrier breed begins in 1870 when a dog of uncertain ancestry, was brought from England. This dog passed through several owners before ending up, in 1875, with one Robert C. Hooper, and the dog was thereafter known as Hooper's Judge.

Early dogs like Hooper's Judge weighed over 20 kg (44 lb), so were closer to bulldog than terrier type. Later breeders bred the Boston down in size – both in body size and in head size – while still managing to retain the dog's unique looks – including its delightful 'bat ears'. Nevertheless, many Boston terriers still have a proportionally large head, and caesarian operations are often required to deliver pups as their heads are to large to pass through the mother's cervix. Three sizes exist in its native America: under 15 lb (6.8 kg); 15-20 lb (6.8-9 kg) and over 20 lb (9 kg).

# BULLDOG

**OTHER NAMES:** English bulldog,
British bulldog

**DATE OF ORIGIN:** 19th century

**PLACE OF ORIGIN:**
Great Britain

**ORIGINAL USE:** Bull baiting

**MODERN USE:** Companion

**SIZE:**

**HEIGHT:** 31–36 cm (12–14 in)

**WEIGHT:** 23–25 kg (50–55 lb)

**COLOURS:** Variety

**RECOGNIZED BY:** K.C.

Widely recognised as the symbol of courage and tenacity – a legacy of its bloodthirsty past as a fighting dog in bull pits – the thickset, heavily boned and 'low–slung' bulldog today is far removed in both looks and temperament from its early ancestors. The first mention of the 'bulldog' as a distinct breed occurs in 1631 in a letter from Prestwick Eaton to George Wellington asking for a mastiff and two 'good bulldogs'. At this time, bulldogs used for bull baiting looked more like Staffordshire bull terriers.

When bull baiting was made illegal in 1835 the breed was in danger of extinction and one breeder, Bill George worked to transform the bulldog into its present form, eliminating the ferocity of the breed. Unmistakable in appearance with its exaggerated shape, stout, strong front legs firmly set, and planted wide apart on the ground, and the distinctive, wrinkled head, the bulldog is one of those breeds that people either love or hate on account of its appearance. Few can truly criticise the bulldog, though, for its temperament: it is one of the most amiable, dependable and good–natured breeds. Despite its essential 'Britishness', the English bulldog has influenced a number of other breeds such as the boxer (see page 233), the Boston terrier (see above), the French bulldog (see page 217), the bull terrier and bull mastiff.

# FRENCH BULLDOG

**OTHER NAMES:** Bouledogue Francais, Frenchie
**DATE OF ORIGIN:** 19th century
**PLACE OF ORIGIN:** France
**ORIGINAL USE:** Bull baiting
**MODERN USE:** Companion
**SIZE:**
**HEIGHT:** 30.5–31.5 cm (12 in)
**WEIGHT:** 10–13 kg (22–28 lb)
**COLOURS:** Pied, black–brindle, red–brindle, fawn
**RECOGNIZED BY:** K.C.

To the horror of many British bulldog breeders, in 1898, a French version – daring to use the appellation 'bulldog' was shown in England! The bulldog was regarded as quintessentially British and although, its blood can be seen in other breeds such as the Boston terrier (see page 216), only the French dared to use the word! Some commentators in the 19th century even went so far to dispute the relationship between the two breeds and suggested that the Frenchie was in fact a descendent of the dogue de burgos, a Spanish bull baiting dog. Nevertheless, the truth is that the little Frenchie is descended from the 'bantam' or miniaturised bulldogs bred in the 19th century in England. Many of these dogs were exported to France where they were crossed with French terriers and their offspring were used for rat hunting before becoming both companion dogs and something of a fashion accessory among the working classes in Paris. Little beyond reducing the bulldog in size had actually been achieved in Europe, so it was left to breeders in the United States to improve and standardise the breed, especially the Frenchie's most distinctive feature – its delightful 'bat ears' which are natural to the breed and not cropped. It was also in the United States that the Frenchie was first recognised as a distinct breed. The 'brutish' appearance is once again deceptive: underneath that often grumpy looking face lies a dog that is charming and playful, small enough to adapt well to urban life, peaceful yet alert to strangers, and with a smooth lustrous coat that requires little grooming. It is no surprise that the French Bulldog is such a popular dog.

# CHOW-CHOW

**OTHER NAMES:** None
**DATE OF ORIGIN:** Antiquity
**PLACE OF ORIGIN:** China
**ORIGINAL USE:** Food, draught animal, guarding
**MODERN USE:** Companion
**SIZE:**
**HEIGHT:** 46–56 cm (18–22 in)
**WEIGHT:** 20–32 kg (45–70 lb)
**COLOURS:** Black, blue, cream–white, fawn, red
**RECOGNIZED BY:** K.C.

The chow–chow has a rather 'unpalatable' history: in Manchuria and Mongolia, it was bred for human consumption, while its coat was used as fur trimming on clothing. Despite the fact that the meat was considered a great delicacy, the name chow–chow does not in fact come from the Cantonese–Chinese word for 'food', nor is it derived from the American cowboy's use of the word 'chow' for food. In the 18th century, British sailors named the dogs chow–chow because these were the words they used to describe miscellaneous ships' cargo. An equivalent English word would have meant that the chow–chow would have been called 'ballast'!

The exact origins of the chow–chow remain a mystery: it is however, a spitz-type dog – a dog from the arctic circle and therefore a member of the same family as the Samoyed (see page 231), the Elkhound (see page 183), the 'husky' dogs, and the smallest of the spitz dogs, the Pomeranian (see page 212). It is likely that the chow–chow is the result of unions between some of these breeds and, perhaps, with some of the eastern mastiffs. Like many other spitz dogs, the chow–chow was used as a draught animal, pulling carts and sleds. The first chow–chow are reputed to have arrived in England in 1780 where their unique black–blue tongue (and inside of the mouth) was noticed. No other canine has such a feature. They also appear to have rather small, and rather 'catlike' feet, are known for their independent streak.

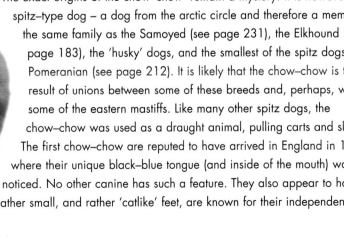

# GERMAN SPITZ

**OTHER NAMES:** Deutscher spitz (gross, mittel and klein) Deutscher gross spitz also known as wolf spitz

**DATE OF ORIGIN:** 17th century

**PLACE OF ORIGIN:** Germany

**ORIGINAL USE:** Companion (gross and klein), farm work (mittel)

**MODERN USE:** Companion (gross, mittel and klein)

**SIZE:**

**HEIGHT:**
Gross: 40.5– 41.5 cm (16 in)
Mittel: 29–36 cm (11½– 14 in)
Klein: 23–28 cm (9–11 in)

**WEIGHT:**
Gross: 17.5–18.5 kg (38½–40 lb)
Mittel: 10.5–11.5 kg (23–41 lb)
Klein: 8–10 kg (18–22 lb)

**COLOURS:** Gross: white, brown, black; mittel & klein: variety of colours

**RECOGNIZED BY:**
F.C.I.: gross;
K.C.: mittel and klein

The German spitz occurs in three sizes: gross (large), mittel (medium or standard) and klein (little, or toy). The gross and klein varieties have always been companion dogs, while the mittel was an efficient herding dog on farms. The breed is most likely descended from the spitz–type dogs of the arctic circle, which arrived in Europe with the Viking invasions. The gross German spitz, or 'wolf spitz' was known in Germany in 1450 and it is said that the white dogs were from Pomerania and the black dogs from Württemberg. When the German Spitz Club was formed in 1899, the gross spitz averaged 43 cm (17 in) at the shoulder, while the tallest of the Klein was a mere 28 cm (11 in) tall at the shoulder. The three types of German spitz are similar in conformation: the ears are compact and triangular, set high on the head and close together; the eyes appear large in proportion to the head; the small feet have insulating hair between the toes; the tail, covered in long hair, lies against the side of the body, and the chest is covered in dense, long rather harsh hair. The three varieties differ only in size, and in colour: the gross occurs in white, black and brown, while the smaller dogs occur in a wider variety of colours. Their glorious coats require a great deal of attention but many of the dogs do resent this! Furthermore they are not the easiest of breeds to obedience–train. Yet they are magnificent dogs and deserve greater and more widespread popularity than they currently enjoy.

# GERMAN PINSCHER

**OTHER NAMES:** Standard pinscher

**DATE OF ORIGIN:** 18th century

**PLACE OF ORIGIN:** Germany

**ORIGINAL USE:** Vermin control

**MODERN USE:** Companion

**SIZE:**

**HEIGHT:** 41–48 cm (16–19 in)

**WEIGHT:** 11–16 kg (25–35 lb)

**COLOURS:** Dark brown, black–tan, fawn

**RECOGNIZED BY:** K.C.

Among Germany's contribution to the terrier breed are the famous schnauzer (see page 221) and the affenpinscher (see page 202) – although in England, the schnauzer (in all three varieties) is placed in the utility (non–sporting) group, and the affenpinscher, on account of its size, is grouped with other toy breeds.

Pinscher is the German word for 'biter' – or 'terrier' – and the German pinscher, or standard pinscher, is now quite a rare breed, being overtaken in the 'popularity stakes' by the miniature pinscher (see page 211), which is a terrier and an equally ancient breed, but which is placed in the toy group) and the relatively modern Doberman pinscher, which is classed in the working group (see page 250). The German pinscher played a pivotal role in developing both the 'min pin' and the Doberman. A tall terrier, the German pinscher was the archetypal 'multipurpose' farm dog: it would chase and kill rabbits, rats and other vermin, it guarded and drove livestock and it made an ideal watchdog on remote country farms. While it is still used in country areas as a watchdog, the German pinscher responds quite well to obedience–training and can, in the hands of an experienced and responsible owner, be a loyal companion dog.

The German pinscher is a medium–sized dog with a well–muscled body and a short, smooth and glossy coat. The long muzzle ends in a blunt tip with a black nose. In countries which prohibit ear cropping, these pinschers have triangular shaped ears with a natural, half fold. Coupled with their dark, oval eyes, they have a very attractive expression. When the ears are cropped however, the Pinscher appears, at first sight, a much more ferocious dog.

# SCHNAUZER (GIANT, STANDARD & MINIATURE)

**OTHER NAMES:**
Giant schnauzer: Riesenschnauzer, Münchener dog
Standard Schnauzer: Mittelschnauzer, Miniature schnauzer: Zwergschnuazer

**DATE OF ORIGIN:** Middle Ages (giant & standard), 15th century (miniature)

**PLACE OF ORIGIN:** Germany

**ORIGINAL USE:** Cattle herding (giant); ratting, guarding (standard); ratting (miniature)

**MODERN USE:** Companion (giant, standard & miniature), service dogs (giant)

**SIZE:**

**HEIGHT:**
Giant: 59–70 cm (23½– 27½ in)
Standard: 45–50 cm (18–20 in)
Miniature: 30–36 cm (12–14 in)

**WEIGHT:**
Giant: 32–35 kg (70–77 lb)
Standard: 14.5–15.5 kg (32–34 lb)
Miniature: 6–7 kg (13–15 lb)

**COLOURS:**
Giant & standard: Pepper–salt, black
Miniature: Black–silver, pepper–salt, black

**RECOGNIZED BY:** K.C.

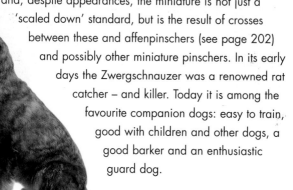

The name schnauzer comes from Schnauze the German word for snout, nose or muzzle. A second word Schnauzbart means moustache. All three breeds of schnauzers are conspicuous for their moustaches and beards – which do make them look like very dignified gentlemen.

The most powerful of all the schnauzers, the giant or Riesenschnauzer, as it is known in Germany today, hails from the south of Bavaria, near to Swabia where it was used as a cattle and drover's dog. When the need of farmers for this type of dog declined, in the 19th century, the Riesenschnauzer became associated with brewers and butchers, who were no doubt more able to feed the dog well! For these owners, the Riesenschnauzer now had a new role as a guard dog and it was this ability that led the giant schnauzer into service in both the police and the military.

The giant schnauzer bears a strong resemblance to another drover's dog, the bouvier des Flandres, although there is no evidence to show that they are in fact related. The dog seems to have been developed by increasing the size of the Mittelschnauzer (standard schnauzer).

The first appearance of the giant schnauzer in a dog show was in Munich in 1909 where it was called the 'Russian Bear Schnauzer' and they created such a sensation that the  Munich Schnauzer Club was formed almost immediately.

The origins of the Mittleschnauzer are also obscure, but it does seem to be the oldest of the three breeds: In Stuttgart, Germany, there is a statue of a watchman and a dog which has the characteristics of the Mittelschnauzer. Furthermore, the German artist, Albrecht Dürer (1471–1528), had a similar dog, whose image he painted several times between 1490 and 1504. Some claim the standard was the result of crosses in the Middle Ages between two now long extinct breeds, others claim it evolved from crosses of the (extinct) Schäferpudel and the wire–haired German pinscher – which led to it being called the schnauzer–pinscher for a time. It seems likely that like the Riesenschnauzer, the Mittelschnauzer originated in the cattle and sheep herding areas of southern Germany, particularly in Bavaria and Württemberg, where it was highly regarded both as a cattle dog and as a ratter. The breed was first shown in Hanover, Germany, in 1879 and, the following year the breed standard was established. Today the Mittleschnauzer is largely a companion dog, and one of the most popular breeds in both Britain and North America where it became well known after World War I.

The miniature, or Zwergschnauzer, is an almost perfect replica of the giant and standard schnauzer. It appeared about 1900 and, despite appearances, the miniature is not just a 'scaled down' standard, but is the result of crosses between these and affenpinschers (see page 202) and possibly other miniature pinschers. In its early days the Zwergschnauzer was a renowned rat catcher – and killer. Today it is among the favourite companion dogs: easy to train, good with children and other dogs, a good barker and an enthusiastic guard dog.

# DALMATION

**OTHER NAMES:** None official, but plenty of nicknames including: spotty dogs, firehouse dogs, dally

**DATE OF ORIGIN:** Middle Ages

**PLACE OF ORIGIN:** Balkans, by way of India

**ORIGINAL USE:** Carriage dog, hunting

**MODERN USE:** Companion

**SIZE:**

**HEIGHT:** 50–61 cm (20–24 in)

**WEIGHT:** 23–25 kg (50–55 lb)

**COLOURS:** White–black, white–liver

**RECOGNIZED BY:** K.C.

Although the breed takes its name from Dalmatia, on the eastern coast of the Adriatic Sea, there is evidence to suggest that these dogs originated first in northern India and were then taken to Greece: ancient Greek friezes dating from some 4,000 years ago show hunting dogs that are similar to the Dalmatian. From Greece it is widely thought that the breed was taken to Dalmatia by gypsies, and where they were used to warn of invasion by Ottoman Turkish forces. By the 17th century, the Dalmatian was evident in western Europe: it seems that the wealthy brought many such dogs home with them as 'holiday souvenirs' from their Grand Tours of Europe: Dutch paintings show the dogs as both household companions and as hunting dogs, while in England, they were put to work as 'carriage dogs'. The Dalmatian was part of the English 'milord's' ostentatious display of wealth and was required to trot with the carriage. Sometimes the dogs worked at the sides of carriages, others were specially trained to trot in front of the lead horse, clearing the road in front and announcing the impeding arrival of someone very important. The finest display however was considered to be when the Dalmatian trotted under the poles, between two horses! Because it worked with horses, the Dalmatian often shared the stables with them, and it proved itself a very capable vermin hunter. Its almost insatiable love of exercise and its familiarity with horses is probably how the Dalmatian became associated with fire engines. With the advent of motorised vehicles, the role of carriage dog ended but the dallie remained the 'mascot' at many fire stations.

# SHIBA INU

**OTHER NAMES:** Japanese shiba inu

**DATE OF ORIGIN:** Antiquity

**PLACE OF ORIGIN:** Japan

**ORIGINAL USE:** Small game hunting

**MODERN USE:** Companion

**SIZE:**

**HEIGHT:** 35–41 cm (14–16 in)

**WEIGHT:** 8–10 kg (18–22 lb)

**COLOURS:** Variety

**RECOGNIZED BY:** K.C.

The shiba inu is one of a number of spitz–type dogs native to Japan and the country's most popular – with a growing fan club in Australia, Europe and North America.
The spitz–type dogs that evolved in the arctic circle regions moved out of northeastern Asia into China and Korea some 4,000 years ago and became the foundation stock for today's chow–chow from China and the Jindo from Korea. Around 2,500 years ago, spitz–type dogs were taken to Japan – possibly from Korea – and these are believed to form the foundation stock of the Japanese spitz–type dogs such as the hokkaido, akita (see page 222), ainu dog, kai dog, shikoku and the shiba inu. (The Japanese spitz however is a much more recently developed breed.)
The shiba inu has existed in the Sanin region of Japan for thousands of years: bones dated at 2,500 years old have been found in archaeological excavations.
The shiba inu is the smallest of all the indigenous Japanese breeds – shiba means small – and, like the primitive basenji (see page 170), it does not bark but has a quite extraordinary shriek! A good–looking dog, with well–developed, strong legs, a deep chest, pointed muzzle and dark nose, and thick strong tail, the shiba inu is set to become even more popular worldwide.

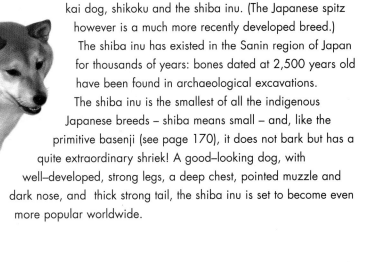

# AKITA

**OTHER NAMES:** Akita inu, Japanese akita,

**DATE OF ORIGIN:** 17th century

**PLACE OF ORIGIN:** Japan

**ORIGINAL USE:** Large game hunting, fighting

**MODERN USE:** Guard dog, companion

**SIZE:**

**HEIGHT:** 60–71 cm (24–28 in)

**WEIGHT:** 34–50 kg (75–110 lb)

**COLOURS:** Any colours

**RECOGNIZED BY:** K.C.

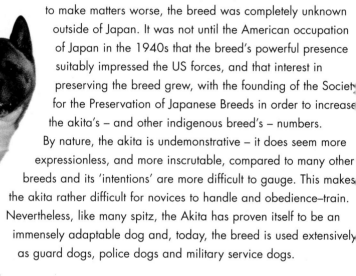

Japanese breeds are classified and named according to their size: akita (large), shika (medium) and shiba (small). There is however only one akita (large) breed and that is of course, the akita inu, which basically translates as 'large dog'! This spitz–type dog was once bred for fighting but, when this sport declined, it was used for hunting wild boar, deer and the Japanese black bear, with ownership restricted to the highest classes in Japanese society. By the 1930s, however, numbers of akitas had declined severely in Japan to near extinction: to make matters worse, the breed was completely unknown outside of Japan. It was not until the American occupation of Japan in the 1940s that the breed's powerful presence suitably impressed the US forces, and that interest in preserving the breed grew, with the founding of the Society for the Preservation of Japanese Breeds in order to increase the akita's – and other indigenous breed's – numbers.

By nature, the akita is undemonstrative – it does seem more expressionless, and more inscrutable, compared to many other breeds and its 'intentions' are more difficult to gauge. This makes the akita rather difficult for novices to handle and obedience–train. Nevertheless, like many spitz, the Akita has proven itself to be an immensely adaptable dog and, today, the breed is used extensively as guard dogs, police dogs and military service dogs.

# JAPANESE SPITZ

**OTHER NAMES:** None

**DATE OF ORIGIN:** 20th century

**PLACE OF ORIGIN:** Japan

**ORIGINAL USE:** Companion

**MODERN USE:** Companion, security

**SIZE:**

**HEIGHT:** 30–36 cm (12–14 in)

**WEIGHT:** 5–6 kg (11–13 lb)

**COLOURS:** White

**RECOGNIZED BY:** K.C.

The Japanese spitz is one of a number of small, white, fluffy breeds. This spitz is a classic example of miniaturisation: the Japanese spitz is half the size of its progenitor, the Samoyed (see page 231) which came from the most northerly regions of central Asia with the nomadic Samoyed tribe, from which it received its name, before being introduced to Japan. It is possible however, that another spitz breed – the Finnish spitz and the Norwegian buhund are possible contenders – contributed to the development of the Japanese spitz.

The Japanese spitz is around 30 cm (12 in) high, with a long, pure white coat, and a magnificent plumed tail. It also shares other common spitz characteristics: tough, lively, nimble and bold. In the 1950s the Japanese spitz became immensely popular in its homeland but, since then, numbers have declined. In contrast, this fluffy 'snowball' of a dog has become enormously popular in the United States and in Europe, where it is both a companion animal and an effective home protector. In some instances, this little – but tough – breed has a successful life as a professional security dog.

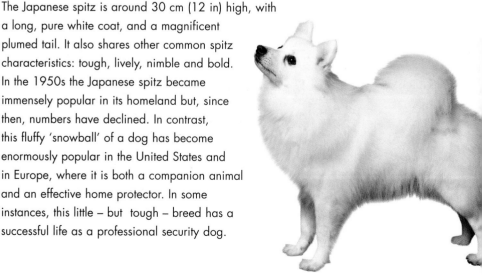

# POODLE (STANDARD AND MINIATURE)

**OTHER NAMES:** Caniche, barbone

**DATE OF ORIGIN:** Middle Ages (standard) 16th century (miniature)

**PLACE OF ORIGIN:** Germany (standard), France (miniature)

**ORIGINAL USE:** Water retrieving (standard), companion (miniature)

**MODERN USE:** Companion, security (standard)

**SIZE:**

**HEIGHT:**
Standard: 37.5–38.5 cm (15 in)
Miniature: 28–38 cm (11–15 in)

**WEIGHT:**
Standard: 20.5–32 kg (45–70 lb)
Miniature: 12–14 kg (26–30 lb)

**COLOURS:** All solid colours

**RECOGNIZED BY:** K.C.

One of the most popular companion breeds today, the poodle – in its standard size – was originally bred as a water retriever in Germany in the Middle Ages: its French name 'caniche' means 'duck dog' and the traditional method of clipping the coat with the hind quarters shaved – known in Europe as the 'lion trim' and in North America as the 'continental cut' – was to make it easier for the dog to swim and retrieve. Later, the little 'bobbles' of hair around the joints were left on to protect them from injury and from rheumatism. The hair on the head was also tied back – first with string and then with brightly coloured ribbons, so the owners could distinguish their dogs from others in the water.

The standard poodle was probably taken from Germany to France in the 16th century and, by this stage, it seems that the poodle had already been 'bantamised' to the reduced size of the miniature poodle, which in turn was used to produce the diminutive toy poodle. Both the miniature and toy poodles were, in the 1950s, the world's most popular dog and a much desired fashion accessory!  The miniature poodle and toy poodle not only inherited the 'make and shape' of their 'big brother', but also their character: while miniaturisation can often bring with it a 'puppy–like' heightened dependence on people, most poodles inevitably retain their sparky independent personalities.

Consequently, all the pleasures of owning a big dog are combined with the advantages of a small one!

Likewise, miniatures and toys are all clipped for show in the same distinctive manner as the standards – although on the smaller dogs this probably takes a great deal less time! In Britain, the toy poodle is classified along with its larger relatives in the utility dogs category. In the USA it is classed as a toy.

# LHASA APSO

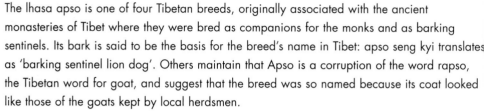

**OTHER NAMES:** Apso seng kyi, Tibetan apso

**DATE OF ORIGIN:** Antiquity

**PLACE OF ORIGIN:** Tibet

**ORIGINAL USE:** Companion

**MODERN USE:** Companion

**SIZE:**

**HEIGHT:** 25–28 cm (10–11 in)

**WEIGHT:** 6–7 kg (13–15 lb)

**COLOURS:** Bicolour, black, brown, white, golden, dark–grizzle

**RECOGNIZED BY:** K.C.

The lhasa apso is one of four Tibetan breeds, originally associated with the ancient monasteries of Tibet where they were bred as companions for the monks and as barking sentinels. Its bark is said to be the basis for the breed's name in Tibet: apso seng kyi translates as 'barking sentinel lion dog'. Others maintain that Apso is a corruption of the word rapso, the Tibetan word for goat, and suggest that the breed was so named because its coat looked like those of the goats kept by local herdsmen.

These dogs were believed to bring good luck and, because of their association with the monasteries, to have a religious significance. Consequently, the breed was treated with the greatest of respect and it was considered an honour to be given one as a gift. The lhasa apso was common in the wealthy 'homes' of Tibet – the royal palaces and the palace of the Dalai Lama. The first lhasa apso was seen in the West in 1921, but was initially grouped in one category with the shih–tzu (see page 225): the confusion may have been caused by the fact that both breeds were evident in Tibet. The Dalai Lama is known to have given palace–bred apsos as gifts to dignitaries, especially those of foreign countries. Consequently apsos went to China, where the Imperial Court practice was to offer shih–tzus – which are probably crosses between the Tibetan apsos and the Chinese Pekingese (see page 213) – as gifts in return. That's how the shih–tzu found its way to Tibet. In 1934, however, the lhasa apso and the shih–tzu were both recognised as distinct breeds. In the USA, lhasa apsos are classed in the non–sporting dogs category.

# SCHIPPERKE

**OTHER NAMES:** 'Little skipper', 'little boatman', 'little captain'

**DATE OF ORIGIN:** 16th century

**PLACE OF ORIGIN:** Belgium

**ORIGINAL USE:** Small mammal hunting, barge guarding

**MODERN USE:** Companion

**SIZE:**

**HEIGHT:** 22–33 cm (9–13 in)

**WEIGHT:** 3–8 kg (7–18 lb)

**COLOURS:** Black

**RECOGNIZED BY:** K.C.

Another small, spitz–type dog, the small, jet–black, tailless schipperke, with its fox–like head and black nose and eyes, hails from Belgium. Its name translates as 'little skipper' or 'little captain' because this dog could be found working on the Flanders and Brabant canal boats, keeping down vermin and warning of any intruders. Schipperke enthusiasts claim that the two black dogs without tails, which are said to have rescued the Dutch prince, William of Orange, from assassins were schipperkes. If this is true, then the breed was well established during the prince's life (1533–1584). One theory is that the schipperke is a small–sized descendent of a now–extinct Belgian sheepdog breed or of yet another extinct small breed, the leunvanaar. Before 1700, however, craftsmen in the St. Gery area of Belgium were known to parade their black, tailless dogs on alternate Sundays, decorated with large brass collars in elaborate designs. These craftsmen didn't call the dogs schipperkes, but simply spitz. This gives rise to the theory that it in fact belongs to the breed of northern dogs, which originated in the Arctic Circle.

Anatomically, it is a spitz–type dog and could therefore be related to other European breeds such as the Pomeranian (see page 212) or the German spitz.

# SHAR PEI

**OTHER NAMES:** Chinese fighting dog

**DATE OF ORIGIN:** 16th century

**PLACE OF ORIGIN:** China

**ORIGINAL USE:** Dog fighting, herding, hunting

**MODERN USE:** Companion

**SIZE:**

**HEIGHT:** 46–51 cm (18–20 in)

**WEIGHT:** 16–20 kg (35–45 lb)

**COLOURS:** Black, red, fawn, cream

**RECOGNIZED BY:** K.C.

The unusual shar pei comes from China's southern province of Guangdong where it descended from mastiffs and spitz–type dogs, and was used as a fighting dog. It is indeed one of the more unusual dogs: the hard, prickly coat is oversized and wrinkled, and the hairs stand on end. The looseness and the texture were said to give the dog added protection during fights. The canine teeth are also curved like scimitars, making it very difficult for the dog to release the jaws once a hold has been established. The shar pei also has the blue–black tongue of another Chinese breed, the chow–chow (see page 217) which suggests there may be a link between the two breeds. To do complete justice to the appearance of the shar pei is the rather poetic Chinese description: "Clamshell ears, butterfly nose, lion–shaped head, grandmother's face, water buffalo's neck, horse's buttocks and dragon's legs".

The shar pei was driven almost to extinction in China in the 20th century following the edict outlawing all dogs on the mainland. Some specimens were in Hong Kong, however, and from these, the breeder Matgo Law was able to successfully re–establish the breed, which was continued in the United States. When the shar pei first arrived in the West, it often suffered from severe eye problems which required surgical intervention. Successive breeding has reduced this problem but not, unfortunately, the high incidence of skin problems which trouble the breed: require frequent medicated shampooing of the dog's 'piggy bristle' coat – with special attention paid to its wrinkles is required. The shar pei has also suffered on account of its fighting past: they can be occasionally aggressive and are not suited to novice owners, but in the right hands they are calm and friendly dogs.

# SHIH–TZU

**OTHER NAMES:** Chrysanthemum dog, lion dog

**DATE OF ORIGIN:** 17th century

**PLACE OF ORIGIN:** China

**ORIGINAL USE:** Imperial Court dog

**MODERN USE:** Companion

**SIZE:**

**HEIGHT:** 25–27 cm (10–11 in)

**WEIGHT:** 5–7 kg (10–16 lb)

**COLOURS:** Any colours

**RECOGNIZED BY:** K.C.

The shih–tzu – pronounced 'shid–zoo' means 'lion dog' in Chinese. It was bred in the Imperial Court of the Chinese Emperors and is thought to be a cross between the Tibetan lhasa apso (see page 224) and the ancestors of today's Pekingese (see page 213). The so–called 'lion dogs' were highly prized in court circles: lions feature prominently in Buddhist mythology and it was believed that the Buddha himself kept a lion as a pet. The pre–Revolutionary Peking Kennel Club standard for the breed is possibly the most poetic description of dog ever: 'a lion head, bear torso, camel hoof, feather–duster tail, palm–leaf ears, rice teeth, pearly petal tongue and the movement of a goldfish.'

Also known as the chrysanthemum dog, this name is derived from the upward–growing beard, whiskers and hair on the nose giving the head a distinctly flower–like – if not exactly a chrysanthemum–like – appearance.

The first pair of shih–tzus were brought to Britain from Peking by General Sir Gordon Brownrigg as recently as 1930. More were imported, but there were insufficient numbers to gain a separate register until 1934. Until then, the shih–tzu was grouped into one category with the lhasa apso and the Tibetan terrier (see page 227). The shih–tzu is less aloof and more playful in character than its Tibetan cousin, and this is enhanced by the dark, round eyes. Shih–tzus are not classed as utility dogs in the USA, but are to be found in the toy group.

# TIBETAN SPANIEL

**OTHER NAMES:** None

**DATE OF ORIGIN:** Tibet

**PLACE OF ORIGIN:** Antiquity

**ORIGINAL USE:** Monk's companion dog

**MODERN USE:** Companion

**SIZE:**

**HEIGHT:** 24.5– 25.5 cm (10 in)

**WEIGHT:** 4–7 kg (9–15 lb)

**COLOURS:** Any colours

**RECOGNIZED BY:** K.C.

The Tibetan spaniel is a spaniel in name only: this breed was never developed to hunt but were trained to turn the prayer wheels of the Buddhist monks in the monasteries of Tibet. Legend has it that the breed was an ancient one – dating back to the time before writing recorded history. Certainly the breed is old, as there is no recorded history of Tibet itself until the 7th century. As the early history of Tibet is linked with China, the custom of giving small dogs as diplomatic gifts may have led to the Tibetan spaniel arriving in China where it was crossed with pugs (see page 214) to produce 'Pekes' (see page 213).

An alternative theory is that Pekes were gifts from China to Tibet, where they lost their breed purity over the centuries to form the Tibetan spaniel. The Peke and the Tibetan spaniel are anatomically similar, although the latter is longer in the leg and longer faced – which gives it fewer respiratory problems than the Pekingese.

The first known Tibetan spaniel was brought to Britain by a Mr. F. Wormald in 1905. In the 1920s a medical missionary, Dr. Grieg, brought more dogs back to England, but the establishment of the breed in Britain really had to wait until after World War II when Sir Edward and Lady Wakefield's pair called Lama and Dolma founded the breed known today.

# TIBETAN TERRIER

**OTHER NAMES:** Dhoki apso, double chrysanthemum dog

**DATE OF ORIGIN:** Middle Ages

**PLACE OF ORIGIN:** Tibet

**ORIGINAL USE:** Guarding

**MODERN USE:** Companion

**SIZE:**

**HEIGHT:** 36–41 cm (14–16 in)

**WEIGHT:** 8–14 kg (18–30 lb)

**COLOURS:** Variety of colours

**RECOGNIZED BY:** K.C.

As the Tibetan spaniel is not a true spaniel, the Tibetan terrier is not a true terrier: it was never bred to 'go to earth' but instead was used as a companion and very vocal guard dog by its Buddhist monk owners. For this reason, in the UK, the Tibetan terrier is not included in terrier group, but in the utility group. The breed is said to be very ancient and dogs were given as gifts by the monks to nomadic tribes as good luck mascots. These tribes seem to have used the dogs for guarding and herding flocks.

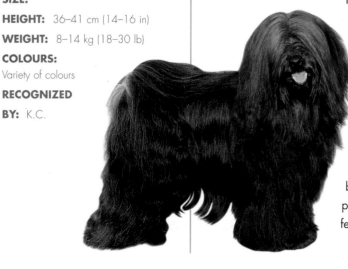

The Tibetan terrier is quite a small dog but it is well muscled. The body and head are a little like a 'miniature' version of an Old English sheepdog (see page 244) – but the tail is quite different. The Tibetan's tail is magnificently plumed, curled and carried elegantly over the back. The 'bangs' or fringes of hair at 'each end' – over the eyes and over the 'rump' of the dog – earned it the nickname of the 'double chrysanthemum dog'. The long coat, which is clipped in hot summer weather was traditionally woven with yak hair to produce a soft, semi–waterproof cloth. Coat colour was therefore important: pure black and pure white being the most highly prized colours. The Tibetan terrier is also presumed to be the only breed in the world required to have large flat feet – although these are hidden under a profusion of fine, long hairs.

# WORKING DOGS

The working group is the largest and is made up of those breeds of dogs which serve mans needs: guard dogs, sledge dogs, herding dogs and drovers (generally referred to as pastoral dogs), rescue and tracker dogs, guide dogs and general helpers, as well as those breeds which, at one time, were used as draught animals. It is often found that many of the breeds included in the working dog group possess a variety of skills.

**ALASKAN MALAMUTE**

**HUSKY**

Dogs were established as the hunting companions of humans well before man began to domesticate other animals such as cattle, horses and sheep. Domestication of 'livestock' only began around

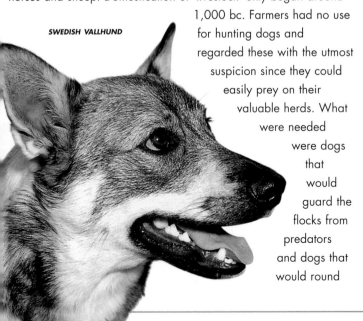

**SWEDISH VALLHUND**

1,000 bc. Farmers had no use for hunting dogs and regarded these with the utmost suspicion since they could easily prey on their valuable herds. What were needed were dogs that would guard the flocks from predators and dogs that would round

up herds without attacking the animals. 'Pastoral' dogs are interesting in that they have a natural instinct to run 'with the pack' – except that the pack is a group of animals that are not dogs – and have no desire to injure or kill their 'quarry'. What seems to have occurred in pastoral dogs, is that the dog's 'desire' to be the pack leader, or 'top dog' has been exploited and developed through breeding and training. Selective breeding of pastoral dogs also encouraged the development of dogs with larger proportions of white in their coats: farmers and shepherds seemed to prefer this, as it made the dogs more distinguishable from predatory wolves. As herd sizes increased over time, individual animals had to be prevented from straying: small, fast, agile dogs were needed to move strays back to the herds, and these dogs became the herding dogs. When herds were required to be moved en masse over, sometimes quite considerable, distances – to markets or to new pastures,– another type of dog was required, the drover. The Old English sheepdog (see page 244), the corgi (see page 249) and the Swedish Vallhund (see page 232) were all cattle droving dogs. These protected and drove the herds along. Large, bulky dogs were needed for livestock such as cattle, while smaller drover dogs were used to move sheep and goats. These became the forerunners of the modern sheepdog. Some other breeds that we don't readily associate with pastoral duties include mastiffs. Used as a weapon of war, the mastiffs were also employed to protect and herd the flocks of animals that were required to accompany (and to feed) armies on the move.

Many of today's mountain dogs are descended from mastiffs: their large size is a legacy of this ancestry of ancient 'war dogs'. As the mastiffs moved across Europe and Asia with conquering armies and traders, they bred with the spitz–type dogs of northern regions and left their legacy in breeds such as the shar pei (see page 225).

The 'husky' type dogs, or sledge dogs of the Arctic Circle are also included in the working group. These were used not only to pull sledges across winter snows, but as pack animals in summer months. Many of these dogs, such as the Alaskan malamute and Siberian huskies still take part in sledge races: teams from across the world compete at the World Championships. Held annually at Anchorage, Alaska, teams race over three 25–mile (40–km) dashes held on consecutive days: drivers may start with any number of dogs in the team – but they must finish each day with the same number – even if they have to ride home one of the sledges themselves! The most famous dog–sledge race from Nenana to Nome, Alaska, in January 1925, was not against other dog teams, but against diphtheria: the Alaskan winter had cut off rail and air links to Nome when the disease struck. Antitoxin was dispatched from Nenana and transported to Nome – a distance overland of 680 miles (1,080 km) – by twenty relays of dog teams in just 127 ½ hours – that's just over five days at an average of 136 miles (220 km) a day.

**MASTIFF**

# CANAAN

**OTHER NAMES:** Kelef k'naani

**DATE OF ORIGIN:** Antiquity

**PLACE OF ORIGIN:** Middle East

**ORIGINAL USE:**
Pariah–scavenger dog

**MODERN USE:** Livestock guarding/herding, tracking/search & rescue, companion

**SIZE:**

**HEIGHT:** 48–61 cm (19–24 in)

**WEIGHT:** 16–25 kg (35–55 lb)

**COLOURS:** Black, brown, sand, white

**RECOGNIZED BY:** K.C.

As wandering groups of people spread out of south–west Asia around 15,000 years ago, 'canny canines' followed them. Pariah, or scavenging dogs, realised that if they 'hung around' humans long enough, there would be edible morsels at hand without having to hunt for them. As self–appointed guard dogs, many would become domesticated. The Canaan dog is one such primitive dog that has existed in the Middle East for thousands of years. Originally a pariah, it then became used by the nomadic Bedouin in the Negev Desert as a guard dog and herder. The breed was developed in the 1930s by Dr. Rudolphina Menzel, who conducted a selective breeding programme in Jerusalem. During World War II a number of Canaans were successfully trained to detect land mines and after the war, some were trained as guide dogs for the blind. In the region today, the Canaan is still used for herding, but its keen senses have also earned it recognition as a search and rescue dog. A medium–sized, very robust dog, the Canaan's coat is straight and harsh. Its most distinguishing feature is the bushy tail, which when the dog is alert, curls up and over the back.

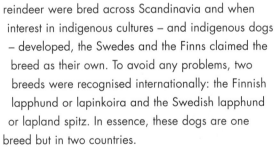

# ALASKAN MALAMUTE

**OTHER NAMES:** Mahlemut

**DATE OF ORIGIN:** Antiquity

**PLACE OF ORIGIN:** North America

**ORIGINAL USE:** Sled pulling, hunting

**MODERN USE:** Companion, sled pulling/sled racing

**SIZE:**

**HEIGHT:** 58–71 cm (23–28 in)

**WEIGHT:** 39–56 kg (85–112 lb)

**COLOURS:** Various shades of grey with black cap or mask

**RECOGNIZED BY:** K.C.

Wolf–like in appearance, the Alaskan malamute is named after the Mahlemut Inuit living on the Kotsebue Sound, on the Arctic coast of western Alaska. The Mahlemuts lived in a fishing and hunting environment, since behind the coast line lies mountainous territory. The Alaskan malamute is the largest of the sledge–dog breeds and is strong enough to haul heavily loaded sleds over difficult terrain. Single dogs were used to haul a travois – a simple platform made by lashing together two poles – while a team of dogs could haul half a ton.

The Inuit often boasted that these dogs were pure–bred tamed wolves, or the result of tamed wolf–dog crosses: while it seems likely that crosses did take place, it was with other dogs than wolves, especially other spitz–type dogs of the Arctic Circle region. The malamute was not only a sledge dog; in summer when sledges couldn't be used, the dogs carried packs strapped under their bellies. The physical strength of the dogs was such that some were able to carry 50 lb (23 kg) packs up to 20 miles (32 km) a day.

The pure–bred malamute dogs could not, however, withstand the onslaught of the Yukon gold rush. Haulage dogs were so badly needed, that animals of all types were shipped into the region and the result was numerous crossbreeding and a distillation of the bloodline. Fortunately enough, malamutes survived to recommence a breeding programme and Canadian and American breeders began to show them in the 1940s.

# FINNISH LAPPHUND

**OTHER NAMES:** Lapinkoira, Lapland dog

**DATE OF ORIGIN:** 17th century

**PLACE OF ORIGIN:** Finland

**ORIGINAL USE:** Reindeer herding

**MODERN USE:** Herding, companion

**SIZE:**

**HEIGHT:** 46–52 cm (18–20½ in)

**WEIGHT:** 20–21 kg (44–47 lb)

**COLOURS:** Variety

**RECOGNIZED BY:** K.C.

The lapinkoira, or Finnish lapphund, is the traditional and historic herding dog of the Sami people. Used for herding reindeer – though today it is mostly to be found herding cattle and sheep – the Finnish lapphund is the result of interbreeding between the spitz–type dogs of the northern regions and the herding dogs from further south in Europe. Semi–domesticated reindeer were bred across Scandinavia and when interest in indigenous cultures – and indigenous dogs – developed, the Swedes and the Finns claimed the breed as their own. To avoid any problems, two breeds were recognised internationally: the Finnish lapphund or lapinkoira and the Swedish lapphund or lapland spitz. In essence, these dogs are one breed but in two countries.

Selective breeding procedures in Finland have maintained the Finnish lapphund's herding instincts but, outside of the country, they are often to be found as companions and well–loved house pets. In many instances, the 'pet' animals have been developed for looks rather than function: their herding instincts have been diminished in favour of a more luxuriously dense and coloured coat which, along with their curled tail, makes them extremely attractive.

# SIBERIAN HUSKY

**OTHER NAMES:** Arctic Husky

**DATE OF ORIGIN:** Antiquity

**PLACE OF ORIGIN:** Siberia

**ORIGINAL USE:** Sledge pulling

**MODERN USE:** Companion, sledge racing

**SIZE:**

**HEIGHT:** 51–60 cm (20–23½ in)

**WEIGHT:** 16–27 kg (35–60 lb)

**COLOURS:** Any colours

**RECOGNIZED BY:** K.C.

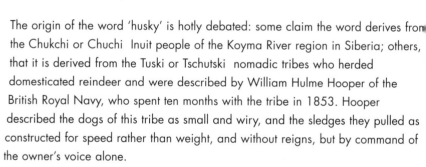

The origin of the word 'husky' is hotly debated: some claim the word derives from the Chukchi or Chuchi  Inuit people of the Koyma River region in Siberia; others, that it is derived from the Tuski or Tschutski  nomadic tribes who herded domesticated reindeer and were described by William Hulme Hooper of the British Royal Navy, who spent ten months with the tribe in 1853. Hooper described the dogs of this tribe as small and wiry, and the sledges they pulled as constructed for speed rather than weight, and without reigns, but by command of the owner's voice alone.

Whatever the exact origins of the name, it has since spread across the arctic regions and come to mean 'sledge dogs' in general. However, the Siberian variety is the only dog to be officially registered as a husky. It is also one of the few breeds to have blue, brown, hazel or non–solid coloured eyes, but, in common with other spitz–type dogs, the Siberian husky seldom barks – but does, like wolves, join in heartily with the communal howling 'songs'!

It was the Yukon gold rush that focussed attention onto sledge dogs, and drivers of teams were proud of their animals, their skill and endurance. Rivalry was expressed in racing, including the famous All–Alaska Sweepstakes covering some 408 miles (669 km). In 1909 the fleet–footed dogs of the Chukchi raced for the first time under the name Siberian huskies and, in the following years, were among the winners. In 1948 a team of Siberian huskies raced a measured 10 mile (16 km) course in a mere 35 minutes.

# SAMOYED

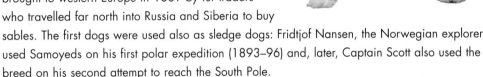

**OTHER NAMES:** Samoyedskaya

**DATE OF ORIGIN:** Antiquity

**PLACE OF ORIGIN:** Russia

**ORIGINAL USE:** Reindeer herding

**MODERN USE:** Companion

**SIZE:**

**HEIGHT:** 46–56 cm (18–22 in)

**WEIGHT:** 23–30 kg (50–66 lb)

**COLOURS:** White, white–biscuit, cream

**RECOGNIZED BY:** K.C.

The Samoyed is a spitz breed which takes it name from the Siberian nomadic tribe of the Samoyedes. The breed was largely unknown until explorers in the 18th century noticed how they were highly valued by their owners who used the dogs to haul sledges, herd reindeer and guard the yurts (the tents) of their owners, and how their hair was used for spinning and weaving into clothes! The first Samoyedes, as they were then called, were brought to western Europe in 1889 by fur traders who travelled far north into Russia and Siberia to buy sables. The first dogs were used also as sledge dogs: Fridtjof Nansen, the Norwegian explorer used Samoyeds on his first polar expedition (1893–96) and, later, Captain Scott also used the breed on his second attempt to reach the South Pole.

In their native lands, Samoyeds could be a variety of shades including black and black and tan but, once they reached Britain in 1900, breeders favoured the pure white–, biscuit–and–cream–coloured dogs and eventually the breed standard was limited to these. Affectionate and lively – but also known to be a little noisy, and sometimes, aggressive with other dogs – the most delightful characteristic of the breed is that it always appears to be smiling! The black lips have an upward curl and, when coupled with sparkling brown eyes, it is very easy to forgive the Samoyed for not being the easiest breed to obedience–train!

# NORWEGIAN BUHUND

**OTHER NAMES:** Norsk buhund, Norwegian sheepdog

**DATE OF ORIGIN:** Antiquity

**PLACE OF ORIGIN:** Norway

**ORIGINAL USE:** Sheep/cattle herding, guarding

**MODERN USE:** Herding, farm/livestock guarding, companion

**SIZE:**

**HEIGHT:** 41–46 cm (16–18 in)

**WEIGHT:** 24–26 kg (53–58 lb)

**COLOURS:** Wheaten, black, red

**RECOGNIZED BY:** K.C.

Fearless and energetic, the Norwegian buhund is a 'jack–of–all–trades': once used to pull sledges and to accompany hunters, on remote farmsteads it could also be found herding ponies and cattle and acting as a guard dog. bu in Norwegian means 'shed' or 'stall' and refers to the breed's later work around domesticated livestock. Such is its herding instinct that the buhund has recently found popularity in Australia as a sheepdog. Although a spitz–type dog, of the type that originated in the intensely cold regions of the Arctic Circle, the Norwegian buhund seems to thrive in the heat of Australia.

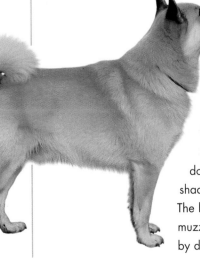

The antipodes is not the only port of call for these well travelled dogs: the buhund is said to have sailed with the Vikings and, almost certainly, it accompanied them to Iceland when it was invaded in ad 874: the Islandsk farehond, or Icelandic sheepdog is most likely a relative as both share the distinctive high–set curly tail.

Some describe the buhund as a rather 'plain–looking' dun–coloured dog, but this is far from the truth. The colours are a beautiful wheaten shading to pearly white or they can be red, or even a beautiful black. The lighter–coloured dogs have an attractive 'smudge' of black on the muzzle and ears, and all have lovely bright, dark brown eyes, outlined by dark eyelids.

# SWEDISH VALLHUND

**OTHER NAMES:** Vollhund, vasgotaspets, Swedish cattle dog

**DATE OF ORIGIN:** Middle Ages

**PLACE OF ORIGIN:** Sweden

**ORIGINAL USE:** Cattle herding/droving, guarding, ratting

**MODERN USE:** Herding, guarding, ratting, companion

**SIZE:**

**HEIGHT:** 30–34 cm (12–14 in)

**WEIGHT:** 11–15 kg (25–35 lb)

**COLOURS:** Grey, grey–brown, red–brown, red–yellow

**RECOGNIZED BY:** K.C.

Classified in Sweden as an indigenous breed, the once rare, short, yet powerfully –legged Swedish Vallhund, like the Pembroke corgi which it resembles, is descended from the European bassets: some do say that corgis were taken to Scandinavia by the Vikings on their return from invading Wales. In Sweden the Vallhund was an 'all–purpose' farm dog: herding and driving cattle, guarding farms and livestock and working as a pest controller, keeping down vermin in the hay and straw barns. Used widely but little considered, it was suddenly realised in the 1940s that the Swedish Vallhund was on the verge of extinction. Fortunately, the breed was rescued and revived by Swedish breeder von Rosen, with official recognition awarded by the Swedish Kennel Club, and the numbers are secure once more. In Sweden it can still be found working on farms, but increasingly it is being seen in both the show ring and in homes as a companion dog.

# MASTIFF

**OTHER NAMES:** English mastiff

**DATE OF ORIGIN:** Antiquity

**PLACE OF ORIGIN:** Great Britain

**ORIGINAL USE:** Guarding

**MODERN USE:** Guarding, companion

**SIZE:**

**HEIGHT:** 70–76 cm (27 ½–30 in)

**WEIGHT:** 79–86 kg (175–190 lb)

**COLOURS:** Apricot–fawn, silver–fawn, dark fawn–brindle

**RECOGNIZED BY:** K.C.

In the years before kennel clubs and pedigree registers it was common to call any large dog a mastiff – including Saint Bernards and Newfoundlands! Today, only a handful of breeds are properly called mastiffs: the English mastiff (known around the world simply as the mastiff); the Japanese tosa inu, the Tibetan mastiff (see page 214), and the Neapolitan mastiff (see page 233). Other dogs do have the name mastiff as well, such as the Spanish, Brazilian, Sicilian and Pyrenean mastiffs, These may well have mastiff ancestry, but they are not 'true' mastiffs and are largely recognised only by the F.C.I. under these names.

One of the heaviest dog breeds in existence, the mastiff existed in Assyria around 700 bc and was perhaps brought to Britain by Phoenician traders. These huge dogs were fighting alongside the ancient Britons when the Romans invaded Britain. So impressed by their size and courage, they sent many mastiffs back to Rome to fight in the 'circus' – the arenas – against lions, bulls, bears, tigers and even gladiators. These fighting qualities have been tied to the breed ever since, although they were also known later in England as 'band dogges' and 'tie dogges', terms used to describe guard dogs. The word mastiff itself is thought to be derived from the Anglo–saxon word masty, meaning 'powerful'. Breeding – and housing – such large breeds is nothing short of a challenge and all breeds, but especially the larger ones, tend to suffer: by the end of World War II only 20 mastiffs remained in Great Britain, but the breed was rescued by re–importing mastiffs from the USA.

# NEAPOLITAN MASTIFF

**OTHER NAMES:** Mastino Napoletano

**DATE OF ORIGIN:** Antiquity

**PLACE OF ORIGIN:** Italy

**ORIGINAL USE:** Fighting, guarding livestock and property

**MODERN USE:** Security, companion

**SIZE:**

**HEIGHT:** 65–73 cm (26–29 in)

**WEIGHT:** 50–68 kg (110–150 lb)

**COLOURS:** Black, blue, brown, grey, black–brindle, red–brindle

**RECOGNIZED BY:** K.C.

Present in Campania in central Italy since ancient times, the Neapolitan mastiff is Italy's contribution to the mastiff group. Although a little smaller than the English mastiff, the Neapolitan has the required broad muzzle, the heavy dewlaps, the desired height and weight, which distinguish the type. The Neapolitan mastiff is most likely descended from the Roman war and fighting 'circus' or arena dogs, which originated in Asia Minor and were transported across the then known world by armies and by traders.

The Neapolitan's coat is short and fine and, on the massive head where the skin is particularly abundant and supple, it has been described as looking like 'baggy velvet'! Like the English mastiff, at the end of World War II, numbers of the Neapolitan mastiff fell dramatically. Thanks to the work of breeder Piero Scanziani, the Neapolitan mastiff was saved from extinction. Once again their sheer size does not make them the first choice as domestic pets, but they are used today in Campania as security/guard dogs and still wear their traditional broad, heavily studded, badger hair–fringed collars.

# TIBETAN MASTIFF

**OTHER NAMES:** Do–khyi

**DATE OF ORIGIN:** Antiquity

**PLACE OF ORIGIN:** Tibet

**ORIGINAL USE:** Livestock guarding

**MODERN USE:** Guarding, companion

**SIZE:**

**HEIGHT:** 61–71 cm (24–28 in)

**WEIGHT:** 64–82 kg (140–180 lb)

**COLOURS:** Black, grey, brown, black–tan, gold

**RECOGNIZED BY:** K.C.

Aristotle is said to have described the Tibetan mastiff as a 'cross between a dog and a tiger', while Marco Polo wrote that they were 'as big as asses'. Either the Tibetan mastiffs they encountered were really enormous or these writers seem prone to a little exaggeration! Nevertheless the Tibetan mastiff is an impressive dog: large boned, a broad and massive head and standing 71 cm (28 in) high. Robert Leighton, in 1907, wrote in The New Book of the Dog that a Tibetan mastiff called Bhotian who was being brought to England by a Major Dougall, needed an entire carriage to himself on the rail journey through India, and every time the train stopped, and Bhotian was exercised on the station platforms, he cleared them of all people!

The 'parent breed' of most of the large mountain, livestock and 'fighting dogs' of Europe, the Americas and Japan, they were used originally to guard livestock in Tibet and the Himalayas. The Tibetan mastiff came close to extinction in the late 19th century, when it was rescued by British breeders. Still rare outside of the show ring, the Tibetan mastiff appears aloof, but they still retain the natural suspicion of strangers and will defend their homes and territory.

# DOGUE DE BORDEAUX

**OTHER NAMES:** French mastiff

**DATE OF ORIGIN:** Antiquity

**PLACE OF ORIGIN:** France

**ORIGINAL USE:** Game hunting, guarding

**MODERN USE:** Guarding, companion

**SIZE:**

**HEIGHT:** 58–69 cm (23–27 in)

**WEIGHT:** 36–45 kg (80–100 lb)

**COLOURS:** Mahogany, golden fawn

**RECOGNIZED BY:** K.C.

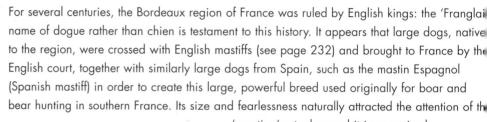

For several centuries, the Bordeaux region of France was ruled by English kings: the 'Franglai' name of dogue rather than chien is testament to this history. It appears that large dogs, native to the region, were crossed with English mastiffs (see page 232) and brought to France by the English court, together with similarly large dogs from Spain, such as the mastin Espagnol (Spanish mastiff) in order to create this large, powerful breed used originally for boar and bear hunting in southern France. Its size and fearlessness naturally attracted the attention of the 'sporting' set who used it in organised animal–baiting and in dog fighting.

The dogue de Bordeaux, with its huge head and furrows of wrinkles, looks very similar to the more recently developed bull mastiff – the product of 60% English mastiff and 40% bulldog root stock. Although the dogue de Bordeaux came briefly to a wider public knowledge in 1989, when one starred with Tom Hanks in the movie Turner and Hooch, the breed is still largely unknown outside of Franc and the show rings.

# GREAT DANE

**OTHER NAMES:** German mastiff, Deutsche dogge, German boarhound

**DATE OF ORIGIN:** Middle Ages

**PLACE OF ORIGIN:** Germany

**ORIGINAL USE:** War dog, large mammal hunting

**MODERN USE:** Guarding, companion

**SIZE:**

**HEIGHT:** 71–76 cm (28–30 in)

**WEIGHT:** 46–54 kg (100–120 lb)

**COLOURS:** Black, blue, fawn, brindle, harlequin (white with black or blue patches)

**RECOGNIZED BY:** K.C.

In spite of its name, the Great Dane has no connection with Denmark. It is the national dog of Germany, where it is referred to as the German mastiff or the German dog. The Great Dane can trace its ancestors back to the dogs brought to Europe by the Scythian tribe called the Alans, from the region known as Asian Russia. During the Middle Ages, the German nobility used this giant breed to hunt boar where size, endurance and courage were more important than looks. Nevertheless, the undisputed elegance of the Great Dane suggests that the earlier mastiffs were at some stage crossed with greyhounds (see page 171). In the 19th century, in Britain, Great Danes could be found escorting the carriages of the wealthy and fashionable: Sydenham Edwards wrote in Cynographia Britannica in 1800 that 'no equipage can have arrived at its acme of grandeur until a couple of harlequin Danes preceded the pomp'.

Harlequin, one of the recognised colours of the breed, is a pure white underground with black or blue patches that have the appearance of being torn at the edges. As with many large dogs with a ferocious history, the Great Dane is so confident in its abilities that it need never pick a fight: they combine elegance with power, grandeur with a good nature, and courage with docility. The sheer size of the noble Great Dane unfortunately attracts more admirers than owners and, as a breed, they suffer a high incidence of arthritis.

# BOXER

**OTHER NAMES:** None

**DATE OF ORIGIN:** 19th century

**PLACE OF ORIGIN:** Germany

**ORIGINAL USE:** Guarding, bull baiting

**MODERN USE:** Police and customs dogs, companions

**SIZE:**

**HEIGHT:** 53–63 cm (21–25 in)

**WEIGHT:** 25–32 kg (55–70 lb)

**COLOURS:** Fawn, brindle

**RECOGNIZED BY:** K.C.

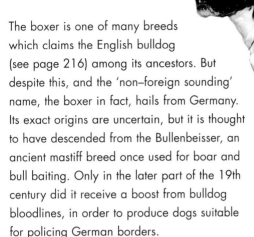

The boxer is one of many breeds which claims the English bulldog (see page 216) among its ancestors. But despite this, and the 'non–foreign sounding' name, the boxer in fact, hails from Germany. Its exact origins are uncertain, but it is thought to have descended from the Bullenbeisser, an ancient mastiff breed once used for boar and bull baiting. Only in the later part of the 19th century did it receive a boost from bulldog bloodlines, in order to produce dogs suitable for policing German borders.

The result was a hardy, alert, strong, powerful dog with an intimidating appearance. But, at the same time, the boxer also has a wonderfully expressive face – an expressiveness enhanced by its tendency to make 'questioning' noises and turn its head to one side – and a great sense of fun. Although not widely known outside of Germany until after World War II, returning servicemen were full of enthusiasm for this delightful breed and, within a few years, the boxer became one of the most popular dogs in Britain and America. Still used by many police forces across Europe, the boxer is more likely thought to be found in the home where it makes an ideal companion dog for active families.

# BERNESE MOUNTAIN DOG

**OTHER NAMES:** Berner Sennenhund, Bernese cattle dog

**DATE OF ORIGIN:** Antiquity, developed further in 20th century

**PLACE OF ORIGIN:** Switzerland

**ORIGINAL USE:** Draughting small carts

**MODERN USE:** Livestock guarding, companion

**SIZE:**

**HEIGHT:**
58–70 cm (23–27½ in)

**WEIGHT:**
40–44 kg (87–90 lb)

**COLOURS:** Black, with rich tan and white markings

**RECOGNIZED BY:** K.C.

The Bernese mountain dog is the most well known of the four Swiss mountain dogs which were split into separate breeds at the end of the 19th century. It is also the largest of the four breeds. Legend says that large, long–haired 'mastiff'–type dogs (although the term mastiff was used to refer to any big dog) were taken to Switzerland by the Roman legions, who needed large, weather–resistant dogs to guard their depots in the Alps. The descendants of these dogs stayed on and took up new roles as guards and as draught animals, pulling small carts to market for the weavers in the canton of Berne.

By the late 19th century, the Bernese had almost disappeared, overshadowed by the more glamourous Saint Bernard (see page 236). Researching the history of Swiss mountain dogs and searching the country for specimens, Franz Schertenleib located a few Bernese still in the region. Collecting the best specimens, he began a breeding programme and formed a breed club to popularise them. The Bernese mountain dog was saved and became firmly established in its native land and officially named in 1908. As the breed standard stresses that the Bernese should be good natured, self–confident and friendly, it is no surprise that this large but lovely dog has become increasingly popular in continental Europe, Britain and in North America.

# SAINT BERNARD

**OTHER NAMES:** Alpine mastiff

**DATE OF ORIGIN:** Middle Ages

**PLACE OF ORIGIN:** Switzerland

**ORIGINAL USE:**
Hauling/draughting, companion

**MODERN USE:** Companion

**SIZE:**

**HEIGHT:** 61–71 cm (24–28 in)

**WEIGHT:** 50–91 kg (110–200 lb)

**COLOURS:** Brown–brindle,
red–brindle, orange

**RECOGNIZED BY:** K.C.

Whether the legendary Saint Bernard ever actually rescued snow–covered travellers and offered them a reviving tot of brandy from the mythical barrel around its neck is debatable! But, like all legends, there is a kernel of truth in the story of the Saint Bernard. Descended from the great mastiff dogs brought to Switzerland by the Roman legions as guard dogs, the once–fierce dog became associated with the Hospice du Grand Saint Bernard – one of the highest human habitations in Europe and one of the oldest for the hospice is built on the site of a Roman temple dedicated to Jupiter.

After centuries of neglect and decay, Saint Bernard of Montjoux (c.996–1081) rebuilt the mountain refuge as a place for weary pilgrims to rest. But it was not until 1707 that there is any record of dogs working at the hospice. The Saint Bernard was not an alpine 'sniffer dog' who looked for and rescued people. Instead, they acted as guide dogs and 'trail breakers', marking safe paths through snowy mountain passes.

These Saint Bernards – or Alpine mastiffs as they were then called until 1865 – were invariably smooth haired and, while large, were more active and less weighty than today's dogs. In the 1830s, however, the breed was close to extinction but was saved by introducing Newfoundland (see page 241) bloodlines. A legacy of this crossing is to be seen in the rough–coated variety of the breed.

# ESTRELA MOUNTAIN DOG

**OTHER NAMES:** Cao da Serra da Estrela, Portuguese sheepdog

**DATE OF ORIGIN:** Middle Ages

**PLACE OF ORIGIN:** Portugal

**ORIGINAL USE:** Livestock guarding

**MODERN USE:** Livestock guarding, companion

**SIZE:**

**HEIGHT:** 62–72 cm (24½– 28½ in)

**WEIGHT:** 30–50 kg (66–110 lb)

**COLOURS:** Black–brindle, red–brindle, fawn

**RECOGNIZED BY:** K.C.

One of the most popular, and one of the oldest, Portuguese breeds, the Estrela, is a descendent of the Asiatic mastiffs brought to the west and used by the Romans as guard dogs. When the Romans left, the Estrela stayed in the rugged Serra da Estrela where, for centuries, it guarded flocks of livestock from wolves. Like many of the mastiff–type dogs from continental Europe, the Estrela developed to suit the location in which it lived and worked: a mountain dog, it required a dense, double coat to insulate it from winter snows and to protect it from marauding wolves. In the early 20th century, crosses with German shepherds took place, but today, thanks to the efforts of breeders in Portugal and overseas – especially in Britain – the Estrela mountain dog was returned to its pure form. The Estrela can still be found today in the mountains of Portugal guarding flocks, while herding is left to breeds such as the cao de castro laboreiro (Portuguese cattle dog) and the cao da serra de aires (Portuguese shepherd dog).

# ROTTWEILER

**OTHER NAMES:** Rottweiler Metzerhund (butcher's dog of Rottweil), 'Rotti'

**DATE OF ORIGIN:** Antiquity, modern version bred in 19th century

**PLACE OF ORIGIN:** Germany

**ORIGINAL USE:** Cattle droving, guarding

**MODERN USE:** Police/military service dog, companion

**SIZE:**

**HEIGHT:** 58–69 cm (23–27 in)

**WEIGHT:** 41–50 kg (90–110 lb)

**COLOURS:** Black with tan/mahogany markings

**RECOGNIZED BY:** K.C.

An ancient breed, the ancestors of the modern Rottweiler may have come to Germany with the Roman legions. As the Romans planned their assaults on foreign territories, they understood that their armies 'marched on their stomachs' but without modern refrigeration, the only way to supply fresh meat was to have it 'on the hoof'. Mass movements of cattle required strong working dogs, that were capable of both herding and guarding. One of the major supply routes led over the Alps and through the St. Gothard Pass: all along the ancient paths that led down from the pass can be found descendants of the Romans' dogs. Some of these dogs travelled further south than the Alps into southern Germany, along the old military road through Württemburg and on to the small market town of Rottweil. Later this region was to become an important cattle area and the Rottweiler Metzerhund – the butcher's dog of rottweil – were said to carry the money of merchants in bags fastened around their necks since no robber would be so foolish as to challenge such a powerful and ferocious–looking dog! As the cattle market declined however, so did the Rotti's fortune: in 1900 the town of Rottweil itself had only one dog to represent the breed. In 1912 the breed was effectively saved from extinction when it joined the police and military services and, since then, it has grown in popularity as both a working guard dog and, because it is an easier breed to obedience–train, as a family pet.

# GERMAN SHEPHERD

**OTHER NAMES:** Deutscher Schäferhund, Alsatian

**DATE OF ORIGIN:** 19th century

**PLACE OF ORIGIN:** Germany

**ORIGINAL USE:** Germany

**MODERN USE:** Guarding/security dogs, 'assistance' dogs for the disabled, and in search & rescue in avalanches/earthquakes, companions

**SIZE:**

**HEIGHT:** 55–66 cm (22–26 in)

**WEIGHT:** 34–43 kg (75–95 lb)

**COLOURS:** Variety (black–tan, black–grey, solid black accepted for exhibition; cream, yellow, and long coats not widely accepted; white accepted in some countries)

**RECOGNIZED BY:** K.C.

The German shepherd is quite possibly the most popular breed in the world. While 'wolf–like' dogs have existed for thousands of years and may well be the ancestors of this and other shepherding dogs like the Dutch and Belgian varieties, the 'modern' German shepherd has much more recent origins. At the end of the 19th century, Max von Stephanitz began a breeding programme using a variety of sheepdogs – long, short, and wire–haired – from the areas of Württemberg, Thuringia and Bavaria to produce a strong, agile shepherding dog. The resulting German shepherd was not only watchful, intelligent, responsive, energetic and obedient, it was also very handsome.

The breed was unknown outside of Germany before World War I, during which German shepherds were trained as messengers crossing shell–torn battle fields, as medical couriers carrying drugs and bandages, as search dogs locating wounded soldiers, and as guard dogs. When hostilities ceased, a number were taken to Britain, where, perhaps to 'disassociate' the breed with Germany, they were known as Alsatians. Indiscriminate breeding in the 1920s led to problems with temperament and incidents involving the dogs were widely reported in the press. The combination of irresponsible breeding and 'media panic' nearly destroyed the German shepherd and its numbers declined severely until they recovered their former popularity in the 1960s. Until 1915 both long–haired and wire–haired varieties were shown, but today, for show purposes, only the shortcoat is recognised.

# HOVAWORT

**OTHER NAMES:** Hofwarth

**DATE OF ORIGIN:** Middle Ages, developed in 19th century

**PLACE OF ORIGIN:** Germany

**ORIGINAL USE:** Livestock guarding

**MODERN USE:** Guarding, companion

**SIZE:**

**HEIGHT:** 58–70 cm (23–28 in)

**WEIGHT:** 25–41 kg (55–90 lb)

**COLOURS:** Variety

**RECOGNIZED BY:** K.C.

Still largely unknown outside its native Germany, the hovawart was first mentioned in 1220 as the 'hofwarth', an estate guard dog, in Eike von Repgow's Sachenspiegel and, later, in the 15th century, it was recorded in Germany as a breed of dogs used to track robbers and fugitives from the law. The modern hovawart was developed by German breeders in the late 19th century in an attempt to recreate the 'great estate' dogs of the Middle Ages and Renaissance. Breeders selected a variety of 'farm dogs' from the Black Forest and Hartz mountain regions and introduced German shepherd (see above), Newfoundland (see page 241) and Hungarian kuvasz (a handsome white guard dog introduced to Hungary by the Kuman, nomadic Turkish shepherds). The hovawart was first recognised in 1936 and is described as an 'elegant worker'. It is indeed an attractive dog and especially distinctive are the forelegs which are fringed with hair at the back of the legs and the well–feathered tail. Any breed that is both attractive and, like the hovawart, that responds well to obedience–training, gets on well with other dogs – and children – is set to become much more widely known in the future as a favoured family dog.

# BELGIAN SHEPHERD DOG

**OTHER NAMES:** Chien de Berger Belge

**DATE OF ORIGIN:** Middle Ages, developed in 19th century

**PLACE OF ORIGIN:** Belgium

**ORIGINAL USE:** Livestock herding

**MODERN USE:** Security/watch/guard dog (groenendael, laekenois, terveuren, Malinois), assistance dog (Malinois, tervueren)

**SIZE:**

**HEIGHT:** 56–66 cm (22–26 in)

**WEIGHT:** 27.5– 28.5 kg (61–63 lb)

**COLOURS AND COATS:**
Groenendael: black, smooth.
Laekenois: Fawn, rough.
Malinois: Red, fawn, grey, smooth.
Tervueren: Red, fawn, grey; hairs are double pigmented black tipped, long, smooth coat.

**RECOGNIZED BY:**

K.C. (four breeds)

Four varieties of Belgian shepherd dog exist, differing only in coat and colour. Classifying Belgian shepherds is a difficult task as national kennel clubs cannot agree on naming them: in the USA, the groenendael, is the Belgian shepherd, while the Malinois, and the tervueren are recognised separately – but the laekenois is not recognised at all. In Britain, the Kennel Club recognises all four breeds as distinct.

They are light–built dogs with slender legs. The ears are erect and the tail is carried low, and all have a distinctive, high head carriage.

At the end of the 19th century, breeders all over Europe began to take a deep interest in 'native' sheepdogs and, in order to preserve these, often ancient, breeds, standards were set to stabilise them into as few breeds as possible. At first Belgium recognised eight standards, which included the groenendael, a breed that was developed and refined by Belgian breeder Nicholas Rose. The groenendael is recognised by its long, smooth black hair which is particularly abundant around the shoulders, neck and chest, well–feathered tail, and long feathering on the forelegs which extends from the forearms to the wrists.

The tervueren also has a long, straight and abundant coat, but the colours include all shades of red, fawn and grey. The coat is double–pigmented: the tip of each light– coloured hair is coloured black. The mature tervueren has a shaded coat which may be especially dark on the shoulders and back. The facial mask is also black. The tervueren descends from stock created by the groenendael: groenendael matings can sometimes produce tervueren offspring. This particular Belgian shepherd dog, which was nearly extinct by the end of World War II, is now favoured as a police and security dog. Its speciality is as a scent detector, sniffing out drugs and explosives. Its willingness to learn has also led the tervueren to be used as an assistance dog for blind and disabled owners.

The Malinois was the first Belgian shepherd dog to establish type, and it became the 'gauge' by which others were to be judged. Named after the area of Malines in Belgium, where this dog was most numerous, the Malinois has a smooth coat and in truth, resembles the German shepherd (see page 235) quite closely. Being eclipsed in popularity by the German shepherd means that the Malinois is still quite a rare breed, although, increasingly, it is being used for police and security work.

The Laekenois is the rarest of the four Belgian Shepherd Dogs: often described as a 'fawn–coloured, untidy, rough, shaggy coated' dog. This description does not really do the Laekenois any justice: it is a very handsome breed with very attractive dark eyes and the 'hint' of a moustache. Of the four Belgian shepherd dogs, only the Laekenois was a favourite of Queen Henrietta of Belgium: the breed in fact takes it name from the Chateau de Laeken, one of the queen's country residences.

# LEONBERGER

**OTHER NAMES:** None
**DATE OF ORIGIN:** 19th century
**PLACE OF ORIGIN:** Germany
**ORIGINAL USE:** Companion
**MODERN USE:** Companion
**SIZE:**
**HEIGHT:** 65–80 cm (26–31½ in)
**WEIGHT:** 34–50 kg
(75–110 lb)
**COLOURS:** Red-brown,
yellow-gold
**RECOGNIZED
BY:** K.C.

In 1855, Heinrich Essig of Leonberg, Germany, tried to produce a dog to look like the lions o the coat of arms of the town in which he lived. As a breeder of Saint Bernards (see page 236 and Newfoundlands (see page 241), Essig crossed these along with the Landseer (the 'black–and–white Newfoundlands which were named after the artist Sir Edwin Landseer) and the Pyrenean mountain dog (see below) to produce the 'gentle giant' that is the Leonberger. It is possible that Essig also used a 'secret ingredient breed, since the desired colour in the Leonberger is a golden yellow – like a lion – with a black mask on the face. Establishing breed type was very difficult: when the Leonberger was first exhibited it was dismissed as a mere crossbreed, and it was not until 1949 that an official standard was published by the F.C.I Until the late 1970s, the Leonberger was a fairly localised breed and not widely known outside of Germany, but has since made 'leaps and bounds' in Britain and the USA. Its Newfoundland ancestry has not only helped to produce a very handsome breed, but one which adores swimming and, to help it along, the breed's large, round feet have webbed toes.

# PYRENEAN MOUNTAIN DOG

**OTHER NAMES:** Chien de
Montagne des Pyrenees, Great
Pyrenees
**DATE OF ORIGIN:** Antiquity
**PLACE OF ORIGIN:** France
**ORIGINAL USE:** Sheep guarding
**MODERN USE:** Guarding,
companion
**SIZE:**
**HEIGHT:** 65–81 cm (26–32 in)
**WEIGHT:** 45–60 kg (99–132 lb)
**COLOURS:** White, with/without
patches of lemon, badger, or grey
**RECOGNIZED BY:**
K.C.

The Great Pyrenees, as the breed in known in North America, is one of the large, white 'mastiff' dogs bred in Europe centuries ago to guard herd and flocks of animals at up to 1,500m (5,000 ft) above sea level. The Pyrenean is probably related to the Italian maremma (see page 247), the Hungarian kuvasz and Turkish karabash, and is to be found on both the French and Spanish sides of the Pyrenean mountains. Because of the nature of the terrain in which it lived and worked the Pyrenean developed its double coat with a woolly undercoat and coarse, thick, straightish outer 'jacket'. These dogs never went under cover so needed the same protection from the weather that the sheep they guarded received from their fleeces. The Pyrenean mountain dogs never herded sheep: this was left to the smaller Pyrenean sheepdogs who worked in pairs, or, to the Pyrenean mastiffs who worked in teams of four or five, herding flocks of up to 1,000 sheep. The Pyrenean mountain dog's role was to guard the flocks against wolf attacks. To protect the dogs throats from the wolves jaws, they traditionally wore a 'carlanca' – a spiked, iron collar. By the 18th century, some Pyreneans had come down from their mountain homes to work as guard dogs on chateaux: the Chateau at Lourdes is said to have sentry boxes large enough to accommodate the sentry and his dog. Madame de Maintenon, who saw the dogs at Barrèges in southwest France, was so impressed that she took several back to Paris and the French royal court.

# NEWFOUNDLAND

**OTHER NAMES:** None

**DATE OF ORIGIN:** 18th century

**PLACE OF ORIGIN:** Canada

**ORIGINAL USE:** Fisherman's assistant

**MODERN USE:** Rescue dog, companion

**SIZE:**

**HEIGHT:** 66–71 cm (26–28 in)

**WEIGHT:** 50–68 kg (110–150 lb) when dry!

**COLOURS:** Black, brown

**RECOGNIZED BY:** K.C.

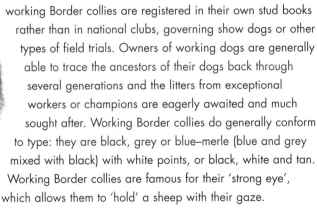

Many say the webbed–toed Newfoundland is a native North American breed descended from the now extinct Greater St. John's Dog; some say Lief Ericson took a black 'bear dog' named Oolum to Newfoundland in the year 1000 ad, others that Biscay fishermen brought big mountain dogs with them to the French settlements on the Newfoundland coast in Canada in 1662, to help them in their war against the British and, for this reason, some canine authorities believe that one of the Newfoundland's ancestors was the Pyrenean mountain dog (see page 240). Whatever its origins, the Newfoundland is one of the most attractive and most friendly of all breeds. It's love of swimming is well known, and the Newfoundland is famous for its impressive record for rescuing people from the water – often regardless of whether the swimmer needs or desires to be saved! The Newfoundland derives its name from the Canadian island where it worked pulling cod fishermen's nets – and their boats – onto the shores. On land they were used to pull loads of firewood cut from the forests of the interior. Today, in France, Newfoundlands are used to assist the emergency services with inshore and offshore rescues.

# BORDER COLLIE

**OTHER NAMES:** None but working dogs are often known as working collies or farm collies to distinguish them from show dogs and pets

**DATE OF ORIGIN:** 18th century

**PLACE OF ORIGIN:** Great Britain

**ORIGINAL USE:** Sheep/cattle herding

**MODERN USE:** Sheep herding, sheep dog trials, companion

**SIZE:**

**HEIGHT:** 46–54 cm (18–21 in)

**WEIGHT:** 14–22 kg (30–49 lb)

**COLOURS:** Black, black–white, brown, tricolour, blue–merle, red

**RECOGNIZED BY:** K.C.

One of the world's finest and best–known sheepdogs, the Border collie takes its name from the border lands between England and Scotland. Nimble, black–and–white farms dogs bred purely for work have been portrayed since the 11th century in Britain, and it is likely that they existed long before that time. The first sheepdog trial held in Britain in Bala, Wales, in 1873 enabled shepherds to test their – and their dogs' – skills at working sheep and the first winner was a dog form the Borders. At subsequent trials, similar dogs from the region were among the winners and so, what had previously been called a 'sheepdog' was to be called a Border collie.

Working Border collies are bred for working abilities rather than type, so only those dogs that have proven themselves to be intelligent and trainable are used for breeding. In most countries,

working Border collies are registered in their own stud books rather than in national clubs, governing show dogs or other types of field trials. Owners of working dogs are generally able to trace the ancestors of their dogs back through several generations and the litters from exceptional workers or champions are eagerly awaited and much sought after. Working Border collies do generally conform to type: they are black, grey or blue–merle (blue and grey mixed with black) with white points, or black, white and tan. Working Border collies are famous for their 'strong eye', which allows them to 'hold' a sheep with their gaze.

*complete DOG*

# ROUGH COLLIE

**OTHER NAMES:** Scottish collie, 'Lassie'

**DATE OF ORIGIN:** 19th century

**PLACE OF ORIGIN:** Scotland

**ORIGINAL USE:** Sheep herding

**MODERN USE:** Companion

**SIZE:**

**HEIGHT:** 51–61 cm (20–24 in)

**WEIGHT:** 18–30 kg (40–66 lb)

**COLOURS:** Sable–white, blue–merle, tricolour

**RECOGNIZED BY:** K.C.

Internationally famous as a the star of numerous Lassie movies – although Lassie was in fact a 'laddie' – the rough collie of today is a much more uniform – and 'prettier' dog than the functional, hard working animal of 100 hundred years ago in the far north of Scotland. Sheep in Scotland at that time were usually dark–coloured animals, and were called 'colleys', from the Anglo Saxon word 'col' meaning black. The dogs that worked them had no breed names, but were frequently called the 'colley dogs'. These colley dogs worked for centuries, but remained largely unknown outside of their working regions but, when Queen Victoria made her first visit to Balmoral in Scotland in 1860, it was 'love at first sight' and she had a number installed at the Royal Kennels at Windsor Castle. With such patronage it was not long before the rough and ready colley dog, which was shorter in the leg and the nose than today's breed, was the object of interest among breeders. The rough collie was one of the first breeds to be 'smartened up' for the show ring and, as appearance became the main criteria, much of the drive, energy, stamina and keenness of the working dog was lost. The once–weatherproof, truly 'rough' coat became longer, more abundant and more magnificent, but required daily grooming to prevent it matting.

# SMOOTH COLLIE

**OTHER NAMES:** None
**DATE OF ORIGIN:** 19th century
**PLACE OF ORIGIN:** Scotland
**ORIGINAL USE:** Sheep herding
**MODERN USE:** Companion
**SIZE:**
**HEIGHT:** 51–61 cm (20–24 in)
**WEIGHT:** 18–30 kg (40–66 lb)
**COLOURS:** Tricolour, blue–merle, sable–white
**RECOGNIZED BY:** K.C.

The smooth collie is the only collie breed without a long coat: it's Lassie without the locks! In every respect except coat, the smooth collie conforms to the same breed standards as the rough collie (see page 242), so it's quite possible that if MGM had chosen a smooth collie to play Lassie in their movies, this breed would be much better known: outside of Britain, the breed is quite rare. A widely held theory is that the rough collies worked the sheep on the hillsides, while the smooth collies were drovers, taking the sheep along the lanes and highways to market. This theory suggests that these were two different breeds but, for most of its history, the smooth collie was classified with the rough, largely because it was not unknown for smooth collies to appear in the litters of roughs. The smooth collie breed foundation dog is generally accepted as a tricoloured puppy called Trefoil, born in 1873. Although overshadowed by its more glamourous relative, the smooth collie is still an immensely attractive breed – it has all the advantages of the rough collie: intelligent and suited to family and urban life, good looks – including the very expressive ears which, when the dog is alert, are semi–erect but with the tips hanging over – without the disadvantages of intensive grooming!

# BEARDED COLLIE

**OTHER NAMES:** Highland collie, beardie
**DATE OF ORIGIN:** 16th century
**PLACE OF ORIGIN:** Great Britain
**ORIGINAL USE:** Sheep droving
**MODERN USE:** Companion
**SIZE:**
**HEIGHT:** 51–56 cm (20–22 in)
**WEIGHT:** 18–27 kg (40–60 lb)
**COLOURS:** Black, brown, blue, fawn, grey
**RECOGNIZED BY:** K.C.

'Shaggy sheepdogs' like the bearded collie appear to have been hard at work herding sheep in Scotland for centuries, but this breed was only officially recognised in Britain in 1944! One theory is that the Highland collie as it was long called, is related to the komondor – the gloriously 'dread–locked' sheepdog from Hungary – which, hundreds of years ago, was taken by the Magyars to Poland, and thence to Scotland: the Poles sent grain (and komondors) and, in return, received Scottish sheep. By this theory, it is also possible that the beardie has Polish lowland sheepdog in its genetic make up: in looks the beardie is closer to this breed than the corded–coated komondor. Until the early 20th century the breed was largely unknown outside of Scotland, where it could be found working as a drover rather than a herding dog.

While a breed club was formed in 1912, the beardie did not make a significant impact on the public and, by the end of World War II, the beardie had almost disappeared as a working dog. The breed was rescued from extinction by a Mrs. Willison, who had acquired a beardie by accident: she was looking for a Shetland sheepdog (see page 244) bred from working parents, but the farmer from whom she had ordered it sent her an 'odd' puppy instead. It took some time to work out what breed the dog was, but Jeannie as the puppy was called (later Champion Jeannie of Bothkennar) was mated with Baillie – another beardie who was fortunately spotted by Mrs. Willison playing happily on Brighton Beach, in Sussex, and these two revived the breed.

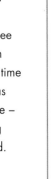
*complete DOG*

# SHETLAND SHEEPDOG

**OTHER NAMES:** Dwarf Scottish shepherd, Sheltie

**DATE OF ORIGIN:** 18th century

**PLACE OF ORIGIN:** Shetland Islands, Scotland

**ORIGINAL USE:** Sheep/pony herding

**MODERN USE:** Sheep herding, companion

**SIZE:**

**HEIGHT:** 35–37 cm (14–15 in)

**WEIGHT:** 6–7 kg (14–16 lb)

**COLOURS:** Black–tan, black–white, blue–merle, sable, tricolour

**RECOGNIZED BY:** K.C.

At first glance, the Sheltie looks like a miniature rough collie (see page 242) and this has led many to believe that the Sheltie was a deliberate bantamisation of the larger dog. This is not the case, as all the domesticated animals of the Shetland Islands – the famous Shetland ponies are the best–known examples, but the sheep and cattle too – tend to be dwarfed compared to their mainland counterparts. This is in part due to the subsistence level of life in the islands which favoured smaller animals and, with an isolated population, inbreeding occurs which also tended to encourage small size. It may well be that the Sheltie descends then from small, rough collies imported to the islands on account of their already suitable size.

Like the rough collie, the Sheltie of 100 years ago was far plainer and, perhaps rougher, in appearance than today's dogs. Few descriptions exist of the dogs except to say that they were often 'speckled' and 'foxy–faced': working ability was more valuable than looks. As well as herding, the Shelties were also used to stop sheep from grazing on the valuable vegetables grown in gardens by the islanders. The modern, very beautiful, Sheltie is of recent origin, for they were only recognised by the Kennel Club in 1909 and, since that time, improvements in the looks of the breed have been made, especially to produce the profuse coat with its abundant frill and mane. An exceptionally gentle and sweet–natured breed, while rarely used today as a working dog, the Sheltie still retains many of its guarding and herding instincts.

# OLD ENGLISH SHEEPDOG

**OTHER NAMES:** Bobtail

**DATE OF ORIGIN:** 19th century

**PLACE OF ORIGIN:** Great Britain

**ORIGINAL USE:** Sheep droving/herding

**MODERN USE:** Companion

**SIZE:**

**HEIGHT:** 56–61 cm (22–24 in)

**WEIGHT:** 29.5– 30.5 kg (65–67 lb)

**COLOURS:** Grey, blue

**RECOGNIZED BY:** K.C.

One of the family of 'shaggy sheepdogs' that spread across Europe – from the south in Italy to the north in Russia, to the east in Hungary and west to Britain – the Old English sheepdog, in spite of its name, is probably only about 200 years old. It is probably a descendant of the bearded collie (see page 234) and foreign breeds such as the briard (see page 239): until a system of registration of pedigrees was introduced in 1873, matings, especially in working breeds, were more indiscriminate than today. Owners who wanted their working dogs to perform specific jobs were more concerned with propagating dogs with the desired working qualities rather than preserving a particular type. For sheep farmers in England's West Country, intelligence, stamina, hardiness and agility were what a dog required, and these could be found in the 'bobtail' as the breed was also called. It earned this name because drover dogs – those that drove the herds to markets – were exempted from taxes and tolls along the road to markets. To prove they were drovers, their tails were docked. The popular belief that the Old English is a tailless breed is false: the majority of puppies are born with tails that require docking. Selective breeding, which began in the 1880s, has altered the Old English somewhat: it is now a much bigger and heavier dog than it was originally, the coat has become longer, more profuse and much softer in texture. Once, grooming would have been difficult, today it's a Herculean task! Nevertheless, the Old English retains it's loud and resonant bark and its deceptively slow, ambling gait – until it turns into a gallop.

# AUSTRALIAN SHEPHERD DOG

**OTHER NAMES:** None

**DATE OF ORIGIN:** 20th century

**PLACE OF ORIGIN:** United States of America

**ORIGINAL USE:** Sheep herding

**MODERN USE:** Sheep herding, service/search and rescue, companion

**SIZE:**

**HEIGHT:** 46–58 cm (18–23 in)

**WEIGHT:** 16–32 kg (35–70 lb)

**COLOURS:** Black, blue–merle, liver, red

**RECOGNIZED BY:** K.C.

Although its ancestors include sheepdogs from Australia and New Zealand, the Australian shepherd dog was 'born' in the United States of America in the 19th century, where is was bred as a working shepherd dog that was suitable for the varied climate of California. Since then, the breed has gone on to distinguish itself in a whole range of fields including search and rescue, and its affectionate and playful yet calm temperament – likened to golden and Labrador retrievers (see pages 102 and 104) – have ensured it a place in many hearts and homes. Currently, the Australian shepherd dog is little known outside of the United States, except for in the show ring, and some breeders are working towards reducing the size of the dog, which would further increase its popularity as a pet. It is already a good–looking dog with a delightful coat, a predominantly brown nose, sparkling eyes and very attractive, well–feathered hind legs. In time, the Australian shepherd dog will become a firm favourite with dog lovers the world over.

# AUSTRALIAN CATTLE DOG

**OTHER NAMES:** Hall's heeler, blue heeler, Queensland heeler, Australian heeler

**DATE OF ORIGIN:** 19th century

**PLACE OF ORIGIN:** Australia

**ORIGINAL USE:** Cattle herding

**MODERN USE:** Cattle herding, companion

**SIZE:**

**HEIGHT:** 43–51 cm (17–20 in)

**WEIGHT:** 16–20 kg (35–45 lb)

**COLOURS:** Blue, red

**RECOGNIZED BY:** K.C.

Australia has developed two of the finest working dogs that ever worked in the service of man: the kelpie and the Australian cattle dog, which predates the former by some 30 years. The first working cattle dogs in Australia, were the now–extinct 'black bobtails', but these were big, clumsy dogs that were unsuited to both the intense heat and great distances involved in driving cattle in Australia. Thomas Smith Hall needed a dog to round up, drive and pen range cattle – which are pretty wild animals – so any dog needed to be rugged, agile, intelligent and capable of delivering a bite to the heel of a bull without crippling it or damaging the hide. Such dogs were generally called 'heelers' and would test the range and speed of cattle by feinting. They snap or bite the heel of the leg bearing the steer's weight. However, a well–aimed kick from a steer is fast and potentially lethal so, after the bite, the heeler drops flat to the ground so it is under the kick. Hall also wanted to exploit the native dingo's ability to sneak silently up on its prey. 'Hall's heeler', as the breed was once called is the result of crosses with dingoes, the now extinct Smithfield, kelpies, blue–merle smooth collies (see page 243), bull terriers and, Dalmatians (see page 221). Like 'dallies' Australian cattle dog puppies are born white (or white with black speckles) regardless of their later colour and, like dingoes, they are wary by nature and need early socialisation with both people and other dogs.

# BRIARD

**OTHER NAMES:** Berger de Brie

**DATE OF ORIGIN:** Middle Ages, developed in 19th century

**PLACE OF ORIGIN:** France

**ORIGINAL USE:** Livestock guarding/herding

**MODERN USE:** Security/guard dog, companion

**SIZE:**

**HEIGHT:** 57–69 cm (23–27 in)

**WEIGHT:** 33.5–34.5 kg (74–76 lb)

**COLOURS:** Black, fawn

**RECOGNIZED BY:** K.C.

Although its exact origins are unknown, the briard, which takes its name from the French province of Brie (most famous for its cheese), is most likely to be a member of the ancient race of sheepdogs that came to Europe from Asia in the company of the invading hoards, which swept across the continent from late Roman times through the early Middle Ages. Other dogs which belong to this group are the Hungarian komondor, kuvasz, and the puli (see page 2248) the bearded collie (see page 243) and the Old English sheepdog (see page 244). While these breeds differ in many respects, they are all roughly similar in both conformation and in the work they were bred to carry out. The briard was once classified as the 'goat–haired' variety of the beauceron: this dog is also from Brie, and shares the same double dew claws and the hind feet. Once used as a herding and watchdog, the briard distinguished itself in World War I in the service of the French army. Wearing specially made backpacks, the briard carried ammunition and gun parts from depots to the front lines and, for the Red Cross, it carried first–aid supplies and located wounded soldiers in the battlefield. Today the briard is one of France's most popular companion dogs, and is gaining a foothold in homes in Britain and the United States of America.

# BERGAMASCO

**OTHER NAMES:** Cane de Pastore Bergamasco, Bergamese shepherd

**DATE OF ORIGIN:** Antiquity

**PLACE OF ORIGIN:** Italy

**ORIGINAL USE:** Livestock guarding

**MODERN USE:** Guarding, companion

**SIZE:**

**HEIGHT:** 56–61 cm (22–24 in)

**WEIGHT:** 26–38 kg (57–84 lb)

**COLOURS:** Various

**RECOGNIZED BY:** K.C.

The most distinctive feature of the Bergamasco is its soft long hair, which forms wavy 'flocks' – though most would call them 'dreadlocks'! A breed that is at least 2,000 years old – if not more – the Bergamasco is named after the Bergamo region of northern Italy where it was used to guard livestock and where its coat developed into a weatherproof jacket that also protected the dog from the flailing hooves of large livestock and from the jaws of wolves. It is possible that the Bergamasco is related to the briard (see above) although its corded coat has more in common with the Hungarian komondor. Like both breeds, the Bergamasco is a highly efficient and enthusiastic worker, but is also little known, even in Italy, and the breed has come close to extinction several times in its recent history: while it is affectionate, it is a breed that is best suited to outdoors, and not to city life. Nevertheless, the breed is secure in the hands of a number of enthusiastic owners and breeders.

# MAREMMA SHEEPDOG

**OTHER NAMES:** Maremma, pastore Abruzzese, central Italian sheepdog

**DATE OF ORIGIN:** Antiquity

**PLACE OF ORIGIN:** Italy

**ORIGINAL USE:** Flock guarding

**MODERN USE:** Security, companion

**SIZE:**

**HEIGHT:** 60–73 cm (23½– 28½ in)

**WEIGHT:** 30–45 kg (66–100 lb)

**COLOURS:** White

**RECOGNIZED BY:** K.C.

The pure white maremma is a native of Tuscany and the Abruzzi region of Italy and is a descendant of the great, white eastern sheepdogs that spread westwards with the Magyars across Europe over 1,000 years ago, leaving their legacy in breeds such as the maremma and the Pyrenean mountain dog (see page 240). The maremma today is smaller than its older relatives, the shorter coated maremmano sheepdog and the Abruzzese mountain dog, but retains its white colour which was preferred by shepherds so that their dogs could be readily distinguished from wolves and so that the sheep the dogs guarded would accept their presence more willingly. Older maremmas show a tinge of biscuit or lemon in their ears, and the youthful black nose becomes slightly pinkish–brown – but no less distinguished – with age. The abundant, long (except on the head) harsh coat is weatherproof, has a slight wave to it, and forms a ruff around the neck. The tail is thickly feathered, forming a magnificent plume. Like many of the flock–guarding breeds, the maremma makes an efficient guard dog, although obedience–training is not easy. The maremma has been shown regularly in Britain since 1931 but it is still rare in other countries outside of Italy.

# POLISH LOWLAND SHEEPDOG

**OTHER NAMES:** Polski owczarek nizinny

**DATE OF ORIGIN:** 16th century

**PLACE OF ORIGIN:** Poland

**ORIGINAL USE:** Hunting

**MODERN USE:** Herding, companion

**SIZE:**

**HEIGHT:** 41–51 cm (16–20 in)

**WEIGHT:** 14–16 kg (30–35 lb)

**COLOURS:** Any

**RECOGNIZED BY:** K.C.

The Polish lowland sheepdog is considered by many to be the 'bridge' or 'link' breed between the Asian corded–coat herding dogs brought to Europe from the east by the Magyars over 1,000 years ago and whose descendants include the Hungarian puli (see page 248) the Bergamasco (see page 246) and the komondor, and the more recent 'shaggy sheepdog' breeds such as the bearded collie (see page 243).

Numerous dogs of this type are to be found across Europe: the Catalan sheepdog in Spain, the Portuguese shepherd dog, and the schapendo (Dutch sheepdog) all bred in their native lands as working dogs. Consequently, except in show rings, breeds like the Polish lowland, are rarely seen outside of their homelands, where many are still, in fact, working dogs. Like many shepherding breeds, interest in 'indigenous' breeds started in the late 19th century – when mechanisation in agriculture was taking over the roles formerly performed by animals. Without this interest, many of these breeds would have become extinct. To add to many such breed's problems, two World Wars did much to speed their decline. The Polish lowland was fortunate, however, in that enthusiastic Polish breeders in the late 1940s were able to successfully revive the breed, which is now a popular household companion in Poland.

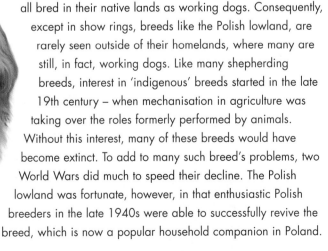

# ANATOLIAN SHEPHERD DOG

**OTHER NAMES:** Coban kopegi, karabas, kangal dog, Anatolian karabash dog

**DATE OF ORIGIN:** Middle Ages

**PLACE OF ORIGIN:** Turkey

**ORIGINAL USE:** Sheep guarding

**MODERN USE:** Sheep guarding

**SIZE:**

**HEIGHT:** 71–81 cm (28–32 in)

**WEIGHT:** 41–64 kg (90–140 lb)

**COLOURS:** Variety

**RECOGNIZED BY:** K.C.

The handsome Anatolian shepherd dog from central Turkey is another of the large guarding breeds used by shepherds across Europe and Asia for centuries. These dogs were not herding dogs – they were not expected to control the flocks – instead their job was to protect them, especially against wolves. The Anatolian is probably related to the mastiff, for it has the size, speed, stamina and broad head which distinguishes this group of dogs. In Turkey, sheepdogs were collectively classified as 'coban kopegi' but in the 1970s breeders began to investigate type and found several regional differences such as the akbash dog from western Turkey. Coban Kopegi was originally the over-arching Turkish term for a number of shepherd dogs such as the Anatolian from central Turkey and the Akbash from western Turkey. These are now seen as distinct breeds- although the KC only recognises the Anatolian and the Akbash is not recognised by anyone except Turkish shepherds and Turkish sheep! The Anatolian's coat is dense and smooth, with a thick insulating undercoat. The most usual colour is fawn – lighter colours in flock–guarding breeds were generally preferred so the dogs could be distinguished from wolves – with a black mask. A white version, and other varied colours are also recognised.

The Anatolian shepherd dog can still be found guarding flocks from wolves, which still range central Asia. Bred specifically for work, the Anatolian is not regarded as a suitable companion dog unless there is early socialisation with humans and other dogs.

# HUNGARIAN PULI

**OTHER NAMES:** Juhasz kutya, puli, Hungarian water dog

**DATE OF ORIGIN:** Middle Ages

**PLACE OF ORIGIN:** Hungary

**ORIGINAL USE:** Sheep herding

**MODERN USE:** Retrieving, companion

**SIZE:**

**HEIGHT:** 37–44 cm (14½–17½ in)

**WEIGHT:** 10–15 kg (22–33 lb)

**COLOURS:** Black, apricot, white

**RECOGNIZED BY:** K.C.

From the great Hungarian sheep–grazing plains known as the Puszta, the Hungarian puli is possibly the best known of the four great Hungarian shepherding breeds. Its most distinctive feature is its coat, which in the case of show dogs, grows to floor length and falls naturally into narrow cords as the dog matures (puppies are born without cording). The overall impression is of a dog hidden by a very large string floor mop! So densely covered is the puli that it's sometimes difficult to tell which 'end' of the dog is which!

The virtually waterproof puli with its distinctive 'dreadlocks' is almost certainly the ancestor of the poodle (see page 223) and there is even a poodle with the same corded coat. Both these breeds have been used as gun dogs, retrieving shot water fowl. In Hungary, the puli and the pumi (created by crosses between puli and softer coated German spitzen) were often classed together under the name juhasz kutya, which simply means 'shepherd's dogs'. The ancestry of the puli is uncertain, but an early mention in 1751 by a Hungarian writer called Heppe, described such a cord–coated dog, and he called it the Hungarian beater dog, and claimed it was used to hunt ducks – and rabbits! Consensus today generally puts the likely contenders for the ancestor of the puli among the Asiatic dogs that came to Hungary with the Magyar invasions. World War II nearly saw the end of the puli in Hungary, but a group of expatriates were able to re-establish the breed abroad. particularly in North America, where it became a popular companion dog. pulis – or more correctly in Hungarian, pulik, the plural of puli – have also been trained for police work in Germany.

# CARDIGAN WELSH CORGI

**OTHER NAMES:** Corgi
**DATE OF ORIGIN:** Middle Ages
**PLACE OF ORIGIN:** Wales
**ORIGINAL USE:** Cattle drover
**MODERN USE:** Livestock drover, companion
**SIZE:**
**HEIGHT:** 27–32 cm (10½–12½ in)
**WEIGHT:** 11–17 kg (25–38 lb)
**COLOURS:** Any
**RECOGNIZED BY:** K.C.

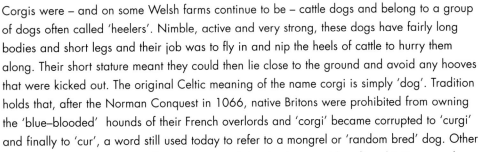

Corgis were – and on some Welsh farms continue to be – cattle dogs and belong to a group of dogs often called 'heelers'. Nimble, active and very strong, these dogs have fairly long bodies and short legs and their job was to fly in and nip the heels of cattle to hurry them along. Their short stature meant they could then lie close to the ground and avoid any hooves that were kicked out. The original Celtic meaning of the name corgi is simply 'dog'. Tradition holds that, after the Norman Conquest in 1066, native Britons were prohibited from owning the 'blue–blooded' hounds of their French overlords and 'corgi' became corrupted to 'curgi' and finally to 'cur', a word still used today to refer to a mongrel or 'random bred' dog. Other however contend that 'cor' means 'dwarf' and 'gi' means dog, but this word does not make any appearance in Middle English writing until around 1360. The Cardigan and the Pembroke (see page below) corgis both come from South Wales but each is a distinct breed in its own right. The isolated nature of the farms in the Welsh valleys meant that the two remained pure breeds.

Whether it came with the Celts over 3,000 years ago, or as other think, it is related to the short legged continental bassets that came to Britain with the Norman's, the Cardigan Welsh corgi has remained relatively unchanged since it arrived in Wales: it still has its long 'fox's brush' of a tail and large, upright ears. The Cardigan is the quieter and more placid of the two corgi breeds – but it is still a very watchful and quite snappy defender of its property.

# PEMBROKE WELSH CORGI

**OTHER NAMES:** Corgi
**DATE OF ORIGIN:** 10th century
**PLACE OF ORIGIN:** Wales
**ORIGINAL USE:** Cattle drover
**MODERN USE:** Livestock drover, companion
**SIZE:**
**HEIGHT:** 25–31 cm (10–12 in)
**WEIGHT:** 10–12 kg (20–26 lb)
**COLOURS:** Black–tan, red, fawn, sable
**RECOGNIZED BY:** K.C.

The Pembroke Welsh corgi is the better known of the two corgi breeds – largely because these are the corgis that are often seen accompanying the British Royal family. There are two main theories regarding the origins of the Pembroke: one is that a dwarf dog was brought to England by Flemish weavers in about 1100. Some of these weavers then moved to the southwest corner of Wales. What weavers would need cattle dogs for is uncertain, except that their small size may have made them the choice for companion dogs. If the Pembroke is of Flemish origins, then it is said this corgi is a descendant of the sptiz–type dogs and is related to the schipperke (see page 224). Both the Pembroke and the schipperke have 'foxy' faces, but where did the long body, short legs and big ears come from! Furthermore, the relationship to the schipperke would not explain the Pembroke's lack of a tail!

The second, more plausible theory is that the Pembroke is, like the Cardigan, descended from the continental short–legged bassets, and that the isolation of the farms and the tendency of farmers to breed for working characteristics accounts for the differences in the two corgi breeds. Another suggestion is that the Pembroke is also related to the Swedish Vallhund (see page 232): it may be possible that, after pillaging Britain, the little heeler was taken back to Scandinavia as booty! In the early part of the 20th century, Cardigan corgis were taken to Pembrokeshire and the two interbred, which reduced the differences between the two breeds. In 1934, the two breeds were recognised as distinct. Like the Cardigan corgi, the Pembroke corgi can still be found working, but it is more likely to be found as a companion dog – both in Wales, and across the world.

# LANCASHIRE HEELER

**OTHER NAMES:** Ormskirk heeler, 'nip 'n duck' dog

**DATE OF ORIGIN:** 17th century, re–created in 1960s

**PLACE OF ORIGIN:** Great Britain

**ORIGINAL USE:** Cattle drover

**MODERN USE:** Companionn

**SIZE:**

**HEIGHT:** 25–31 cm (10–12 in)

**WEIGHT:** 3–6 kg (6–13 lb)

**COLOURS:** Black–tan

**RECOGNIZED BY:** K.C.

Recognised only as recently as 1981 in Britain: with mechanisation, the work of many of heeler breeds was no longer necessary and the Lancashire heeler, along with the Yorkshire and Norfolk heelers, and the Smithfield collie (so called because it worked at London's Smithfield meat market) all became extinct. The modern Lancashire heeler is therefore a re–creation of the breed that took place in the 1960s and is the result of crosses between Welsh Corgis (see pages 249) – themselves heelers and providers of the Lancashire's conformation – and Manchester terriers (see page 195) who provided the smooth, glossy black coat with its rich tan markings. The 'new breed' is almost identical to its ancient namesake, which was used in the district around Ormskirk in Lancashire, northwest England, by butchers and slaughter men to control and direct cattle. The dogs were generally called 'nip'n duck' dogs, which described perfectly their method of working. The modern breed is not used as a cattle dog, but instead displays more of its terrier ancestry in its enthusiasm for chasing rabbits and squirrels!

# DOBERMAN PINSCHER

**OTHER NAMES:** Doberman

**DATE OF ORIGIN:** 19th century

**PLACE OF ORIGIN:** Germany

**ORIGINAL USE:** Guarding

**MODERN USE:** Security/guard dog, companion

**SIZE:**

**HEIGHT:** 65–69 cm (251/2–27 in)

**WEIGHT:** 30–40 kg (66–88 lb)

**COLOURS:** Black, brown, blue, fawn

**RECOGNIZED BY:** K.C.

The elegant, obedient and often very affectionate Doberman is a relatively recent and deliberately 'manufactured' breed. In the 1870s German tax collector, Louis Dobermann of Apolda, in Thuringia, Germany, began experimental breeding to produce a guard dog 'par excellence'. He used Rottweilers (see page 237), German Pinschers (see page 219), Weimaranas (see page 161), English greyhounds (see page 171) and Manchester Terriers (see page 195). By 1890, Herr Dobermann had arrived at a type which suited his requirements: a giant terrier with the strength and guarding abilities of the famed Thuringian shepherd dogs. According to early commentators on the breed, the Doberman was certainly fearless and most thought that a good deal of courage was needed to own one: legend tells of one Doberman exported to the USA that was awarded Best in Breed three times before any judge dared to open the dog's mouth. It was only then that a serious fault was discovered: the Best in Breed had missing teeth! Following the wishes of Herr Dobermann, a later breeder, Otto Goeller added pinscher (meaning 'terrier') to the name. Today, the Doberman pinscher is perhaps the most famous, and perhaps the best, guard dog in existence and is used the world over by police and security companies. But with socialisation in infancy, Dobermans have also proved themselves to be excellent companion dogs.

# GLOSSARY

**Bat ear** — An erect ear, broad at base and rounded at top

**Bay** — The prolonged sound of a hunting dog

**Beard** — Thick long hair on the muzzle

**Blaze** — White stripe running up the centre of the face

**Blenheim** — Chestnut and white colour

**Blue–merle** — Marbled blue and grey, mixed with black

**Bobtail** — Naturally tailless dog or one with docked tail (see below )

**Breed standard** — Description of the breed against which dogs are judged at shows

**Brindle** — Mix of black hairs with brown, light gold, red or grey hairs

**Broken coat** — Wire–haired coat

**Button ear** — An ear where the flap folds forward with the tip close to the skull

**Corded coat** — A coat of separate, rope–like twists of hair, formed from intertwined top and undercoat hairs

**Cropping** — Amputating the ears to enable the remaining part to stand erect

**Crossbreed** — The offspring of parents of two different breeds

**Dam** — Female parent

**Dew claw** — Fifth digit (thumb) on inside of leg

**Dewlap** — Loose pendulous skin under throat

**Docking** — Amputating the tail

**Domed skull** — An evenly rounded head

**Double coat** — Warm and waterproof undercoat and weather resistant outer coat

**Drop ear** — Folded, drooping ear

**Feathering** — Long fringes of hair

**Flews** — Pendulous upper lips

**Giving tongue** — The barking or baying (see above) of hounds

**Grizzle** — Mix of colours including bluish–grey, red and black

**Hackney action** — High lifting front feet

**Harlequin** — Patched colours of black or blue on white

**Height** — Distance from top of withers (see below) to the ground

**Hock** — The tarsal bones, forming the joint between the knee and toes

**Inbreeding** — Mating closely related dogs

**Interbreeding** — Breeding together dogs of different varieties of a breed

**Line breeding** — Mating of related dogs in a family or to a common ancestor

**Mask** — Dark shading on the fore face

**Merle** — Blue–grey with flecks of black

# GLOSSARY

| | |
|---|---|
| Moult | Shedding of the coat |
| Muzzle | The fore face, the face in front of the eyes |
| Occiput | The highest, upper point of the skull |
| Pads | Thickened cushions beneath the toes and on soles of the feet |
| Part–coloured | Two colours in variegated patches |
| Pastern | The region between the wrist and the toes |
| Pedigree | A dog's ancestry |
| Pied | Unequally proportioned patches of white and another colour |
| Plume | A long fringe of hair hanging from the tail |
| Pointing | Freezing on sight of game and pointing in direction of game |
| Pricked ears | Erect, pointed ears |
| Pure bred | A dog whose parent belong to the same breed |
| Random bred dog | A dog whose parents do not both belong to a recognised breed |
| Retrieve | The act of bring back game or other item to a handler |
| Roan | A fine mix of coloured hairs alternating with white hairs |
| Rose ear | A small drop ear folding over and back |
| Runt | The weakest, often the smallest puppy in a litter |
| Sable | Black tipped hairs on a background of gold, silver, grey or tan |
| Sabre tail | A tail carried in a curve |
| Scent hound | A hound that hunts by ground scent |
| Self colour | Whole colour except for lighter shading |
| Setting | Freezing on sight of game and flushing game on command |
| Sickle tail | A tail carried out and up in a semicircle |
| Sight hound | A hound that hunts more by sight than scent |
| Sire | Male parent |
| Stop | The depression before the eyes between the skull and the muzzle |
| Topknot | Longer hair on top of head |
| Trail | To hunt by following ground scent |
| Tricolour | Three colours – black, white and tan |
| Wheaten | Pale yellow or fawn colour |
| Withers | The highest point on the body just behind the neck |

# INDEX

# CREDITS

## Acknowledgements

With thanks to Vic Swift at the British Library, London for assistance, and to all owners, breeders and enthusiasts who placed details of dogs, dog breeds and 'shaggy dog stories' on the internet.

## Selected Bibliography

Dr. Bruce Fogel **The New Encyclopaedia of the Dog** Dorling Kindersley, 1995

**Collins Gem Dogs** Harper Collins, 1996

Stanley Dangerfield and Elsworth Howell (eds.)

**The International Encyclopaedia of Dogs** Pelham Books, 1971

Kay White **The Wonderful World of Dogs** Hamlyn, 1976

## Associations

The British Kennel Club
1–5 Clarges Street,
Piccadilly,
London
W1Y 8AB
www.the–kennel–club.org.uk

Federation Cynologique Internationale (FCI)
Place Albert 1,
13 B–6530,
Thurin,
Belgium
www.fci.be

American Kennel Club
260 Madison Ave
New York
NY 10016
www.akc.org

United Kennel Club
100 East Kilgore rod
Kalamazoo
Missouri 49002–5584
www.ukcdog.com